D0706864

HENSLOWE'S DIARY

HENSLOWE'S DIARY

EDITED WITH SUPPLEMENTARY MATERIAL
INTRODUCTION AND NOTES

BY

R. A. FOAKES

AND

R. T. RICKERT

CAMBRIDGE
AT THE UNIVERSITY PRESS
1961

PUBLISHED BY
THE SYNDICS OF THE CAMBRIDGE UNIVERSITY PRESS

Bentley House, 200 Euston Road, London, N.W. 1
American Branch: 32 East 57th Street, New York 22, N.Y.
West African Office: P.O. Box 33, Ibadan, Nigeria

Printed in Great Britain at the University Press, Cambridge
(*Brooke Crutchley, University Printer*)

To the memory of

SIR WALTER GREG

CONTENTS

INTRODUCTION

THE DIARY

APPENDICES

INDEXES AND GLOSSARY

PLATES

Between pp. lii and liii

PREFACE

The main purpose of this edition is to make available again the text of the chief source for theatrical history between 1590 and 1604, Henslowe's *Diary*, and the fragments and manuscripts associated with it, in as convenient a form as possible. The monumental edition of 1904–8 by Sir Walter Greg has long been out of print and unobtainable; but his interpretation of the *Diary* has taken its place as the basis of all studies of the Elizabethan theatre in the last fifty years, and was used extensively by E. K. Chambers in his *Elizabethan Stage* (1923). Chambers modified a few of Greg's conclusions, but the only general attempt to reassess the evidence in the *Diary*, so far as it relates to the structure of the Admiral's Men as a company in the period 1590–4, was made by T. W. Baldwin in his ingenious and rather too schematic book, *The Organization and Personnel of the Shakespearean Company* (1927), pp. 321–31; Baldwin did not accept Greg's view that Henslowe's arrangements with his company were exceptional in the period (see below, pp. xxx–xxxi), and emphasised the similarities between the customs followed in the conduct of various theatres (pp. 1–45), so that his book has an important bearing on the broader implications of the *Diary*. It is time, however, to reconsider the meaning of Henslowe's entries and Greg's detailed interpretation of them, and we hope that this new edition, based on a fresh transcript of the material, will encourage further scrutiny of the evidence. Some new possibilities of interpreting difficult entries are examined in the Introduction to this edition.

We are grateful to the Governors of Dulwich College for giving us permission to complete this edition, and to use the facilities of the College library. Mr W. S. Wright, the Librarian, has been most kind in giving us all the help in his power. Our thanks go also to Professor Allardyce Nicoll, with whom the idea of the edition was first discussed, and who put the resources of the Shakespeare Institute at our disposal, to Professor C. J. Sisson for his advice, to Professor Thomas B. Stroup, who provided us with a transcript of the notes written by E. K. Chambers in his copy of Greg's edition of the *Diary*, and to Mr Remington Patterson, who kindly communicated to us his independent discovery of the correct date of a document discussed on p. 299 below, namely Manuscripts, Volume III, Article I. The skill and patience of the printer and publisher have contributed much to the final shape of the edition. The Durham Colleges have materially assisted the progress of this work over several years with grants from their Research Fund.

R. A. F.
R. T. R.

DURHAM
July 1960

INTRODUCTION

I. HISTORY OF THE MANUSCRIPT

The history of the manuscript is well known from Sir Walter Greg's account,[1] to which the following summary is heavily indebted. The book was first used by John Henslowe, the brother of Philip, to enter accounts relating to mining and smelting operations in Ashdown Forest during the years 1576–81. Possibly upon the death of John, which occurred before 1592,[2] the book passed to Philip, who used it to record business matters and occasionally more private affairs until 1604, and thereafter for infrequent jottings until 1609. Later, no doubt at his death in 1616, the volume passed to Edward Alleyn, who had married Philip's step-daughter, and so eventually became part of the library of the College of God's Gift which Alleyn founded at Dulwich.

The book seems to have been first used for scholarly purposes by Edmond Malone, who printed portions of a transcript made of those sections he thought important in his *Historical Account of the English Stage* in 1790.[3] Malone's transcript, which he collated with the original, and which contains some notes and corrections he made, was acquired by Dulwich College in 1895, and now reposes in the same library as the original. The manuscript was later used by J. P. Collier in preparing his *History of Dramatic Poetry*, and he reprinted the theatrical material in a separate edition of *Henslowe's Diary* (1845). The volume was described and a list of forgeries given in G. F. Warner's *Catalogue of Manuscripts and Muniments of Alleyn's College of God's Gift* (1881).[4] Finally, in 1902 Sir Walter Greg obtained permission to prepare a new edition, which appeared in

(1) *Diary*, I, xiii–xiv.

(2) He predeceased Edmond, who died before 23 May 1592; *Diary*, II, 16–17.

(3) It is in vol. I, part II, pp. 288–329.

(4) Pp. 157–63; it is listed as MS. no. VII.

1904, and which was followed in 1908 by a second volume containing a detailed commentary and an interpretation of the material in the account-book.

2. DESCRIPTION OF THE MANUSCRIPT

The manuscript is a folio of 242 leaves, measuring approximately 13¼ × 8 inches; it was originally bound in a limp vellum wrapper which was inserted at the beginning when the volume was rebound. It is very well preserved, but has suffered a certain amount of mutilation; the edges of some leaves are frayed or torn, and a number of pages have been removed or partially cut out. It seems likely that most of 69 or 70 missing leaves were lost early in the book's history, and, as Greg noted,(1) the fact that accounts span several of the gaps with no apparent omissions suggests that these were present when Philip Henslowe began to use it. Probably little theatrical material was lost in this way.(2)

The absence of leaves is indicated by the original foliation, written in ink, and numbering the leaves from that end of the book used by John Henslowe; possibly they represent his numeration. The numbers run from 1 through to 100, and from 102 (altered to 101, as 103 is altered to 102, but 104 left standing, so that 103 is simply omitted) to 308: and the following leaves are missing according to this numeration; the modern foliation is given in brackets: 3 leaves at the beginning, before 6 (f. 236v), where only two leaves (ff. 237, 238) remain, both lacking numbers; 8 (between f. 234 and f. 235); 33 (between f. 210 and f. 211); 40–2 (between f. 204 and f. 205); 47 (between f. 200 and f. 201); 63 (between f. 185 and f. 186); 72 (between f. 177 and f. 178); 78 (between f. 172 and f. 173); 80 (between f. 171 and f. 172); 87 (between f. 165 and f. 164); 98 (between f. 154 and f. 155); 111 (between f. 143 and f. 144); 116 (between f. 139 and f. 140); 124 (between f. 132 and f. 133); 128 (between f. 129 and f. 130); 132–3 (between f. 126 and f. 127); 135, 139–41, 143–4 (these blank leaves were not numbered by Warner); 147 (between f. 123

(1) *Loc. cit.* p. xvii.

(2) It is possible that some pawn accounts are lost, before f. 55, where they begin abruptly; in the original foliation f. 54v is 20045, f. 55v is 20041, so some leaves are missing here.

and f. 124); 150–2 (between f. 121 and f. 122); 154–6 (between f. 120 and f. 121); 167–8 (between f. 110 and f. 111); 175–7 (between f. 104 and f. 105); 181–2 (between f. 101 and f. 102); 185–6 (between f. 99 and f. 100); 188 (between f. 98 and f. 99); 196–7 (between f. 91 and f. 92); 1 leaf between 205 and 208 (between f. 82 and f. 84; the numbered corner is missing from f. 83); 213 (between f. 77 and f. 78); 218 (between f. 73 and f. 74); 221 (between f. 71 and f. 72); 236–8 (between f. 57 and f. 58); 242–4 (between f. 54 and f. 55); 251 (between f. 48 and f. 49); 255 (between f. 45 and f. 46); 1 leaf between 269 and 273 (f. 29 and f. 32), where the remaining leaves (ff. 30, 31) have lost numbered corners; 277 (between f. 25 and f. 26); 281 (between f. 22 and f. 23); 285 (between f. 19 and f. 20); 288 (between f. 17 and f. 18); 295 (between f. 11 and f. 12); 300–1 (between f. 7 and f. 8); 306 (between f. 3 and f. 4). A leaf may also be missing after the last numbered one (308; f. 2), for if, as Greg suggests,[(1)] f. 1, which has lost its old number, is the original last leaf, as the scrawls on it may indicate, then it should have an even number (?310), and at least one leaf must be lacking here. One other leaf, f. 167, is not so far accounted for; this was at some time inserted in the volume, and since it is rather larger than the other leaves, so that one edge has had to be folded in, it cannot ever have been part of the book. But, as Greg notes, it may always have lain folded inside the *Diary*, for it contains on one side mining accounts, and on the other, some words in Philip Henslowe's hand.

The numbering is a little strange, for when the scribe reached 100, he simply retained this figure, and began again at 1, so that pages have numbers like 10025 or 20078. These numbers appear upside down in the bottom left corner of each leaf as the manuscript was used for his main entries by Philip Henslowe. The present transcript follows the modern foliation inserted in pencil in accordance with his use of the book, but for this main sequence of theatrical entries (section 2), the original foliation is given too, as evidence of what leaves are missing.

A number of mutilations are comparatively recent, and have

---

(1) *Diary*, I, xvii.

probably occurred since Malone had possession of the book. Several scholars have worked with it, and doubtless many people have had access to it. It is clear that several excisions have been made for the sake of the signatures on them of well-known dramatists, and eleven fragments of the account-book have been traced.[1] Perhaps more are in existence; excisions from the following leaves remain unaccounted for: ff. 5, 12, 29, 30, 31, 33, 60, 83, 88, 111, 114, 132, 187, 189, 190, 191, 199, 200, 206, 207, 208, 209, 228, 229, 231, 236.

3. CONTENTS OF THE MANUSCRIPT

It seems most convenient to divide the contents into four groups of items for the purpose of this Introduction, and to consider them not in the order in which they are printed in this edition, but in such a way that comments on the theatrical accounts are not separated from the introductory note on the other theatrical entries (in fragments from the *Diary*, and supplementary manuscripts) which are included in the edition. For this reason, the theatrical accounts are dealt with last of all. First are the mining accounts, which belong to a time prior to Philip Henslowe's ownership and use of the volume; these, which Greg described as forestry accounts, were omitted from his reprint of the manuscript, and although they are not included here, a description of them is given because of their intrinsic interest as a detailed record of operations in iron-smelting at an early period, and also because they provide further knowledge of the Henslowe family, and of Philip's background. Secondly, there are Philip's notes of private matters of various kinds, ranging from the buying of property to recipes for the alleviation of various diseases. Like the mining accounts, these have much intrinsic interest, and also throw light on Henslowe's personal relationships. A third group consists of the pawn accounts, which relate to a business carried on, it seems, largely through agents, though most of the transactions are recorded in the book in Philip Henslowe's hand. Most of these accounts were omitted from Greg's reprint, and are now given in full for the first time. Again, they have an interest in their own right, but may, in

(1) See below, pp. 265–9.

addition, have a relation to the theatre; their significance is discussed further below. Finally, the major part of Philip's entries concern his theatrical affairs, chiefly his financial relationship with companies of players, principally the Admiral's Men, and accounts relating to the building and maintenance of the theatres in which he was interested.

4. THE MINING ACCOUNTS

These accounts occupy chiefly what, in Warner's foliation, are the verso pages from f. 237v to f. 137v, though there are many blank leaves; as John Henslowe used the book, these would, of course, have been recto pages. Since f. 137v is numbered 10019 (i.e. 119), it can be inferred that eighteen leaves are missing from this section, but it is very doubtful whether anything of consequence is lost. Philip Henslowe occasionally used blank pages, or spaces between old entries, to add items of his business, and also entered various theatrical reckonings on the first few versos (rectos for him) at this end of the book.

The mining accounts extend in time from January 1576 to 10 December 1580 or 1581. However, there are only twelve entries dated specifically in 1576, none in 1579, one in 1580, and one in 1581, which may be 1580. The bulk of the dated accounts relate to 1577 and 1578, and it may be conjectured that most of the undated entries belong also to this period. They are concerned mainly with operations in the Ashdown Forest in Sussex, particularly in the area extending for some miles around Buxted and Maresfield, north of Lewes and south-east of East Grinstead. The father of John and Philip Henslowe was master of the game in the forest and at Brill Park,[1] and it was perhaps natural for one of the sons at least to find an occupation in that area. In the earliest accounts of 1576 and in 1577 John seems to be acting as an agent for his brother-in-law Ralph Hogg, who had married his sister Margaret; for he is to be found reckoning up moneys which he has delivered to 'my brythier hogg', and assessing the debts to him of a miner, Gilbert Ford. Later on this relationship may have been modified, for while John Henslowe continues, as it

(1) *Diary*, II, 1–2.

seems, to act as general payee of miners and cutters, and receiver of their goods, Hogg himself, at times, becomes the intermediary in payments, and in 1578 entries appear of the form, 'More my bryther payd ffor hem. . . Mor my bryther must Anser for hem'. Perhaps by this time John had achieved a partnership with Ralph Hogg; or possibly he remained a kind of financial manager for the latter, who was a large-scale ironfounder,[(1)] in his dealings with his employees and customers.

Employees is not an accurate term by which to describe the 190 or so people mentioned in these accounts, for they were nearly all free agents as far as the evidence shows, being paid by piece-rates for work actually performed, or deliveries made. Five main trades are involved, though many of the workmen seem to have been adept at more than one. First, as perhaps occupying more space than the others, is that of cutting wood in various parts of the forest, chiefly at Log Hill, the Swynfall, names which seem to have fallen out of use, at Harne Gate, probably the modern Horney Gate and Common just outside Maresfield, Echen Wood, the modern Etchingwood, a mile from Buxted, and 'Ryes Bryge', perhaps to be identified with Rice Bridge, about ten miles west of Buxted. The wood cut is described specifically on occasion by one of six names, 'log wood', 'top wood', 'stub' or 'stubble' wood, 'chux', 'bronds', and 'chepes'. It seems clear that log wood and top wood were used to make charcoal, as payments for 'Collynge at loge heyll tope wodd' and 'colling in the Swynffall of logge wodd' indicate. It seems likely that where the kind of wood is not specified, it is one of these two that is meant, and that it was used to make charcoal, the main fuel of the smelting furnaces. The 'chux', presumably chucks or chipped logs, 'bronds', and 'chepes' or chippings were probably used directly as fuel, since the accounts suggest that these were brought to the furnaces in the same way as coals.

The second trade, also a forest occupation, is 'collyng', or coaling, making charcoal from cut wood. The third, the trade of mining, produced the other raw material necessary for making iron goods,

---

(1) See Ernest Straker, *Wealden Iron* (1931), especially pp. 147–52, 398–9.

the ore. The main areas of mining were in Etchingwood, at the 'Baye', that is, Oldlands, about four miles north of Buxted, and on the land of a certain Angell. One or two of the miners had their own ground to work. The next trade, that of hauling, was involved with the other three, cutting (for though charcoal was often made on the site where the wood was cut, there are payments for transport of wood, especially to Log Hill, which seems to have been a centre of charcoal-making), coaling, and mining. In consequence, a large part of the accounts record payments made for the carriage of materials, usually to the furnaces of Langley, Marshalls, the name of a manor-house owned by Hogg, and Hyndoll, which may be a person, or perhaps identifiable with the place known as Hendall Wood. Lastly, John Henslowe records payments for the founding of iron, making moulds, blowing the furnace, pulling the bellows, filling the founds, cleaning the chimneys, beating shot, and other tasks connected with the furnaces.

There are some indications of the way in which the workmen operated. A number combined two or more trades, cutting and hauling, or mining and hauling, but certain men seem to have specialised in their trade. So James Alcock, 'Alcoke the collier', and a certain Gyllat, were charcoal makers who sent their coals out of the forest by a number of different carriers. These two were perhaps fairly important and prosperous men, and in one entry is noted the delivery of a ton of iron to them; Alcoke had a partner, Giles the collier, and there is mention of Gyllat's son, so that they were not working alone. Other partnerships are indicated; Gilbert Ford, a miner, had at least two partners, William Collin and John Paccom, and Andrew Humphreys and Harry Curd were partners in cutting wood. Possibly a more complicated partnership is revealed occasionally; Thomas Bartlet, a cutter, had two associates: Thomas Sanders, who is also named as John a Ford's partner, and 'Parssons man', who may be connected with John Parson, partner of Thomas Penfold. It is clear that the colliers, miners and cutters worked in small groups, partnerships of two or more.

Many of them were free agents, selling their services and goods, and, as noted above, some miners owned their own workings. But there is one entry recording payment of a half year's wages to Peter Bartholomew of Lewes, and there may have been other hired servants. Occasionally, too, there is reference to more powerful figures in the background; so John Paccom, named as partner in mining with Gilbert Ford, is elsewhere described as 'S^r^uant to Mr John Waruntc', possibly a landowner. Several men are paid for mining in Angell's land, and Lord Buckhurst is mentioned as the owner of Ashdown Forest, so that some of the men may have been dependents of these in some sense. However, they are paid for the work they do, generally by John Henslowe.

Further connections between workmen can be traced in the frequent payments to one on behalf of another; the most complicated of these transactions is the payment to 'Symans yemans wyddow' on behalf of Giles, James Alcock's partner. Sometimes wives or fathers are paid on behalf of men, and once there is specific mention of the wife of the founder, Peter Bartholomew, being employed in carrying coals, so that the womenfolk sometimes worked also at what must have been heavy labour.

Among the peripheral figures who enter into John Henslowe's dealings are a number of tradesmen of a different kind. One or two, like John a Wood the miller, who passes payment for John Henslowe to John Geffere, a charcoal-maker, or John a Smith, the carpenter of Blackboys, who turned his hand to haulage, perhaps while business was slack, enter very briefly. Several are specialist tradesmen, whose work was connected with mining and smelting, like Alcock the smith, Roger Sherman the 'hamar man', and John Dyne the 'ffyller' of founds. Among others named are Paris, a butcher, William Wallington the butcher and Elliot the mercer of Uckfield, and the miller at Barkham. It is just possible that butchers and millers had to do with the occasional payments in kind for work; meat is not mentioned in this connection, but payment sometimes takes the form of a hundredweight or a barrel of herring, or a quarter of wheat. Other payments in kind include a load of hay, and amounts of iron, ranging from a hundredweight to a ton.

The controller of all these operations seems to have been Ralph Hogg, who dealt in iron, and more specifically in guns or 'pesses' (pieces) and shot. John Henslowe was his financial manager or partner, and kept accounts. Two other men, George Kenyon and Samson Colstokes, also kept account-books. The first may have shared some of John Henslowe's labours; his book seems to have duplicated John's occasionally, and once he is recorded as acting as payee on behalf of John Henslowe. The second appears to have been an agent for Lord Buckhurst. Although Ralph Hogg dealt directly in iron, presumably pig-iron, his large-scale business was in shot and guns. The biggest transaction listed is the sale to Sir Thomas Griffin and Mr Turberville at Lewes of 41 tons of demi-cannon shot at a price of over £300; these two were acting for the Earl of Warwick, who was Master of the Ordnance at this time (1576). A buyer on a smaller scale was a Mr Harman of Lewes, who paid for 'pesses wth Rynges Appon ther nosse', guns with rings presumably at the muzzle.(1) Other deals involve a certain Sharples, agent for Turberville, Thomas Jansson of London, and a Mr Leche. The last-named was an agent of Lord Buckhurst, and it is not clear why John Henslowe carried money to him in London at one time, and took delivery of wood from him in Ashdown Forest at another. One interesting note in connection with Hogg's business is a stocktaking of March 1577 which lists all the round shot of his remaining with his brother, Brian Hogg, a total of 2338 cannon balls of various sizes. His dealings in London took there not only John Henslowe, but some of the hauliers too, who were evidently not all mere country labourers, although some local Sussex names, such as Sleche, do appear.

Two miscellaneous items among these accounts have connections with material in the *Diary*. An undated note of the sale of some sheep to 'Mr Langworth' almost certainly belongs to the period of the mining accounts, for it contains a reference to 'my Brythe r', Ralph Hogg; it provides a link between the Henslowes and the Langworths of Brill, Sussex, at this early time. Philip Henslowe later had many dealings with Arthur Langworth, who seems to have been his close friend. In 1578 John Henslowe recorded the payment of

---

(1) *O.E.D.* records 'nose' (*sb.* 12b) as meaning only the muzzle of a gun; the first example cited is of 1598. For Harman, who shipped ordnance to London, see Straker, *op. cit.* p. 150.

rent to a Mr Welles; this is perhaps the same person as the Robert Wells who was later, in 1592–3, to cause so much trouble over the transfer of a property called Lockyers (*Diary*, ff. 41, 122v–124, 127v, and Dulwich MSS., vol. III, article 6). Eventually Philip Henslowe was driven to seek an interview with Lord Buckhurst about the matter (*Diary*, ff. 41, 123). A further personal note among these accounts lists the prices of shoes for members of Ralph Hogg's family; beside it is written the following snatch of verse:

> The mi^r^o^r^s of mighte
> & patterns of Loue
> Reste heare day & nyghte
> and Can not remoue

5. PHILIP HENSLOWE'S PRIVATE AFFAIRS

The majority of the miscellaneous items concern loans made by Henslowe to many people, friends like Arthur Langworth, family, for instance his nephew Francis Henslowe, players and a variety of other people. Occasionally the purpose of the loan is specified, and this can be of interest; so, for instance, he lent money to Thomas Heywood to buy silk garters (f. 114), provided funds to enable Mrs Birde to release her husband from gaol, and to release Chettle from arrest (f. 62). There are also records of payments of rent, and some lists of his tenants in 1602 (ff. 177v–178). Of the more personal transactions recorded, several relate to affairs or property in Sussex: evidently Philip kept up his connections there, acquiring the property of 'Locyers' in Buxted in 1593[(1)] (f. 128; see also below, p. xli), selling the property of his dead sister-in-law to Langworth, and having dealings with Thomas Chaloner (ff. 19, 124), who became the uncle by marriage of Arthur Langworth's son John, and left him his property as his heir and nephew.[(2)] Philip also acted as executor

(1) In the *Sussex Manors, Advowsons, Etc. Recorded in the Feet of Fines* (Sussex Record Society, vol. XX, 1915), 2 vols., II, 335, is recorded a suit of 1592 between Arthur Langworth, Rose his wife, and John Langworth on the one party, and John and Robert Welles on the other, relating to tenements in Buxted; perhaps Henslowe and Langworth, who is known to have lived at Ringmer, had mutual interests in Buxted. As noted above, John Henslowe had paid rent to a Mr Welles.

(2) When Arthur died his son John intended to marry Mary Chaloner, which he evidently did; see *Notes of Post Mortem Inquisitions*, ed. F.W. T. Attree (Sussex Record Society, vol. XIV, 1912), pp. 139, 49.

on behalf of Edmund Henslowe's children in Sussex (f. 72). A few entries reflect interests of Philip's outside the normal range of his dealings; so, for instance, he considered buying a farm in Gloucestershire (f. 111v), and invested in a starch business (f. 204). Other items include some rather horrifying remedies for diseases and hurts, and miscellaneous notes concerning such matters as sending his horse out to grass, and paying the charges for his soldier Peter, including fitting him out with equipment and with drinking money (ff. 20, 21). The curious item on f. 159, relating to a bargain between E. Alleyn and T. Lawrence regarding the bringing by water of the wood of eleven trees, may relate to one of the two wharfs connected with Henslowe's name,(1) but whether the wood came from Sussex property it is impossible to say.

6. THE PAWN ACCOUNTS

There are three sets of pawn accounts, on ff. 55–61, 73–81 and 133–6. The first extend from 16 January 1593 to 19 December 1593 on f. 60, and are followed by two additional entries of 14 February and 18 May 1594. In most cases the form of entry is 'Lent unto Frances Hensley upon a...', indicating that he was acting as an intermediary, and that Philip advanced money to him on goods deposited by customers. The second set, comprising entries from 10 December 1593 to 22 January 1595, is clearly a continuation of the first; but Francis Henslowe drops out after December 1593, and Philip Henslowe records elsewhere (f. 2v) the loan of £15 to him in May 1594(2) to buy a share in the Queen's Men, so presumably Francis took up acting at this time. Another entry, on f. 6, noting loans totalling 55*s*. to Francis in January 1593 may have recorded money advanced to set him up in the pawn business, in which his career seems to have lasted a little more than a year. Thereafter Philip may have carried on the business himself for a time, but the evidence is uncertain. A Goody Watson becomes prominent midway through this set of entries, and may have been an agent for him, but many entries continue to list names of customers with whom he possibly

(1) Greg, *Diary*, II, 28.

(2) The text has '1593', but see Chambers, *E.S.* II, 114.

dealt directly. The third set is headed 'm[r]s grantes Recknynge 1593', and the first page contains accounts dating from 17 January 1593/4 to March 1594. The second page goes back to 26 March 1593, and thenceforward the entries record loans made at intervals of from two days to several months, until 12 April 1596. The first page possibly refers to dealings by an agent, Mrs Grant, whom Philip employed in addition to Francis; she is not mentioned in the second set, which extends through and beyond the same period of time. The remainder of this third set, which overlaps both the first and second sets in time, frequently mentions Anne No(c)kes, who also seems to have acted as an agent. It would therefore appear that Philip Henslowe carried on a pawn business employing several agents from January 1593 until April 1596. There is no certain evidence that it ceased at this time; it is conceivable that it began in 1593 as a means of finding employment for Francis, his nephew.(1)

The pawn accounts have considerable human interest. The objects pawned range from clothes and household linen to a set of silver buttons, a pint pot, a lease, a silver whistle, an 'edward angell', and one odd collection of objects: a looking-glass, a comb, a pair of scissors, three ear-pickers and a pair of small compasses. Several women were reduced to pawning wedding-rings, and there is a note at once pathetic and ironic about the posies or mottoes recorded as being on some of them, for instance, on f. 59, 'hope helpeth hevenes' (i.e. heaviness), on f. 77v, 'as thow haste vowed vnto me so ame I thine vntell I die', and on f. 80v, 'god hath Apoynted I ame content'.

The names of a considerable number of customers are given, most of them women. Occasionally there is an indication of their social standing, in descriptions such as butchers' wives, the woman who sells raisins, a tailor's wife, the midwife's daughter. A number of men also figure in the accounts, and one or two of these were of higher rank. The most interesting name is that of 'my lord Burte' (f. 76v, 77v), by whom Greg thinks Henslowe may just possibly

(1) A letter from him to Philip asking for assistance in order to obtain his release from the Wood Street Counter (MSS. III, 5; see below, p. 300) must have been written before 23 May 1592, and is the only earlier notice of him so far found.

have meant Baron Willoughby, whose family name was Bertie.[1] An alternative identification might be William Herbert, later Earl of Pembroke; this may seem a remote possibility, since he was born in 1580, but he was old enough to be betrothed in 1595, and E. K. Chambers is inclined to regard him as the likeliest candidate for identification with 'W.H.', the only begetter of Shakespeare's *Sonnets*.[2] In March and June 1593 doublets and hose of 'w^m^ harbutes', or 'William harbarte' were pawned, and in both cases a marginal entry records payment of interest up to 16 December 1593 (ff. 55v, 58). In January 1593/4 a loan was made on articles of clothing, two of which were redeemed as 'my lords' on 18 May (f. 74v); further loans on a doublet of 'my lord Burtes man' and a cloak of 'my lord Burtes' were made in March and April 1594 (ff. 76v, 77v). The entries make no connection between William Herbert and my lord 'Burte', but it is possible that the same person is meant.[3]

Two loans are made on a lease and a pair of venetians of Mr Dorington (ff. 73v, 134), who may be the same John Dorrington, later Sir John, who was to become Master of the Game of Bears, Bulls and Mastiff Dogs in August 1598, and a tenant of Henslowe's (f. 151),[4] though in 1598 Henslowe referred to him as 'one Mr Dorington'.[5] Other interesting names include those of a ship's captain, Captain Swan, who pawned his sea-gown, and a certain Captain Hannam, who deposited sheets and other linen in January and February 1593/4 (ff. 75, 76). This provides a tenuous and early link between the financier of the Admiral's Men, for whom both Jonson and Dekker were to write, and a Captain Hannam, and it is quite conceivable that this is the same 'honest Captain *Hannam*' whom Dekker accused Jonson of imitating as Tucca in his *Poetaster*.[6]

---

(1) *Diary*, II, 246–7.
(2) *William Shakespeare. A Study of Facts and Problems* (2 vols., 1930), I, 565–7.
(3) 'My lord Burte' also appears in the *Diary* (f. 3v) as owing money to Francis Henslowe in June 1595.
(4) See *Diary*, II, 261–2.
(5) See Warner, *Catalogue*, p. 65.
(6) 'To the World', preface to *Satiromastix* (1602), in *Dramatic Works*, ed. Fredson Bowers, vol. I (1953), pp. 309–10.

These consist of four types of entries.(1) The first lists the daily receipts, or that portion of the daily receipts, which Henslowe took from performances at his theatres between 19 February 1591/2 and 5 November 1597. There are several breaks in the sequence of performances, and the form of entry was twice changed. The following are typical forms:

Until 16 May 1594:

ne—Rd at harey the vj the 3 of marche 1591 . . . . iij^{li} xvj^{s} 8^{d}

3 June 1594 until 22 January 1596/7:

¶28 of novembȝ 1595 ne—Rd at harey the v . . . . . . iij^{li} vjs

24 January 1596/7 until 5 November 1597:

Aprelle 1597 1 tt at blinde beger . . . . 00 05 03 – 00 – 00

After this time daily entries cease, and there are records for various periods of time of weekly receipts from the galleries and payments received from the company; these continue until July 1600 (f. 62v).(2)

The second type of entry relates to expenditure on behalf of the companies of Admiral's or Worcester's Men from 21 October 1597, and continues with many breaks until 1604; these accounts are closed out with a final reckoning casting up 'all the acowntes from the begininge of the world' on 14 March 1604 (f. 110). The form of entry, typically 'Lent (Paid) unto...at the appointment of the company (or some officer of the company)', shows that these were loans made on behalf of the company, for which Henslowe was acting as banker and moneylender, and periodically he totals up their debt to him. A third group of entries affords detailed lists of payments Henslowe made in connection with the building and repair of two theatres in which he had an interest, successively the Rose and the Fortune. Lastly, there remains a mass of notes of many kinds, relating to such matters as the hiring of actors, payments to the

(1) *Diary*, I, xxii–xxiii.

(2) There are, however, just two entries of October 1600 (f. 83) which repeat the form of the earlier daily entries. With these the notes of takings for three days at the Fortune and Beargarden in 1608 (ff. 127, 126v) should perhaps be listed.

Master of the Revels, various legal proceedings and other miscellaneous transactions.

This material, supplemented by other items from among the papers and muniments in the collection at Dulwich, enabled W. W. Greg to reconstruct a detailed history of Henslowe's relations with theatrical companies and the theatres they worked in, and so to amplify considerably the history of the stage between 1584 and 1613. Indeed, Greg's account in the *Diary*, II (1908), has remained one of the main bases for the discussion of the theatrical history of this period, and his findings were used throughout E. K. Chambers's *Elizabethan Stage* (1923), and in particular, were embodied in the sections on the Admiral's Men, the theatres, and the economics of acting.(1) This is not the place to attempt further analysis of the material, except so much as is necessary to draw attention to the need for further close scrutiny of the evidence the volume offers. For brilliant as is Greg's commentary, it includes some doubtful assumptions and dubious interpretations, and has come to be treated not merely with the great respect it deserves, but as an ultimate authority on matters relating to the Admiral's Men.(2)

One assumption, which Greg took over from Fleay and passed on, was the view of Henslowe as 'an illiterate moneyed man...who regarded art as a subject for exploitation', and who was ignorant of stage management and of dramatic literature; his company was contrasted with the Chamberlain's Men, who were 'managed by the housekeepers or principal sharers, whose interest was that of the whole company'.(3) It might be supposed that the Chamberlain's Men were also interested in making money out of art, but the view stemming from Fleay and Greg was taken up and developed at length by R. B. Sharpe in his *The Real War of the Theatres* (Boston, 1935). He analysed the repertory of the Admiral's Men between 1594 and 1603, compared it with that of the Chamberlain's Men, and sought to show that the former company chose to make a 'prole-

(1) See especially I, 358ff.; II, 128–240 and 405ff.

(2) It should be noted that E. K. Chambers did not accept all Greg's conclusions, and stated his main differences in a review of the *Diary*, *Modern Language Rev.* IV (1909), 407–13; and that Greg has revised some of his views, as may be best seen in his *Dramatic Documents* (1931).

(3) *Diary*, II, 112, 113, citing Fleay.

tarian appeal' to a lower-class audience, purveying romance, plays on biblical themes, domestic crime plays, and other kinds alien to the fashionable gallants and ladies whom he supposes to have frequented the Globe in anticipation of a kind of Third Programme. The difficulty with his argument is twofold; the known repertory of the Chamberlain's Men, apart from Shakespeare's plays, is very slight and affords no sufficient body of evidence for comparison; and the whole thesis is based on a conception of Henslowe as 'an ignorant man, whose spelling bears witness to a complete lack of acquaintance with literature'.(1) It is true that Henslowe's spellings are sometimes odd, but they are little stranger than those of many Elizabethan writers.

The question of Henslowe's literacy would not be important if it had not led to other beliefs. Greg noted some irregularities on Henslowe's part, for instance, that he occasionally carried over old-style year-dates well after 25 March, writing for example April 1591 when the true date was 1592 (ff. 7–7v). He also observed some errors of dating, especially in the daily entries of receipts,(2) and having once caught Henslowe out, he, and other scholars since, have been the more ready to accuse him of other mistakes; the belief in Henslowe's illiteracy has made it easier to regard discrepancies in the accounts as errors on his part. Greg, for instance, claimed that whenever the lines dividing daily receipts into weekly groups do not show performances on weekdays and the omission of Sunday there is a mistake, and also, that when the letters 'ne' appear against a play known to be old and not newly revived, 'the one or two cases not thus covered are apparently slips on Henslowe's part'.(3) He may be right about both points, but it is worth drawing attention to other possible interpretations of the evidence.

His correction of dates makes sense, but it should be observed that the 'weekly' groups range from one to ten performances, and though the norm is six (108 groups), there are twenty-five groups of five performances, nine of four, and eleven of three. As the accounts now stand, at least one lined entry appears against every day of the

(1) *The Real War of the Theatres*, p. 5.

(2) See *Diary*, II, 116, 46–7, 324–7.

(3) *Diary*, II, 324–7 and 148.

week; and again, while the norm is Monday (ninety-one times), lines appear against Sunday dates on thirty occasions. In some instances, as where there is a duplication of a date or dates, for example the repetition of 6 October on f. 13, an error on Henslowe's part is almost certain; but Greg's corrections also include the emendation of a date at the head of a sequence, as on f. 8v, where Henslowe wrote 'begninge the 27 of desembʒ', a date which Greg thinks should be 26 December; the correction of dates in straightforward runs, such as 19 December (f. 25v), which he claims should be 18 December; and one or two corrections of dates revised by Henslowe himself, such as a Sunday, 28 September 1595 (f. 13), altered by Henslowe from 27 September, which Greg would correct to Monday, 29 September. It is true that from about 1583 onwards the performance of plays on Sundays seems to have been prohibited, but the regulation was certainly neglected in 1587 and 1591,(1) and Greg's claim that his 'corrections are to all practical intents certain'(2) should not perhaps be accepted too easily. It assumes, in any case, what is perhaps not certain, that Henslowe made his entries regularly from day to day.

Two other factors, which Greg did not consider, need to be taken into account here. First, Henslowe sometimes seems to have written a column of dates before entering titles and receipts opposite them (cf. f. 9v, note 2, p. 23, and f. 12v, note 5, p. 30); on f. 9v dates and titles eventually fall completely out of alignment, and after trying to restore order by drawing a connecting line between dates and entries, he gave up at 5 August, and simply levelled off the entries at this point; two titles, *galiaso* and *the Jewe of malta* are both connected by lines to this date.(3) If this is a correct interpretation of what Henslowe did on this page, it suggests that individual dates may not have been of much significance to him, and also that entries may not necessarily have been made from day to day on the dates written, but possibly in batches. In other words, the date opposite a title may not

---

(1) Chambers, *E.S.* I, 314–15.

(2) *Diary*, II, 324; they were accepted by Chambers, *E.S.* II, 142; I, 314–15.

(3) Greg printed the second of these plays as unattached to a date, and merely noted, 'There is some confusion among the entries at this point' (*Diary*, I, 18, 220); see Plate II.

always represent the date of performance of that play, or the day on which Henslowe made the entry in his book.

This has a bearing on the second factor, which is the question, not fully solved, of why Henslowe made these daily entries at all. Greg brilliantly showed that in all probability the sums listed represent Henslowe's half-share of the gallery moneys which he received as landlord of the theatre,[1] that is to say, the rent paid by the company to him. In attempting to account for the sums entered later in the *Diary* (f. 48) under the heading 'Here I Begyne to Receue the wholle gallereys', Greg himself observes

> I suppose Henslowe...to have been from the beginning to the end of his recorded career in receipt of one half of the takings of the galleries as rent for his house. As this was a constant payment there was no need to specify it and as it was all profit there was no need to keep a record.[2]

If there was no need for Henslowe to keep a record at this time (1598), it may be wondered why he should have troubled to keep one earlier. A possible answer could have been provided by the contract Henslowe made with Cholmley to build the Rose in 1586/7; this specified that receipts were to be divided equally between them.[3] This contract, however, was due to expire in April 1595, and there is no evidence of its renewal, but the daily accounts run on into 1597. Moreover, Henslowe speaks, presumably of the Rose, as 'my playe howsse' in 1592 and 1595 (ff. 4, 2v), and Cholmley's name appears only once in the *Diary*, in the scribble on f. 1. It is inferred by Chambers that Cholmley was dead before entries in the *Diary* commence;[4] at any rate, it is reasonable to assume that the partnership had been dissolved. It is better to look for some other reason why Henslowe kept a list of his daily receipts.

A reason may be embedded in the frequent entries of payments to the Master of the Revels, at first by the week, later fortnightly or by the month. These payments seem to have constituted fees paid to the Master for permission to stage plays in the theatre.[5] The entries take

---

(1) *Diary*, II, 128–34; his conclusion was accepted by Chambers, *E.S.* I, 360–1; II, 139–40.

(2) *Diary*, II, 134.

(3) See below, p. 306.

(4) *E.S.* II, 408–9.

(5) Greg, *Diary*, II, 116–17; Chambers, *E.S.* I, 319–20.

several forms, a list of weekly payments in 1592 (f. 6v), a number of acquittances by servants of the Master of the Revels for payments by Henslowe (the first, for two weeks of playing in 1596, appears on f. 20v; the first acquittance for a monthly payment, on f. 23v, is dated 31 May 1597),[(1)] and notes within the columns of daily receipts, usually of the form 'm^r^ pd', as on ff. 14, 14v. Clearly, over the years from 1592 to 1597 the system of paying the Master was modified; what began as a weekly payment had become by the summer of 1597 a monthly payment. The daily entries come to an end in November 1597, about the time when Henslowe seems to have become not merely landlord but banker to the company;[(2)] the payments to the Master of the Revels continued, and in October 1598, Henslowe made a single payment covering the previous three months (f. 23v). It may be that as the basis of payment changed, it became no longer important for Henslowe to keep a list of daily performances, if one reason for doing so initially was to provide evidence for the Master or his man of actual performances, and a check for himself of what he should be paying; a close relationship between performance and payments may have decayed until the payments became a customary formality. Or possibly, when Henslowe became banker as well as landlord, the job of keeping a daily record was deputed to someone else.

If some such explanation of the daily entries is possible, it may be that their day-to-day accuracy is not significant, and that Henslowe entered plays against dates which do not always indicate the day of actual performance.[(3)] To correct the dates on the assumption that they should provide an accurate record from day to day may be an action based on incorrect presuppositions about both the character of the entries and the character of Henslowe himself.

---

(1) These occur irregularly in the *Diary*, and the existence of one for July 1602 on a slip of paper among the Dulwich manuscripts (MSS. I, 37; see below, p. 296) shows that acquittances were not necessarily written in Henslowe's account-book.

(2) *Diary*, II, 127, 131; Chambers, *E.S.* I, 361–2.

(3) Another point of interest in interpreting these entries is the fact that, if plays marked 'ne' are excluded, for which entrance charges to the theatre seem to have been raised, the average daily receipts, according to Henslowe's figures, were highest on Tuesdays and Mondays, and lowest on Saturdays. Averages based on Greg's corrected dates show little alteration in the picture.

Concerning the meaning of 'ne', there is no reason to think that Henslowe made errors in his use of this unexplained note;(1) it is better to find an interpretation of 'ne' which fits all its occurrences. Some of the plays so marked were not new; for instance, *2 Tamar Cam* is marked twice as 'ne', on 28 April 1592 (f. 7v), as played by Strange's Men, and again on 11 June 1596 (f. 21v), as played by Admiral's Men; *Alexander and Lodowick* is marked 'ne' on 14 January 1597 (f. 25v), and again on 11 February 1597 (f. 26). If the first of these repetitions is explicable as relating to a play new to the Admiral's Men, the second is not, and Chambers, in a cautious and balanced consideration of the meaning of 'ne', rejects this as an error by Henslowe.(2) Like Greg, he thinks that 'Two explanations are possible' of the use of 'ne' by Henslowe, that a play was new to the repertory, or 'had undergone...substantial process of revision before revival',(3) to be so marked. But the most significant common factor about the entries marked 'ne' is that the takings for these performances were always high; this includes both 'ne' performances of *Alexander and Lodowick*, which took respectively 55*s.* and 65*s.*, when the daily average of plays not marked 'ne' ranges at different periods from about 20*s.* to 30*s.*, and on the day of highest receipts (Tuesday or Monday) only rises above 40*s.* during the 1592 season. Clearly either a higher charge was made to spectators at these plays or they attracted much larger audiences. One possibility which covers all occurrences of 'ne' is that this refers to the licensing of a play-book for performance by the Master of the Revels. Several instances of Henslowe paying 7*s.* for this purpose are recorded in the *Diary* from 1598 onwards (the first appears on f. 44), but these are entered in the *Diary* apparently by chance, and others must be lost.(4) The company would need increased takings for such plays in order to

---

(1) See *Diary*, II, 148.

(2) *E.S.* II, 143–6.

(3) *E.S.* II, 146.

(4) Cf. MSS. I, 37, p. 296 below. Greg and Chambers (*E.S.* II, 143 n.) take the entry '17 p' and 'from hence lycensed' in the daily entries of March 1595 on f. 11v to refer to plays, and the commencement of the need for licensing of this kind; but it might equally refer to payments for licensing performances: there is no other reference to licensing plays for performance within the daily entries, or during the period (1592–7) during which these are made in the *Diary*. But the position of the Master of the Revels as a licenser and censor of plays was well established by 1589 (*E.S.* I, 319), and he must have taken a fee for each play.

recoup the sum spent on licensing, and a new licence may itself have been a good advertising point. A licence was required for a new play, presumably for a revival, at least when substantial revision had been made of the play, and also, it is probable, in a variety of other circumstances. So, possibly, *Alexander and Lodowick* had for some reason to be withdrawn and relicensed; this may have been news, for on its second appearance as 'ne' it was an unusual success, taking more money than any play between the preceding Christmas and the phenomenal *The Comedy of Humours* in the following summer.

Solutions to such problems as the meaning of the lined entries, or the meaning of 'ne', can at best be offered as probabilities, and the most acceptable are those which can most easily be reconciled with the evidence of the *Diary*; Henslowe certainly made some mistakes, but it is unfortunate that a view of him has been accepted which encourages a trust in his deficiencies. It is better to assume that he is right unless he can be proved wrong.

Together with a belief in Henslowe's illiteracy, Greg took over another assumption of Fleay's which may have hampered evaluation of the evidence in the account-book. He quoted Fleay's argument:

One prevailing error has been the assumption that Henslowe's was a typical management, and that other companies were conducted in the same manner. This was not so...the especial value of Henslowe's document lies not, as I have seen it asserted, in its showing us what the inner arrangement of Shakespeare's company must also have been, but in setting before us the selfish hand-to-mouth policy on which its principal rivals were guided, and consequently an explanation of their ultimate failure, in spite of the excellence of many of their plays, and the genius of their authors.[1]

To this Greg added an endorsement of his own:

I quite agree with Fleay that Henslowe's methods were not those best adapted to the free development of the dramatic energies of the company, being such as were forced upon them by their want of capital, and I believe his comparison to be in the main a true one. What it is important to bear in mind is that the financial arrangements which we find obtaining in the groups of companies under Henslowe's control were the exception rather than the rule.[2]

---

(1) *Diary*, II, 112.

(2) *Ibid.* II, 113.

There are no grounds for calling Henslowe's arrangements with his companies 'the exception rather than the rule'. He had dealings with all the principal companies of his time; from 1594 until 1602 he financed one of the two main companies, and in 1602–3 two (Admiral's and Worcester's) of the three officially recognised companies. The lack of evidence about the working methods of the Chamberlain's Men makes difficult any comparison with those of the Admiral's; but it is worth noting the superficial parallel between the two companies, one having as its leading actor (Richard Burbage) the son of the owner, the other having as its leading actor (Edward Alleyn) the son-in-law of the owner. The account-book reveals a friendly and, on the whole, harmonious relationship between Henslowe and the players, a harmony which strongly contrasts with the quarrels and lawsuits that embittered relations between Francis Langley, the one other landlord about whose dealings much is known, and the companies at the Swan and Boar's Head theatres.(1) Moreover, James Burbage's arrangement with his company at the Theatre, whereby he, as owner of the playhouse, took half the gallery moneys,(2) seems to have been similar to Henslowe's; and when, upon the building of the Globe in 1599, five sharers of the Chamberlain's Men were admitted as housekeepers, with a share in the theatre and ground lease, the new agreements were made for a sound business reason, namely in order to keep the Globe in the hands of the members of the company, or the longest survivors among the housekeepers, and prevent its passing to heirs, and so out of their control.(3) So although it would be unwise to press these analogies far, for we do not know whether Henslowe's arrangements with his companies were typical of the period, there is little justification for drawing a contrast between Henslowe, as a mercenary

---

(1) See C.W.Wallace, 'The Swan Theatre and the Earl of Pembroke's Servants', *Englische Studien*, XLIII (1910–11), 340–95; Chambers, *E.S.* II, 131ff.; C.J. Sisson, 'Mr and Mrs Browne of the Boar's Head', *Life and Letters Today* (winter 1936–7), pp. 99–107, and 'The Red Bull Company and the Importunate Widow', *Shakespeare Survey 7* (1954), pp. 57–68. It should be noted that much later, in 1615, Henslowe was accused of harsh dealing by actors, and, rather extravagantly, of breaking five companies in three years; but there is no sign of discord before this; see *Papers*, pp. 86–90, and *E.S.* I, 365–8.

(2) Chambers, *E.S.* II, 384ff.

(3) This point was made by C. W. Wallace; see Chambers, *E.S.* II, 417–18.

capitalist, and the Burbages;[1] the evidence suggests that they were all capitalists.

If some of the general assumptions handed down from Greg need to be reconsidered, the material in the account-book is also open to fresh interpretation. Two examples may serve to illustrate how valuable a careful re-examination might prove to be. The first is one which has exercised the minds of several scholars, the problem of the meaning of the five-column entries which extend from January to November 1597 (ff. 26–27v); this is an important question, because the change to these from the earlier form of entry may indicate a change in Henslowe's relationship with the Admiral's Men. Greg observed that the first two columns represent pounds and shillings, the last three, allowing for certain errors on Henslowe's part, pounds, shillings and pence; but he could find 'no mutual dependence whatever' between the two sets of figures. The first two columns, which correspond fairly well with previous receipts, he interpreted as a continuation of daily entries and as indicating the owner's takings of half the gallery money; the three-column entries he explained as listing the 'sums which Henslowe was able every now and then to squeeze out of the company towards the repayment of the moneys advanced' in the previous year to various members of the Admiral's Men and the company as a whole.[2]

Different interpretations were put forward by C. W. Wallace and E. K. Chambers. Wallace suggested that the last three columns represent the players' door-receipts;[3] but Chambers rejected this argument by pointing out[4] that '(*a*) these (the sharers' door-receipts) would not all pass through Henslowe's hands; (*b*) the amounts are often less than half the galleries, and (*c*) the columns are blank for some days of playing'. He in turn put forward a suggestion that the disputed entries represent money that Henslowe advanced to the players. The proposal of Wallace was taken up again by T. W. Baldwin, who argued that the figures in the last three columns, which include pence, are a record of the actors' door-receipts; he based this view on his observations that Henslowe changed his style

---

(1) As Chambers does, *ibid.* I, 360ff.; see especially p. 368.

(2) *Diary*, II, 131. (3) *Loc. cit.* p. 361. (4) *E.S.* II, 143n.

of entry at this time from 'Rd' (Received) to 'tt' (ttottalis), and that the second set of figures is frequently smaller than the first and therefore cannot include them. The blank entries in these three-column figures he regarded as being due to Henslowe's ignorance since he 'was not necessarily in a position to know these receipts accurately all the time'.(1)

There are objections to each of the three theories. When this system of entries in five columns began, Henslowe already had a current account of advances and repayments with the players (f. 22v and f. 23) which corresponds in no way with the amounts appearing in the five-column entries. This account became inactive after 14 March 1597 and Henslowe closed it out on 25 March 1597 with an advance of £5. 14*s*. which brought the total due from the players to an even £30. The theories of Greg and Chambers that the entries in question represent either repayments or advances from him therefore involve an assumption that he kept two parallel accounts with the players, at least for the period from 24 January to 14 March 1597, one of which is not in the account-book, and that, on some basis not known, he was able to separate his advances and repayments between the two accounts. The theory of Wallace (and Baldwin) seems to collapse entirely, as Chambers noted, on the lack of correlation between the entries in the columns on any given day. Of all these writers, only Chambers noticed that the character of the entries in the last three columns changes after a few weeks;(2) he drew no inference from this fact, but another interpretation of their meaning might be deduced from it.

From 24 January to 14 March 1597 (5 weeks of playing), there seems to be a rough correlation between the first two and last three columns on a weekly basis; the three-column entries of this period are marked off from the later ones, both by the comparatively large sums listed, a point Chambers observed, and by the fact that there are no all-zero entries. On 15 March, the day following the last regular advance made by Henslowe to the players and recorded in

(1) 'Posting Henslowe's Accounts', *J. English and Germanic Philology*, XXVI (1927), 42–90; the quotation is from p. 71.
(2) *E.S.* II, 143.

the current account, the first of the all-zero entries appears, and the weekly correlation between the two sets of figures either ceases, or rests on a quite different basis for the remainder of these accounts. Henslowe had been advancing money to the players from 2 May 1596, and was to resume doing so from October 1597 onwards; but between 15 March and October 1597 the account-book seems to indicate no financing of the company at all. It is possible that his loans of this period, and the players' repayments, are buried in the three-column entries. During the period (24 January to 14 March 1597) when Henslowe maintained another account with the players, the weekly totals average out at about £20, and there are no days with all-zero entries. As soon as he ceased to record advances in the old account, the amounts listed in the three-column entries drop to an average of £6 or £7 a week, and all-zero entries occur frequently. The explanation may be that for the duration of these entries Henslowe was responsible for collecting all the receipts;[1] that in the first two columns he listed one half of the gallery money, continuing his former practice, and in the three-column entries recorded the door money due to the players; and that he maintained a separate account of advances to the players until 14 March, after which date the fall in weekly totals of the three-column entries indicates that he was repaying himself out of current takings, and listing the net amounts turned over to the company after he had deducted what was owing to him. There would thus be no need for a separate account of advances and repayments. According to this hypothesis the first two columns would be likely to represent the players' half of the gallery moneys, and not Henslowe's, and 'tt' (ttottalis[2]) opposite each entry might be taken to indicate a sum Henslowe was holding on behalf of the company. The variations in amount in the three-column entries, and the occurrence of all-zero entries, suggest that these were not reckoned daily, as the gallery moneys seem to have been, but irregularly, and that the deductions Henslowe had to make sometimes took all the door money. This explanation of the five-column entries has the virtue, if it is a virtue, of reconciling all

(1) As Wallace and Baldwin suggested. (2) So spelt out on f. 19, p. 43, and elsewhere.

the solutions so far proposed without assuming that Henslowe kept another account-book, or that he was incompetent.

The second example of the value of a fresh examination of the material in the account-book is based on the one error of consequence which Greg made in a reading. He noted that the book contains five lists of names of members of the Admiral's Men; these are on ff. 3; 43v (11 October 1597); 44v (March 1598); 70 (July 1600); 104 (July 1600). In the first of these Greg found what he read as 'lame Charles alen', whom he took to be a person otherwise unknown.(1) These words are written one under the other, and respectively opposite 'J syngr', 'R Jonnes' and 'T towne'; it seemed more likely that they might refer to three separate persons, a suspicion confirmed when the first letter, which is smudged, proved to be *s*, so that the column reads 'same Charles alen'. These probably represent Samuel Rowley (cf. 'same Rowley', f. 52v), Charles Massey (who later appears frequently in conjunction with Rowley; they figure as 'sam' and 'Charles' in the plot of *Frederick and Basilea*), and Richard Alleyn (not Edward, who heads the adjacent list).

If this identification is correct it raises several issues. In the first place, this list occurs between entries of 14 December 1594 and 14 January 1595, and, as Greg argues,(2) it belongs probably to the month between these dates, although there is a possibility that the list was added later in a blank space.(3) The first known mention elsewhere of Rowley and Massey is in the plot of *Frederick and Basilea*, which belongs to June 1597,(4) and therefore this list may provide the earliest record of them. It must in any case be the earliest of the lists Greg noted, for Slater, Donstone and Edward Alleyn, who are named in it, had left the company by October 1597, and do not appear in the later ones.

The date of this first list is affected by a sixth list of names, which Greg left out of account,(5) perhaps because of its shortness: this

---

(1) *Diary*, II, 99–100, 237. (2) *Diary*, II, 99 n.

(3) See p. 8, note 3.

(4) See below, p. 328. A Samuel Rowley, who may be the same man, was married in April 1594; see G. E. Bentley, *The Jacobean Stage* (1941), II, 555.

(5) As did Chambers in *E.S.*, and Greg again in his reconsideration of sharers in *Dramatic Documents* (1931), I, 31 ff.

occurs on f. 23, contains only four names, those of Edward Alleyn, Slater, Donstone, and Juby, and is dated 14 October 1596. It belongs to a period when Jones and Downton had left to form what was to be Pembroke's Men at the Swan Theatre,[(1)] and when Towne and Singer were missing for a time from the Admiral's Men, and it is connected with attempts, as it seems from entries on the same page, to attract new actors or sharers to join the company. In other words, the company seems to have been reduced at this time to four sharers. The likely history of the Admiral's Men, then, is a development from the first list (which includes Jones and Downton), through a period of decline in numbers which is reflected in the October 1596 list, to a recovery of strength in 1597, when Jones and Downton returned from the Swan with Shaa and Bird, and Towne and Singer also reappear. The existence of a list belonging to 1596, then, tends to reinforce the conclusion that the likeliest date of the first list of names is December–January 1594–5.

Other questions raised by the new reading are the exact nature of these lists, and the status in the company of the men named. Richard Alleyn appears only in the first list, and his name last appears in the account-book in an entry of May 1600 (f. 53).[(2)] Rowley and Massey became sharers presumably by 1600, when their names are incorporated in the company lists; but they are named in the first list, and again in the list of March 1598, and in both, their names are set apart from the rest, although in the latter they seem to be joined with the sharers in acknowledging a debt of the company.

The matter is complicated by two other pieces of evidence. One is the set of agreements made between Henslowe and various actors in 1597 and 1598 (*Diary*, ff. 233–229v, and Fragment 5), when the company was reconstituted after a number of its principal members had seceded for a period.[(3)] Greg argues that unless these contracts specify wages, they relate to sharers in the company; and he thinks that the agreements concerning Richard Alleyn, binding him as a

---

(1) C. W. Wallace, *loc. cit.* pp. 350, 357ff.

(2) But Henslowe lent money to his widow in September 1602 (f. 230).

(3) See Chambers, *E.S.* II, 149–58, where the agreements are printed in their chronological order.

'hired servant', and Thomas Heywood, Rowley and Massey, binding them as 'covenant servants' for two years, indicate 'the inception of sharership' for these men.[1] The agreements with Alleyn and Heywood are dated March 1598, that with Rowley and Massey, November 1598. It is true that in the two appearances of Richard Alleyn in the *Diary* as authorising payments for the company in 1599 and in May 1600 (ff. 53 and 69; the second of these, it may be noted, is dated after the termination of his 1598 contract), Greg was able to find support for his view that Alleyn was a sharer at this time; but there is no evidence in the *Diary* about Thomas Heywood. In making this claim Greg may be glossing over a significant difference, in form as well as date, between these agreements and the four of 1597 relating to Jones, Downton, Bird and Shaa, all sharers, which simply bind these men to play in Henslowe's theatre.[2]

The other piece of evidence is provided by the actors' names in the extant dramatic plots.[3] In these a number of men are given the honorific 'Mr', which Greg thinks indicates a sharer: 'In a few exceptional cases a sharer appears without the honorific, but no non-sharer is ever graced with it.'[4] Thomas Hunt, Richard Alleyn, Rowley and Massey all appear without the addition of 'Mr' in the plot of *Frederick and Basilea* (*c.* June 1597), and with it in the plot of *The Battle of Alcazar.*

Neither Hunt nor Alleyn appears in the lists of sharers noticed by Greg in the *Diary*; he therefore argued that Alleyn, whose agreement is dated 25 March 1598, and Hunt, for whom no agreement is recorded, and who appears only once in the *Diary*, as paid 6*s.* 8*d.* in 1596 (?a week's wage as an actor), were sharers for two years from March 1598, after the list on f. 44v was drawn up, and had left the company before the list of July 1600 (f. 70) was entered. He also argued, as a consequence of this, that the plot of *The Battle of Alcazar*, in which these appear with 'Mr' against their names, must on their account be dated within this two-year period, and probably in the

---

(1) *Dramatic Documents*, I, 34.

(2) See *Two Elizabethan Stage Abridgements* (Malone Society Reprints, 1923), pp. 88–90.

(3) See below, pp. 326–33.

(4) *Dramatic Documents*, I, 38.

winter of 1598/9.[1] This theory involved Greg in two difficulties. First, Edward Alleyn is named in the plot of *The Battle of Alcazar*, but he retired from acting between 1597 and late in 1600; Greg explains his presence in this as an 'occasional appearance' in emergence from retirement.[2] Secondly, the agreement between Henslowe and Rowley and Massey marking, as Greg thinks, the commencement of their status as sharers is dated November 1598, but their names appear, set apart, it is true, from the others, in the list of March 1598 (f. 44v); Greg was therefore driven to argue that their names were added retrospectively to this list, months later; this is, of course, mere supposition.[3]

A correct reading of the first list alters the whole picture and casts some doubt upon the assumptions that only sharers are named in the lists in the *Diary*, and that 'Mr' in the plots is used only of sharers. This list must be earlier than any of the others, and it contains, also set apart from the main sharers, the names of Rowley, Massey and (Richard) Alleyn. This suggests that, perhaps as early as the end of 1594, certainly before 1597, these three had positions of some prominence with the company. There is no reason to think that they were sharers then, and the fact that their names are set apart from the sharers both in this list and in that of March 1598 perhaps indicates that they had a different standing. It is possible that they had some status between that of sharer and hired man, were master actors;[4] or alternatively, held a fractional share before they became full members. Some such arrangement might also explain the curious appearance of Thomas Hunt as 'Mr' in the plots of *Troilus and Cressida* and *The Battle of Alcazar*, though he never figures in the

(1) *Dramatic Documents*, I, 40; and cf. his article, 'The Evidence of Theatrical Plots for the History of the Elizabethan Stage', *Rev. English Studies*, I (1925), 257–74, especially pp. 272–4.

(2) *Ibid.* I, 39.

(3) See *Dramatic Documents*, I, 34. On the same basis of argument, the names of Alleyn, Heywood and Hunt should also have been included, as Greg notes; but he thinks that 'with Henslowe's methods it would be mainly a matter of chance whether new sharers were called upon to acknowledge the company's debt'.

(4) If part of a sharer's return to the company was his service as an actor (see *E.S.* I, 352ff.), and Henslowe owned shares in the company, he might, as a non-actor, have come to an arrangement with certain actors whereby they received special terms, better than those of a hired man, perhaps some return from a share, while he kept the shares in his control. This might explain the word 'servant' in the contracts of 1598 between him and Alleyn, Rowley and Massey.

Diary as a sharer; and the status of Thomas Heywood, who bound himself, with Alleyn, Rowley and Massey, as hired or covenant servant to Henslowe for two years in 1598, but for whose membership of the company neither the plots nor the *Diary* afford any evidence.(1) The appearance of the names of Alleyn, Rowley and Massey in an early list of the Admiral's Men thus affects in some measure the interpretation of all the lists, and, possibly, the dating of the dramatic plots associated with the company.(2)

These examples may serve to illustrate that the possibilities of interpreting Henslowe's account-book are by no means exhausted. The entries relating to companies and theatres are closely interconnected, so that a new explanation of the five-column entries, a new reading, or a reconsideration of the lists of names of members of the Admiral's Men, may affect in some measure the meaning of the whole body of material in the book. As the primary source for the theatrical history of the Elizabethan age, it deserves constant and careful study, for many assumptions are grounded upon it; and by its nature as a private record of transactions which are often ambiguous or unexplained in their context, numerous difficulties of interpretation arise. It is the purpose of this edition to make the material readily available again, and to encourage a fresh scrutiny of the evidence which is set out in the following pages.

8. FRAGMENTS AND SUPPLEMENTARY MATERIAL

In this edition the text of the *Diary* is followed by a reprint of the five major fragments that have been found, and a note of authors' signatures apparently cut from the *Diary* and pasted in books in the Bodleian Library. For comment on these, reference should be made to the headnotes on pp. 265–8 below.

The collection of manuscripts at Dulwich contains a number of

---

(1) It might also account for the equally curious appearance in the *Diary* of William Juby as authorising payments for the company between 1598 and 1602, though he does not appear in lists of sharers or in the plots.

(2) See below, pp. 326–33. In the lists of names of actors in the plots printed here, 'Mr' is interpreted as 'Master Actor' rather than the specific 'sharer'; and a later date than Greg's is preferred for the plots of *The Battle of Alcazar* and *2 Fortune's Tennis* for reasons stated in the headnotes. But the evidence for both of these plots is inconclusive.

items which relate very closely to entries in the *Diary*, and which are printed here from new transcripts in Appendix I. Most of the items included here were printed, together with much other material not relating to the *Diary*, in Greg's *Henslowe Papers* (1907); the excerpts from manuscripts, vol. I, article 25, and from vol. III, were not included in Greg's collection. The relationship of the items to material in the *Diary* is pointed out in the headnote to each. As the items are printed here in order of their numbering in Warner's *Catalogue*, it may be helpful to indicate what different kinds of material they contain. Many of these documents are of a personal kind; there is a group of letters interchanged between Edward Alleyn, while he was on tour during the plague of 1593, and his wife and Henslowe who remained in London, and one letter from his wife, Joan, to Edward Alleyn, who was in the country, during the plague of 1603. These letters (MSS. I, 9–15, 38) throw much light on personal relationships in Henslowe's *ménage*, and on some members of the company. A number of other letters amplify the evidence of the *Diary* concerning actors or concerning Henslowe's family and private affairs. The best-known is Henslowe's letter to Alleyn in September 1598, during the latter's retirement from acting, which announces the death of Gabriel Spenser in a duel with Jonson (MS. I, 24). Others in this category are the begging letters from Bird to Henslowe in 1599 (I, 105), and from Francis Henslowe to Philip, *c.* 1590–2 (MS. III, 5), and the letter from William Henslowe to Philip of 1592 concerning the property of Lockyers and other family affairs (III, 6). Reference is made to two other items (MSS. III, 1 and 2) concerning Henslowe's dealings in property with Isabel Keys, principally because Warner was followed by Greg in misreading the date of one as 1576, and so taking it to be the earliest known reference to Philip; in fact the date must be 1596.(1) In addition, the bonds from Richard Bradshaw to William Bird of 1598/9 (MS. I, 25), and from Francis Henslowe to Philip of March 1605 (MS. I, 42), are noted because they help to explain references in the *Diary*.

The documents also include a group of business letters (MSS. I, 26,

(1) See below, p. 299; this date (1576/7) was taken over by Chambers, *E.S.* I. 359.

31–6; see also p. 315) of the period 1599–1602, concerning the purchase of play-books for the company, which amplify entries of payments in the *Diary*, and give information not in the theatrical accounts. These items provide examples of a kind of document, a letter from a principal member of the company asking for an advance to be paid on a new play-book, which perhaps never existed in quantity; for it may be supposed that such requests were often, perhaps normally, made by word of mouth, and Henslowe's own notes in the *Diary* of a loan advanced would then be the only record in writing. There also appears in these miscellaneous manuscripts one acquittance (MS. I, 37) from William Playstowe to Henslowe on behalf of the Master of the Revels, dated 1602, which is of special interest as listing the titles of five plays for which Henslowe owed a licensing fee.

The remaining documents are in many ways the most important as concerning the theatre and the companies. Among them are the deed of partnership of 1586/7 between Henslowe and Cholmley for the erection of the Rose (Muniment 16), and the contract between Peter Street and Henslowe for the building of the Fortune Theatre in 1599/1600 (Muniment 22); two warrants and a petition (MSS. I, 27–9) also relate to the establishment of this theatre. In addition, there are two petitions and a warrant relating to the temporary closure of the Rose, probably in 1594 (MSS. I, 16–18), and Edward Alleyn's notes of his expenses on the Beargarden and the Fortune from 1594 onwards (MSS. VIII and XVIII, 7). Some jottings of Henslowe regarding a performance at Court by Worcester's Men, probably in 1602, are also printed (MS. XI). Finally, two important items concern company property. One is the deed by which Richard Jones sold his share in theatrical property to Edward Alleyn in 1588/9 (MS. I, 2); it is interpreted by Chambers as indicating that at this time Alleyn, with his brother John, 'bought up the properties [i.e. of the first company known as Admiral's Men] and allied himself with the Lord Strange's men',(1) and it is thus of considerable significance for the interpretation of the earliest theatrical accounts in the *Diary*. The second is a list of costumes in the hand of Edward Alleyn

(1) *E.S.* II, 137–8; see also Greg, *Dramatic Documents*, I, 12–16.

(MS. I, 30). This mentions a few parts in plays, Henry VIII, Will Summers, Daniel (though this may be an actor), Candish (? Cavendish, also an actor), Faustus and the Guise, and Priam. Faustus and the Guise belong to popular plays of Marlowe, which were revived after many years, the former, for instance, in 1602 (f. 108 v), the latter in 1601 (f. 94 v). The allusions to Henry VIII and Will Summers (there is also listed a cardinal's gown) may well relate to the two-part play on *Cardinal Wolsey*, which was in production in 1601 and 1602 (*Diary*, ff. 93, 94 v, 105 v, 106), that to Priam may be connected with *Troilus and Cressida*, written in 1599 (ff. 54 v, 63), or *Troy*, acted July 1596 (f. 21 v). On the whole, a probable date for this list is after Alleyn's return to acting in 1600 or early 1601; but these indications of date are at best tenuous. A late date is, however, preferable to Greg's conjecture that it belongs to the same period (1598) as the inventories, apparently in Henslowe's hand, which were printed by Malone, and which are included in this edition in Appendix 2.

There seems no reason to doubt that these inventories, now lost, were genuine, and the spelling suggests Henslowe's hand. Many clues within the lists confirm the March 1598 date at the head of the inventory of goods, costumes and properties. The list of titles, and note of goods bought after March 1598, can also be dated with reasonable accuracy as belonging to about August–October 1598. The headnote and footnotes to the text of these inventories present the evidence for this dating, and point out the many connections the inventories have with items in the *Diary*.

A third Appendix contains lists of actors' names in the seven extant dramatic plots or fragments of plots, all of which seem to have been associated at some time with Alleyn or his company. The later plots, the five which can be dated between 1597 and 1603, were certainly acted by Admiral's Men, and provide useful evidence of the composition of the company. The problems raised by these plots are discussed in headnotes to them, where reference is made to discussions of them elsewhere.[1]

---

(1) See also above, p. xxxviii.

9. HENSLOWE'S HANDWRITING

The main purpose of this section is to draw attention to the possibilities of error in transcription to which all editors of a document such as Henslowe's account-book are subject. The major sources of confusion are listed below separately under each letter and numeral, and representative examples are cited. These will indicate how uncertain a number of readings must remain. Some difficulties are due to a combination of careless writing and peculiar spelling, but the implications of Greg's casual phrase, 'Henslowe's handwriting is irregular and uneducated like his spelling',(1) should not be too readily accepted. Certainly the handwriting is irregular, but the account-book is a private notebook, kept for jottings of accounts over a period of more than twelve years, and a good deal of variation in the writing is to be expected; at best there is no reason to regard it as better than the equivalent of a dramatist's 'foul papers'. Henslowe's spelling is often very individual, and his curious handling of some historical and classical names may indicate ignorance; but English spelling was not settled at this time, and his odd spellings are not much stranger than those found in many other manuscripts of the period.(2) It is extremely doubtful whether they can be used as evidence of his education or lack of it; this is a matter of which nothing is known. At the same time, Greg's insistence that the editor is forced to compromise at times between what he can read, and what he knows or supposes the author to have intended, needs to be reiterated. Many of the sources of confusion are of a kind well known, extremely common in secretary hand, and often the cause of errors in printed texts; and the length of the list of difficulties given below is not due to an unusually obscure hand. Henslowe's writing, though often, as is natural, careless and hurried into a scrawl, is generally fairly easy to read.

a

This letter is easily exaggerated into a majuscule form by elaboration of the pen's upstroke, and it frequently appears much larger than

(1) *Diary*, I, xxiv.

(2) For example, in Hand *D* of *Sir Thomas More* (Shakespeare's, it is presumed), there occur *loff* (=loaf), *scilens* (=silence), *deule* (=devil), *ffraunc* (=France), *Jarman* (=German).

other letters, especially where it stands alone as the word 'a', or separated from the rest of the word to which it belongs (it is especially liable as an initial letter to become detached from the rest of the word, as in *A men*, f. 7). Greg generally treated these large forms as minuscules,[1] and printed them in lower-case, but in the present text they are printed as capital letters. This seems to be nearer to the original, and is in line with the frequent appearance of majuscule *C*, *R*, *I*, *L*, *B*, *D*, *K*. Minuscule *a* is liable to confusion, when carelessly formed, with a number of other letters. The most common difficulty arises when the final down-stroke is not completed, and the letter becomes almost indistinguishable from *o*. Examples may be found on f. 2 (*bonde*; *bande* Greg), f. 83 (*RadeRicke*; *RodeRicke* Greg). If the down-stroke is carelessly raised to become nearer to the horizontal than the vertical, then *a–e* confusion is also possible; so on f. 24 occurs *parsonege* (*parsonage* Greg), and on f. 61 *Remnant* (*Remment* Greg); this, however, is rare. A more natural difficulty may be caused by the omission of the cross-stroke, or its attenuation, which leaves a form like *u*; the best example of this confusion is on f. 67v, *pethyas* (*pethyus* Greg).

b

Again, as the majuscule is often little more than an elaborated minuscule, it is not always easy to determine which is intended. Otherwise this letter offers only one difficulty; the fully formed majuscule is similar to majuscule *R*, and where the bottom loop is not closed, confusion may arise. There is one example in this text, on f. 55, where *Baggete* or *Raggete* may be read; this proper name occurs nowhere else.

c

As commonly in secretary hand, it is hard to distinguish carelessly written *c* from *r* (cf. f. 6v; n. 4, p. 15) or from a small *t*, and wch and wth are often almost identical (as on f. 19v, w^{th}; wch Greg). Other possibilities of minuscule confusion are described under *e* and *o*. One

(1) He printed them as capitals in his transcription of a sample page of the *Diary* (f. 65) in *English Literary Autographs* (1932), Plate I.

curious form of majuscule *C* is indistinguishable from majuscule *S*, and occurs several times, near the bottom of f. 11 (*Comodey*; so Greg), f. 127 (*Chilldermas*; *Shilldermas* Greg), and f. 221 (*Complayneth*; *Somplayneth* Greg).[1] One other peculiar form of majuscule *C* is used solely to represent the Roman numeral, as in the lists of articles bought for theatre repair, f. 5.

d

The minuscule varies in size, and when small is indistinguishable from *e*; this may cause difficulties, as at f. 55 (*gardiners lane* or *land*); f. 93 v (see note 1, p. 182: *strowd*; *strowe* Greg); f. 98 v (see note 1, p. 191: *Lyngard*; *Lyngare* Greg). Also, the majuscule is commonly an enlarged minuscule, and the use of upper-case must often indicate an editor's interpretation of what is on Henslowe's page (cf. the last entry on f. 66, *Downton*; *downton* Greg).

e

The letter is often attenuated into a mere squiggle or dash, especially at the end of a word, so that it sometimes disappears altogether, and will be found italicised in the present text more frequently than any other letter. It is not surprising, then, that it is sometimes easily confused with other letters besides *a* and *d*, discussed above. A carelessly looped *e* may look like *o*, and this causes numerous difficult readings, as on f. 7 (see note 4, p. 17: *mvle*; *mvlo* Greg); f. 12 (see note 2, p. 29: *setto*; *sette* Greg); f. 178 (see note 1, p. 247: *whetley*; *whotley* Greg). Or again, it may look like an erratic *l*, as on f. 5, near the foot of the page, where we at first read *nayllls*, and print *nayells*. One form of the letter may also be confused with *c* (as on f. 9 v, entry of 30 July, where *eamden* might be read as *camden*, and f. 57 v, second entry, where *Whittcakers* or *Whitteakers* is possible).

f

This letter is occasionally liable to confusion with the long *s*, if the cross-stroke is omitted, or if, as sometimes happens, a cross-stroke is

---

(1) Greg observed in relation to this, 'Were I starting afresh I should deliberately disregard the form and render the letter according to the evident intention of the writer only; a form such as "Somplayneth" should not appear' (*Diary*, I, xxvi).

made on an *s*; an example occurs on f. 37v (see note 2, p. 73: *sleavse*; *sleavfe* Greg). The majuscule, as was common practice, was indicated by doubling the letter.

g

The minuscule is normally differentiated from *y*, but confusion arises in a very few instances, where Henslowe seems to have written *g* in error for *y*, as on f. 45v (see note 1, p. 89: *cangones* = canions), and f. 73 (see note 1, p. 142: *sage* is probably an error for *saye*). On f. 43 (see note 2, p. 84), we read *wayghte* where Greg has *wagghte*. The majuscule is rare in Henslowe's hand.

h

There are two forms of minuscule *h*, and both may become majuscule by enlargement, so that there is no fixed borderline between minuscule and majuscule. But the letter raises no problems.

i

This vowel is subject to confusion with other minims when carelessly dotted, or not dotted at all (see notes on *n* and *m* below); and, more rarely, may also be mistaken for *o*, where the loop of the *o* is lost, or the *i* has acquired one through the crossing of the up- and down-strokes of the pen (see f. 4v, *ij lode of lome*; *lime* Greg; and the note on the numeral *1* below), or even for *r*, a letter often casually written (as on f. 85v, entry of 6 March, *hares*; *haies* Greg, but corrected in his *Corrigenda*). The majuscule is very frequently used for initial *i*. For *j*, see p. lvii below.

k

The minuscule may rarely, when casually written, be confused with *l*; see f. 178 (note 2, p. 248: *skedmore*; *sledmore* Greg). The majuscule is frequently developed by elaboration from the minuscule, and, as in the case of *d*, is not easily distinguished.

l

Sometimes this letter is crossed (apparently to indicate a majuscule form as a rule, but not always), so that when the loop is attenuated it may resemble *t*, as on f. 51v, entry of 16 November, *valtinge*;

vattinge Greg. For a rare confusion with *e*, see note on this letter. The majuscule is sometimes an elaborated minuscule, and what is intended has to be guessed.

m

Like many other writers of his time, Henslowe was casual about the number of strokes he made in his minim letters, and *m*, *n*, *un*, *in*, *im*, *mi*, *nu*, *ui*, *mm*, *nn* etc., are often liable to be misread. See, for instance, f. 8 v, *begninge* (any combination of letters is possible): f. 12, *ensuienge*; *ensiuenge* Greg: f. 33 v, entry of 4 October, *Jonnes*; *Jones* Greg: f. 124 v, *Sonne*; *Somme* Greg (altered in his *Corrigenda*). Terminal *m* is very liable to lose its final stroke, and appear as *n*, so that *them* is often written as *then*. Majuscule *M*, like *d*, *h*, *l*, is often enlarged from the minuscule, and the borderline is indeterminate; a full-scale majuscule is reserved for the initial letter of certain entries like the memorandum on f. 233.

n

This letter is virtually interchangeable with *u*, and some readings are uncertain, chiefly in proper names; see f. 1 v (*glene* or *gleue*); f. 12 v (*heugenyo*; *hengenyo* Greg); f. 96 (see note 1, p. 187: *ponescioues*: *ponesciones* Greg). Majuscule *N* rarely appears.

o

As noted above, *o* is liable to be confused with *e* and *i*, but usually stands free, whereas the other vowels are cursive and joined to the letter following. If the loop of the *o* is not closed, it may resemble *v* or *u*, as on f. 7 v, *whittsvn*; *whittson* Greg, and can also be mistaken for *c* as on f. 31 v, *tooke*; *tocke* Greg: f. 36 v, last line, *locke*; *looke* Greg. After *t* it may degenerate into little more than a curl of the cross-stroke.

p

Minuscule *p* and *x* are often indistinguishable, and confusion is possible occasionally, as at f. 24 v (see note 4, p. 53: *xd*; *pd* Greg).

q

A rare letter, which causes no difficulties.

r

Possible confusion with *c* and *i* has been discussed above. The major difficulty in transcribing this letter is its tendency to degenerate into a casual pen-stroke, even to disappear altogether (see f. 11v, *godfey*; *godfrey* Greg: f. 41, *cownseler*; *cownsele* Greg). The majuscule, which is much used, is once or twice difficult to distinguish from *B*, as noted above.

s

Occasional confusion with *f* has already been discussed under that letter; and the peculiar use of a majuscule *C* that is identical with a form of majuscule *S* has been described under *c*.

t

As noted above, *t* is sometimes indistinguishable from *c*. One form of majuscule *T* is very similar to majuscule *E*, but no confusion is caused by this.

u, *v*

See the remarks on *m* and *n* above. These letters are, of course, interchangeable, except that the initial is always written as *v*. Sometimes the initial flourish of *v* is much attenuated, and it is hard to know whether *v*, *u* or *w* is intended (see note on *w* below). As pointed out under *n*, *u* and *n* are often identical, and serious difficulty is caused in some proper names. There is one instance of *u*-*m* difficulty, on f. 105v (see note 3, p. 201: *wouon*; *womon* Greg). For other sources of confusion with *u*, see under *a* and *o*.

w

Like *v*, this letter also has an initial flourish which is sometimes lost in hurried or careless writing, and it may be mistaken for *u* or *v* (cf. f. 6v, *Rownd*; *Round* Greg, and f. 86, entry of 4 April, *Samwell*; *Samvell* Greg).

x

Its occasional confusion with *p* was noted above.

y, *z*

For occasional confusion of *y* with *g*, see under this letter; *z* is rare and causes no difficulties.

Numerals

Of the numerals, *2* and *8* require no discussion. *0* may lose its loop in the writing, or *1* gain one, and examples of difficulty may be found on f. 26 (see note 1, p. 57), *03*; *13* Greg; f. 32v (see note 2, p. 67), *031*; *131* Greg. The numeral *1* is frequently dotted, but is printed as the Arabic figure, except where the long *j* form is used, which is represented so. When either figure is carelessly written, *3* and *5* can look alike, as on f. 12v (see note 6, p. 29), where *2*[*3*]*4* may be *2*[*5*]*4*, and on f. 63 (see note 1, p. 122) *586*; *386* Greg. Occasionally the figure becomes so straightened out that it can be mistaken for *7*; examples may be found on f. 22v (see note 3, p. 49), *3 of Julye*; *7 of Julye* Greg, and f. 26v (see note 2, p. 58), where *03* could be *07*. On rare occasions *4* may be confused with *9*, as on f. 6v (see note 2, p. 15), *14 of ap*^{r}*ell*; *19 of ap*^{r}*ell* Greg. Besides the similarity noted above between *3* and *5*, the latter sometimes closely resembles *6*, as on f. 11 (see note 5, p. 26), *15*; *16* Greg, and f. 86v (see note 2, p. 169), *63 18 6*; *63 18 5* Greg.

10. OTHER HANDS IN THE DIARY

A large number of hands besides that of Philip Henslowe appear in the *Diary*.[(1)] These are recorded, and where possible identified, in the footnotes; individual entries may be traced by referring to the Index for the name of the person concerned. It is important, however, to comment here upon some doubts and difficulties. Many of these identifications should be regarded as probable rather than certain, particularly where, as in a number of instances, only one entry or signature of a person is found in the *Diary*. Even in the case of men who figure prominently in the accounts, like Downton, Shaa, Haughton or Alleyn, uncertainties still arise. Edward Alleyn is a special instance, for his name recurs many times as a witness for Henslowe, when clearly Henslowe has himself written it in. Greg pointed out that in autograph signatures in the *Diary* the name is always spelt *Alleyn* (*Alleȳ* once, f. 38), but this is no certain guide, for though Henslowe sometimes spells it *Al*(*l*)*en*, as on f. 3, he also,

(1) Listed by Greg in his edition, I, xxx–xxxiii.

as on f. 19v, writes it with a *y*. It may be that in accepting Greg's rejection of all but nine of the signatures in the *Diary* as not autograph we have been too rigorous, and a slight element of doubt must remain about some of what appear to be pretty good imitations by Henslowe.

Alleyn's was not the only signature imitated by Henslowe; he forged Gabriel Spenser's signature on f. 40 (writing *D* for *G*), and again on f. 42; and on f. 68 a signature of Haughton's is forged by Henslowe, or, Greg thinks, Shaa. Greg also came to think that the signature 'Raffe Bowes' on f. 72v was a copy by Henslowe.(1) On f. 100 the signature of Wentworth Smyth appears to have been written by Hathaway, though Greg thinks it is autograph. If the possibility that one man might imitate another's hand, or simply sign his name for him, complicates the identification of hands, further occasional difficulties are caused by the different styles of writing used by the same man, or by similarities between the hands of two people. The two most prominent examples of different styles used by one man are afforded by the signature of Day on f. 31, which differs from his usual signature, and Chapman's signature on f. 90 in an Italian script, which differs markedly from the more casual secretary hand which he seems usually to have employed, as in his signature on Fragment 2.(2) The variations of Day's hand may perhaps appear in the troublesome entry on f. 69, where the words 'by John day to the vse of Th Dekker Harry Chettle and himselfe' are written in two different styles, but, Greg suggests, are all in the hand of Day. We think the first words 'by...of' are in Henslowe's hand; the rest may be in Day's or Dekker's, though the wording does not support an attribution to the latter. The passage is much disputed, and a facsimile and references may be seen in *English Literary Autographs*, plate VII.

In this instance there is enough similarity between the hands of Day and Dekker to raise doubts about which of them wrote a brief

---

(1) *Diary*, II, 37, 377.

(2) See below, p. 266. These signatures of Chapman are reproduced in *English Literary Autographs*, plate XII; a number of Day's signatures are also reproduced, including the two mentioned here, on plates VI and VII.

note. Another pair whose hands sometimes, in very brief passages, may be confused are Shaa and Downton. Both of these write usually in a flowing secretary hand, but each on occasion uses a more formal, quasi-Italian script, especially for proper names. This is most noticeable in Shaa's entries, but in some signatures, and occasionally in entries, such as that on f. 64v, Downton also adopts a formal hand.[1] There is enough likeness between these to raise doubts about the titles added in a formal hand on f. 108; these Greg thought were in Shaa's hand, but Shaa had left the company many months before the date (October–November 1602) of these entries (see f. 104), and in any case these may just as well be in Downton's hand, as we think they are. A more difficult problem is raised by the list of names on f. 104, representing principal members or sharers of the company at some time between 7 and 23 February 1601/2. Greg thinks this is in Shaa's hand, as at first sight it appears to be; but Shaa is not in the list, and had just, it seems, left the company; he is last named on 21 January 1601/2 on this page, and the list of names is followed by a note recording the departure of Shaa and Jones. The list was originally headed by the name of Downton,[2] and was probably written by him.

It remains only to note other instances where we differ from Greg and to comment on forgeries. We think that the name 'm^{r} porter' added in a clumsy hand on f. 46 may be a forgery; and that the interlined 'm^{r} mastone' on f. 64v is genuine. The quittance on f. 88, which Greg thinks is in Langworth's hand, we feel sure is in Henslowe's, and the entry on f. 132v, which Greg thinks is in Henslowe's writing, seems rather to be in Shaa's. The forged entries observed by Warner and Greg are omitted from the text of the *Diary* in this edition, but are given, for the sake of reference, in footnotes.

---

(1) In the example of Shaa's hand reproduced at the top of plate I in *English Literary Autographs*, a facsimile of f. 65 of the *Diary*, it will be observed that he writes the name 'H. Chettle' in his formal manner. The two styles of Downton may be seen by comparing the entry of his reproduced also on this plate, with his signature as a witness reproduced on plate II from f. 85 of the *Diary*.

(2) It is now headed by that of Singer, whose name was written third in the list, deleted, and inserted again above Downton's.

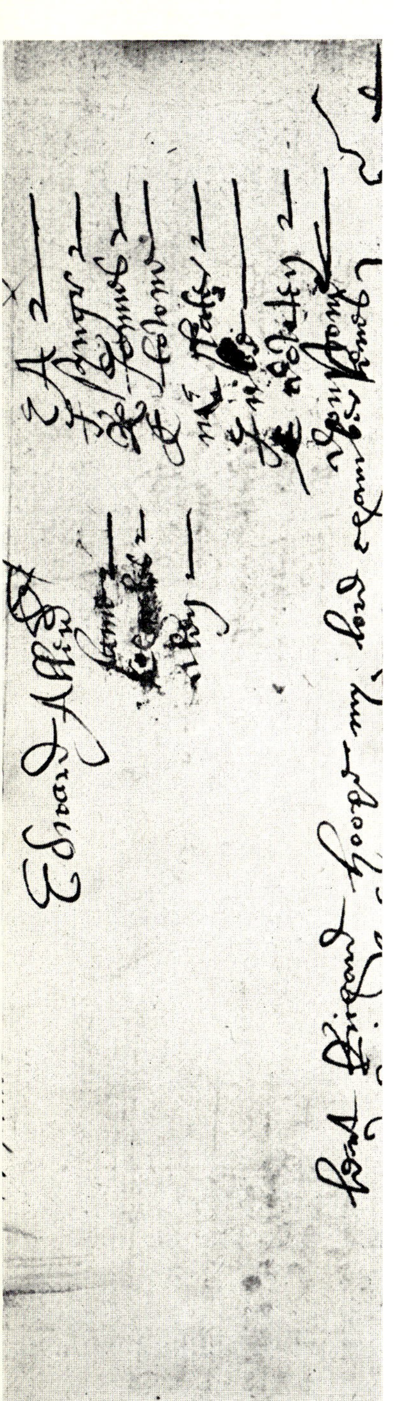

(*a*) F. 3. This seems to be the earliest (?1595) list of sharers or members of the Admiral's Men, with three names set apart from the rest (see Introduction, p. xxxvi)

(*b*) F. 26. The arrangement of the daily entries of 1596–7 is shown here. The line marking a break in playing from 12 February to 3 March is omitted in print, together with the vertical rules. A few letters which run into the binding could not be included in the photograph

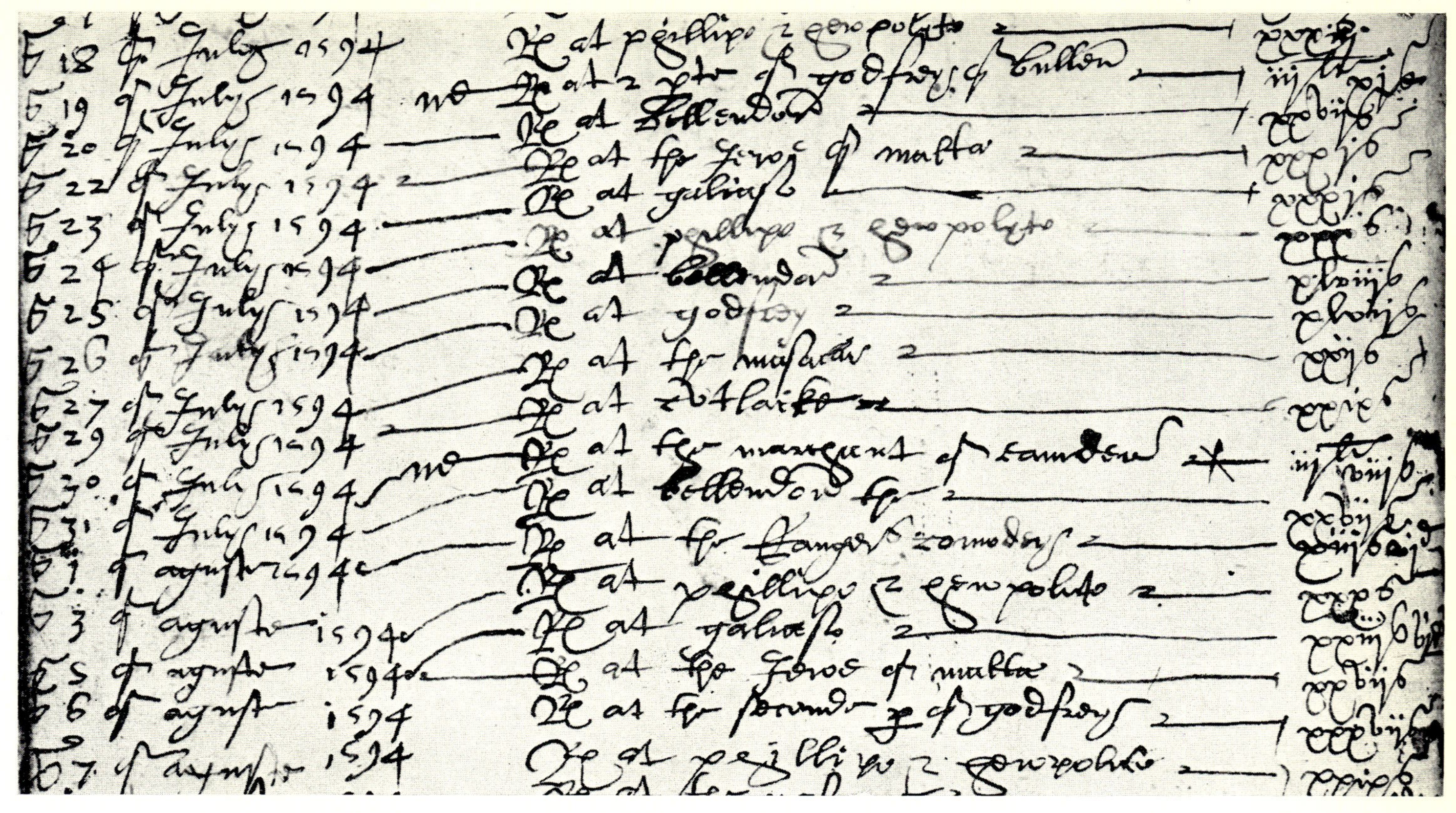

F. 9v. The form of the daily entries, 1594. The lines joining dates and receipts from 20 July to 5 August seem to have been added to mark alignment (see note, p. 23)

PLATE III

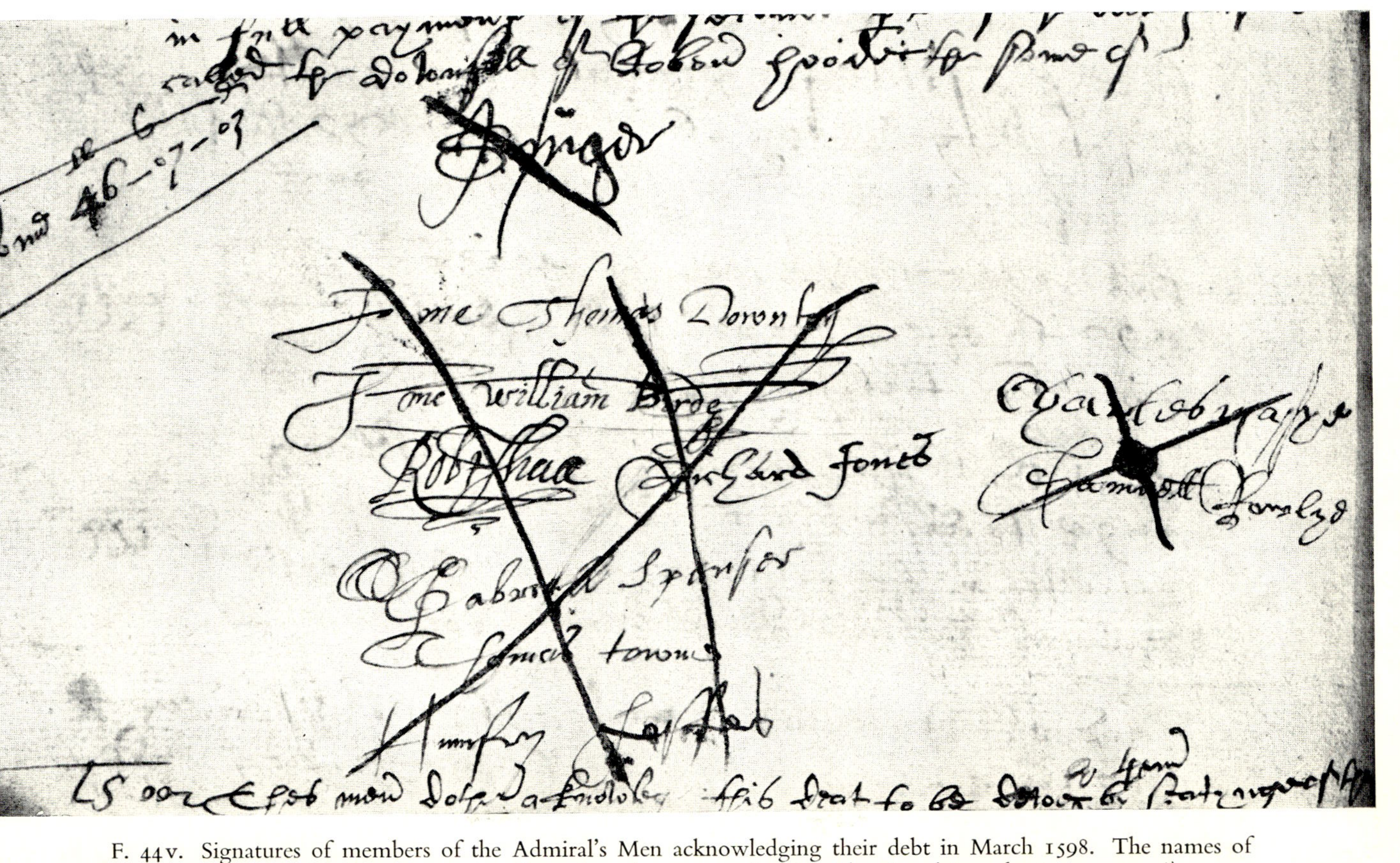

F. 44 v. Signatures of members of the Admiral's Men acknowledging their debt in March 1598. The names of Massey and Rowley are set apart from the others, as on f. 3 (see Plate I and Introduction, p. xxxvi)

PLATE IV

(*a*) F. 48. The form of weekly entries commencing July 1598 when Henslowe began to receive all the gallery moneys

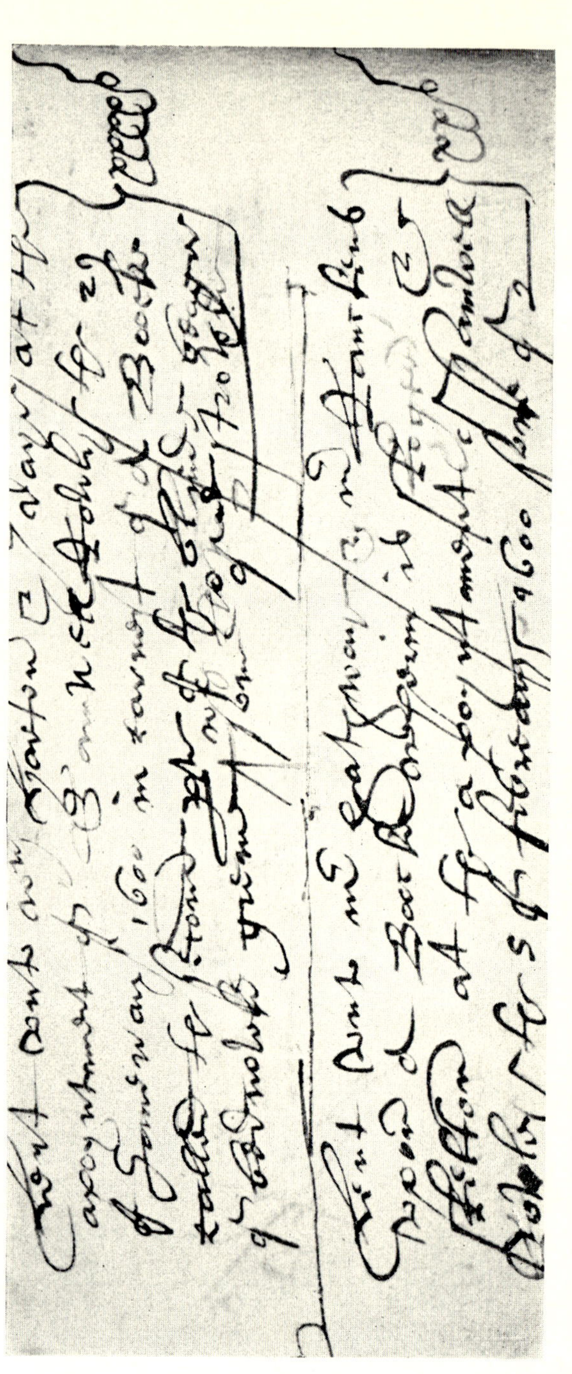

(*b*) F. 85v. The form of loan entries, 1600, showing inserted play titles

II. ARRANGEMENT OF THE PRESENT EDITION

The text of the *Diary* is printed in four sections, which are not all treated in the same way. The first contains a selection from the scribble on the vellum wrapper and the end-pages, which are covered with writing, most of it signatures of Philip Henslowe and copies of other names. Some of these scribbles date from John Henslowe's ownership of the volume, but the majority are of Philip's time, and in his hand. Many of the proper names are repeated several times, but only one or two versions are given here. All legible phrases or sentences which may be of significance are also printed, but not necessarily odd words or letters, for instance *I*, *P*, *moste*, which stand in isolation. The second section contains ff. 1v–125v, the main theatrical and pawn accounts, in the sequence in which they appear in the *Diary* as it was normally used by Philip Henslowe. The original is not reproduced page for page, but otherwise the relative position of the entries is preserved as far as possible. Reference to the foliation will enable the reader to visualise what pages face one another, and blank pages and spaces are indicated within the text. The original numeration is also given in this section, as a guide to indicate what leaves are missing from the book. The third section prints the occasional entries which Philip made from the other end of the book, and which are interspersed among mining accounts. Blank pages are not noted, since the inclusion of this information would serve no purpose, but the original numeration of leaves is indicated in this section. The last section reprints the fragments which have been identified as belonging to the book.

The text of the *Diary* is followed by three Appendices containing supplementary material. The first reprints those manuscripts in the Dulwich collection which relate most closely to the *Diary*. Most of these were printed by Greg in his *Henslowe Papers*, but the present text is from a fresh transcript. These documents are treated more simply than the *Diary*; footnotes are for the most part avoided, and hands are not identified except where indicated in the headnotes, which comment on each item and its relation to the *Diary*. Appendix 2 reprints the inventories of plays, properties and costumes, as given by Malone in 1790 from a manuscript now lost; it appears to have been in Philip Henslowe's hand, and is dated 1598. A third appendix provides lists of actors' names from the extant dramatic plots, most of which certainly belonged to the Admiral's Men, and are of the period spanned by the material in the *Diary*. It should be noted that unnamed supernumeraries such as attendants and gatherers are not included in these lists.

12. CONVENTIONS AND USAGES

(*a*) *In the Text of the Diary*

1. *Foliation and blank pages.* This is not a page-for-page reprint, and the text is printed continuously. Warner's foliation, now the usual form of reference to the *Diary*, is printed in bold-face type within square brackets. The original foliation is printed with this in sections 2 and 3 (the lack of a number indicates that the corner of the leaf is missing), and is not given in the other sections. Blank pages are also noted, between square brackets, in these sections only, where their existence may be of importance in interpreting the sequence of accounts. A note in italic and within brackets is made of space left blank within a page, or at the head or foot of a page.

2. *Lineation.* The original lineation is preserved as far as possible, and is kept always in the single-line entries. Elsewhere, the exceptional length of some lines, or the reduction of interlineations to the line, have made it impossible to keep to the lineation of the manuscript in some paragraph entries. The manuscript lineation is indicated by lines turned under on f. 72, p. 140, line 13; f. 97, fourth line from the foot of the page; f. 100v, p. 194, first line of the folio; also in the Appendices, Articles 16, 17 and 18, pp. 283–5; Article 28, p. 289, lines 3–7; Article 6, pp. 300–1; and Muniment 16 and 22, pp. 304–10. Elsewhere the original lineation is disturbed at the following points: f. 27v, p. 60, in the marginal note, *the xj...penbrockes*; f. 118, eleventh line of the page; and p. 313, last line of the marginal note.

3. *Interlineations.* These are printed in the line, and noticed in footnotes. The formula 'interlined with caret' indicates that the letters or words are interlined above the line in which they are

printed, and that a caret marks the point of insertion; they are not always written above the caret mark. The formula 'interlined above [below]' indicates that there is no caret mark. The formula 'interlined' indicates that the words concerned are inserted above a rule joining parts of an entry; such words are normally printed within the rule, cf. 'satterdaye', f. 7, n. 3, p. 16.

4. *Alterations and deletions.* Letters deleted or altered are enclosed within square brackets. Alterations, but not deletions, are recorded in the footnotes.

5. *Rules.* Many entries are marked off from surrounding ones by rules, as for instance all the loan entries from f. 44 on. The columns of figures on ff. 26–27v are set off by vertical rules. These rules are not printed, but a note is made in the footnotes of those few which may have a bearing on the interpretation of the text, such as those dividing accounts on f. 9 (n. 2, p. 21), f. 11v (n. 3, p. 28), and elsewhere. Lines within the text, such as the weekly division lines in the theatre accounts from f. 7 on, are printed.

6. *Marginal crosses.* Marginal crosses which appear to be in Henslowe's hand are included in this reprint, without comment; they were omitted by Greg. The pencilled crosses and others added in modern hands are ignored.

7. *Marginal and other cramped entries.* In order to get them on the page, some marginal entries, as on f. 4v, are printed in a smaller fount than the rest of the text; and some words, as in the original, are cramped between date and title in the play entries, such as 'S steuens day', f. 14. These are in Henslowe's normal handwriting, which, it should perhaps be noted, varies a good deal in size according to the space available for an entry, and from one page to another.

8. *Special and conventional signs.* Certain signs of Henslowe's, such as his brackets and lines, which are often irregular or sloping, are represented here by conventional printed forms. His signs for the pound sterling (*l*, *li*, *le*, *ll*), are regularised as *li*. His abbreviated form for 'Received', [sign], and its variants are here printed as *Rd* (R7 Greg). One other frequent sign in the manuscript, which precedes the date in all the early entries of daily receipts, and appears occasionally

elsewhere before a date, seems to be some kind of paragraph mark; its normal form is [illegible]. Greg printed this as *y^e^*, but it is treated here simply as a sign, and is represented by ¶.

Many of Henslowe's entries are cancelled, usually by a cross, and to indicate this a convention is used of a heavy bracket at the beginning and end of a cancelled passage. Sometimes he used a marginal sign, which was normally of this form, [illegible], that is, like four letters *t* crossed twice or three times, and which also seems to have been for him a cancellation sign. It is treated in this reprint as equivalent to the more usual crossing out, and represented in the same way. These signs occur at the following places: f. 19v, against the entries of March 1595; f. 28, against the entry of 14 December 1598; f. 33v, against the entry of 6 April 1598; f. 40v, against the entry of 25 April 1598; f. 43v, against the entry of January 1597/8; f. 44, against the entries of 3 and 8 January 1597/8; f. 45v, against the entry of 2 May 1598; f. 234, against the group of three entries beginning 'Itm lent vnto my sonne...'.

9. *Brackets.* The only forms of bracket used within the text are square brackets, as noted, for deletions and alterations; and pointed brackets to indicate letters or words that are quite illegible, mutilated, or cut away.

10. *Italics.* Difficult readings, attenuated or blotted letters, are italicised, without comment in the footnotes. Italic is simply an indication that a measure of interpretation on the part of the editors is involved in the reading.

11. *Footnotes.* In these are noted significant differences from Greg, but not differences of spelling, spacing or punctuation, except where, as in a number of proper names, it is of significance, or where sense is affected. Alterations in the manuscript, interlineations, forgeries, and a few obscurities, difficulties or unusual spellings, are noted; for the rest, reference should be made to the Index.

Greg printed a list of Errata before the text in his edition, and these are treated as if they had been included within his text; in other words, where our text follows them, no comment is made in footnotes. But he also printed a list of Corrigenda at the end of his Commentary (*Diary*, II, 377–8), which are probably not seen by many users of his edition. For this reason, they are ignored in the footnotes to the present edition, and treated as if non-existent; the footnotes record differences from Greg at the following points where he revised his reading in his Corrigenda: ff. 7, note 2, p. 16; 17v, note 2, p. 40; 19v, note 1, p. 44; 48v, note 1, p. 96; 62, note 1, p. 120 (both Greg's readings are given here); 89v, note 2, p. 174 and note 4, p. 174; 118v, note 2, p. 221; 178, note 11, p. 247. On f. 123v Greg corrected 'kacke' (printed text) to 'tacke' (Corrigenda), where we have 'Kacke', so written, though 'take' is clearly meant.

12. *Hands in the Diary*. All entries are in Philip Henslowe's hand, so far as we can tell, unless otherwise stated in the footnotes.

13. *Use of* I *and* J. The modern *J* was not fully differentiated from *I* as a letter in Henslowe's time, although its sound as a consonant was different from that of the vowel. Henslowe uses the same form for both, but it seems unnecessary to represent both, as a sixteenth-century printer would have done, by *I*, or by *J* as Greg did. In the present text modern forms are used, as in, for instance, *Itm* and *Jonnes*.

(b) In the Text of the Supplementary Material in Appendix I

The text of these manuscripts is not footnoted, except in the case of MS. I, 30, but a few major differences from Greg are recorded in the headnotes to the separate items. In these, interlineations are incorporated without comment in the line, and deletions and alterations are included without distinction in square brackets. The original lineation is not always kept, as is indicated in the headnotes. Hands are not identified, except as stated, and italic is not used. The treatment of signs, and the use of pointed brackets, are similar to those in the text of the *Diary*.

13. A NOTE ON THE TEXT

In this reprint the modern pencilled foliation used by Greg, and now the standard form of reference, is kept. The original numeration, which runs from the other end of the book, and which is useful as often indicating where leaves are missing, is also given. The text is printed in four sections. The first includes a selection of the miscellaneous material on the vellum wrapper and the two end-pages, f. 1

and f. 238v. The second contains ff. 1v–125v, in sequence as the book was normally used by Philip Henslowe. John Henslowe had made his entries from the other end, with the book reversed, and interspersed among his mining accounts are a number of entries by Philip, who also occasionally used the book in this way. Section 3 contains these entries, printed in order from f. 238 to f. 126v. The last section reprints fragments from the *Diary* now scattered in various libraries.

From time to time Philip reversed the book within his two sequences of entries, from f. 1v to f. 125v and from f. 238 to f. 126v, so that a few entries appear upside down in these sequences; such entries are marked by the footnote 'entered with the book reversed'. A note is made of pages left blank in section 2, the main sequence of entries by Philip Henslowe, but not in the other sections.

14. A NOTE ON FORMS OF REFERENCE

A few abbreviated forms of reference are used in this edition. Philip Henslowe is often referred to simply as 'Henslowe'; other members of his family are identified by their Christian names. His account-book has for long been known generally as his *Diary*, and although this is not an accurate title, it seemed best to keep it throughout this work, even at the risk of some confusion between references to the manuscript and to Greg's edition (see below). The context in any passage will make clear which is meant. Some dates cited from the *Diary* are given as 1597/8 or 1599/1600; this indicates that Henslowe entered the particular date according to the Old Style calendar, in which the year began on 25 March, and the later year-date given is that of the modern calendar. In addition to these usages, some books to which frequent reference is made are cited by short titles. In the following list, the short title is given first, before a colon; the names in brackets are not always used in references:

(Chambers,) *E.S.* I, II, III, IV: E. K. Chambers, *The Elizabethan Stage* (4 vols., Oxford, 1923); reprinted with corrections, 1951.

Collier: J. P. Collier, *The Diary of Philip Henslowe from 1591 to 1609. Printed from the Original Manuscript Preserved at Dulwich College* (London, for the Shakespeare Society, 1845).

(Greg,) *Diary*, I and II: W. W. Greg, *Henslowe's Diary. Part I, The Text; Part II, Commentary* (2 vols., London, 1904 and 1908).

(Greg,) *Papers*: W. W. Greg, *Henslowe Papers, being Documents Supplementary to Henslowe's Diary* (London, 1907).

(Greg,) *Dramatic Documents*, I and II: W. W. Greg, *Dramatic Documents from the Elizabethan Playhouses. Stage Plots: Actors' Parts: Prompt Books* (2 vols., Oxford, 1931). The volume headed 'Commentary' is here referred to as I, and the volume of 'Reproductions and Transcripts' as II.

(Greg,) *English Literary Autographs*: *English Literary Autographs 1550–1650*. Selected for reproduction and edited by W. W. Greg in collaboration with J. P. Gilson, Hilary Jenkinson, R. B. McKerrow and A. W. Pollard (Oxford, 1932).

Malone: The extracts from Henslowe's *Diary* printed among the 'Emendations and Additions' to his 'Historical Account of the Rise and Progress of the English Stage' in *The Plays and Poems of William Shakespeare* (1790), vol. I, part II, pp. 288–322. These were reprinted in the 'Variorum' edition of Shakespeare in 1821, vol. III, pp. 295–335.

O.E.D.: *The Oxford English Dictionary*, edited by J. A. H. Murray, Henry Bradley, W. A. Craigie and C. T. Onions (13 vols., 1933).

(Warner,) *Catalogue*: George F. Warner, *Catalogue of the Manuscripts and Muniments of Alleyn's College of God's Gift at Dulwich* (London, 1881).

THE DIARY

1. THE VELLUM WRAPPER AND THE END PAGES

These are covered with scribble, mostly in Henslowe's hand. Only the more substantial entries and proper names are given here. The most frequent entry is Philip Henslowe's own signature. All the entries on f. 238 v except the recipe and name at the head are entered with the book reversed. Some of these scribbles are repeated or amplified on ff. 229, 221, 215 v, 168, 167 v and 162.

Names[1] on the wrapper:

thomas downton
Phillippe Henslow
John willsone
Jhon whitte
henerie hallowed
Thomas homer

Selected entries on f. 1:

yf thow wiste what thinge yt weare
wheneuer I lente I was a frendeę
when I asked
layd owt A bowt w h
as ffoloweth
Itm lent vj d
Itm lent v s
Itm layd owt goinge to the corte & westmester } iiij[s] ij[d]
for when I lent I wasse A
frend & when I asked I wasse vnkind
Chomley when
Clement Bowle Bowle wth owt mersey
Chemley Chomley
Bowghte wth mersey

---

(1) Not recorded by Greg.

A man wth owt mer
mersey of mersey shalle
Bowles willsone^{s}
timberd stone
John willsone
Bowland
In R m^{r}. . . . . 103 – 0^{s} – 0^{d}
A man withe owte mercye of mersey
shall myse & he shall haue mersey y^{t}
mersey full ys

Selected entries on f. 238v:

for the agew
Take brianey Roote & steape yt in alle all a nyght
then drincke yt lucke warme a fore the fite come
& good vpon yt

palle yonge
yonge

By me John Henslowe
This by me williamsones p̷ me Johne williamsone
This is John Henslow Boke
John Hod the fyrst Lefe This is my md^{ixs} ^{xd}
W^{m} wellꝭ
This is John Henslow
By me willson
willsones Bowghte P Henslow
The Boke of Reconyg̅ꝭ ffor this for when I lent I
yeare 1576 & 1577 wasse a frend
doinnge yowe to vnderstand y^{t} I haue Receued
masse willsones Ᵽ me John willsone
m^{rs} D m went to [pay t] of name heycrosse
the 19 of June 1593 on a wendesday
p̷ me John Willson henslow Phillipp
p̷denamy
m^{r} D m̄ wente to grenstead the 14 of July
1593
Phensley Phillippe 1593 lord god
w^{m} come to towne the 28 of July & wen a waye
the 6 of aguste 1593 moste

2. THE TEXT; FF. 1v–125v

[1v]

Jonne allen Receued for Rente as folowthe(1) 1593

Rd of the duchewoman the for(2) mydsomer qt 1593	xv^{s} viijd
Rd of the carpenter for mydsomer qte(3) 1593	xvijs vjd
Rd of goody Rowden for mydsomer qte(3) 1593	xs
Rd of goodman hudson the 14 of aguste 1593	xv^{s}
Rd of goodman glene(4) the 16 of aguste 1593	xxxx^{s}
Rd of goody Rowden the 18 of octob3 1593	vijs x^{d}

ffor tremynge of the ffolles
head as foloweth

Itm for selynge of the ij chambers & mendynge of the walles & whittinge & blackynge the same	xxx^{s}

[2½ *inches blank*]

A note what m^{r}s allen hath payd sence
her husband went into the contrey as foloweth

1593

Itm pd for howsse Rente & for naylles	xx^{s}
Itm pd vnto hime for Kepinge of you^{r} horsse	ixs xd
Itm pd vnto the Joyner for the beadstead	xvs
Itm pd for coshenes	vs

the 28 of Janewary 1597 I payd
Jo. ffa

[1¼ *inches blank*]

---

(1) *folowthe*] *wthe* altered from a faint *weth*.
(2) *the for*] *sic*.
(3) *qte*] *qtr* Greg.
(4) *glene*] or possibly *gleue*.

[2]

Bowght th*e* 18 of June 1592 A gyllte gyllte goblette wayinge 17 & ½ at v^{s} vj d o^{z} th*e* some . . . . iiij^{li} xix^{s} ij^{d}

Bowght th*e* same time j beacker of persell gyllte wainge viij o^{z} j q at vj^{s} 8^{d} some is	l[iij]vj^{s} [1] vj^{d}

Edward[2] alen wasse maryed vnto Jone Woodward the 22 of daye of octobȝ 1592 In the iiij & thirtie yeare of the Quene[3] Matie Rayne elyzabeth by th*e* grace of god of Ingland france & Iarland defender of the fayth[2]

Pearsyvalle Craffte hath geuen his word*e* for th*e* foschen dier in grobstreat wch persyvall lise in watlynge streate at th*e* syne of th*e* crosse Keayes‸ a crysmas eue last 1592 for iiij^{li}

A E ծ H

Rd of Thomas newman th*e* 10 of Jenewary 1593 In ꝑte of paymente of a more some as a pereath*e* vpon A bonde I saye Rd by me phillipe Hensley.	xxxx^{s}

The wenscot belo*w* in the halle of Edwardes Allenes howsse Is three score & fyve yardes & iij foote at ij^{s} A yardes wch comes to . . . . . .

Rd of Richarde waltame the 27 of desembȝ 1593 in ꝑte of payment of a bande of Thomas newmanes the some of	xxxx^{s}

[1¾ *inches blank*]

[2v] **3008**

A nott what I haue layd owt abowt my playhowsse ffor payntinge & doinge it a bowt wth ealme bordes & other Repracyones as ffoloweth 1595 in lent

Itm bowght iij hunderd & a ꝗter of elmebordes	xxiiij^{s}
Itm pd the carpenters ther wages	viij^{s}
Itm geuen the paynter in earneste	xx^{s}
Itm geuen the paynter more	x^{s}

---

(1) *l[iij]vj^{s}*] *vj* altered from *iij*.

(2) *Edward. . .fayth*] This entry is written in a lighter ink than the surrounding entries, except for *22* and the initial *i* of *iiij* (so Greg).

(3) *Quene*] *Quenes* Greg.

Itm geuen more vnto the paynter	xx^{s}
Itm pd vnto the paynter	x^{s} (1)
Itm pd the carpenters ther wages	xvj s
Itm pd for iij henges	ij s
Itm pd for a borde	ij s ij d
Itm pd for v pownde of spickes	xv^{d}
Itm pd th*e* carpenters	v^{s} iiij^{d}
Itm pd the paynter	v^{s}
Itm pd for ij bundell of lathes	ij s ij d
Itm pd for j lode of sande	xiiij d
Itm pd for hallfe a thowsen of lathe naylles	viij d
Itm pd the paynter	vj s
Itm pd the paynter	iiij s
Itm pd for j lode of lyme	xiiij d
Itm pd for wages	iiij s vj d
Itm pd the paynter	v^{s}
Itm pd the paynter In fulle	xvj s
Itm pd for naylles	ij s iiij d
Itm pd the smyth for naylles In fulle	xij s iij d

li s d

Some is 108 – 19 – 00

Itm pd for carpenters worke & mackinge the throne In the heuenes the 4 of June 1595 } vij^{li} ij^{s}

Lent vnto frances henslow the 8 of maye 1593 to laye downe for his share to the Quenes players when they brocke & went into th*e* contrey to playe the some of fyften pownd to be payd vnto me at his Retorne owt of the contrey I saye lent } xv^{li}

wittnes John towne
Hew daves &
Richard alleyn

[3]

[¶ 2 of Jeneware 1593 — lent vnto m^{r} hareye draper the second of Jeneware 1593 In Redey money th*e* some of twenty pownd to be payd a gayne wth in on moneth next folowinge } xx^{li}

---

(1) This entry appears to have been interlined (so Greg).

lent vnto m^r harey draper the 4 of ap^r ell 1593 in Redey money the some of . . } xvj^li

lent m^rs Draper the 29 of marche 1594 . . . in Redye money the some of. . . . . } v^li

8 – 16 – o(2) lent m^r John(1) sheaperd the 14 of desemb3 1594 In Redey mony to be payd wth In one monethe after the date herof the some of fyve pownd wittnes] . . . . } v^li

Edward Allen

same(3) . . .
Charles. . .
alen(3) . . .

E A(3). . . . .
J syngr . . . .
R Jonnes. . . . . . .
T towne. . . . . . .
m^r slater. . . . . . .
Jube . . . .
T dowten . . . . . .
donstone(3). . . . . .

lent Richard Hoope my lord chamber lenes man the 14 of Jenewary 1595 In Redey money to be pd at easter next cominge the some of . . } [xx^s] iij^li

wittnes his owne man
william ferney &
edward allen

lent vnto the master of the Reuelles man w^m stonard the 8 of ap^r ell 1595 the some of seuen shillinges to be pd vnto me at his next cominge to london. . . . . } vij s

wittnes hew daves & John
tayller owermaker & hew daves &
his wiffe

[1¼ *inches blank*]

[3 v] **3007**

lent vnto w^m Blackwag*e* my lord camberlenes man fyve pownd &s a pereth by his Bylle . . } v^li

[lent vnto m^r Rafe Raye my lorde chamberlenes man tenne pownd as a pereth by his bell } x^li]

(1) *John*] interlined with caret. (2) *8 – 16 – o*] not recorded by Greg.

(3) The columns of names are in a different ink from the surrounding entries, and *donstone* appears to be written over *lenes* in the line below. Greg reads *lame* for *same*; *s* is smudged, but not obscured. See Introduction, p. xxvi, and Plate I (*a*).

lent vnto ffrances henslow the j of June 1595
In Readey mony to laye downe for his hallfe share
wth the company wch he dothe play wth all to be
payd vnto me when he doth Receue his mony w^ch^
he lent to my lord burte or when my asyenes dothe
demand yt wittnes I saye nyne pownd . . . . . } ix^li^

w^m^ smyght player
gorge attewell player
Robard nycowlles player

bowght the Jemes is head the 24 of aguste 1595 for . xxx^li^
& bowghte more as foloweth

Itm wanscotte in the halle	xiiij yardes at 16^d^ p y^r^d
Itm paynted clothe in the halle	xvj yrdes at vj d p y^r^d
Itm wanscott setlynge in the parler	x yardes at xvj d y^r^d
Itm turnde pellers in the parler	iij yrdes at xvj^d^ yrd
Itm a lowd for dores	iiij yrdes at xvj d y^r^rd
Itm paynted cloth in the parler	v yrdes at vj d yrdes

layd owt a bowte John allen
adminestracyon as folowethe

[¶ 4 of maye layd owt a bowt the admenestracyon	x[iij] s ij d
pd for her[1] balle	xiiij d
pd the sargentes & other charges	iij s
pd for all carges in yeald halle	viij s j d
pd the carman for bringinge the stvffe	iij s iiij d
p the carman for bringinge the stvffe	ij s
pd going to stanes by water	v^s^
& spente in charges for meat & drincke	xiij s
Itm pd ffor the Ingrossynge of the Inventory .	x^s^ vj d]

[4]

Jesus 1592

A note of suche carges as I haue layd owt a bowte
my playe howsse in the yeare of o^r^ lord 1592 as ffoloweth

Itm pd for a barge	iij^li^ xs
Itm pd for breacking vp & palynge	xx^s^
Itm pd for wharfyng	viij^s^
Itm pd for tymber & bryngen by watter	vij^li^ ix^s^
Itm pd for lyme	ixs ij s[2]
Itm pd for wages	xixs

(1) *her*] i.e. their; cf. f. 65 v (note 1, p. 127). (2) *ij^s^*] *ij^d^* Greg.

Itm pd for bryngen of dellberds	ijs vjd
Itm pd for ij hunderd of lyme	xjs
Itm pd for iij quarters of A hunderd of deall bordes	iij^{li}
Itm pd for A maste	xij^{s}
Itm pd for A some of lathe naylls & hafe	
Itm pd for wages	iiij^{li} xs
Itm pd for iiij hundred of iij peny naylls	xijd
Itm pd for j lode of Rafters	
Itm pd for j lode of quarters	
Itm pd for j thowsen of lathe naylles	
Itm pd [for] vnto the thecher	vijs
Itm pd for bryngen of stvfe	vjd
Itm pd for j hunderd of lyme	v^{s} vjd
Itm pd for iij dayes for A w*or*kman	iijs vjd
Itm pd for A⟨...⟩er (1) for iiij dayes	iijs 4^{d}
Itm pd vnto th*e* thecher	xxs
Itm pd for sande	iiijs vjd
Itm j thowsen of lath nayelles	
Itm pd for xxvj fore powlles	xs vj^{d}
Itm pd vnto my workmen for A weckes wages	vj^{li}
Itm pd for a hundred of syngell tennes	x^{d}
Itm pd for iiij lode of sande	iiijs
Itm pd vnto th*e* thechers man	iijs
Itm pd for ij hundered of syxpenynaylles	xijd
Itm pd for hallfe A lode of lathes	
Itm pd for hallfe A some of lath*e* naylles	
Itm pd for ij hundred & A hallfe of dubell tennes	
Itm pd for v hundred of syxpenynaylles	
Itm bowght hallfe A lode of lathes of J gryges	
Itm pd for iij hundred of syxpeny naylls to brader	xviijd
Itm pd for *ch*ake & bryckes	iijs 4^{d}
Itm pd for j hundred of dubell tennes	xd
Itm pd for ij hundred of lyme	xj^{s}
Itm pd vnto the thecher	⟨ ⟩^{s} (2)

[4v] **3005**

Itm pd for sande	xijd
Itm pd for wages	vj^{s} jd
Itm pd for turned ballyesters ij^{d} q A pece ij d*o*ssen	iiijs vj^{d}

(1) ⟨...⟩*er*] *naler* Greg; the first three letters are illegible.

(2) Sum worn away.

	Itm pd for wages.	iijs 4d
	Itm bowght xx furpowell at vj^{d} A pece	xs
	Itm pd vnto th*e* thecher	xs
	Itm pd for naylles to brader	ijs 4^{d}
	Itm pd th*e* vj of febreary for wages	iiij^{li} iij^{s} 4^{d}
	Itm pd for v hundred of syxpeny naylles	
Reste ij^{s} x^{d}[1]	Itm pd steuen coke iij^{s} for his manes wages	
	Itm bowght of J gryges ij C & iij qt & x foote bords[2] . .	xixs
	Itm bowght of J gryges ij bundell of lathes	ijs
	Itm pd the thecher	vs
+	Itm bowght of the Iermonger in sothwarke ½ *C* lath naylls	
	Itm bowght at th*e* fryngpan v hund [s]tennes	ijs vj^{d}
	Itm bowght at th*e* fryngpan ij hund^{r} dubl tennes	iij^{s} 4^{d}
	Itm bowght at th*e* fryngpan j m[3] of vj^{d} naylles	iiijs vjd
	Itm pd for *A* thowsen of vj^{d} naylles	
	Itm pd for ½ some of ij^{d} nayl*l*es	
	Itm bowght j lode of Rafters & j lode of quarters.	
	Itm pd for ij lode of l*o*me & j lode of sande	iijs
	Itm pd for brycklaynge	ijs ijd
smyth had	Itm bowght at th*e* fryngpan ½ some of ij^{d} naylles	
iiij[li].ij li of	Itm pd the laborers wages	viijs ixd
Iorne[4]	Itm bowght at the fryinge pan v hundred vj^{d} naylles . . .	
	Itm bowght at the fryingpan j q m singell tennes	
	Itm pd for j hund*r*ed of lyme	v^{s} vjd
	Itm bowght iiij hundred of quarter bordes.	xx^{s}
	Itm bowght v hunded of ynche bordes	xxv^{s}[5]
	Itm bowght halfe a lode of Rafters	
	Itm pd the thecher	xs
	Itm pd for naylles	viijd
	Itm bowght of J gryges halfe a lode of lathes[6]	[ij] xvs[7]
	Itm bowght at the fryingpan j q m dubell tennes[8]	
	Itm pd vnto the carpenters for wages	iiij^{li} *v*s[9]
Rd of th*e*	Itm pd for carege of tymbȝ	vijd
smyth 18^{li}	Itm pd for iij fore bordes sayed	iiijs vjd
& 18^{li} & 15^{li}	Itm pd for payntinge my stage.	xjs
	Itm pd for v hundred of vjd naylles at fryingpan	

(1) *ij^{s} x^{d}*] so Greg; possibly *ij^{s} pd*.

(2) *bords*] interlined; *bored* Greg.

(3) *j m*] *7 m* Greg.

(4) *Iorne*] i.e. iron; *Jane* is a possible reading.

(5) *xxv^{s}*] *xx^{s}* Greg.

(6) *halfe...lathes*] interlined.

(7) [*ij*] *xvs*] *xv* altered from *ij* (from *vj* Greg).

(8) *j...tennes*] interlined.

(9) *vs*] *x^{s}* Greg; Henslowe began to write *x*, but altered the loop to make *v*.

Itm pd for a q of a m of dubell tennes at fryingpan . . . .
Itm pd for a q of a m of syngell tennes fryingpan . . . .
Itm bowght of brader ij hundred of 4^d naylles . . . . . . viij d

[5]

Itm pd for ij dossen of turned ballysters . . . . iiij s
Itm bowght at braders iij C & ½ iiij d naylls . . . .
Itm bowght at th*e* fryingpan v C vj d naylls . . . .
Itm bowght at th*e* fryingpan a q m dubell tennes . . . . . .
Itm bowght at th*e* fryingpan a q m singell tennes. . . . . .
Itm bowght at th*e* fryingpan a q m singell tennes . . . . . .
Itm bowght at the fryingpan a m of vj d naylles . . . . . .
Itm bowght at th*e* fryingpan a q of some of lathe naylles . .
Itm bowght j lode of syngell quarters . . . .
Itm pd for bryngng of stufe by watter . . . .
Itm bowght of brader v C of 4^d naylles . . . .
Itm bowght iij score & ix corsse deall at iij d ob . . . . . . xx s
Itm pd for bryingin them by water . . . . viij d
Itm pd the thecher . . . . v^s
Itm bowght at th*e* fryingpan ½ a q m of singell x . . . . . .
Itm bowght at th*e* fryingpan ½ a q m dubell x . . . .
Itm bowght at th*e* fryingpan a q m vj^d naylles . . . .
Itm bowght at th*e* fryingpan ½ C of singell x . . . .
Itm bowght at th*e* fryingpan j q of m singell x . . . . xvij d
Itm bowght of brader ij C of 4 d naylles. . . . .
Itm bowght of J gryges iij C of q bordes . . . . xvj s
Itm *b*owght at th*e* fryingpan j q *m* singell tenes . . . . xvij d *ob*
Itm bowght at th*e* fryingpan j q *m* dubell tennes . . . . .
Itm bowght at th*e* fryingpan j q *m* vjd nayells . . . . . .
Itm bowght of brader ij C 4 d nayells . . . .
Itm bowght at the fryingpan j q m singell tenes . . . . . . xvij d
Itm bowght at th*e* fryingpan j q vj d nayells . . . .
Itm pd vnto th*e* thecher a bondell of lathes . . . . xij d
[*Itm of brader*[(1)]] ½ C of vj d naylles . . . .
⟨. . . . .⟩ lockes[(1)] ⟨ ⟩

[*The rest of the leaf, measuring* 4 *inches at the inner margin and* 3½ *inches at the outer margin, is torn away*]

---

(1) *Itm of brader . . . lockes*] these words are partly torn away.

[5v]

Receaued[1].By me.Jeameę.Borne.the 2 of March[2].1591.
of M^{r}.Phillipe.Hinchlie for.the vse.of.
henerie A ddameę: the: some.of.three.pound.
[I]and[4].is in [parte] fulle[5].of paiment of.a. } – 3^{li} – [*o*]8^{s}[3] – o
recconieng I.saye.Receaued in payte.[1]
pd in fulle paymente the 7 of march 1591
vnto th*e* Iormonger in sothwarke at the } iij^{li} xij s
fryingpan three pownd & xij^{s} I saye R
pd in fulle paymente th*e* 28 of marche 1591
vnto m^{r} lee tymber man for Rafters & } v^{li} xiiij^{s}
quarte*rs* & laths & bordes th*e* soms[6] of . .
pd vnto my^{r}[7] cossen adren for money wch I owght } vij^{li}
him th*e* 28 of marche 1591 . . . .
pd vnto th*e* paynters th*e* 28 *of* marche 1591 . . . xxvj^{s}
pd vnto my cossen adren th*e* 13 of ap^{r}ell 1591 . . xxij^{li} x^{s}
li s d 4[8]
103 – *02* – 03 pd for sellynge th*e*[9] Rome ouer th*e* tyerhowsse . xs
pd for[10] wages to th*e* plasterer . . . . iiij s
\+ pd for sellinges my lords Rome . . . . xiiij s
pd for makenge th*e* penthowsse shed at th*e* tyeringe } xs
howsse doore as foloweth pd for owld tymber .
pd for bordes & quarte*rs* . . . . xviij s vj d
pd for bordes . . . . xiij s vj d
pd for naylles & henges & bowlltes . . . . xix s
pd the carpente*rs* for wages . . . . ix s

[*Torn as on recto*]

[6]

A not what mony I haue layd owt of my owne
to frances henslow as ffolloweth 1593

lent th*e* 14 of Jeneway 1593. . . . . xxv^{s}
lent th*e* 16 of Jeneway 1593. . . . . xxx^{s}

---

(1) *Receaued...payte*] in James Borne's hand, except for the interlined *fulle*, added by Henslowe. Greg reads *parte* for *payte*.
(2) *March.*] interlined above.
(3) [*o*]*8*] alteration.
(4) [*I*]*and*] *a* altered from *I*, which is not fully deleted.
(5) *fulle*] interlined above.
(6) *soms*] *some* Greg.
(7) *my^{r}*] *sic*; neither *r* nor *y* is deleted.
(8) 4] not recorded by Greg.
(9) *sellynge the*] *sellynge of the* Greg.
(10) *for*] *the* Greg.

A not what I haue layd owt A bowt
the howsse w[ch] was hew Daueses as ffoloweth
1595 locke the next leafe

	Itm pd vnto the nayllman for naylles	iiij s
	Itm pd vnto the tyller	xviij d
	Itm iiij long peces of tymber.	vj s
	Itm ij thowssen of lath naylles	ij s viij d
	Itm pd th*e* tyller & laberer	xviij d
	Itm pd for Rege tylles	xviij d
	Itm pd for tylle pennes	ij d
	Itm pd a[(1)] hundered of tylles	xviij d
	Itm pd for a hunderd of qter bordes	vij s ij d
	Itm pd for vj syngell qters.	ij s ij d
	Itm j longe pece of tymber	xvj d
	Itm halfe a hunderd of lyme	iij s
	Itm pd for heare	
	Itm pd for lome	xiiij d
	Itm j thowsen of lath naylles.	xvj[d]
	Itm *pd* for iiij qter bordes	iiij s xj d
	Itm pd for a payer of henges.	xiij d
	Itm pd for halfe a thowsen of lath naylles	xvj[d]
	Itm pd the *l*aborer his wages.	x d
	Itm pd for bordes & quarters	v s viij d
	Itm pd grymes for his wages & his man	vij s
¶ 16 of octob3 1595	Itm j longe pece of temb3	xvj d
	Itm pd for a locke	iij s j d
	Itm pd for j lode of lome	xij d
	Itm pd setyng vp the porthole	ij s vj d
	Itm pd the carpenters	xiij s 8 d
	Itm pd the laborer	v[s]
	Itm pd for henges latches & bowltes	
	Item pd for a thowsen of lath naylles	xvj d
	Itm pd th*e* smyth for naylles.	v s j d
	Itm pd vnto th*e* carpenters	ij s viij d
	Itm pd for a hel*mee*bord[(2)].	viij[d]
	Itm pd for wages.	iij s vj d

(1) *pd a*] *sic*; *pd for a* Greg.

(2) *helmeebord*] *sic*; *helme bord* Greg: possibly *helmde* or *helmed bord*, but Henslowe elsewhere duplicates *e*, cf. *redreffee*, f. 24 v.

Receued as foloweth

0 - 02 - 00
00 - *03* - 00
00 - 07 - 00
00 - 04 - 04

Itm pd vnto m^r^ tyllnes man th*e* 26 of febreary 1591	v^s^
Itm pd vnto m^r^ tyllnes man th*e* 4 of marche 1591	v^s^
Itm pd vnto m^r^ tyllenes man th*e* 10 of marche 1591	v^s^
Itm pd vnto m^r^ tyll*nes* man th*e* 17 of marche 1591	v^s^
Itm pd vnto m^r^ tyllnes man th*e* 24 of marche 1591	vs
Itm pd vnto m^r^ tyllenes man the 28 of marche 1591	vs
Itm pd vnto m^r^ tyllnes man th*e* 7 of [marche] ap^r^ell (1) 1591	v^s^
Itm pd vnto m^r^ tyllnes man th*e* 14 (2) of ap^r^ell 1591	vs
Itm pd vnto m^r^ tyllnes man th*e* 2[7]1 (3) of ap^r^ell 1591	v^s^
Itm pd vnto m^r^ tyllnes man th*e* 28 of ap^r^ell 1591	vs
Itm pd vnto m^r^ tyllenes man th*e* 5 of maye 1592	vs
Itm pd vnto m^r^ tyllnes man th*e* 10 of maye 1592	v^s^
Itm pd vnto m^r^ tyllnes man th*e* 13 of maye 1592	xij s
Itm pd vnto m^r^ tyllnes man th*e* 20 of maye 1592	vj s 8^d^
Itm pd vnto m^r^ tyllnes man th 9 of June 1592	vj s 8^d^
Itm pd vnto m^r^ tyllnes man th*e* 14 June 1592	vj^s^ 8^d^

Layd owt a bowte the howsse w^ch^
hewe daves dwelt in laste in
the yeare 1595 as foloweth

Itm hallfe a lode of lathes	xv^s^ vj^d^
Itm elme bordes	viij s 4^d^
Itm j hunderd of syngell tennes	x d
Itm j Rownd polle	xx^d^
Itm j bar*e* (4) of Iorne	iiij s viij d
Itm j lode of sand	xij d
Itm ij thowssen of lathe naylles	ij^s^ viij d
Itm j thowsen of lath naylles	xvj d
Itm pd the carpenter wages	ij s vj d
Itm pd for furpowles	v^s^
Itm j hunderd of vj^d^ naylles	vj d
Itm pd for ij gystes to beare the chymne	iiij s vj^d^
Itm pd for v bundell of lathes	v^s^ v^d^

(1) [*marche*] *ap^r^ell*] alteration. (2) *14*] *19* Greg; both readings are possible.

(3) *2[7]1*] *1* altered from *7*; Greg reads as *7* altered from *1*, but *21* fits the sequence of dates better.

(4) *bare*] so Greg; just possibly *bace*.

Itm j lode of sande for grymes . . . . xij[d]
Itm geven grymes in mony . . . . xiiij s
Itm pd for ij qters . . . . xiiij d
Itm j hunderd of lyme . . . . vj[s]
Itm j manteltre . . . . xij.[d] [J.ħa] (1)
Itm pd to grymes . . . . vij[s]
Itm pd to grymes . . . . xij[d]
Itm pd for A gvtter of leade . . . . xij[s] iij[d]
Itm pd the ij carpenters for wages . . . . xv[s] vj d
Itm pd the laberer . . . . vj d

[7]

In the name of god A men 1591
beginge the 19 of febreary my
lord stranges (2) mene A ffoloweth
1591

Rd at fryer bacvne the 19 of febreary . . satterdaye (3) . . xvij s iij d
Rd at m*v*lomvr*co* the 20 of febreary . . . . xxix s
Rd at orlando th*e* 21 of febreary . . . . xvj s vj d
Rd at spanes comodye donne oracioe (4) th*e* 23 of febreary . xiij s vj d
Rd at sy[r] John mandevell th*e* 24 of febreary . . . . xij[s] vj d
Rd at harey of cornwell th*e* 25 of febreary 1591 . . . . . xxxij[s]
Rd at the Jewe of malltuse th*e* 26 of febrearye 1591 . . . . l s
——Rd at clorys & orgasto th*e* 28 of febreary 1591 . . . . . . xviij s
Rd at mvlamvlluco the 29 of febrearye 1591 . . . . xxxiiij s
Rd at poope Jone the 1 of marche 1591 . . . . xv[s]
Rd at matchavell the 2 of marche 1591 . . . . xiiij s
ne—Rd at harey the vj the 3 of marche 1591. . . . . iij[li] xvj[s] 8 d
Rd at bendo & Richardo th*e* 4 of march*e* 1591 . . . . . . xvj s
——Rd at iiij playes in one th*e* 6 of marche 1591 . . . . xxxj s vj d
Rd at harey the vj (5) the 7 of marche 1591 . . . . iij li
Rd at the lockinglasse th*e* 8 of marche 1591 . . . . vij[s]
Rd at senobia the 9 of marche 1591 . . . . xxij s vj d
Rd at the Jewe of malta th*e* 10 of march*e* 1591 . . . . . . lvj s
Rd at harey the vj the 11 of marche 1591 . . . . xxxxvij[s] vj[d]
——Rd at the comodey of doneoracio th*e* 13 march 1591–×– . xxviiij[s]

(1) *xij.[d] J. ha*] *xi* is written over *J*, *d* over *h*, and *a* stands free. The letters *J. ha* appear to be in the ink of the opposite page, which is dated 1591; they occur again on f. 7.

(2) *stranges*] *strangers* Greg.

(3) *satterdaye*] interlined.

(4) *oracioe*] so Malone; *oracoe* Greg; *i* and *o* are run together.

(5) *harey the vj*] *hary vj* Greg.

Rd at Jeronymo th*e* 14 of march 1591 . . . . iijli xj s
Rd at harey the 16 of march*e* 1591 . . . . xxxj s vj d
Rd at mvlo mvllocco th*e* 17 of marche 1591 . . . . xxviij s vj[d]
Rd at the Jewe of malta th*e* 18 of march*e* 1591 . . . . . . xxxix s
——Rd at Joronymo th*e* 20 of march*e* 1591 . . . . xxxviij s
Rd at constantine th*e* 21 of march*e* 1591 . . . . xij s
Rd at Q Jerusallem the 22 of march*e* 1591 . . . . xviij s
Rd at harey of cornwell the 23 of march*e* 1591 . . . . . . xiij s vj d
Ester⟨.⟩(1) Rd at fryer bacon the 25 of marche 1591 . . . . xv[s] vj[d]
——Rd at the lockinglasse the 27 of march*e* 1591 . . . . lv[s]
Rd at harey the vj the 28 of march*e* 1591 . . . . iij[li] viij s
Rd at mvlimvlucko(2) the 29 of march*e* 1591 . . . . iij[li] ij s
Rd at doneoracio the 30 of marche 1591 . . . . xxxix s
Rd at Joronymo(3) th*e* 31 of march*e* 1591 . . . . iij li
Rd at mandefell the 1 of ap[r]ell 1591 . . . . xxx s
——Rd at matchevell the 3 of ap[r]ell 1591 . . . . xxij s
Rd at the Jewe of malta th*e* 4 of ap[r]ell 1591 . . . . xxxxiij s
Rd at harey the vj th*e* 5 of ap[r]ell 1591 . . . . xxxxj s
Rd at brandymer th*e* 6 of ap[r]ell 1591 . . . . xxij s
Rd at Jeronymo th*e* 7 of ap[r]ell 1591 . . . . xxvj s
Rd at mvle(4) mvloco the 8 of ap[r]ell 1591 . J . h . – 01 – 10 – 00(5) xxiij s

[7v] 3002

——Rd at the comodey of Jerony*m*o the 10 of ap[r]ell 1591 . . xxviij s
ne—Rd at tittus & vespacia th*e* 11 of ap[r]ell 1591 . . . . . . iij[li] iiij s
Rd at byndo & Richardo *the* 12 of ap[r]ell 1591 . . . . . xxiij s
Rd at harey the vj the 13 of ap[r]ell 1591 . . . . xxvj s
Rd at Joronymo th*e* 14 of ap[r]elle 1591 . . . . xxxiij s
Rd at mandevell th*e* 15 of ap[r]ell 1591 . . . . xxvj s
·9·——Rd at mvllo mvlluco th*e* 17 of ap[r]ell 1591 . . . . xxx s
Rd at the Jewe of mallta the 18 of ap[r]ell 1591 . . . . . xxxxviij s vj d
Rd at the lockingglasse th*e* 19 of ap[r]ell 1591 . . . . . . xxiiij s
Rd at tittus & vespacia th*e* 20 of ap[r]ell 1591 . . . . . . lvj s
Rd at harey th*e* vj th*e* 21 of ap[r]ell 1591 . . . . xxxiij s
Rd at th*e* comodey Jeronymo the 22 of ap[r]ell 1591 xvij s
——Rd at Jeronymo the 24 o*f* ap[r]ell 1592 . . . . xxviij s
Rd at Jerusalem th*e* 25 of ap[r]ell 1592 . . . . xxxxvj s
Rd at fryer bacon th*e* 26 of ap[r]ell 1592 . . . . xxiiij[s]

(1) ⟨.⟩] a blot may conceal a letter.
(2) *mvlimvlucko*] *mvlomvlucko* Greg; the letters *vli* are smudged, but the third letter is dotted.
(3) *Joronymo*] *Jeronymo* Greg.
(4) *mvle*] *mvlo* Greg.
(5) *.J.h–01–10–00*] interlined.

Rd at mvlo mvloco the 27 of ap^r^ell 1592 . . . . xxvj^s^
ne—Rd at the second pte of tamber came the 28 of ap^r^ell . . iij^li^ iiij s
Rd at harey of cornwell the 29 of ap^r^ell 159[1]2(1) . . . xxvj s
Rd li24. . . . Rd at mvlo mvlluco the 30 of ap^r^ell 159[1]2(1) . . . . . lviij^s^
Rd at Jeronymo the 2 of maye 159[1]2(1) . . . . xxxiiij s
Rd at titus & vespacia the 3 of maye 159[1]2(1) . . . . . lvij s vj d
Rd at harey the vj the 4 of maye 159[1]2(1) . . . . . . lvj s
Rd at the Jewe of mallta 5 of maye 159[1]2(1) . . . . . xxxxj s
Rd 32.14. . . Rd at fryer bacon the 6 of maye 1592 . . . . xiiij s
——Rd at brandimer the 8 of maye 1592 . . . . xxiiij^s^
Rd at harey the vj the 7 of maye 1592. . . . . xxij s
34. . . . Rd at tittus & vespacia the 8 of maye 1592. . . . . xxx s
Rd at Jeronymo the 9 of maye 1592 . . . . xxvj s
Rd at the 2 pte of tambercam ye 10 maye(2) 1592 . . . . xxxvij s
whittsvn tyde Rd at the Jew of mallta the 11 of maye 1592 . . . . . . xxxiiij^s^
Rd at Jeronymo the 13 of maye 1592 . . . . iij^li^ 4^s^
Rd at harey the 6 the 14 of maye 1592 . . . . l s
51–10(3) Rd at tittus & vespacia the 15 of maye 1592 . . . . . . iij^li^
[49–10] . . . . Rd at mandevell the 16 of maye 1592 . . . . xxxx^s^
Rd at mvllomvloco the 17 of maye 1592 . . . . xxxvj^s^ vj^d^
Rd at harey of cornwell the 18 of maye 1592 . . . . . xxvj s
——Rd at harey the vj the 1[0]*9*(4) of maye 1592 . . . . . . xxx^s^
Rd at the Jewe of mallta the [11]*20*(4) of maye 1592. . . liiij s
Rd at the comodey of Jeronymo the [12]21(4) of maye 1592 xxviij s
Rd at Jeronymo the [13]22(4) of maye 1592 . . . . . . xxvij s
ne—Rd at the taner of denmarke the [14]23(4) maye 1592 . . iij^li^ xiij^s^ vj d
Rd at titus & vespacia the [16]24(4) of maye 1592 . . . . xxx s
——Rd at harey the vj the [17]25(4) of maye 1592 . . . . . xxiiij s
Rd at tambercame the [18]26(4) of maye 1592 . . . . . xxxvj s vj d
Rd at Jeronymo the [19]27(4) of maye 1592 . . . . . . xxiij s
066. . . . . . Rd at matchevell the 2[0]9(4) of maye 1592 . . . . . . xxvj s
Rd at the Jewe of malta the [21]30(4) of maye 1592 . . . xxxiij s
Rd at mvlemvloco the [22]31(4) of maye 1592 . . . . . xxiij^s^

[8]

1587(5) the(5)
——Rd at Bendo & Richardo the [24]5(6) of [*maye*] June(7) 1592 xxxij s
Rd at tittus & vespacia the 6 of June 1592 . . . . xxxxij s

(1) *159[1]2] 2* altered from *1*.
(2) *10 maye] 10 of maye* Greg.
(3) *51–10]* interlined above.
(4) The dates are all altered.
(5) *1587...the]* not recorded by Greg; in an unidentified hand.
(6) *[24]5] 5* altered from *2*; *4* deleted.
(7) *[maye] June]* alteration.

Rd at th*e* lockinglasse the 7 of June 1592 . . . . xxix s
Rd at the tambercame the 8 of June 1592 . . . . xxxx^{s}
76......Rd at Jeronymo th*e* 9 of June 1592 . . . . xxviij s
ne—Rd at a knacke to knowe a knave 1592 . . 10 day[1] . . . iij^{li} xij s
——Rd at harey th*e* vj th*e* 12 of June 1592 . . . . xxxij s
Rd at mvlemvloco th*e* 13 of June 1592 . . . . xx s
Rd at th*e* Jewe of malta th*e* 14 of June 1592 . . . . xxxviij^{s}
Rd at th*e* Knacke to knowe a Knave the 15 of June 1592 . lij s
.80...Rd at mandevell the 16 of June 1592 . . . . xx^{s}
——Rd at Joronymo the 18 of June 1592 . . . . xxiiij s
Rd at harey th*e* vj the 19 of June 1592 . . . . xxxj s
Rd at th*e* comodey of Jeronymo th*e* 20 of June 1592 . . . xv s
Rd at tambercame the 21 of June 1592 . . . . xxxij s
Rd at th*e* knacke to knowe A knave th*e* 22 of June . . . . xxvij s

In the Name of god Amen 159[2]3[2]
beginnge th*e* 29 of desemb3 . . . .

Rd at mvlomulluco th*e* 29 of desemb3 1592 . . . . iij^{li} x^{s}
Rd at Joronymo th*e* 30 of desembe3 1592 . . . . iij^{li} viij s
Rd at the cnacke th*e* 31 of desemb3 1592 . . . . xxx s
Rd at th*e* Jewe th*e* 1 of Janewary 1592 . . . . lvj s
Rd at th*e* cnacke th*e* 3 of Jenewary 1592 . . . . xxix s
Rd at mandevell th*e* 4 of Jenewary 1592. . . . . xij s
ne—Rd at th gelyous comodey the 5 of Jenewary 1592 . . . . xxxxiiij^{s}
——Rd at titvs th*e* 6 of Jenewary 1592 . . . . lij s
——Rd at Jeronymo th*e* 8 of Jenewarye 1593 . . . . xxij s
Rd at mvlo mulocko th*e* 9 of Jenewary 1593. . . . . . . xx s
Rd at frier bacon th*e* 10 of Jenewary 1593 . . . . xxiiij s
Rd at the comodey of cosmo th*e* 12 of Jeneway 1593 . . . xxxxiiij^{s}[3]
Rd at mandevell th*e* 13 of Jenewary 1593 . . . . ix s
Rd at the cnacke the 14 Jenewary[4] 1593 . . . . xxiiij^{s}
——Rd at tittus th*e* 15 of Jenewary 1593 . . . . xxx s
Rd at harey th*e* 6 of 16 of Jenewary 1593 . . . . xxxxvj s
Rd at frer bacon th*e* 17 of Jenewary 1593 . . . . xx s
Rd at th*e* Jew th*e* 18 of Jeneway 1593 . . . . iij^{li}
Rd at tambercam th*e* 19 of Jenewaye 1593. . . . . xxxvj^{s}
Rd at m*v*lomvloc[5] th*e* 2*o* Jeneway 1593. . . . . xx^{s}
——Rd at Jeronymo th*e* 22 of Jenewary 1593 . . . . xx^{s}

---

(1) *10 day*] interlined
(2) *159[2]3*] *3* altered from *2*.
(3) *xxxxiiij^{s}*] *xxxxvij^{s}* Greg.
(4) *14 Jenewary*] *14 of Jenewary* Greg.
(5) *mvlomvloc*] *mvlomvlco* Greg.

Rd at *cossmo* the 23 of Jeneway 1593 . . . . xxx s
Rd at the knacke the 24 Jenewye(1) 1593 . . . . xxiiij s
Rd at titus the 25 Jenewaye(2) 1593 . . . . xxx s
ne—Rd at the tragedey of the gvyes 30 . . . . iij li xiiij s
Rd at mandevell the 31 *of Jenewarye* ⟨.... ⟩ . . . *xij* s(3)

[8 v] **20099**

——Rd at frier bacon the 30 of [July] Jenewarye 1593 . . . . . . xij s
Rd at harey the vj the 31 of Jenewarye 1593 . . . . xxvj s
Rd at the Jewe of malta the j of febreary 1593 . . . . xxxv s

In the name of god Amen begninge th 27 of desembȝ 1593 the earle of susex his men

Rd at good spede the plowghe . . . . iij li j s
Rd at hewen of burdoche the 28 of desembȝ 1593 . . . . . iij li x s
Rd at gorge a gren the 29 of desembȝ 1593 . . . . iij li x s
Rd at buckingam the 30 of desembȝ 1593 . . . . lj s
Rd at Richard the confeser the 31 of desembȝ 1593 . . . . . xxxviij s
——Rd at buckingam the j of Jeneway 1593 . . . . lviij s
Rd at gorge a grene the 2 of Jene*w*arye 1593 . . . . xviij s
Rd at hewen of burdo*c*kes the 3 of Jeneway 1593 . . . . . xiiij s
Rd at william the conkerer the 4 of Jeneway 1593 . . . . . xxij s
Rd at god spead the plowe the 5 of Jeneway 1593 . . . . . xj s
——Rd at frier frances the 7 of Jeneway 1593 . . . . iij li j s
Rd at the piner of wiackefelld the 8 of Jeneway 1593 . . . . xxiij s
Rd at abrame & lotte the 9 of Jenewarye 1593 . . . . lij s
Rd at buckingam the 10 of Jenewarye 1593 . . . . xxij s
Rd at hewen the 11 of Jenew*a*rye 1593 . . . . v s
Rd at the fayer mayd of ytale the 12 Jeneway 1593. . . . . ix s
——Rd at frier frances the 14 of Jeneway 1593 . . . . xxxvj s
Rd at gorge a grene the 15 of Jene*w*arye 1593 . . . . xx s
Rd at Richard the confeser the 16 of Jenewar*y*e 1593 . . . . xj s
Rd at abr*am* & lotte the 17 of Jenewar*y*e 1593 . . . . xxx s
Rd at Kinge lude the 18 of Jenewarye 1593 . . . . xxij s
——Rd at ffrier ffrances the 20 of Jenewarye 1593 . . . . xxx s
Rd at the fayer mayd of ytaly the 21 of Jeneway. . . . . . xxij s
Rd at gorge a grene the 22 of Jenewar*y*e . . . . xxv s

---

(1) *24 Jenewye*] *sic*; *24 of Jenewarye* Greg.

(2) *25 Jenewaye*] *sic*; *25 of Jenewarye* Greg. Malone read *29*.

(3) *Jenewarye...xij s*] *Jenewarye 1593...xij s* Greg; the writing is smudged, and the paper frayed and rotted.

ne—Rd at titus & ondronicus th*e* 23 of Jenew*ary* . . . . iij[li] viij s
——Rd at buckengam th*e* 27 of Jenewarye 1593 . . . . xviij s
Rd at titus & ond*ro*nicous th*e* 28 of Jenewary . . . . xxxx[s]
Rd at abrame & lotte th*e* 31 of Jenewary 1593 . . . . xij s
——Rd at th*e* Jewe of malta th*e* 4 of febery 1593 . . . . l s
Rd at tittus & ondronicus th*e* 6 of febery 1593 . . . . xxxx[s]

[⅞ *inch blank*]

[9]

In the name of God Amen begininge at easter 1593
the Quenes men & my lord of Susexe to geather

Rd at frier bacone the j of [marche] Aprell(1) 1593 . . . xxxxiij[s]
Rd at the Rangers comodey 2 of [*marche*] Aprell(1) 1593 . iij[li]
Rd at the Jew of malta the 3 of ap[r]ell 1593 . . . . . . iij[li]
Rd at the fayer mayd of Italey ¶ 4 of ap[r]ell 1593 . . . . xxiij s
Rd at frier bacon the 5 of ap[r]ell 1593 . . . . xx s
Rd at kinge leare the 6 of ap[r]ell 1593 . . . . xxxviij s
——Rd at the Jewe of malta the 7 of ap[r]ell 1594 . . . . . . xxvj s
Rd at Kinge leare th*e* 8 of ap[r]ell(2) 1594 . . . . xxvj s

In the name of god Amen begininge the 14 of
maye 1594 by my lorde admeralls men

Rd at the Jewe of malta 14 of maye 1594 . . . . xxxxviij s
Rd at the Rangers comodey the 15 of maye 1594 . . . . xxxiij s
Rd at Cvtlacke the 16 of maye 1594 . . . . xxxxij s

In the name of god Amen begininge at newing
ton my Lord Admeralle men & my Lorde chamberlen
men As ffolowethe 1594

¶ 3 of June 1594	Rd at heaster & asheweros	viij s
¶ 4 of June 1594	Rd at the Jewe of malta	x s
¶ 5 of June 1594	Rd at andronicous	xij s
¶ 6 of June 1594	Rd at cvtlacke	xj s
¶ 8 of June 1594	ne—Rd at bellendon . . . . . × . . .	xvij s
¶ 9 of June 1594	Rd at hamlet	viij s
¶ 10 of June 1594	Rd at heaster	v s

(1) [*marche*] *Aprell*] alteration.
(2) *Rd...8 of ap[r]ell*] A rule in the left margin seems intended to mark this entry off from those above.

¶ 11 of June 1594		Rd at the tamynge of A shrowe . .	ix s
¶ 12 of June 1594		Rd at andronicous	vij s
¶ 13 of June 1594		Rd at the Jewe	iiij s
¶ 15 of June[1] 1594		Rd at bellendon	iij^{li} iiij s
¶ 17 of June 1594		Rd at cutlacke	xxxv s
¶ 18 of June 1594		Rd at the Rangers comodey	xxij s
¶ 19 of June 1594		Rd at the Gwies	liiij s
¶ 20 of June 1594		Rd at bellendon	xxx^{s}
¶ 22 of June 1594	——	Rd at the Rangers comodey	lviiij s
¶ 23 of June 1594		Rd at the Jewe	xxiij s
¶ 24 of June 1594		Rd at cvtlacke	xxv^{s}
¶ 25 of June 1594		Rd at the masacer.	xxxvj s
¶ 26 of June 1594	ne—	Rd at galiaso	iij^{li} iiij s
¶ 27 of June 1594		Rd at cvttlacke	xxxvj *s*

[9v] **20098**

¶ 30 of June 1594	——	Rd at the Jewe of malta	xxxxj s
¶ 2 of Julye 1594		Rd at bellendon	xxxxij s vj d
¶ 3 of Julye 1594		Rd at the masacer	xxxj s
¶ 4 of Julye 1594		Rd at cvtlacke	xxiiij s
¶ 5 of Julye 1594		Rd at the Rangers comodey . .	xviij s
¶ 6 of Julye 1594		Rd at bellendon	xxxiiij s
¶ 8 of Julye 1594	——	Rd at the masacer	xxvij s
¶ 9 of Julye 1594	ne—	Rd at the phillipo & hewpolyto .	iij^{li} ij s
¶ 10 of Julye 1594		Rd at the Jewe	xxvij s
¶ 11 of Julye 1594		Rd at bellendon	xxvij s
¶ 12 of Julye 1594		Rd at galiaso	xxxxvj s
¶ 13 of Julye 1594		Rd at phillipo & hewpolyto . .	xxxx s
¶ 15 of Julye 1594	——	Rd at cvtlacke	xxxv^{s}
¶ 16 of Julye 1594		Rd at masacare	xxxj^{s}
¶ 17 of Julye 1594		Rd at the Rangers comodey. . .	xv^{s}
¶ 18 of Julye 1594		Rd at phillipo & hewpolyto . .	xxxiij^{s} [2]
¶ 19 of Julye 1594	ne—	Rd at 2 pte of godfrey of bullen .	iij^{li} xj s
¶ 20 of Julye 1594	——	Rd at bellendon	xxvij s
¶ 22 of Julye 1594	——	Rd at the Jewe of malta	xxxj^{s}
¶ 23 of Julye 1594	——	Rd at galiaso	xxxj^{s}
¶ 24 of Julye 1594	——	Rd at phillipo & hewpolyto . .	xxx^{s}
¶ 25 of Julye 1594	——	Rd at bellendon	xlviij s

(1) *¶ 15 of June...*] There is a rule across the page between this entry and the one above.

(2) *xxxiij^{s}*] *xxx^{s}* Greg; Henslowe wrote *xxx^{s}*, then added *iij*.

¶ 26 of Julye 1594	——Rd at godfrey.	xlvij s
¶ 27 of Julye 1594	——Rd at the masacar	xxij s
¶ 29 of Julye 1594	——Rd at cvtlacke	xxix^{s}
¶ 30 of Julye 1594	ne—Rd at the marchant of eamden ×	iij^{li} viij s
¶ 31 of Julye 1594	——Rd at bellendon the	xxvij s
¶ 1 of aguste 1594	——Rd at the Rangers comodey . .	xiij s vj^{d}
¶ 3 of aguste 1594	——Rd at phillipo & hewpolito . . .	xxx s
¶ 5 of aguste 1594	——Rd at galiaso	xxiij s vj d
	Rd(1) at the Jewe of malta . . .	xxvij s
¶ 6 of aguste 1594	Rd at the seconde ꝑ of godfrey .	xxxvij s
¶ 7 of aguste 1594	Rd at phillipo & hewpolito . . .	xxix s
¶ 8 of aguste 1594	Rd at the masacare	xxiij s vj d
¶ 7 of aguste 1594	Rd at the Jewe of malta	xvij s vj d
¶ 8 of aguste 1594	Rd at cvttlacke	xiij s vj d
¶ 10 of aguste 1594	——Rd at bellendon	xxxiij s
¶ 11 of aguste 1594	ne—Rd at tassoes mellencoley	iij li iiij s
¶ 12 of aguste 1594	Rd at galliaso	xviij s
¶ 13 of aguste 1594	Rd at godfrey of bullen	xxix s
¶ 14 of aguste 1594	Rd at mahomett	iij li v s
¶ 15 of aguste 1594	Rd at phillipo & hewpolyto . .	xxj s
¶ 17 of aguste 1594	——Rd at the masacar	xx s
¶ 18 of aguste 1594	——Rd at tassoes mallencoley	xxxxvij s
¶ 19 of aguste 1594	Rd at bellendon	xxj s
¶ 20 of aguste 1594	Rd at the Rangers comodey . .	xiiij s vj d
¶ 21 of aguste 1594	Rd at galiaso	xxj^{s} vj^{d}
¶ 22 of aguste 1594	Rd at cvttlacke	xxiij s vj^{d}

0111– 6–00(2)

[10]

¶ 24 of aguste 1594	Rd at phillipo & hewpolyto . .	xxviij s
¶ 25 of aguste 1594	ne—Rd at the venesyon comodey .	l s vj d
¶ 26 of aguste 1594	Rd at godfrey	xxvij s vj d
¶ 27 of aguste 1594	Rd at mahemet	xxxx s
¶ 28 of aguste 1594	j Rd at tamberlen	iij^{li} xj s
¶ 29 of aguste 1594	Rd at belendon	xx^{s} vj d

(1) *Rd*] linked by a slanting line to *5 of aguste*, which has two plays attached to it; Greg does not note this. Henslowe seems to have written the dates as a column before entering titles; when they got seriously out of alignment, he went back to the entry of 19 July, and began to join dates and titles by connecting lines; but he abandoned this at the entry of 5 August, where he levelled off by joining two titles to one date. See Introduction, p. xxvii.
(2) – *6–00*] A smudge before *6* may conceal *1* or *0*. This total is in a different ink from the rest of the entries on this page; cf. note 1, p. 25.

¶ 2 of septmbȝ 1594	——	Rd at the Jew of malta . . .	xxiij s vj d
¶ 3 of septmbȝ 1594		Rd at Tasso.	xxxxvj s
¶ 4 of septmbȝ 1594		Rd at phillipo & hewpolito .	xxij s
¶ [7]5(1) of septembȝ 1594		Rd at the venesyon comodey .	xxxvj s vj d
¶ 6 of septmbȝ 1594		Rd at cvtlacke.	xj s
¶ [6]7(2) of septmbȝ 1594		Rd *at* masacar(3)	xvij s vj d
¶ 8 of septmbȝ 1594	——	Rd at godfrey	xxxx^{s}
¶ 9 of septmbȝ 1594		Rd at mahemett	xxxv^{s}
¶ 10 of septmbȝ 1594		Rd at galiaso	xxv^{s}
¶ 11 of septmbȝ 1594		Rd at bellendon	xxiiij^{s} vj d
¶ 12 of septmbȝ 1594		Rd at tamberlen	xxxxv^{s}
¶ 13 of septmbȝ 1594		Rd at phillipo & hewpolito . .	xx s
¶ 15 of septmbȝ 1594	——	Rd at the venesyon comodey .	xxxvj s vj d
¶ 16 of septmbȝ 1594		Rd at the Rangers comodey .	xv^{s}
¶ 17 of septmbȝ 1594	ne—	Rd at palamon & a^{r}sett	lj s
¶ 18 of septmbȝ 1594		Rd at tasso	xxvij s vj d
¶ 19 of septmbȝ 1594		Rd at phillipo & hewpolyto . .	xiiij s vj d
¶ 20 of septmbȝ 1594		Rd at godfrey	xxx^{s}
¶ 21 of septmbȝ 1594	——	Rd at mahemett	xxviij s
¶ 22 of septmbȝ 1594		Rd at the venesyon comodey .	xxv s
¶ 23 of septmbȝ 1594		Rd at bellendon	xvj s vj d
¶ 24 of septmbȝ 1594	ne—	Rd at venesyon & th*e* love of & Ingleshelady	xxxxvij
¶ 25 of septmbȝ 1594	——	Rd at masacar	xiiij^{s}
¶ 26 of septmbȝ 1594	——	Rd at cvttlacke	xiij s
¶ 28 of septmbȝ 1594	——	Rd at tamberlen	xxxj^{s}
¶ 29 of septmbȝ 1594		Rd at galiaso	xvij^{s}
¶ [2]30(4) of septmbȝ 1594		Rd at docter ffostose	iij^{li} xij^{s}
¶ 2 of octobȝ 1594		Rd at the Rangers comodey . .	x s
¶ 3 of octobȝ 1594		Rd at the venesyon comodey .	xvij s
¶ 4 of octobȝ 1594		Rd at th*e* love of a gresyan lady .	xxvj s
¶ 6 of octobȝ 1594	——	Rd at godfrey of bullen . . .	xx^{s}
¶ 7 of octobȝ 1594		Rd at phillipo & hewpolito . .	xij s
¶ 8 of octobȝ 1594		Rd at tasso	xxvij s
¶ 9 of octobȝ 1594		Rd at docter ffostus	xxxxiiij s
¶ 11 of octobȝ 1594		Rd at venesyon comodey . . .	xvj s
¶ 13 of octobȝ 1594	——	Rd at bellendon	xxij s
¶ 14 of octobȝ 1594		Rd at mahemett	xxvj s
¶ 15 of octobȝ 1594		Rd at tamberlen	xxviij s
¶ 16 of octobȝ 1594		Rd at palaman & arset	xxvij s

(1) [7]5] alteration. (2) [6]7] alteration.

(3) *at masacar*] *at the mesacar* Greg; *masacar* retraced. (4) [*2*]*30*] *3* altered from *2*.

¶ 17 of octob3 1594 Rd at tamberlen . . . . xxxx^s
¶ 18 of octob3 1594 Rd at the frenshe docter . . . xxij s

060–06 – 03 (1)

[10 v] **20097**

¶ 20 of octob3 1594 ——Rd at the Jewe of malta 1594 . . . xiij s
¶ 21 of octob3 1594 Rd at docter ffostus 1594 . . . . . xxxiij s
¶ 22 of octob3 1594 ne—Rd at a Knacke (2) to Know a noneste xxxx^s
¶ 23 of octob3 1594 Rd at tasso . . . . xxiij s
¶ 24 of octob3 1594 Rd at love of & Ingleshe ladey . . xxiij s
¶ 25 of octob3 1594 Rd at galleaso . . . . xj s
¶ 27 of octob3 1594 ——Rd at pallaman & harset . . . . . xxxxvij s
¶ 28 of octob3 1594 Rd at the frenshe docter . . . . . xv^s
¶ 29 of octob3 1594 Rd at the Knacke to Knowe & oneste man xxxxvij s
¶ 30 of octob3 1594 Rd at bullen . . . . xv s
¶ 1 of novemb3 1594 Rd at the Knacke to Knowe & onest man iij^li iij s
¶ 2 of novemb3 1594 Rd at bellendon[t] . . . . vij s
¶ 4 of [octob3]novēb3 (3) 1594 ——Rd at tamberlen . . . . xxxix^s
¶ 5 of novemb3 1594 Rd at docterfostes . . . . xxxviij s
¶ 6 of novemb3 1594 Rd at mahemette . . . . xv s
¶ 7 of no*v*mb3 1594 Rd at th*e* Knacke . . . . xxxxiiij^s
¶ 8 of novemb3 1594 ne—Rd at seser & pompie . . . . . . iij^li ij s
¶ 9 of novemb3 1594 Rd at palamon . . . . xij s
¶ 11 of novemb3 1594——Rd at the venesyon comodey . . . xxj s
¶ 12 of novemb3 1594 Rd at tasso. . . . . xxv^s
¶ 13 of novmb3 1594 Rd at the gresyan ladye . . . . . xv^s
¶ 14 of novemb3 1594 Rd at sesor & pompie . . . . . . xxxv^s
¶ 15 of novemb3 1594 Rd at bellendon . . . . xij s
¶ 16 of novmb3 1594 ne—Rd at deoclesyan . . . . liiij s
¶ 18 of novmb3 1594 ——Rd at the frenshe docter 189–08–00 (4) xxvij s
¶ 20 of novmb3 1594 Rd at docter fostes . . . . xviij s
¶ 21 of novmb3 1594 Rd at the Knacke . . . . xx^s
¶ 22 of novmb3 1594 Rd at deoclesyan . . . . xxxxiij^s
¶ 23 of novmb3 1594 Rd at th*e* greasyon comody . . . x s
¶ 25 of novemb3 1594——Rd at seser & pompey . . . . . . xxxij^s
¶ 26 of novmb3 1594 Rd at the venecyon comodey. . . xiij s
¶ 27 of *no*vmb3 1594 Rd at tamberlen . . . . xxij s

---

(1) The total is in a different ink from the rest of the entries on this page, the same ink as the total on f. 9 v.

(2) *a Knacke*] *the knacke* Greg

(3) [*octob3*] *novēb3*] alteration.

(4) *189–08–00*] interlined.

¶ 28 of novmbʒ 1594	Rd at worlamchester	xxiijˢ
¶ 29 of novmbʒ 1594	Rd at the Knacke	xx s
¶ 30 of novmbʒ 1594	Rd at warlamchester	xxxviij s
¶ 1 of desembʒ 1594	——Rd at the gresyan comody	iiij s
¶ 2 of desembʒ 1594	ne—Rd at the wise man of chester . .	xxxiij s
¶ 3 of desembʒ 1594	Rd at tasso	vj s
¶ 4 of desembʒ 1594	Rd at mahemet	xj s
¶ *6* of desembʒ 1594	Rd at wiseman of *we*schester . . .	xxxiiij s
¶ 8 of desembʒ 1594	——Rd at docterfostus.	xvˢ
¶ 9 of desembʒ 1594	——Rd at the Jew	iij s
¶ 10 of desembʒ 1594	——Rd at seser	xijˢ (1)
¶ 12 of desembʒ 1594	Rd at warlamchester	xvˢ
¶ 13 of desembʒ 1594	Rd at the Knacke	xij s
¶ 14 of desembʒ 1594	ne—Rd at the mawe	xxxxiiij s

058–08–0(2)

[11]

¶ 17 of desembʒ 1594	Rd at tamberlen	xxxj s
¶ 19 of desembʒ 1594	Rd at the 2 ꝑte of tamberlen. . .	xxxxvj s
¶ 20 of desembʒ 1594	Rd at docter fostes	xviij s
¶ 25 of desembʒ 1594	S steuen—Rd at the greasyane comodey	xxxxvj s
¶ 26 of desembʒ 1594	Rd at the [g]sege(3) of london . .	iijˡⁱ iij s
¶ 27 of desembʒ 1594	Rd at Docter fostes.	lij s
¶ 29 of desembʒ 1594	——Rd at the wissman of weschester .	iijˡⁱ ij s
¶ 30 of desembʒ 1594	Rd at tamberlen	xxij s
¶ j of Jeneway 1594	Rd at the 2 ꝑte of tamberlen. . .	iijˡⁱ ij s
¶ 2 of Jeneway 1594	Rd at the seat at mawe	xxiiij s
¶ 3 of Jeneway 1594	Rd at the frenshe docter	xxj s
¶ 4 of Jeneway 1594	Rd *at* valy a for.	xj s
¶ 7 of Jeneway 1594	——Rd at the knacke.	xxij s
¶ 9 of Jeneway 1594	Rd at docter fostes	xxij s
¶ 10 of Jeneway 159[*4*]5(4)	Rd at the greasy*o*n comodey . .	xxviij s
¶ 11 of Jeneway 159[*4*]5(4)	Rd at tasso	xxˢ
¶ 13 of Jeneway 159[*4*]5(4)	——Rd at the Knacke	xxxiij s
¶ *14* of Jeneway 1594	Rd at th*e* seage of london	xxviij s
¶ 15(5) of Jenew*a*rye 1594	Rd at the wiseman of weaschester.	iij li

(1) *xijˢ*] so Greg; *i* could be a compressed *v*.

(2) The total is in a different ink from the rest of the entries on this page, the same ink as the totals on ff. 9v and 10.

(3) [*g*]*sege*] *s* altered from *g*.

(4) *159*[*4*]*5*] *5* altered from *4*.

(5) *15*] *16* Greg; both readings are possible.

¶ 17 of Jeneway 1594		Rd at th*e* mawe	xxv^{s}
¶ 18 of Jeneway 1594		Rd at seaser	xxv^{s}
¶ 19 of Jeneway 1594		Rd at the Rangers comodey . . .	xv^{s}
¶ 21 of Jenew*ar*y 1594	——	Rd at tasso	xxxvj s
¶ 22 of Jenew*ar*y 1594		Rd at the seage of london	xxxij s
¶ 23 of Jeneway 1594		Rd at the wiseman of weascheaster	iij^{li} vj s
¶ 24 of Jeneway 1594		Rd at docter fostes	xxiiij s
¶ 25 of Jeneway 1594		Rd at the greasyan	xv s
¶ 27 of Jeneway 1594	——	Rd at tamberlen	xxx^{s}
¶ 28 of Jeneway 1594		Rd at th*e* mawe	xxvij s
¶ 29 of Jeneway 1594		Rd at the 2 pt of tamberlen . . .	xxxxvij s
¶ 30 of Jenew*ar*y 1594		Rd at the frenshe doct*er*	xviij s
¶ 31 of Jeneway 1594		Rd at the gresyan comody . . .	xxviij s
¶ j of febreary 1594		Rd at seaser	xxiiij s
¶ 3 of febreary 1594	——	Rd at th*e* sege of london	xxxxv^{s}
¶ 4 of febreary 1594		Rd at wysman of weschester. . .	iij li iiij s
¶ 5 of febreary 1594		Rd at mahemett	xxvj s
¶ 6 of febre*ar*y 1594		Rd at the Knacke	xxiiij s
¶ 7 of febreary 1594		Rd at the frenshe docter	xxj s
¶ 8 of febreary 1594		Rd at docter fostes	xviij s
¶ 10 of febreary 1594	——	Rd at th*e* venesyan	xx s
¶ 11 of febreary 1594	ne—	Rd at the frenshe Comodey . . .	l s
¶ 12 of febreary 1594		Rd at wisman of weschester . . .	liij s
¶ 13 of febre*a*ry 1594		Rd at the sege of london	xxix s
¶ 14 of febreary 1594	j	Rd at longe mege of westmester .	iij^{li} ix s
¶ 15 of febreary 1594		Rd at tasso	xix s

[11 v] **20096**

¶ 17 of febreye 1594		Rd at tamberlen	xxx^{s}
¶ 18 of febreary 1594		Rd at 2 pte of tamberlen	xxxvj s
¶ 19 of febre[ary]y(1) 1594		Rd at wisman of weschester . . .	xxxxvj s
¶ 20 of febreary 1594		Rd at longe mege	xxxxviij s
¶ 21 of febre*a*ry 1594	ne—	Rd at the macke . . . . × . . .	iij^{li}
¶ 22 of febre*a*ry 1594		Rd at the gresyan comodey . . .	xx s
¶ 24 of febre*a*ry 1594	——	Rd at th*e* frensh docter	xxxxxiiij^{s}
¶ 25 of febreary 1594		Rd at th*e* venesyan comodey . .	xx s
¶ 26 of febreary 1594		Rd at the *Knacke*	xxiiij s
¶ 27 of febreary 1594		Rd at the frenshe Comodey . . .	xxxx^{s}
¶ 28 of febreary 1594		Rd at the wisman of weschester .	xxxix s

(1) *febre*[*ary*]*y*] *y* altered from a faint *ary*.

¶ 29 of febreary 1594		Rd at lo*n*ge mege	xxxviij s
¶ 3 of marche 1594	——	Rd at the sege of london	xxvj s
¶ 4 of marche 1594		Rd at longe mege on sraftusdaye[1]	iij^{li}
¶ 5 of marche 1594	ne—	Rd at seleo & olempo	iij^{li}
¶ 6 of marche 1594		Rd at seaser	xx^{s}
¶ 10 of marche 1594	17 p——	Rd at th*e* Knacke from hence lycensed[2]	xxiiij s
¶ 11 of marche 1594		Rd at fyrste ꝑt of tamberlen	xxx^{s}
¶ 12 of marche 1594		Rd at 2 ꝑt of tamberlen	xxij s
¶ 13 of marche 1594		Rd at longe mege	xxviij s
¶ 14 of marche 1594		Rd at sege of london	xiiij s
easter mondaye[3] 1595	easter	Rd at the ffrenshe doctor	liij s
¶ 23 of ap^{r}ell 1595		Rd at the knacke	lv^{s}
¶ 24 of ap^{r}ell 1595		Rd at the grecian comody	lj s
¶ 25 of ap^{r}ell 1595		Rd at the wissman	lviij s
¶ 26 of ap^{r}ell 1595		Rd at the wisseman of weschester	iij^{li}
¶ 27 of ap^{r}ell 1595	——	Rd at godfrey of bullen	xxix s
¶ 29 of ap^{r}ell 1595	——	Rd at warlamchester	xxix s
¶ 30 of ap^{r}ell 1595	——	Rd at longe mege	xxvij s
¶ 31 of ap^{r}ell 1595	——	Rd at fastes	xxij s
¶ 1 of maye 1595	——	Rd at longe mege	l s
¶ 2 of maye 1595	——	Rd at seleo & olempa	l s
¶ 3 of maye 1595		Rd at[4] frenshe docter	xj s
¶ 5 of maye 1595	——	Rd at the Knacke	xxiij s
¶ 6 of maye 1595		Rd at the wiseman	xxxx^{s}
¶ 7 of maye 1595	—ne—	Rd at th*e* firste ꝑte of herculous	iij^{li} xiij s
¶ 8 of maye 1595	——	Rd at th*e* venesyon comody	xxx s
¶ 9 of maye 1595		Rd at selyo & olympo	xxvj s
¶ 10 of maye 1595		Rd at warlam chester	xxix s
¶ 12 of maye 1595	——	Rd at th*e* frenshe comodey	xxviij s
¶ 13 of maye 1595		Rd at longe mege	xxviij s
¶ 14 of maye 1595		Rd at tasso	xx^{s}
¶ *1*5 of maye 1595		Rd at th*e* wisse man of weschester	xxxvij s
¶ 16 of maye 1595		Rd at th*e* greasyan comodey	xxxiij s
¶ 17 of maye 1595		Rd at godfey[5] of bullen	xxij s[6]

(1) *sraftusdaye*] enclosed in a rectangle.

(2) *from...lycensed*] interlined.

(3) *easter mondaye*] There is a rule across the page between this entry and the one above.

(4) *at*] *at the* Greg.

(5) *godfey*] *sic*; *godfrey* Greg.

(6) Below this line is a modern forgery which reads: ¶ *18 of maye 1595* . . . . . . *Rd at galfrido & Bernardo* . . . . *xxxj^{s}*. The title does not occur again, and the entry was not recorded by Malone.

[12]

[Beyt[1] knowen vnto all men by thes pñtę
y^t I John griggs cyttezin and Butcher of
London do owe vnto phillipe hinchley
cyttezin and dyer of london the some
of fyveten poundę of good and lawfull
money of England to be payd vnto
the sayd phillipe hinchley his ex̄ adm̄e
and assignes the xiij^th day of August
next ensuienge the datte hereof vnto
the wch payment I the sayd John griggę
do bynd me my heires ex̄ adm̄ and assignes
by thes presentę In wyttnes wherof I
the sayd John griggę have setto[2] my
[3]hand [the] and seale the [da] xiij^th day
of July 1592 ///]

p me Joh[a]n[4] Griggę://[1]
p me John Griggę
lamentable ..
p me J [5/8 × 1 3/8 *inches cut out*] 51 8

47
48

[3 3/4 *inches blank*]

[12v]		20094
¶ 1[7]9[5] of maye 1595	Rd at olimpo	xxiij s
¶ 20 of maye 1595	Rd at hercolas	iij^li ix^s
¶ 21 of maye 1595	Rd at j pt of tamberlen	xxij s
¶ 22 of maye 1595	Rd at 2 p of tamberlen	xxv^s
¶ 23 of maye 1595	ne—Rd at 2 p of hercolas	iij^li x s
¶ 2[3]4[6] of maye 1595	*R*d at frenshe docter . . 12[7] . .	xxij s
¶ 26 of maye 1595	——Rd at weschester	xxxj s
¶ 27 of maye 1595	Rd at j pte of herculos	iij li[8]
¶ 28 of maye 1595	Rd at 2 pte of herculas	iij^li ij s
¶ 29 of maye 1595	Rd at olimp*o*	xxix s

---

(1) *Beyt...Griggę://*] in Grigg's hand; the rest is in Henslowe's.
(2) *setto*] *sic*; *sette* Greg.
(3) A smudge in the left margin obscures some figures, perhaps tests of a nib.
(4) *Joh*[*a*]*n*] *n* altered from *a*.
(5) *1*[*7*]*9*] *9* altered from *7*
(6) *2*[*3*]*4*] *4* altered from *3*.
(7) *12*] interlined.
(8) *iij^li*] *ij^ll* Greg.

¶ 30 of maye 1595 Rd at warlamchester . . . . . . ixs
¶ 31 of maye 1595 —pd—Rd at frenshe comodye . . . . . xvs
¶ 3 of June 1595 ne—Rd at the vij Dayes of the weack*e*. iij[li] xs
¶ 4 of June 1595 Rd at th*e* wisman of weschester . . xxij s
¶ 5 of June 1595 Rd at doctor ffostus . . . . xvij s
¶ 6 of June 1595 Rd at the vij dayes of the weack . xxxxiiij s
¶ 7 of June 1595 Rd at olimpio . . . . xvs
¶ 9 of June 1595—whittson daye(1)—Rd at the Knacke . . . lv[s]
¶ 10 of June 1595 post 83[li]–0 Rd at the vij dayes of the wecke iij[li] vj s
¶ 11 of June 1595 Rd at wissman of weschester . . . xxxxvij s
¶ 12 of June 1595 Rd at the j ꝑt of herculos . . . . iij[li] j s
¶ 13 of June 1595 Rd at the 2 ꝑt of herculos . . . . iij[li] ij s(2)
¶ 14 of June 1595 Rd at the vij dayes of the wecke . iij[li] ixs
¶ 16 of June 1595 ——Rd at warlamchester . . . . . . xxvs
¶ 17 of June 1595 Rd at the frenshe comodey . . . . xxj s
¶ 18 of June 1595 ne—Rd at the 2 ꝑte of sesore . . . . . lv[s]
¶ 19 of June 1595 Rd at longe mege . . . . xxij s
¶ 20 of June [*Cut out as on recto*(3)] Rd at antony & vallea . . . . . xxs
¶ 21 of June . at the Knacke . . . . xiij s
¶ 23 of June Rd at the vij dayes of th*e* wecke. iij[li] v[s]
¶ 24 of June mydsomerday*e* Rd at th*e* frenshecomodey . . xxx[s]
¶ 25 of June 1595 Rd at th*e* j ꝑte of seaser . . . . . xxij s
¶ 26 of June 1595 Rd at the 2 ꝑte of seaser . . . . . xx[s]

¶ 25 of aguste(4) 1595 Rd at the Knacke to Know a nonest man xvij s
¶ 26 of aguste 1595 Rd at the wisman of wescheaster . xxxixs
¶ 27 of aguste 1595 Rd at *t*he weacke . . . . liij s
¶ 28 of aguste 1595 Rd at longe mege . . . . xvij s
¶ 29 of aguste 1595 ne—Rd at longe shancke . . . . xxxxs
¶ 30 of aguste 1595 Rd at the seage of london . . . . xviij s
¶ 1 of septmbȝ 1595 ——Rd at j ꝑte of hercvlos . . . . . . iij[li] iiij s
¶ 2 of septmbȝ 1595 ——Rd(5) at 2 ꝑte of hercvlos . . . . iij li
¶ 3 of septmbȝ 1595 ——Rd(5) at the vij dayes of the weacke lij s
¶ 4 of septmbȝ 1595 ——Rd(5) at olempeo & heugenyo . . xviij s
¶ 5 of se*p*tmbȝ 1595 ne—Rd at cracke me this nvtte . . . . iij li j s
¶ 6 of septmbȝ 1595 Rd at valia & antony . . . . . . xiij s

---

(1) *daye*] interlined below. (2) *ij s*] *li* in the next entry is written over *ij*.

(3) The piece missing was cut out after the entry was made on the recto (1592), and apparently before the entries on this page; the year of the date (1595) was never entered in these lines.

(4) ¶ *25 of aguste*] A rule across the page separates this entry from the one above.

(5) Faint lines join the dates and entries of plays, which are out of alignment here.

¶ 9 of septmbȝ 1595 ——Rd[1] at th*e* wise man . . . . . . xxxxiiij s
¶ 10 of septmbȝ 1595 ——Rd[1] at longshanck*e*. . . . . . . iij li
¶ 11 of septmbȝ 1595 ——Rd[1] at docter fostes . . . . . . xxx s ij[2]
¶ 12 of septmbȝ 1595 ——Rd[1] at cracke me this nutte . . . iij li
¶ 13 of septmbȝ 1595 ——Rd[1] at the vij dayes . . . . . . xxxviij s
poste 17[6]3[3]–00–0[4] Rd at longe mege. . . . . xvj s

[13]

¶ 15 of septmbȝ 1595 Rd at j p̱te of tamberlen . . . . . xxj s
¶ 16 of septmbȝ 1595 Rd at godfrey of bullen . . . . . xx^s
¶ 17 of septmbȝ 1595 ne—Rd at th*e* worldes tragedy . . . . iij^li v^s
¶ 18 of septmbȝ 1595 Rd at the Knacke . . . . xvij^s
¶ 19 of septmbȝ 1595 Rd at the frenshe docto^r . . . . . xvj s
¶ 20 of septmbȝ 1595 Rd at the sege of london . . . . . xviij s
¶ 22 of septmbȝ 1595 ——Rd at the vij dayes . . . . xxxxiiij s
¶ 22 of septmbȝ 1595 Rd at j p̱te of herculos . . . . . . xxxj s
¶ 23 of septmbȝ 1595 Rd at 2 p̱t of herculos . . . . . . xxiij s
¶ 24 of septmbȝ 1595 Rd at cracke me this nvtte . . . . xxxxij s
¶ 25 of septmbȝ 1595 Rd at the worldes tragedy . . . . xxxviij s
¶ 26 of septmbȝ 1595 Rd at docter fostes . . . . xiij s
¶ 2[7]8[5] of septmbȝ 1595 ——Rd at cr*a*ck me this nvtte . . iij^li vj^s
¶ 29 of septmbȝ 1595 Rd at th*e* wiseman . . . . xv s
¶ [2]30[6] of septmbȝ 1595 Rd at longe shancke . . . . . . xxxij s
¶ 2 of octobȝ 1595 ne—Rd at the Desgysses . . . . xxxxiij s
¶ 3 of octobȝ 1595 Rd at olempeo . . . . xv s
¶ 4 of octobȝ 1595 Rd at longe mege . . . . xj s
¶ 6 of octobȝ 1595 ——Rd at the vij dayes . . . . xxxx^s
¶ 6 of oct*o*bȝ 1595 ——Rd[7] at th*e* wisman . . . . xvij s
¶ 7 of oc*t*obȝ 1595 Rd at the worldes tragedy . . . . xxxij s[8]
¶ 8 of octobȝ 1595 Rd at cr*a*cke me this nvtt . . . . xxvj s
¶ 9 of octobȝ 1595 Rd at the gresyan comody . . . . x s
¶ 10 of octobȝ 1595 Rd at the desgyses . . . . xxix s
¶ 12 of octobȝ 1595 ——Rd at j p̱te of hercul*o*s . . . . . . xxix s
¶ 13 of octobȝ 1595 Rd at 2 p̱te of herculus . . . . . xxv^s
¶ 14 of octobȝ 1595 Rd at the vij dayes . . . . xvij s

---

(1) Faint lines join the dates and entries of plays, which are out of alignment here.
(2) *xxx s ij*] ? *xxxij s* (so Greg).
(3) *17[6]3*] *37[6]3* Greg; *1* is caught up in the tail of the preceding *e*; *3* altered from *6*.
(4) *poste 17[6]3–00–0*] interlined.
(5) *2[7]8*] *8* altered from *7*. (6) *[2]30*] *3* altered from *2*.
(7) ¶ *6 of octobȝ...Rd*] The line linking date and entry is faint.
(8) *xxxij s*] *xxxj^s* Greg.

¶ 15 of octobȝ 1595	ne—Rd at the wonder of a womon . .	liij s
¶ 16 of octobȝ 1595	Rd at desgysses(1)	x s
¶ 17 of octobȝ 1595	Rd at th*e* vij dayes	xxviij s
¶ 19 of octobȝ 1595	——Rd at the wisman	xvij s
¶ 20 of octobȝ 1595	Rd at cracke me this nvtte	xxj s
¶ 21 of oct*o*bȝ 1595	Rd at long shancke	xxx s
¶ 22 of oct*o*bȝ 1595	Rd at the worldes tragedy	xxxiij s
¶ 23 of *o*ctobȝ 1595	Rd at the w*o*nder of a wom*a*n . .	xxiij s
¶ 24 of octobȝ 1595	Rd at cracke me this nvtte	xxiij s
¶ 25 of octobȝ 1595	——Rd at j ꝑt of herculos	xxxij s
¶ *26* of octobȝ 1595	Rd at valia & antony	xxvij s
¶ 27 of octobȝ 1595	Rd at the desgyses	xix s
¶ 28 of octobȝ 1595	ne—Rd at barnardo & philameta(2) . .	xxxxij s
¶ 29 of octobȝ 1595	Rd at the vij Dayes	xiij s
¶ 30 of *octobȝ* 1595	Rd at the desgysses	xxix s
¶ 2 of novmbȝ 1595	——Rd at 2(3) ꝑt of hercolas	xxviij s
¶ 3 of nov*e*mbȝ 1595	Rd at the new worldes tragedy . .	xxix s
¶ 4 of novembȝ 1595	Rd at the wonder of a wom*on* . .	xxvij s
¶ 5 of novmbȝ 1595	Rd at *cr*acke me this nvtt	xxiiij s
¶ 6 of novmbȝ 1595	Rd at barnardo	xvij s
——m^r^ pd	——Rd at weschester	xx^s^

[13v] **20093**

praysed the 28th of Aprill 1595 thes parssell*s*
A Remnaunt of Black sattin of 7 yardę & A black
Cloke of cloth w^t^ out lyning cape or Lace both
Together att the some of fouer powndę tenn shillings
By vs

the*e* mark of [mark] hugh davis

by me EAlleyn(4)

[Lent vnto m^r^ Jonnes player the 17 of
novmbȝ 1599 in Redy mony fortie
shellenges wch is boye Jemes feched
I saye . . . . } xxxx^s^]

wittnes m^rs^ alleyn

[5½ *inches blank*]

(1) *at desgysses*] *at the desgysses* Greg.
(2) *philameta*] *phvlameta* Greg. (3) *at 2*] *at the 2* Greg.
(4) *praysed...EAlleyn*] in Alleyn's hand, except for the mark.

¶ 9 of novmbȝ 1595 Rd at longshancke . . . . xxxiij s
¶ 10 of novmbȝ 1595 Rd at Desgysses . . . . xv^s
¶ 12 of novmbȝ 1595 Rd at j ꝑte of tamberlen . . . . xviij^s
¶ 13 of novmbȝ 1595 Rd at 2 ꝑt of tambrlen . . . . . xxxij s
¶ 14 of novembȝ 1595 ne—Rd at a toye to please my ladey . lj s
¶ 15 of novmbȝ 1595 Rd at vij Dayes . . . . xviij s
¶ 18 of novmbȝ 1595 ——Rd at cracke me this nvtte . . . xxiiij s
¶ 19 of novmbȝ 1595 Rd at barnardo . . . . vj s
¶ 20 of novmbȝ 1595 Rd at wonder of A womon . . . xx s
¶ 21 of novmbȝ 1595 Rd at a toye to please chaste ladeyes xxj s
¶ 22 of novmbȝ 1595 Rd at olempo . . . . iiij s vj d
¶ 24 of novmbȝ 1595 ——Rd at j herculos . . . . xx s
¶ 25 of *no*vmbȝ 1595 Rd of 2 pt of herculos . . . . . xvj s
¶ 26 of novembȝ 1595 Rd at longshancke . . . . xviij s
¶ 27 of novembȝ 1595 Rd at the newes wordles tragedy . xviij s
¶ 28 of novembȝ 1595 ne—Rd at harey the v . . . . iij^li vj s
¶ 29 of novmbȝ 1595 Rd at the welche man . . . . . vij s
¶ 31 of novmbȝ 1595 ——Rd at th*e* t*o*ye to please chaste ladeyes xij s
¶ 2 of desembȝ 1595 Rd at hary the v . . . . xxxv^s
¶ 3 of desembȝ 1595 Rd at barnardo . . . . vij s
¶ 4 of desembȝ 1595 Rd at wonder of A womon . . . xiiij s
¶ 6 of desembȝ 1595 [——](1) Rd at Crack me this nvtt . . xv^s
¶ 8 of desembȝ 1595 ——Rd at hary the v . . . . xxxxiij s
¶ 10 of desembȝ 1595 Rd at prynce longshanke . . . . xxx s
¶ 12 of desembȝ 1595 Rd at the new worldes tragedy . xxxj s vj d
¶ 14 of desembȝ 1595 ——Rd at the vij dayes . . . . xxiiij s
¶ 16 of desembȝ 1595 Rd at hary the v . . . . xxix s
¶ 18 of desembȝ 1595 m^r pd—Rd at j ꝑt of herculos . . . . xiij s
¶ 22 of desembȝ 1595 ——Rd at the newe worldes tragedie . xx s
¶ 25 of desembȝ 1595 S steuens day Rd at the wonder of A womon iij^li ij s
¶ 26 of desembȝ 1595 Rd at barnardo . . . . lviij s
¶ 28 of desembȝ 1595 ——Rd at harye the v . . . . lvj s
¶ 29 of desembȝ 1595 Rd at longshanckes . . . . xxxij s
¶ 30 of desembȝ 1595 Rd at the wisman of weschester . xxij s
¶ 1 of Jenew*ar*y 1595 Rd at t*he* wecke . . . . xxxxij s
¶ 2 of Jenew*a*ry 1595 Rd at cracke me this nvtt . . . . ix s
¶ 3 of Jeneway 1595 ne—Rd at chinone of Ingland . . . . l s
¶ 5 of Jeneway 1595 140–1[0]1(2)–0^d—Rd at harey the v . [140](3) . . xxvj s

---

(1) A line joining the date and the play entry has been erased.
(2) *1*[*0*]*1*] the second *1* altered from *0*. (3) *140*] interlined.

¶ 6 of Jenewary 1595 Rd at hurculos the j pte . . . . . iij li
¶ 7 of Jenewary 1595 Rd at a Knack to Know & onest man xx s
¶ 8 of Jenewary 1595 Rd at new worldes tragedie . . . xviij^{s}
¶ 9 of Jeneuerye[1] 1595 Rd at the Jew of malta . . . . . lvj s
¶ 10 of Jenewary 1595 Rd at a toye to please chaste ladeys xviij s
¶ 12 of Jenewary 1595 ——Rd at chynon of Ingland . . . . l s
¶ 13 of Jenewary 1595 Rd at the sege of london . . . . xv^{s}
¶ 14 of Jenew*ary* 1595 Rd at cracke me this nvtte . . . xxiij s
¶ 15 of Jenew*ary* 1595 Rd at the wonder of A wom*o*n . xxvij s
¶ 16 of Jenewary 1595 ne—Rd at pethageros . . . . iij li j s
Rd at wissman of weschester . . xviij s

[14v] **20092**

¶ *18* of Jenew*ary* 1595 Rd at the Jewe of malta . . . . . xxxviij s
¶ *19* of Jene*wary* 1595 Rd at harye th*e* v . . . . xx s
¶ 20 of Jenewary 1595 Rd at barnardo & phiameta . . . xj s
¶ 21 of Jenewary 1595 Rd at chinon of Ingland . . . . xxxiij s
¶ 22 of Jenewary 1595 ne—Rd at the 2 wecke . . . . iij li
¶ 23 of Jenewary 1595 Rd at pethagorus . . . . xxxvj s
¶ 25 of Jenewary 1595 ——Rd at the new worldes tragedy . xiiij s
¶ 26 of Jenew*ary* 1595 Rd at the 2 weake . . . . . . xxiiij s
¶ 27 of Jenewary 1595 Rd at chinon . . . . xxj s
¶ 28 of Jenew*ary* 1595 Rd at pethagoros . . . . xxx^{s}
¶ 29 of Jenewary 1595 *R*d at the Jew of malta . . . . . xxv s
¶ 30 of Jenew*ary* 1595 m^{r} pd—Rd at the wonder of a womon xj s
¶ 2 of febereary 1595 ——Rd at the Jew of malta . . . . . lvij s
¶ 3 of febreary 1595 Rd at the j p of forte*w*natus . . . iij li
¶ 4 of febreary 1595 Rd at wissman of weschester . . xij s
¶ 5 of febreary 1595 Rd at longshancke . . . . xiiij s
¶ 6 of febreary 1595 Rd at hary the 5 . . . . xviij s
¶ 7 of febreary 1595 Rd at crackme this nvtt . . . . . xix s
¶ 9 of febreary 1595 ——Rd at pethagores . . . . xx^{s}
¶ 10 of febreary 1595 Rd at fortunatus . . . . xxxx^{s}
¶ 11 of febreary 1595 Rd at chinon of Ingland . . . . xx^{s}
¶ 12 of febreary 1595 ne—Rd at the blind beger of elexandrea iij^{li}
¶ 13 of febreary 1595 Rd at fosstes . . . . xxv^{s}
¶ 15 of febreary 1595 ——Rd at pethagores . . . . xxxv^{s}
¶ 16 of febre*ary* 1595 Rd at the blinde beager . . . . . iij^{li} vj^{s}
¶ 17 of *feb*reary 1595 Rd at the Jew of malta . . . . . xx s
¶ 18 of feb*r*eary 1595 Rd at olempeo . . . . x s

(1) *Jeneuerye*] *sic*; *Jenewary* Greg.

¶ 19 of febreary 1595 Rd at the blind beager . . . . . liijs
¶ 20 of febreary 1595 Rd at ffortunatus. . . . . xxijs
¶ 22 of febreary 1595 Shroue monday(1)—Rd at the blind beager xxxvjs
¶ 23 of febreary 1595 shroft tewsday(2) Rd at pethagores . . xxxiiijs
¶ 24 of febre*aye* 1595 Rd at chinone . . . . lvjs
¶ 25 of febreary 1595 Rd at wecke . . . . xxs
¶ 26 of febre*ary* 1595 Rd at the blind beager . . . . . iijli
¶ 27 of febreary 1595 Rd at longshancke . . . . xxxs
the master of th*e* Revelles payd vntell this time al wch I owe hime

[2½ *inches blank*]

[15]

[Sowld mr Richard Jones player A manes gowne of Pechecoler In grayne the 2 of septmbȝ 1594 to be payd by fyveshellenges a wecke Imedyatly folowinge & beginynge as ffowloweth]

[Rd of mr Jones the 7 of septmbȝ . . 1594(3). . . . . . vs
Rd of mr Jones the 13 of septmbȝ . . . . vs
Rd of mr Jones the 20 of septmbȝ 1594. . . . . vs
Rd of mr Jones the 4 of octobȝ 1594 . . . . vs
Rd of mr Jones th*e* 11 of octobȝ 1594 . . . . vs
Rd of mr Jones the 18 of octobȝ 1594 . . . . vs
Rd of mr Jones the 24 of octobȝ 1594 . . . . vs
Rd of mr Jones the 2 of novembȝ 1594. . . . . vs
Rd of mr Jonnes the 9 of novmbȝ 1594 . . . . vs
Rd of mr Jonnes the 16 of novmbȝ 1594 . . . . vs
Rd of mr Jones the 23 of novmbȝ 1594. . . . . vs
Rd of mr Jonnes In fulle payment the 30 of novmbȝ 1594 . vs]

[1½ *inches blank*]

Sowld vnto william Sley the 11 of octobȝ 1594 A Jewell of gowld seat wth A whitte safer [to b*e*]for(4). . . viijs to be payd after xijd A weacke as ffolloweth

Rd of wm sley the 18 of octobȝ 1594 . . . . vjd
Rd of wm sley th*e* 24 of octobȝ 1594 . . . . vjd
Rd of wm sleye th*e* 2 of novembȝ 1594 . . . . vjd

(1) *Shroue monday*] interlined. (2) *shroft tewsday*] interlined.
(3) 1594] interlined. (4) [*to be*]*for*] *for* altered from *to*; *be* deleted.

Rd of wm sleye the 9 of novmbȝ 1594	vj d
Rd of wm sley the 16 of novmbȝ 1594	vj d
Rd of wm sley the 30 of n*o*vmbȝ 1594	xij d
Rd of wm sley the 14 of desembȝ 1594	xij d
Rd of wm sley th*e* 17 of Jenewar*y* 1594	ij s

[1½ *inches blank*]

[15 v] **20091**

1596

¶ 12 of ap[r]elle ester mvnday(1)	Rd at barnardo & fiameta. .	xxx s
¶ 13 of ap[r]ell 1596	Rd at toye to please chaste ladeys .	xxxix s
¶ 14 of ap[r]ell 1596	Rd at fortunatus	xviij s
¶ 15 of ap[r]ell 1596	Rd at the blynd beger	xxxx s
¶ 16 of ap[r]ell 1596	Rd at the Knacke	xj s
¶ 17 of ap[r]ell 1596	Rd at th*e* wisman of weschester . .	xxx s
¶ 1[8]9(2) *of ap*[r]ell 1596——	Rd at Doctor fostes	xij s
¶ 20 of ap[r]ell 1596(3)	Rd at the Jewe.	xx[s]
¶ 21 of ap[r]ell 1596(3)	Rd at longshancke	xiiij s
¶ 22 of ap[r]ell 1596(3)	Rd at pethagorus.	xviij s
	Rd at chin*o*n	xx s
¶ 23 of ap[r]ell 1596(3)	Rd at hary the v	xv[s]
¶ 24 of ap[r]ell 1596(3)		
¶ 26 of ap[r]ell 1596 m[r] pd—	Rd at the blind beger	xxxx s
¶ 27 of ap[r]ell 1596	Rd at new worldes tragedy	xxix s
¶ 28 of ap[r]ell 1596	Rd at longshancke	xx s
¶ 29 of ap[r]ell 1596 ne—	Rd at Julian the apostata	xxxxvij s
¶ 30 of ap[r]ell 1596	Rd at wisman	x s
maye Daye 1596	Rd at wonder of a womon	xxij s
¶ 2 of maye 1596 ——	Rd at chinon	xx s
¶ 3 of maye 1596	Rd at the blinde beger	xxxv[s]
¶ 4 of maye 1596	Rd at pethagorus.	xx s
¶ 5 of maye 1596	Rd at Docter ffostes	xx s
¶ 6 of maye 1596 ne—	Rd at tambercame	xxxxvij s
¶ 7 of maye 1596	Rd at cracke me this nvtte	xviij s
¶ [9]10(4) of maye 159[5]6(5) m[r] pd—	Rd at Julian apostata. .	xxvj s
¶ 11 of maye 159[5]6(5)	Rd at fortunatus	xviij s
¶ 12 of maye 159[5]6(5)	Rd at tambercame	xxxxv s

(1) *mvnday*] interlined. (2) *1*[*8*]*9*] alteration.

(3) The dates and entries of plays were written in separately, and are not aligned; there is no entry against *24 of ap*[r]*ell*. Greg regularises them.

(4) [*9*]*10*] alteration. (5) *159*[*5*]*6*] *6* altered from *5*.

¶ 13 of maye 159[5]6(1) Rd at blind beger . . . . xxxx s
¶ 14 of maye 1596 Rd at the Jew of malta . . . . . . xxiiij s
¶ 16 of maye 1596 ——Rd at chynone . . . . xxxiij s
¶ 17 of maye 1596 Rd at tambercame . . . . xxxxvj s
¶ 18 of maye 1596 Rd at beger . . . . xxxxix s
¶ 19 of maye 1596 ne—Rd at tragedie of ffocasse . . . . . xxxxv^s
¶ 20 of maye 1596 Rd at Julyan apostata . . . . xiiij s
¶ 22 of maye 1596 m^r pd—Rd at pethagoros . . . . xxvij s
¶ 23 of maye 1596 Rd at tragedie of ffocasse . . . . . xxxix s
¶ 24 of maye 1596 Rd at ffortunatus . . . . xiiij s
¶ 25 of maye 1596 Rd at tambercame . . . . xx s
¶ 26 of maye 1596 Rd at hary the v . . . . xxiij s
¶ 27 of maye 1596 Rd at chinone . . . . ix s

[1 *inch blank*]

[16]

Sowld vnto Jeames donstall player the 27 of aguste 1595 a manes gowne of purpell coller cloth faced wth conney & layd on the sleues wth buttenes for xxxxiij s iiij d to be payd xx^s in hand & xxiij^s iiij d at mychellmase next cominge after the datte a boue written I saye for . . . . } xxxxiij s iiij d

[1 *inch blank*]

Rd in pte of payment the same daye beinge the 27 of aguste 1595 of Jemes danstall the some of } xs

Rd in pte of payment the 28 of aguste 1595 In mony of Jemes donstall the some of . . . . } xs

Reste to paye . . 23^s . . iiij d

[1½ *inches blank*]

ssome is xvj s to paye

Sowld vnto steuen magett the 20 of Jeneway 1595 A dublet of fuschen playne & a payer of venesyones of brade cloth wth ij laces of belement for xvj s to be payd by xij^d a wecke begenynge the 23 of Jeneway 1595 beinge saterdaye & so forth Receued as foloweth

(1) *159*[*5*]*6*] *6* altered from *5*.

[Rd the 23 of Jeneway 1595 . . . . xij d
Rd the 30 of Jeneway 1595 . . . . xij d
Rd the 7 of febreary 1595 . . . . xij d
Rd the 13 of febreary 1595 . . . . xij d
Rd the 20 of febreary 1595 . . . . xij d
Rd the 27 of febreary 1595 . . . . xij d
Rd of maye daye 1596 . . . . iiij s
Rd the 6 of maye 1596 . . . . iiij[s]
Rd in full payment the 3[(1)] of maye 1596 . . . . ij s]

[1 *inch blank*]

[16v] **20090**

A	T	G	C	L	V	Li	SCO	SA	CAP
.1.2	345	678	9.10	11.12.13	14.15.	16.17	18.19.20	21.22	23.24

A q	P
25.26.27	28.29

		take th*e* name of Chilld m or wom & th*e* name of th*e*
.m	A thowsan	mother her o*w*ne naturall name & the chylldes name
.C	A hundred	& then youe moste take owt all the m & c & l & x &
.d	v hundred	& d & v & n & J [the take] & owt of & m & owt of
.l	for fifte	& l & a n & J & JJ owt of 100 owt of 40 $\overset{4}{\text{owt}}$ of 30 owt
.x	for tenne	(2 2 1 2 [2]4 4 6)
.v	for five	of 20 owt of 500 owt o[(2)] 800 owt of 700 owt of 400 owt of 200 owt of
n	for two	(8 8 8 4 4 8)
.J	for one	160 owt of 140 owt of 80 owt of 50
JJ	for two	(4 8 8 2)

To dryue A waye A greaues agew
or A agew cotedian

Take stebıvm [the ⟨. .⟩[(3)]] & beate yt in powder verey
\+ fyne then tacke a stewed pryne and plucke owt th*e*
stone & put in as mvch*e* as will fylle yt & swalowe
yt downe wholle & yt will healpe you by the grace
of god pobtm

ffor A greaues ache or strayne
in th*e* back*e* pb*a*tm

Take th*e* oylle of meaderey*d*atom & wth A chafyngdishe
\+ of coles warem yt & A noynt the back wth yt as hoote

(1) *3*] *sic*; (? error for *13*, Greg).
(2) *o*] *of* Greg. (3) ⟨. .⟩] The deleted letters may be *oz*, for ounce

as thow canest sufer yt & warminge of th*e* *h*ande
chaf yt weall in & by godes grace yt will healpe the

[2½ *inches blank*]

[17]

To make A fowle ffalle downe

+ picture yt in paper & when yt is makinge leat one say[(1)] m.a.n to th*e* eand wth battes blude behold her wth thine eies & pricke the picture in the head wth A pyne & she will falle downe Imedyatley

To know wher a thinge is y[t] Is stolen

+ Take vergine waxe & write vpon yt Jasper + melchiser + [Beth] Balthasar + & put yt vnder his head to wh*o*me th*e* good partayneth & he shall knowe in his sleape wher th*e* thinges is become

[To[(2)] make a fowle fall dead]
[Picture yt in paper & when it is making lett one say]
[m.a.n. to the]

for the falling evill

Take the blood of his little finger that is sicke & wryte these iij verses & hang them abowte his necke
Jasper fert mirrum̄ Thus melchior Balthazar aurum
Hæc quicunq̄ secū[(3)] portat tria nomina Regum
solvitur a morbo domini pietate caduca.

for to know of a stolne thing

Lay this vnder yor head in parchem[t] when yo[u] go to bed
3.f.g.f.y.&[(4)].x.g.y.&[(4)].

si vis refrænare sanguinem alicuius fac[(5)] + in fronte et scribe Beronix et si fæmina Beronixa

against frensye or one that
is bytt wth a dogg

wryte on crust of cheese piga cera dera effema give yt the sicke to eate/ Also give the sicke petty morell blossomes o[r]*f*[(6)] eldars, Rue, and sootherne wood. stampt in wyne˙/.

---

(1) *say*] interlined with caret.
(2) *To...have*] in an unidentified hand; the Latin passages are written in an Italian style.
(3) *secū*] *serū* Greg.
(4) *&....&*] representing a sign like a tilted *8*.
(5) *fac*] *fur* Greg.
(6) *o*[*r*]*f*] *f* altered from *r*.

+ wryte these wordꝭ in virgins parchement wth the blood of a batt vppon tewseday morning betwixt v or vj in the morning or at nighte. halia J K. turbutzi & tye yt abowt thy left arme and aske what ye will have./.(1)

[1 *inch blank*]

[17v] **20089**

A Proved & good medysen for the pluresie when leattinge of blud will not Searue or healpe or & exstreame s*t*yche(2)

Take A sheafe(3) of browne bread cut yt square to the quantetie of your hande then take a sheate of browne paper & wrape yt A bowte the breade then weat the paper & bread in the watter & so donne then put yt in hotte embers & so backe(4) the same this done then spread vpon the bread treackelle & laye to the plasse greved xij owers & vsse yt iij tymes youe mvste laye yt to the bare skenne as hoote as you maye sufer yt

A medyson for deafnes in the eares wch hathe benne proved

Take antes eages & stampe them & strayne them throwght A cloth then take swines greasse ore cnotte grasse stamp*e* the same & tak*e* the Jusse & myxe wth the other straninge of the eges & put in to the eare searten dropes yt will healpe & owld deafnes yf god permet ꝑbatm

A nother for deafnes in the eares proved

ffrie earthwormes wth goosegreasse then strayne the same & drope A lytell therof into the deafe & payned eares warminge the same & so vsse yt hallfe A dossen time*s* at th*e* least A trewe med*e*sen ꝑobāt

To healpe fayer cleare eysse that be blynde

Tak*e* smaledge Read fenel Rewe verven beatten(5) & eg^ramone fyve leaued grasse peampernell eighbrig*h*t Sage selendine of eache ½ A pounde washe the*m* clean & stampe them in a panne

---

(1) *To...have*] in an unidentified hand; the Latin passages are written in an Italian style.

(2) *styche*] *stythe* Greg.

(3) *sheafe of*] *sheafe* Greg.

(4) *backe*] *sic*; (? error for *black*).

(5) *beatten*] *boatten* Greg.

or bassen or morter(1) beinge cleane then take the powder of xv peper cornes finely searced A pinte of white wine & mixe wth the earbes then tak*e* iij sponfull*e* of Ingleshe honey xv sponfulle of the vrine of a boye beinge ane enosent*e* mix*e* all & boylle all to geath^r^ ouer the fier a litell whille then strayne all th*rowg*ht A A clothe & kepe in a glasse weall*e* stoped & wth A feath*er* drop*e* yt in then eysse wch by godes grase y*t* will cure *in* 15 dayes yf they be curable yf the medicen drie put in to yt white wi*n*e

[18]

To cleanes A hurte
wou*n*de & healle yt

\+ Mixe valencia svger wth freashe butter for beinge layd to yt plaster wisse yt consvmethe th*e* superflueshe fleash*e* a euell corvpted mater yt healleth yt allso moste exselent proued

for to healle all woundes

\+ Take grekee(2) piche & Brymstone & whitte osibanū(3) wch is a Kinde of frencomsence of eache a litell quantitie stampe all them then mixe the*m* wth th*e* whitte of eages then washe the wounde afor wth whitte wine once or twise the*n* mack plaster & laye to yt & yt will healle yt

A Salve for all sores

\+ Tacke [tare](4) cere(5) j^li^ Rosien j^li^ of fine sheapes suet tried ij^li^ of turpentine ℥4(6) of bolle armonecke ℥ij(6) leat you^r^ wax & rosen & talowe boylle & be myxed to geather or you put in you^r^ bolle torpentine & laste of all put in you^r^ bolle armoneck*e* & yf you will haue yt sweat of savover(7) put in to yt ℥f(8) camphora & stear yt weall tyll yt be cowld then youse yt as you haue ocasion ꝑobtm̄

A Rewle to Knowe vnder what planet A chillde
Is borne in

of 1000	– 14	of 160	– 24
of 900	– 1	of 140	– 24
of 800	– 17	of 120	– 4
of 700	– 4	of 100	– 13
of 600	– 20	of 80	– 22
of 500	– 6		

(1) *morter*] *anorter* Greg.
(2) *grekee*] so Greg; *k* altered from another letter. Henslowe perhaps first wrote *greate* or *greace.*
(3) *osibanū*] ? error for *olibanū.*
(4) *tare*] *taw* Greg.
(5) *cere*] interlined.
(6) ℥] i.e. an ounce, apothecaries' weight.
(7) *savover*] *sic*; *favover* Greg.
(8) ℥*f*] *sic*; ?=*of,* Greg.

of 400	– 23	of 60	– 2
of 300	– 10	of 50	– 21
of 200	– 26	of 40	– 11
of 180	– 6	of 30	– 1

The naturall leatters Signifinge the numbʒ

n – 2	l – 50
J – 1	C – 100
JJ – 2	D – 500
v – 5	m – 1000
x – x	

[18v] 20087

A watche at cardes to tell a man at what ower he thincketh to Risse proved trewe

tacke xij cardes [w^th] and (1) the Knaue of clubes & laye them Rownd licke A clocke turnynge them all ther faces Downward but the knaue of clubes & laye hime vnder neth licke your watche & laye them this (2)— then aske [k]the (3) ptie at what ower he will Risse & leat him kepe yt to hime seallfe & yf he thincke vij then poynte hime A a card to teall frome & bead hime yf he thincke vij to teall the card viij observinge this Rewle frome your leafte hand a cownt that j for xv always & when you will haue the ptie tell (4) a poynt hime to tell toward your Right hand to what card you will a poynte hime you mvste tell to your seallfe as before toward your leafte hand be ginynge at the j wch is xv & so tell them vpward as thus 15 16 17 18 19 20 21 22 23 24 25 26 & wch of al thes nvmbers that you poynte vpon bead him tell frome that wch he thinketh in his mind tel he haue towld to so maney toward his Right hand & then leat hime turne yt vp & yt shalbe that wch he thincketh a proved

[m^r gelbarte (5) Rocket the 16 of June 1596 afermed me to be his caldeste sone & ayer & gave me that howsse wch the widow dwelles in wch was m^r wistowes wch was geven at the hinde one the banck syde the daye a bowe written & wittneses to yt John whitte & his wiffe
william tvrner & his wiffe]

---

(1) *and*] interlined above.
(2) *this*] *sic.*
(3) *[k] the*] *t* altered from *k.*
(4) *tell*] interlined with caret.
(5) *gelbarte*] interlined with caret.

[19]

Mr malthowse Recknynge what I
haue layd owt as ffoloweth by me phillipe
henslow

Itm m^r harys for mackynge al the writtinges . . . . . . xiij s j d
Itm for drawinge the fyne . . . . xs vj d
Itm for a knowleginge the fyne . . . . x^s 8^d
Itm for gowinge by wat^r & Dryncky nge at westmēn . . ij s
Itm pd m^r Docter stanap for settynge his hand . . . . . xij^d
Itm pd for goinge by water . . . . iij d
Itm pd for drawinge of the fynne . . . . iij s
Itm pd for writtinge in pchmente . . . . iij s
Itm pd for writtinge of covenantes . . . . iij s
Itm pd for the othe(1) & writtinge . . . . ij s
Itm pd for the cvstus bre*ūīū*(2) . . . . vj s
Itm pd for entrynge therof . . . . iiij s
Itm pd for the Quenes sylu*e*^r . . . . ij s
Itm pd for the syghegraphes . . . . xvj s
Itm pd for the pclemation . . . . iiij s
Itm pd for sewinge of the fine forthe . . . . vj s viij d

li s d — li s d
ttottalis –131 – 06 – 11 — Some – 04 –12 – 11

[m̄(3) that I Thoms̄ Chalon^r do owe vnto
m^r phylip*e* Hensley vij^li x^s to be payed
vnto p the Last*e* day of June 1592
By me Thoms̄
Chalon^r
Witnes willi henslye(3)]

[19v] 20086

[Lent w^m atkynsone leather dreaser the 6 of Jeneway
1597 in Readey money fortishillinges to be payd
me agayne the [7]13(4) day of the same moneth*e* in
wittnes of the leandinge of this money is . . . . . } xxxx^s]
EAlleyn pd(5)

---

(1) *for the othe*] *for othe* Greg.
(2) *breūīū*] *bremn^r* Greg; =*brevium*, presumably, but a flourish after the second *u* looks like a raised *r*.
(3) *m̄...henslye*] entered with the book reversed; in Chaloner's hand.
(4) [7]*13*] *3* altered from *7*, and then *1* inserted.
(5) *pd*] added in a different ink.

[lent m^{r} Jonnes player the 8 of Jenewary 1597
vpon iiij Rynges j gemer of gowld j sparke of a dimon
j Ringe wth v sparkes of Rewbes j small sell Rynge
of gowld the some of fortyshyllinges I saye } xxxx^{s}

lent vnto m^{r} Jonnes player the 21 of ap^{r}ell 1598
I*n* Redy money tenne shilling*e* wth(1) williame
Cartwrighte I say lent(2). . . . . } x s]

dd(3) vnto goody watsone the march 1595 severalle
garmentes of my owne to be sowld as foloweth

Itm j payre of venysyones of brodcl*o*th layd wth ij belementes
laces to be sowld for . . . . } xvj s
Itm j womones gowne of frease adowe blacke for . . . . . xx s
Itm j paye*r* of fuschen venesyanes for . . . . iij s
Itm j payer of breches fuschen payned & layd wth gowld lace [v^{s}]
Itm j ceartell of villet bradecloth wth ij belement laces &
bodeyes to yt for. . . . . } [xvij s]
000000000000 8 Itm j fuschen Dublett cvtt vpon grene sylke . . . . xvj^{s}(3)

[20]

Rd(4) by me, of m^{r} Phillipp Hynsley for my M^{r} the master of
the Revells this second daie of Januarye 1594 in full
payement of a bonde of one hundreth powndes the some
of tenn powndes & in full payement of what soever is
due fr*o*m the daie above wrytten vntill Ashwednesdaie
next ensuinge after the date hereof. In wittness
whereof I have put to my hande/

p me Tho. Stonnard.(4)

A(5) notte whot carges my soger peter
hath stode me in this yeare 1596

---

(1) *wth*] *w^{ch}* Greg.

(2) Below this line is a modern forgery which reads:

pd vnto Thomas dickers the 20 of desembr 1597
for adycyons to ffostus twentie shellings and fyve
shellinges more for a prolog to Marloes tembelan
so in all I saye payde twentye fyve shellinges.

(3) *dd...xvj^{s}*] entered with the book reversed.

(4) *Rd...Stonnard.*] in Stonnard's hand. (5) *A...xviij d*] repeated from f. 21.

Itm pd for iiij dayes traynynge . . . . v^s 4 d
Itm fownd hime viij li of powder . . . . vj s 8^d
Itm pd for his lyvery & mony in his pursse . . . . xiij s 8^d
Itm fownd A head pece wch cosste . . . . vij s
Itm fownd a sorde & a dager . . . . vij s
Itm fownd A bealt & a geardell . . . . xij *s*
Itm geuen at his goinge awaye for powder & to dryncke by the waye . . . . v^s
Itm pd for featchenge of my head pece frome graues end . . . . ij s iiij d

laide owt for my soger this laste traynynge the seamste*rs* husband

Itm pd for j dayes traynge & halfe a j^li of powder . . . . . xviij d(1)

[20 v] **20084**

Rd for ij weckes paye w^ch [is]*w*as(2) dew vnto the m^r of the Revelles frome the 12 of ap^rell 1596 vnto the 26 of the same moneth xx s I saye Rd . . . . xx^s

mihell MB Blvenson
marke(3)

Lent vnto Johne tomsone player the 22 of desemb*ʒ* 1598 In Redey money th*e* some of . . . . v^s

[Thomas downton the 25 of Janewary 1599 ded hire as his couenante servante(4) for ij yers to beg[*a*]yne(5) at shrofe tewesday next & he to geue hime viij s a wecke as longe as they playe & after they lye stylle one fortnyght then to geue hime hallfe wages wittnes P H & edward browne & charlles masey]

Lente vnto Roger [L*a*leye] evanes(6) grome of the [chamber] Quenes chamb*ʒ* 1598 as foloweth in Redy money

lent hime the 28 of marche 1598 . . . . viij s
lent hime th*e* 16 of ap^rell 1598 . . . . vj s

---

(1) *A...xviijd*] repeated from f. 21. (2) [*is*]*was*] *w* altered from *is*.
(3) Below the word *marke* is a modern forgery, the name *downton*.
(4) A space is left for the name. (5) *beg*[*a*]*yne*] *y* altered from *a*.
(6) *evanes*] interlined above.

lent hime the 8 of June 1598 . . . . iijs
lent hime the 6 of Jenewary 1598 . . . . vijs
lent hime the 9 of Janewary 1598 . . . . vjs

[21]

[*263*] (1) 8–[4]o (2)

[Lent m^r artur Lagworthe In Redey mony as apereth 1595

5 4
13– 8
16
12
05
[59]60 [4]o (3)

lent him In Redy mony . . . . x^li
lent him mor In mony . . . . xvijs
lent himme mor In mony . . . . iijli
lent hime more In mony . . . . xs
lent hime the 15 of maye 1595 In mony . . . . . xiijs]

54
80
138
16
11
05
———
590 (1)

A notte of what charges my Soger petter hath stode me in this yeare 1596

[Itm pd hime for 4 dayes traynynge . . . . v^s 4d
Itm fownd hime viij^li of powder for viijs
Itm pd for his levery & mony in his pursse . . . . . xiijs viijd
Itm fownd a head pesse wch coste me . . . . viijs
\+ Itm fownd a sorde & a dager . . . . viijs
Itm fownd a bealte & a gerdell . . . . xijd
Itm geuen at his gowinge awaye for powder & to dryncke . . . . } v^s]

A notte of the charges wch my wharffe coste me mendinge as folowethe 1596

---

(1) [*263*]...*590*] marginal figures not recorded by Greg.
(2) [*4*]*o*] alteration. (3) [*59*]*60* [*4*]*o*] alterations.

Itm pd for grene tember	xs
Itm pd for planckes iij hunderd	ls
Itm pd worckmen	xiij s
Itm pd for naylles	v^s iiij d
Itm pd for worcke	ij s viij d

[21 v] **20083**

1596

¶ 31 of maye whittsenmvnday		Rd at pethagores	iij^li
¶ 1 of June 1596		Rd at chinone of Ingland	iij^s
¶ 2 of June 1596		Rd at longshancke	iij^li
¶ 3 of June 1596		Rd at the blinde beager	xxxxj s
¶ 4 of June 1596		Rd at the tragedie of focas	xxxj s
¶ 5 of June 1596		Rd at tambercame	xxviij s
¶ 7 of June 1596	m^r pd—	Rd at cracke me this nvtte	xxviij s
¶ 8 of June 1596		Rd at wisman of weschester . . .	xx s
¶ 9 of June 1596		Rd at the chaste ladye	xviij s
¶ 10 of June 1596		Rd at tambercame	xxviij s
¶ 11 of June 1596	ne—	Rd at 2 pte of tambercame	iij^li
¶ 12 of June 1596		Rd at Docter fostes	xvij^s
¶ 14 of June 1596	——	Rd at sege of london	xxx^s
¶ 15 of June 1596		Rd at pethagores	xxiij^s
¶ 16 of June 1596		Rd at ffocase	xx^s
¶ 17 of June 1596		Rd at hary the v	xxvij s
¶ 19 of June 1596	m^r pd—	Rd at j pte of tambercame	xxxvj s
¶ 20 of June 1596		Rd at 2 pte of tmbercame(1) . . .	xxxv s
¶ 21 of June 1596		Rd at Jew of malta	xiij s
¶ 22 of June 1596		Rd at focas.	l s
¶ 22 of June 1596	ne—	Rd at troye	iij^li ix s
¶ 23 of June 1596		Rd at cracke me this nvtt	xij s
¶ 25 of June 1596	——	Rd at the beager	xix s
¶ 26 of June 1596		Rd at j pte of tambercame	xxx s
¶ 27 of June 1596		Rd at 2 pte of tambercame	xx s
¶ 1 of Ju[ne]ly(2) 1596	ne—	Rd at [peth] paradox.	xxxxv^s
¶ 2 of Julye 1596		Rd at troye	xxiiij^s
¶ 3 of July 1596		Rd at fostes	xiiij^s
¶ 5 of July 1596	m^r pd—	Rd at focasse	xxij^s
¶ 6 of July 1596		Rd at sege of london	xv^s
¶ 7 of July 1596		Rd at wisman of weschester . . .	xvj^s
¶ 8 of July 1596		Rd at 2 p of tambercame	xxiij^s

(1) *tmbercame*] *sic*; *tambercame* Greg. (2) *Ju*[*ne*]*ly*] *ly* altered from *ne*.

¶ 4 of July 1596 Rd at frenshe dacter . . . . xiiij s
¶ 5 of July 1596 Rd at [w]the(1) beager . . . . . . xvij s
¶ 7 of July 1596 ——Rd at troye . . . . xxix s
¶ 8 of July 1596 Rd at j pte of tambercame . . . . xiiij s
¶ 9 of July 1596 Rd at longshancke . . . . xv s
¶ 10 of July 1596 Rd at hary the v . . . . xiiij s
¶ 11 of July 1596 Rd at bellendon . . . . xxxv s
¶ 12 of July 1596 mr pd——Rd at the toye(2) . . . . x s
¶ 1[3]4(3) of July 1596 Rd at pethagores(2) . . . . xxij s
¶ 15 of July 1596 Rd at hary v . . . . xxij s
¶ 16 of July 1596 Rd at troye . . . . xxj s
¶ 17 of July 1596 Rd at focas. . . . . xxix s
¶ 18 of July 1596 ne—Rd at the tyncker of totnes . . . . iij li

[22]

[Reseved(4) the xix of desember 1595 mon(5) in part of mr phellepe henslow the some of fortty shyllyngꝭ I say . . . . xl s/
In part of the bargen for the Tenymtꝭ on the bankꝭ syd]

By me John mavlthowse /(4)

[Reseved(6) ye 21th of January 1596 of philype
henslowe the some of tenn powndꝭ of
lafull money of Inglannd by me hughe wrene
of kunskleer in the county of south tanar, for
the vse and by the apoyntment of John malth[u]ous(7)
wch is in part of payment t[h]o(8) the sayd John malthous
of A more some . . tenn powndꝭ I saye . . . . . x li]

[Rd ye 21th of January 1596 of philype
henslowe the some of twentye powndꝭ of
lafull money of Ingland by me hughe wrene
of kingskleer in the county of south tanar, for } xx li
the vse and by the appyntment of John malthous
wch is in part of payment the sayd John malthous
of A more some [tenn powndꝭ I saye. . . . . xli]]

the marke hwr(9) of hugh wrene(6)

---

(1) [*w*]*the*] *t* altered from *w*.

(2) The dates and titles are badly aligned here, and *12 of July* is written level with, and linked by a line to, *pethagores*.

(3) *1*[*3*]*4*] *4* altered from *3*; Greg thinks *12* in the line above is a mistake for *13*.

(4) *Reseved...mavlthowse*] in Maulthouse's hand.

(5) *mon*] *noon* Greg, which is just possible. The day was a Friday.

(6) *Reseved...wrene*] in an unidentified hand.

(7) *malth*[*u*]*ous*] *o* altered from *u*.

(8) *t*[*h*]*o*] *o* altered from *h*.

(9) *hwr*] *hwe* Greg; the last letter is a mere scrawl.

[Reseved(1) of m^r henslow the second day of febrearey in part of a mor som the som of ffower pound of lawfull Englyshe mony I say . . iiij^li
By me John mavlthowse/(1)]

[lent vnto marter(2) slather the 22 of June 1596 the some of viij li of good & lafulle mony of Ingland to be payd the same daye moneth folowinge or els to forfete for not paying of the same xvj^li where vpon he hath bownd hime selfe by tackynge of a j d vpon & a sumsett wittnes to this edward alleyn & his wiffe]

[22v] 20082

[Sowld vnto m^r Jonnes player the 27 of maye 1596 ij y^rdes & iij quarters of brode clothe for eyghtene shelynges to be payd by iiij s a weacke as foloweth]

[Rd the 5 of June of m^r Jonnes . . . . . . iiij s
Rd the 12 of June of m^r Jonnes . . . . . . iiij s
Rd the 19 of June of m^r Jonnes . . . . . . iiij s
Rd the 23 of June of m^r Jonnes . . . . . . ij s
Rd in fulle payment the *3*(3) of Julye 1596 . . iiij s]

[deliuered vnto the company the 2[3]5(4) of marche beinge good frydaye 1597(5) the some of fyve pownd & fortenshelyngs wch mackes vp the some of thirtie powndes as her vnder writen maye be sene wch they owe vnto me I saye . . . . xxx^li wittnes edward allen]

[lente vnto my lord admerall players at severall tymes in Redey money as foloweth 1596

lent vnto Jeames donstall for to by thinges for the playe of valteger . . . . v^li
lent vnto marten slater to by coper lace & frenge for the playe of valteger the 2[9]*8*(6) of novmbʒ 1596. xxxx s
lent vnto marten slather the 29 of novmbʒ 1596 to by for the play of valteger lace & other thinges . . . . xxv^s

---

(1) *Reseved...mavlthowse*] in Maulthouse's hand.
(2) *marter*] *sic.*
(3) *3*] 7 Greg.
(4) *2*[*3*]*5*] *5* altered from *3*.
(5) *1597*] interlined above.
(6) *2*[*9*]*8*] *8* altered from *9*.

dd vnto steuen the tyerman for to delyver vnto the company for to bey a headtier & a Rebata & other thinges the 3 of desemb3 1596 } iij^{li} x s

——lent vnto my sonne to by the saten dublet wth syluer lace . [xxxx^{s}] iiij^{li} (1)

some – xv^{li} x[s] v^{s} (2) the wholl some of this & the other syd is

22^{li} – 15^{s} – 00^{d}

Lente more the 8 of desemb3 1596 for stewtleyes hosse . . . iij^{li}

lent donston & marten the 11 of desemb3 1596 . . . . xxxx s

li s d

lent marten the 14 of desemb3 1596 . . . . xx s

35–15–00 (3) dd vnto m^{r} porter the 16 of desemb3 1596 . . . . . . [iiij] [v]^{li} v^{li} (4)

li s d

payd vnto the carman (5) for fetcheng you^{r} wagen . . . . . ij s

4[0]4 (6)–06–00 lent vnto m^{r} porter the 7 of marche 1597 . . . . iiij^{li}

lent vnto my sonne for to by sylckes & other thinges for gvido the 14 of marche . . . . iiij^{li} ix s]

[23]

Sowld vnto steven maget the 27 of maye 1596 A clocke of sade grene to be payde by xij d A weacke wch clocke is sowld for . . . . } xviij s

Receued as ffoloweth

[Rd the 5 of June of steuen . . . . xij d

Rd the 12 of June of steuen . . . . xij d

Rd the 20 of June of steuen . . . . xij d

Rd the 26 of June of steuen . . . . ij s

Rd the 12 of July of steuen . . . . xij d

Rd the 22 of septemb3 of steuen . . . . vij s]

[A note of Suche money as I haue lent vnto thes meane whose names folow at seaverall tymes edward alleyn martyne slather Jeames donstall & Jewbey

all this lent sence the 1596 14 of octob3

lent vnto martyne to feache fleacher . . . . vj s

lent vnto theme to feache browne . . . . x s

lent vnto my sonne for thomas honte . . . . vj s 8^{d}

lent vnto them for hawodes bocke . . . . xxx s

---

(1) *iiij^{li}*] interlined above.

(2) *x[s]v^{s}*] *v* altered from *s*.

(3) *35–15–00*] *36–18–00* Greg.

(4) *[iiij] [v]^{li} v^{li}* *v* altered from *iiij*, then deleted and a fresh *v* written.

(5) *carman*] *carmen* Greg.

(6) *4[0]4*] the second *4* altered from *o*.

[1]lent vnto them at a nother tyme . . . . ls
lent vnto marteyn at a nother tyme . . . . xxx s
lent vnto the tayller for the stocke . . . . xxx s
lent them[2] to by a boocke . . . . xxxxx s[3]
lent the company to geue fleatcher /& the hauepromysed[4] me payement who promysed me is marten donston Jewby } xx[s]

Rd in pt of payment the 29 of octob3 1596 . . . . . . xx[s]
Rd in pt of payment of al holanday 1596 . . . . xx s
[Rd in pt of paymente the 13 of desemb3 1596 . . . . . xxxx s[1]]

[Some is vij[li]] [viij[li] xs] ttottalles . . 31[li] [o]15[s(5)] – 00[d]
Some ixli

Rd at the second time of playinge that wilbe shalbe the 4 of Janeway 1597 the some of. . . . . } xxxx s
Rd at Joronymo the 7 of Jane[y]wary[6] 1597 in pte. . . of payment . . . . } vij[li]
Rd at elexsander & ladwicke the 14 of Janewarye the fyrste time yt wasse playde 1597 in pte . . . . } v[li]
Rd at a womon hard to please the 27 of Janewary 97 . . iiij[li]]

[23 v] **20080**

vltimo[7] die maij Anno Regni
dm̄e Nr̄e Regine Tricessimo Nono

Receiued y[e] daie & yeare aboue written by me Robert[h] Johnson to the vse of y[e] M[r] of y[e] Reuellϱ of Phillippe Henslaye the full & whole some of fortie shillingϱ dew ffor this pn̄te Monthe afore saide/. } xl[s]

xxvij[th] of June 15.97

Receiued the daie and yeare aboue written, by me Robert Johnson to the vse of ye M[r] of ye Reuellϱ of Phillipp Henchley the *full* ⟨ ⟩[8] & whole some of fortie shillingϱ of Lawfull English monney dew for y[is] pn̄t monthe aforesaide[7]. . . . . } xl[s]/

---

(1) *lent...xxxxs*] These entries are marked off by rules forming a large bracket in the left margin.
(2) *them*] *vnto them* Greg.
(3) *xxxxxs*] the first *x* added later, and written over the line connecting entry and sum.
(4) *the hauepromysed*] *sic*.
(5) [*o*]*15*] *1* altered from *o*.
(6) *Jane*[*y*]*wary*] *w* altered from *y*.
(7) *vltimo...aforesaide*] in Johnson's hand.
(8) ⟨ ⟩] a blot may conceal a letter.

Receaved[(1)] this xixth of Julij 1597 of m[r]
hēchlay the some of fortie shillingę
and is to the vse of the m[r] of the
revells as appeareth by a quyttās
wch m[r] blewmsone haith in keapinge
I saye Rde the so*me* of . . . . xl s

p me w[m] hatto/[(1)]
octobris[(2)] xij[o]: 1598:/

Receiued y[e] daie & yeare aboue Written . by me.
Robert Johnson . of . m[r] Henchlay the full . &.
whole . some . of . vj[li] . to . the vse of y[e] M[r] of y[e]
Reuellę . for . iij Monethes . endinge the daie a fore . said
after xl[s] . a . monethe[(2)] . . . . vj[li]/

[3½ *inches blank*]

[24]

This agremente & bargen Betwene edward alleyn &
m[r] arthour lengworth as foloweth was made the 5 [of] daye
of July 1596 yt was agreed vpon that m[r] langworth
shold geue vnto edward alleyn for the leasse of the parsonege
of fvrll*e* – iij thowssen powndeę of lafful mony of england
to be payd in xx[th] yeares in maner folowinge by a hundered
& ffiftie powndeę a yeare & to be g[e]ine[(3)] payment at ou[r]
ladey daye next folowinge & so to paye [t]eue[r]y[(4)] halfe yeare the
hallfe of the hundreth & fiftie powndę or w[th] in one moneth after
being xxviijdayes & for the performence of this xx yeares paymen[t]
hath promesed to potte hime in such a suerence as by his
learned cownsell he shall deuise [in wittnes wher] at his
neth cominge to towne after the daye a bowe written i*n*
wittnes wher of to this I haue seate to my hand

Phillippe henslow

[Rd of Bengemenes Johnsones
Sharre as ffoloweth 1597]

Rd the 28 of July 1597 . . . . iij s ix d

Sowld vnto Thomas Towne player
A Blacke clothe clocke layd w[th] sylke lace
for xxvj s viij d to be payd by xij d a weck*e*

---

(1) *Receaved . . . hatto/*] in Hatto's hand.
(2) *octobris . . . monethe*] in Johnson's hand.
(3) *g[e]ine*] *i* altered from *e*.
(4) *[t]eue[r]y*] *e* altered from *t*.

& to be gyne payment the 2 of Jenewary 1597
& so to contenew weckely payment as

lent vnto Thomas towne the 20 of march*e* 1598 Redy money . . . . } xij d

Lent vnto thomas Towne [to b]vpon(1) A skarffe v[s]

[2 *inches blank*]

[24v] **20079**

[sent my horsse to grasse th*e* 9 daye of Ap*r*e*ll*e being tewsdaye(2) 1600 to m[r] Kellocke at redreffee for xx d a wecke////]

bouroud(3) of m[r] henslow . . xx[s]

by me Charles massye(3)

[1¼ *inches blank*]

sent my horsse to grasse one tewesdaye beinge
the 30 of ap[r]ell 1600 to m[r] Kellocke at
Rede*r*effe x d to thomas(4)

Removed my horsse one [s.] whitsone sondaye beinge
the xj of maye 1600 to m[r] wodcoke of Redereffe
to grasse

sent my horsse to grasse one [sondaye] saterday
at nyght beinge the 7 day of June 1600
to m[r] *wod*cokes at Redereffe

sent my horsse to grasse one frydaye beinge
the v daye of septm̄b3 1600 to m[r] wodcoke
at Redreffe

Lent vnto charlles massey the 3 of desemb3 1600 in Redy mony to be payd a gayne at crysmas next the some of . . . . } xs

[2 *inches blank*]

(1) [*to b*]*vpon*] *v* altered from *b*; *to* deleted.
(2) *being tewsdaye*] interlined with caret. (3) *boroud*...*massye*] in Massey's hand.
(4) *xd to thomas*] added in a different ink; *pd* Greg, a possible reading.

[25]

ag[d (1)] that the xxixth daye of september/ 1596/beinge Mihelmas daye the some of one hundred[th] and xxvj[li] was tendered and redye to be payd yn the house of m[r] Phillipe henslowe the day and year aforesayd w[ch] sayd some was to be payd by Edwarde Allene as afore sayd before the settinge of the svnne of the same daye yn the p[r]sentę of thos whose names ar hervnder Wryten vnto Arthure Langworthe gent.[(1)]

In the name of god Amen
begynynge one simone & Jewd*es* daye
my lord admeralles men as ffoloweth
1596

¶ 27 of octob3 1596 Rd at chynon . . . . lij s
¶ 28 of octob3 1596 Rd at doctore foster[(2)] . . . . xxvij s
¶ 29 of *o*ctob3 1596 Rd at the frenshe docter . . . . xv[s]
——[(3)]
¶ 1 of novmb3 1596 Rd at longe meage . . al holanday[(4)] . . xxxxvij s
¶ 2 of novmb3 1596 Rd at chinone of Ingland . . . . xvij s
¶ 3 of novmb3 1596 Rd at th*e* cnacke to knowe . . . xv s
¶ 4 of novmb3 1596 Rd at doctor fostes. . . . . xvij s
¶ 5 of novmb3 1596 Rd at longe meage. . . . . v s
¶ 6 of novmb3 1596 Rd at the beager. . . . . xxx[s]
¶ 8 of novmb3 1596 ——Rd at the toye . . . . xiij s
¶ 9 of novmb3 1596 Rd at the frenshe docter . . . . xiiij s
¶ 10 of novmb3 1596 Rd at chinon . . . . x s
¶ 11 of novmb3 1596 Rd at the vij dayes. . . . . . . xxxv[s]
¶ 12 of novmb3 1596 Rd at the beager. . . . . xvj s
¶ 13 of novmb3 1596 Rd at tambercame . . . . xvij s
¶ 15 of novmb3 1596 ——Rd[(5)] at the vij dayes . . . . . . xij s
Rd

[2¾ *inches blank*]

---

(1) *ag[d]. . .gent.*] in an unidentified hand. *ag[d]*] *m[d]* Greg. (2) *foster*] *sic.*

(3) This rule was apparently inserted between the lines to mark a weekly division, as at the entry of 8 November below.

(4) *al holanday*] interlined.

(5) *1596——Rd*] Greg omitted the connecting line.

In the name of god Amen beginynge th*e*
25 of novmbȝ 1596 as foloweth
the lord admerall play*ers*

¶ 25 of novmbȝ 1596	Rd at long meage.	xj s
¶ 26 of novembȝ 1596	Rd at weake	xvij s
¶ 27 of novmbȝ 1596	Rd at the toye	xj s
¶ 2 of desembȝ 1596	Rd at the beager	xx s
¶ 4 of desembȝ 1596	ne—Rd at valteger	l s
¶ 8 (1) of desembȝ 1596	——Rd at valteger	xxxv^{s}
¶ 10 of desembȝ 1596	Rd at the beager	x s
¶ 11 of desembȝ 1596	ne—Rd at stewtley	xxxx s
¶ 12 of desembȝ 1596	Rd at the vij dayes	ix s
¶ 14 of desembȝ 1596	——Rd at stewtley	xxxx^{s}
¶ 16 of desembȝ 1596	Rd at valteger	xxxv^{s}
¶ 17 of desembȝ 1596	Rd at *d*octerfostes	ix s
¶ 19 of desembȝ 1596	ne—Rd at nabucadonizer	xxx^{s}
¶ 21 of desembȝ 1596	——Rd at valt*e*ger	xxv^{s}
¶ 22 of desembȝ 1596	Rd at nabucadonizer	xxvj s
¶ 23 of desembȝ 1596	Rd at the beager	iij s
¶ 24 of desembȝ 1596	Rd at valteger	xij s
¶ 2[8]7 (2) of desembȝ 1596 *crismas* day (3)	——Rd at nab*u*cadonizer	iij^{li} viij s
¶ 2[9]8 (2) of desembȝ 1596	Rd at stewtley	iij^{li} iiij s
¶ 3[0]9 (2) of desembȝ 1596	Rd at valteger	xxij s
¶ 30 of desembȝ 1596	ne—Rd at that wilbe shalbe	l s
¶ 31 of desembȝ 1596	Rd at vij d*aye*s	vj s
¶ 1 of Jeneway 1596	Rd at valteger	xxxxv^{s}
¶ 3 of Jenewa*r*y 1597	——Rd at that wilbe shalbe	xxxxij s
¶ 4 of Jeneway 1597	Rd at nabucadonizer	xvj s
¶ 5 of Jeneway 1597	Rd at docter fostes	v s
¶ 6 of Jeneway 1597	Rd at that wilbe shalbe	xxxxij s
¶ 7 of Jeneway 1597 [ne] (4)	Rd at *J*oronymo	iij^{li}
¶ [7]8 of Jeneway 1597	Rd at valteger	xij s
¶ 10 of Janeway 1597	——Rd at stewtley	xxviij s
¶ 11 of Janeway 1597	Rd at Jor*on*ymo	xxxx s
¶ 12 of Janeway 1597	Rd at nabycadnazer	xiij s

(1) *8*] or, just possibly, *3*.

(2) *2*[*8*]*7*...*2*[*9*]*8*...*3*[*0*]*9*] *7* altered from *8*, *8* from *9*, *9* from *0*; *3* not corrected.

(3) *crismas day*] not recorded by Malone; *crismas*] interlined.

(4) *ne*] erased at some time. Noted in Greg's Errata but not in his text. Recorded by Malone.

¶ 13 of Janeweary 1597		Rd at that wilbe shalbe	xxij s
¶ 14 of Janeweary 1597	ne—	Rd at elexsander & lodwicke . .	lv[s]
¶ 15 of Janeweary 1597		Rd at the blinde Beager	ix s
¶ 17 of Janeweary 1597	——	Rd at Joronymo	xx s
¶ 18 of Janeweary 1597		Rd at that wilbe shalbe	xv[s]
¶ 19 of Janeweary 1597		Rd at nabucadonyzer	x s
¶ 20 of Janeweary 1597		Rd at stewtley	xj s
¶ 21 of Janeweary 1597		Rd at valteger	xij s
¶ 22 of Janewarye 1597		Rd at Joronymo	xix s

[26]

Janeweary[1] 1597	24	——	Rd at that wilbe shalbe	0	17	00.19 –	07
	25		Rd at the blinde beager	0	19	03 08 –	00
	26		tt at Nabucadonizer	0	09	02 00 –	03
	27	ne—	tt at womane hard to please . .	2	11	06 07 –	08
	28		tt at long mege	0	07	01 30 –	11
	29		tt at womon hard to please . .	02	03	04–14 –	00
	31	——	tt at Joronymo	01	04	01.15 –	06
ffebreary	01		tt at womones hard to pleasse .	01	05	02 11 –	02
1597 Candlemaseday	2		tt at what wilbe shalbe	01	18	01 03 –	00
	3		tt at oserycke	01	09	03.02 –	01
	4		tt at womon hard to pleasse . .	01	08	04–03 –	00
	5		tt at valteger	01	09	05–13 –	09
Shrove mvnday	7	——	tt at oserycke	00	14	07 16 –	00
Shrove tewesday	8		tt at womon hard to please . .	01	09	01 02 –	01
	9		tt at Joronymo	00	17	04 15 –	02
	10		tt at stewtley	00	18	01.01 –	00
	11	ne—	tt at elexsander & lodwecke . .	03	05	00 17 –	00
	12		tt at elesxander & lodwicke . .	01	14	09 13 –	00[1]
[2]begynyng in leant marche 1597	3		tt at what wilbe shalbe	00	09	00 16 –	00
	5		tt at elexsander & lodwicke . .	01	15	00 13 –	00
	7	——	tt at A womon hard to pleasse .	01	05	06.02 –	01
	8		tt at JoRonymo	01	01	00.03 –	04
[not pd]	[10]9[3]		tt at lodwicke	01	16	07.04 –	00

(1) *Janeweary...oo*] The varying shades of ink in these entries led Greg to argue that they were written in this order: (*a*) the entries of 24 and 25 January, with two columns of figures; (*b*) the entries from 26 January to 5 February, with two columns of figures and the first figure of the third; (*c*) the entries from 7 February to 12 February, when the last five figures were added to the previous entries.

(2) There is a rule across the page between the entries of 12 February and 3 March.

(3) [*10*]9] alteration.

	12	tt at valteger	00	18	*09*	01	04
pd	14	——tt at the beager	00	18	03	00	00
	15	tt at stewtley	01	05	00	00	00
	19	—ne—tt at gvido	02	00	00	*03* (1)	01
	20	tt at elexsander & lodwicke (2) .	00	17	00	04	02
	21	tt at nabucadnazer	00	05	00	00	03
	22	tt at gvido	01	04	00	03	00
Easter mvnday	28	——tt at a womon hard to pleasse .	01	11	00	00	*00*
tewsday	29	tt at elexsander & lodwicke . .	02	01	00	04	03
wensday	30	tt at gvido	02	17	00	00	00
m^r pd	31	tt at belendon	01	15	00	04	00
Aprelle 1597	1	tt at blinde beger	00	05	03	00	*00*
	2	tt at valteger	00	04	01	01	00
	4	——tt at gvido	01	08	00	04	03
	5	tt at elexsander & lodwicke . .	01	02	00	03	05
	6	tt at what wilbe & shalbe . . .	00	07	03	00	*08*
	7	ne—tt at v playes in one	02	01	00	18	01
	8	tt at womon hard to pleasse . .	00	05	03	00	00

[26 v] **20076**

Ap^r ell 1597	11	—11—tt at belendon.	01	00	00	14	00
	12	tt at elexsander & lodwicke . .	00	14	03	00	01
	13	tt at times triumpe & fortus .	01	05	01	00	03
	14	tt at stewtley	00	17	00	12	00
	15	tt at v playes in one	01	08	02	00	00
	16	tt at womon hard to please . .	00	05	03	00	00
	18	—ne—tt at a frenshe comodey . . .	02	00	01	01	03
	19	tt at belendon.	00	09	02	00	00
	20	tt at v playes in one	00	19	00	07	*01*
	21	tt at Jeronymo	00	17	00	03	04
	22	tt at frenshe comodey	01	02	00	17	01
	23	tt at gvido	00	16	01	11	00
	25	——tt at v playes in one	01	13	01	00	00
	26	tt at frenshe comodey	01	02	00	17 (3)	*00*
	27	Rd at elexsander & lodwick .	01	[1]02 (4)	00	00	00
	28	m^r pd Rd at belendon	o[o]1 (5)	00	00	13	00

(1) *03*] *13* Greg. (2) *lodwicke*] *lodovicke* Greg.
(3) *17*] *11* Greg; a doubtful reading.
(4) [*1*]*02*] *o* altered from *1* (so Greg), or *1* altered from *o*.
(5) *o*[*o*]*1*] *1* altered from *o*.

	29	ne—tt at vterpendragon	02	14	01	– 01 – 03
	30	tt at what wilbe shalbe	00	14	00	– 17 – 08
Maye 1597	2	——tt at frenshe comodey	01	*00*	00	– 09 – 03
	[4]3	tt at vterpendagon.	01	05	00	– 01 – 00
	4	tt at Jorenymo	00	11	03	– 14 – 00
	5	tt at frenshe comodey	01	07	*01*	– 00 – 00
	6	tt at v playes in one	00	16	00	– 03 – 00
	7	tt at pendragon	00	14	*00*	– 04 – 00
	9	——tt at lodwicke & elexsand . .	00	14	00	– 00 – 00
	10	tt at womon hard to plesse . .	00	17	03	– 10 – 00
	11	ne—tt at the comodey of vmers . .	02	03	00	– 13 – *00*
	12	tt at pendragon	0	[0]17[(1)]	00	– 00 – 00
	14	tt at v playes in one	00	07	00	– 00 – 00
whittsone mvnday. . }	16	——tt at pendragon	02	19	00	– 14 – 00
T	17	tt at elexsander & lodwicke . .	03	00	00	– 03 – 04
W	18	tt at stewtley	01	12	01	– 17 – 00
	19	tt at the comody of vmers . .	02	15	00	– 00 – 00
	20	tt at bellendon	00	10	00	– 00 – 00
	21	tt at frenshe comodey	00	14	00	– 13 – 06
	23	——tt at v playes in one	01	00	03[(2)]	– 00 – 01
moste[(3)]	24	tt at comody of vmers	02	18	00	– 03 – 02
	25	tt at Joronymo	00	19	00	– 14 – 06
	26	ne—tt at harey the firste life & deth	02	10	01	– 03 – 09
	27	tt at womon hard to pleasse .	00	05	00	– 00 – 00
	28	m^r^ pd tt at elexsander & lodwicke . .	00	*13*	01	– 10 – 00

[27]

	30 3[1]0[(4)]	tt harey the fyrste life & dethe.	00	19	06	– 00 – 00
	31 31	tt at the vmers	03	04	01	– 03 – 00
June 1597	1	tt at frenshe comodey	00	13	00	– 04 – 06
	2	tt at pendragon	00	*16*	00	– 04 – 06
	3	ne tt at frederycke & basellia . .	02	02	01	– 13 – 04
	4	tt at the comodey of vmers . .	03	06	02	– 14 – 06
	6	——tt at what wilbe shalbe	00	10	00	– 16 – 00
	7	tt at the comodey of vmers . .	0[4]3[(5)]	[0]10[(5)]	00	– 00 – 00
	8	tt at harey the firste liffe & death	00	12	06	– 00 – 00
	9	tt at fredericke & baselia . . .	01	00	00	– 00 – 00

(1) [*0*]*17*] *1* altered from *0*.
(2) *03*] so Greg; just possibly *07*.
(3) *moste*] written slantingly in the margin.
(4) *3*[*1*]*0*] *0* altered from *1*.
(5) *0*[*4*]*3*...[*0*]*10*] *3* altered from *4*; *1* from *0*.

	10		tt v playes in one	00	11	03 – 01 – 00
	11		tt at the vmers	02	18	00 – 00 – 00
	o					
	13	——	tt at pendragon	01	00	00 – 00 – 00
	14		tt at harey the fyrste life & death	00	14	00 – 00 – 00
	15		tt at bellendon	00	13	00 – 00 – 00
	16		tt at frenshe comodey	00	07	00 – 13 – 06
	17		tt at comodey of vmers . . .	02	10	01 – 04 – 01
	18		tt at fredericke & basilia . . .	00	11	00 – 14 – 06
	o					
	20	——	tt at Joronemo	00	14	00 – 00 – 00
midsomer daye	21		tt at the comodey of vmers . .	03	00	00 – 00 – 00
	22		tt at henges.	00	06	00 – 11 – 06
	23		tt at frenshe com*o*dey	00	08	00 – 00 – 00
	24		tt at harey the f*irs*te	00	14	00 – 00 – 00
	25		tt at bellendon	00	07	00 – 00 – 00
	o m^r^ pd					
	27	——	tt at stewtley	00	14	00 – 01 – 06
	28		tt at v playes in one	01	00	00 – 13 – 11
S petters daye	29		tt at elexsander & lodwick . .	01	02	00 – 14 – 00
	30	ne	tt at liffe & death of marte*n* swarte	02	08	01 – 11 – 06
July 1597	1		tt at harey the firste	00	06	01 – 12 – 11
	2		tt at frenshe comodey	00	04	02 – 00 – 13
	o					
	4	——	tt at fredericke & baselia . . .	01	00	01 – 14 – 06
	5		tt at what wilbe *s*halbe	00	10	02 – 00 – 00
	6		tt at life & deth of marten swarte	02	10	01 – 13 – 09
	7		tt at Comodey of vmers . . .	01	18	02 – 17 – 01
	8		tt at the wismane[1] of weschester	01	00	01 – 00 – 03
	9		tt at life & death of marten swarte	01	13	02 – 13 – *01*

[27v] **20075**

July 1597	12		tt at wismane of weschest*er* .	00	18	00 – 01 – 0*0*
	13		tt at comodey of vmers . .	01	10	01 – 11 – 01
	14		tt at the wiche of Islyngto*n* .	01	07	02 – 00 – 0*0*
	15		tt at elexsander & lodwicke .	00	08	00 – 13 – 00
	16		tt at frenshe comodey . . .	00	09	00 – 14 – 00
	⊗ m^r^ pd					

(1) *at the wismane*] *at wismane* Greg.

marten slather went	18	——tt at wisman	01	10	00 – *0*0 – 00
for the company of	19	tt at Jeronemo	01	00	01 – 13 – 01
my lord admeralles					
men the 18 of July	20				
1597	27	tt at v playes in one	00	14	03 – 14 – 00
	28	tt at the wich*e* of Iselyngton	01	08	00 – 13 – 00
octob3 1597[1]					
In the name					
of god a men					
the xj of octobe[4]	11	tt at J*o*roneymo	⟨.⟩2[2]	⟨..⟩[3]	01 – 13 – 00
be gane my lord		tt at the com*o*dey of vmers .	⟨.⟩2[3]	00	00 – 19 – 0
admerals & my		tt at docter fostes	o.[5]		
lord of penb*ro*ckes		tt at			
men to playe at		tt at			
my howsse 1597		tt at			
	19[6]	tt at			
		tt at ha*rdicute*[7]	00	16	00 – 00 – 1–
octob3	31	ne—tt at fryer spendelton . . .	02	00	01 – 014– *00*
novemb3 1597	2	tt at burbon	00	16	30 – 12 – 00
	3	tt at knewtus	00	10–	00 – 14 – *00*
	4	tt at vmers	0*0*	16	03 – 00 – 14
the mr payde the 26 of novmb3 1597 for iiij *w*eckes the some of xxxx s	5	tt at fryer spendelton . . .	00	14	01 – 14 – *00*[8]

[3 *inches blank*]

[28]

Lent vnto Harey daves the 20 of aprell 1598 In Redy mony the some of . . . . } vj s

[1 *inch blank*]

Leant vnto arthure langworthe the 23 of maye 1598 In Redy money fortishillinges I saye lent by my wiffe . . . . } xxxxs

(1) There is a rule across the page below *octob3 1597*.
(2) ⟨.⟩2] the first figure is illegible. (3) ⟨..⟩...⟨.⟩2] figures smudged and illegible.
(4) *octobe*] *sic*. (5) *o*.] a second figure was begun, but not completed.
(6) *19*] linked by a slanting line to *tt at hardicute*. (7) *hardicute*] *hardwute* Greg.
(8) *14 – 00*] *14 – 0* Greg; the last figures are doubtful.

Leant vnto m^r^ arthure Langworth the 27 of maye 1598 In Readey money twentishillinges I saye Leant the some of . . . . xx^s^

[2 *inches blank*]

Lent vpon a Raper & hangers the 1[2]4(1) of desembȝ 1598 in Redey money to be payd wth in one moneth the some of . . . . viij^s^

lent vpon iij payer of worsted stockens the [*11*]25(2) of desembȝ 1598 to be payed wth in one moneth next the some of . . . . xs

[3¼ *inches blank*]

[28v] 20074

[Lent vnto my felow m^r^ vallantyne Haris one of the gromes of her ma^tis^ chamber the 8 of aguste 1598 in Redey money the some of three powndes to be payd me agayne at his Retorne owt of the contrey I say lent. . . . . iij^li^
wittnes hareys brother in lawe]

[1 *inch blank*]

Lent vnto phillippe Hearen the 4 of Jeneway 1599 in Redy mony the some *of*(3) [of teneshellenge] I say . . . . x^s^x(4)
Phillip Herne(5)

pd–xs [1 *inch blank*]

[Lent vnto Thomas towne the 3 of ma^rch^ 1600
pd vpon a [gowld](6) Ringe wth a grene stone in it the some of . . . . xxs]

---

(1) *1[2]4*] *1[3]4* Greg; *4* altered from *2*. (2) [*11*] *25*] alteration.
(3) *of*] interlined with caret. (4) *x^s^x*] Henslowe wrote *x^s^*, then added another *x*.
(5) Herne's signature autograph. (6) *gowld*] deletion not recorded by Greg.

Lent vnto Thomas towne by my wiffe the 13 of marche 1601 vpon a payer of sylcke stockens tenneshellens wch stockens he fetched agayne & payd vs not so oweth vs stylle. . . . . } x^s^

[2 *inches blank*]

[29]

[1599.(1)

Receiued of m^r^ Henseslowe in earnest of the tragedie of merie the some of xx^s^. . the 27th. of noueb.

. . . . xx^s^

W̄ Haughton·(1) J D.(2)

stete(3) Receiue*d*(4) of m^r^ Henselow in earnest of the orphanes T⟨. . . .⟩d⟨.⟩(5) the somme of x·^s^ the 27th of noūeber./(4)

[¾ *inch cut out*]

Rec*^d^*(6) of m^r^ Hinchloe more in ernest of The Tragedy of Thomas Merrye 20^s^

Joh· Day·

W̄ Haughton

Rec*^d^* more of m^r^ Hinchloe vpō the *same*(7) book*e* 10^s^

By John Day·(6)]

lent vnto harey chettell the 27 of novmbʒ 1599 in earneste of A Boock*e* called the orphenes tragedie th*e* some of xs as maye A peare a bowe by his hand crossed some of } xs

[Lent vnto w^m^ harton the 2 of febreary 1599 th*e* some of. . . . . } vs]

[Lent vnto m^r^ Jonnes th*e* 4 of aguste 1601 . . . . . . in Redy mony th*e* some of twenty shelleng*e* wch he leant vnto Richard weabe . . . . } xx^s^]

---

(1) *1599*. . .*Haughton*.] in Haughton's hand.

(2) *J D*.] in Day's hand.

(3) In Henslowe's hand.

(4) *Receiued*. . .*noūeber*./] in Chettle's hand.

(5) *T*⟨. . . .⟩*d*⟨.⟩] the missing letters are cut away, and only the tops of *T* and *d* remain.

(6) *Rec^d^*. . .*Day*·] in Day's hand, except for Haughton's autograph signature.

(7) *same*] a mere scrawl.

Receiued(1) in pt of paiment of [⟨..⟩i](2) damon and Pytheas this 16 of ffebruary 1599. . . . . } xx^s.

By me henry chettle./(1)

[1¼ *inch blank*]

[¾ *inch cut out*](3)

[6¾ *inches blank*]

[30]

[3¾ *inches cut out*]

Lent(4) harey porter the 11 of ap^r ell 1599 the some of . . . . . ijs vjd
pd [Lent hary porter the 16 of ap^r ell 1599 the some of . . . . . . xijd]
Lent harey porter th*e* 5 of may 1599 th*e* some of . . . . ijs vjd
Lent harey porter th*e* 15 of may*e* 1599 the some of . . . . . . ijs vjd

Henry(5) Porter(4)

Be it knowne vnto all men that I henry
Porter do owe vnto phillip Henchlowe
the some of xs of lawfull money of England
wch I did borrowe of hym the 26 of
maye a° dom 1599

Henry(5) Porter

[2¼ *inches cut out*]

---

(1) *Receiued...chettle./*] in Chettle's hand.
(2) ⟨..⟩*i*] *Gri* Greg; the first two letters are not clear.
(3) Below the cut-out is a modern forgery which reads:

> *Lent the 14 may 1597 to Jubie vppon a notte*
> *from Nashe twentie shellinges more for the Iylle*
> *of dogges wch he is wrytinge for the company.*

Cf. the parallel forgery on f. 33.
(4) *Lent...Porter*] in Porter's hand.
(5) *Henry*] *Henr* Greg; the tail of *y* continues into *P*.

[30v]

[3¾ *inches cut out*]

[Receued[1] of m^r^ phillipp Hinchlow the som of six shilling I say receud 6^s^ for my selfe . . . . } vj^s^]
Bme Thomas Downton[1]

pd [Lent vnto John daye the 4 of Jeneway 1599 in Redy *mony* the some of . . . } v^s^
wittnes edward alleyn

Receiued[2] by me william Haughton for the vse of Thomas dickers on the 30th. of Januarie the some of . . . . 20^s^ } 20^s.^]
In parte of payement for the booke of truths supplycation to candle light[2]

[2¼ *inches cut out*]

[31]

I[3] receued forty shillinge of m^r^ Phillip Hinslowe in part of vj^li^ for the playe of Willm̄ longsword to be deliu^r^d p^r^sen*t* wth 2 or three dayes the xxj th of January / 1598 / } xxxx^s^
Mi*h* Drayton[3]

[the 1 of novmbȝ 1599
W̄.[4] Haughton receiued of m^r^.
Hunselowe in parte of payement. of the the tragedie of John Co*x* the *some* of . . . . [iij] 20^s^[4]
Willyam[5] Haughtonn receyued of m^r^ Hinchloe in part of payment of the Tragedy of Cox of Collunptō the som of . . . . 20^s.^[5]
pd & quite.[6] John Daye[7]]

---

(1) *Receued. . . Downton*] in Downton's hand.
(2) *Receiued. . . light*] in Haughton's hand; this entry is enclosed in rules.
(3) *I. . . Drayton*] in Drayton's hand.
(4) *W̄. . . 20^s^*] in Haughton's hand.
(5) *Willyam. . . 20^s^*] in Day's hand.
(6) *pd & quite*] in Henslowe's hand.
(7) Autograph signature; as Greg notes, it differs from that on f. 29.

Receiued(1) in earnest of patient Grissell by vs Tho: dekker, Hen: Chettle and willm Hawton the sume of 3.li.of good & lawfull money, by a note sent from m[r] Robt Shaa: the 19th of december.1599: . . . . 3[li]

By me henry chettle.(1)
W̄ Haughton(2)
Thomas Dekker.(2)

[2¾ *inches cut out*]

[31v]

Lent vnto John pallmer grome of the Quenes Chamber the 5 of febreary 1598 the some of twentishillinges in Redy money & wittnes to the lendinge of the same — xx[s]

Lent vnto John pallmer the 8 of July 1599 when he playd a shove g[o]rate(3) at the cort Redy mony . . — v[s]

m[r] griffen at the hachette
m[r] drayton
[m[r]]
harey Chettelle

Lent vnto John pallmer grome of the Quenes chamber the 7 of aprell 1599 the some of fortye shellenges I say. — xxxx[s]

wittnes hewe daves
as maye a pere by his Bande

John pallmer oweth me mor the some of . . . . . . w[ch] was my wages w[ch] he tooke vp & spent at his wiffes linge in . . . . — lv[s]

Receaved(4) by vs Richard hathway & willm Rankins in p̱t of payment for the play of Hanniball & Scipio the sūme of forty shillyngę we say receaved the 3 day of Januarye 1600 . . . . .xxxx[s]
By vs Wi: Rankins Ri: Hathwaye.(4)

[2¾ *inches cut out*]

---

(1) *Receiued...chettle.*] in Chettle's hand. (2) Autograph signatures.

(3) *g[o]rate*] *r* altered from *o*; Henslowe forgot to add another *o*.

(4) *Receaved...Hathwaye.*] in Hathaway's hand, except for Rankins's autograph signature.

[32]

pd for bylldinge of my howsse
vpon th*e* bancksyd wch was goodman
deres 1599 wth m^{r} strette carpenter
as followeth 1599

	Lent m^{r} strette th*e* 13 of desembʒ 1599	v^{s}
	Lent m^{r} strette th*e* 14 of desmbʒ 1599.	xx^{s}
	pd vnto m^{r} strete the 22 of desembʒ 1599	viij^{li} xv^{s}
	pd vnto m^{r} *s*trete in hande th*e* some of	x^{li}
	pd vnto [m^{r}] grimes at the apoyntment of strette.	vj s
	pd vnto grymes in earnest of the ij chemnes	x s
	Lent vnto m^{r} streteꝭ man to by naylles	xv^{d}
	Lent vnto m^{r} strete the 9 of Jeneway 1599	xx^{s}
no	pd for A gvter of leade	xxiij^{s}
	Lent vnto grymes at the apoyntment of stret for to bye ij thowsen of lathe naylles some of	ij s iiij d
	Lent vnto m^{r} strette the 18 of Janeway 1599	xx^{s}
	Lent vnto m^{r} streteꝭ man w^{m} Blackeborne the 21 of Janeway to bye Lathes & naylles some of.	x^{s}
	Lent vnto m^{r} strete the 19 of Janeway*e* 1599	iiij^{li}
	pd vnto the plasterer the 24 of Janeway 1599	iij s
	pd vnto the Laberer the 24 of Janeway 1599	iij s
no	pd for a payer of henges	xiiij d
no no	pd for iij payer of hengeꝭ . . . . & a locke & stapell	v^{s}
	pd vnto the laborer.	vj d
	Lent vnto m^{r} stretes man w^{m} Blackborne the j of febreary 1599 to bye lathes naylls & heare s*o*me of	ix s
	Lent vnto good man grimes th*e* *2* of febrea*r*y 1599 to paye for a thowssen of tylles	xvj s
	Layd o*w*t for j bundell of lathes	xj d(1)
	Layd owt for j thowsen of lath naylles	xiiij d

[32 v] **20069**

pd vnto the plasterers	xij s
pd vnto the laberer	vj s
pd vnto the man for lome	ij s

(1) *Layd...xjd*] A short rule in the left margin separates this and the following entries from those above.

	pd vnto the lyman for sande & lyme	iijs vjd
grimes	pd for ij bushells of heare	xviijd
	geuen to the laberer for j bundell of lathes	xijd
	pd for ij d naylles	vjd
	pd for heare	xiiijd
	pd to ij plasterers for [*ij*]4[(1)] dayes work*e*	vjs
	pd for lyme & sande	v^s iiijd
li s d	pd for hallfe a hunder*d* of lyme half lod of sand	iijs vjd
031[(2)] – 11 – 1[1]o	Layd owt for iij hunder*d* of tylles	iiijs vjd

[6½ *inches blank*]

li s d
grimes 3 – 4 – 10

[33]

Rd of w^m Birde at severalle times
as foloweth begininge th*e* 17 of June
1598

Rd the 17 of June 1598 . . . . v^s

[½ *inch blank*]

[2 *inches cut out*][(3)]

[4¾ *inches blank*]

[33v] **20068**

Rd of gabrell spencer at severall tymes
of his share in the gallereyes as foloweth
be gynynge th*e* 6 of ap^r ell 1598

---

(1) [*ij*] *4*] alteration. (2) *031*] 131 Greg; just possibly 091 (? *9* altered from *3*).
(3) Below the cut-out is a modern forgery which reads:

pd this 23 of aguste 1597 to harey porter
to carye to T Nashe nowe at this tyme in the
flete for Wrytinge of the eylle of dogges ten
shellings to be paid agen to me when he canne
I saye ten shillinges . . . . xs.

It is in the same hand as that on f. 29v; both concern Nashe, who does not figure in the *Diary*.

[Rd the 6 of ap^r^ell 1598. . . . dd to dowton(1) . . . . . [v^s^ vj d]]
Rd the 14 of [ap^r^ell] maye(2) 1598 . . . . vij s
Rd the 27 of maye 1598. . . . . iiij s
Rd the 17 of June 1598 . . . . v^s^
Rd the 24 of June 1598 . . . . iiij s

[2 *inches cut out*]

[Lent vnto m^r^ Jon*n*es Robart shawe Thomas dowton
w^m^ Birde the same time they pd m^r^ langleyes his money
for the agrement & feched home the Riche clocke frome pane } iij^li^]
wch the stocke is not to paye but thes meane I saye lent
in Read*e*y money th*e* some of iij^li^ the 4 of octob3 1598 . .
wittnes Jewby
John syng*er*
thomas towne

[Lent vnto antoney Jeaffes the 11 of Ap^r^ell
1599 In Redey money to by divers thinges A } xx^s^]
geanst sente gorges daye the some of . . .
wittnes Beattres(3)

[1 *inch blank*]

[34]

A Juste acownte of all suche money as I dooe
Receue for vmfrey Jeaffes and antoney Jeaffes begenynge
the 29 of ap^r^ell 1598 as foloweth of the companey

Rd th*e* 29 of ap^r^ell 1598. . . . . ij s vj d
Rd th 7 of ap^r^ell 1598. . . . . ij s vj d
Rd the 14 of [ap^r^ell] maye(4) 1598 . . . . ij s vj d
Rd the 20 of maye 1598. . . . . ij s vj d
Rd th*e* 27 of maye 1598. . . . . ij s vj d
Rd the 3 of June 1598 . . . . v^s^
Rd th*e* 10 of June 1598 . . . . ij s vj d
Rd th*e* 17 of June 1598 . . . . ij s vj d

---

(1) *dd to dowton*] interlined. (2) *maye*] interlined above.
(3) Below this line is a modern forgery which reads:

*pd vnto Mr Blunsones the M^r^ of the Revelles
man this 27 of aguste 1597 ten shellinges for
newes of the restraynte beinge recaled by the
lordes of the Queenes counsel . . . . . x^s^.*

It is in a hand similar to that on f. 19v, but in a darker ink.
(4) *maye*] interlined above.

Rd the 24 of June 1598 . . . . [v^li vijs] ijs vjd
Rd the 31 of June[1] 1598 . . . . ijs vjd
Rd the 8 of July 1598 . . . . ijs vjd
Rd the 14 of July 1598 . . . . ijs vjd
Rd the 21 of July 1598 . . . . ijs vjd

[1 *inch blank*]

[Lente vnto vmfrey Jeaffes the 6 of ap^rell 1598
In Redy money xxs

Lent vnto vmfrey Jeaffes the 5 of septmbȝ 1598 to by a payer of sylke stockenes . . } xv^s]

pd & quite [Lent vnto vmfrey Jeffes the 12 of desembȝ 1599 the some of . . . . } x^s]

[1¾ *inches blank*]

[34 v] **20067**

[Lent vnto m^r Richard Jonnes player the 2 of June 1599 to be payd me agayne by xs A wecke the some of fyve pownds to be gene at the daye A bowe written I saye lent Redy mony . . . . } v^li
pd & quite]

[3½ *inches blank*]

Rd of m^r Jonnes player of this v^li a boue written as foloweth 1599

[Rd the 7 of June 1599 . . . . xs
Rd the 14 of June 1599 . . . . xs
Rd the 21 of June 1599 . . . . xs
Rd the 28 of June 1599 . . . . xs
Rd the 6 of Julye 1599 . . . . xs
Rd the 13 of July 1599 . . . . xs
Rd the 20 of Julye 1599 . . . . xs
Rd the 27 of July 1599 . . . . xs
Rd the 5 of aguste 1599 . . . . xs
Rd the 15 of septmbȝ 1599 . . . . xs
pd & quite]

[2 *inches blank*]

---

(1) *31 of June*] *sic.*

[35]

Receued as ffolowethe of the company of my lorde admeralles mean fo͠r[1] the 2 of ap^{r}rell 1598 at diuers tyme as foloweth

	Rd the 2 of Ap^{r}ell 1598	xxvj s
	Rd the 9 of Ap^{r}ell 1598	iij li vij s vj d
	Rd the 14 of Ap^{r}ell 1598	lvij^{s}
	Rd the 22 of Ap^{r}ell 1598	vj li iij s vj d
	Rd the 29 of Ap^{r}ell 1598	lij s vj d
	Rd the 6 of ap^{r}ell 1598	iiij li ij s vj d
	Rd the 14 of [ap^{r}ell] maye 1598	v^{li} ij s [vj d]
	Rd the 20 of maye 1598	iiij^{li} vj s
	Rd the 27 of maye 1598	iij^{li} iiij s vj d
	Rd the 3 of June 1598	lij s vj d
	Rd the 10 of June 1598	v^{li} xvj s vij d
	Rd the 17 of June 1598	iij^{li} xvj s
s	Rd the 24 of June 1598	v^{li} vij s
56[1]– 11 – 10	Rd the 31 of June[3] 1598	v^{li} xviij s iij d
	Rd the 8 of July 1598	lj s vij d

[1 *inch blank*]

Lent vnto thomas towne the 26 of ap^{r}ell 1600
in Redy mony the some of . . . . } x^{s}

[4 *inches blank*]

[35 v] **20066**

[*Blank*]

[36]

[Borrowed[4] of m^{r} phyllip Henslowe the xjth of november 1597 the some of xls. [By me] to be payd on the xth of december next ensuinge By me Robt Shaa[4] **]**

[2 *inches blank*]

---

(1) *fo͠r*] *sic*; =*fro* (Greg), cf. f. 97 (note 4, p. 189).

(2) *56*] A blot seems to conceal a figure after *6*, and *s* tails from the line above.

(3) *31 of June*] *sic*.

(4) *Borrowed...Shaa*] in Shaa's hand.

A Juste acownte of the money wch I
haue Receued of humfreye Jeaffes hallffe
sheare beginynge the 14 of Jenewary 1597
as foloweth

[Rd the 21 of Jenewary 1597 . . . . viij^s^
Rd the 28 of Janewary 1598 . . . . iij s 4^d^
Rd the 4 of febreary 1598 . . . . xj s vij d
Rd the 11 of febrearye 1598 . . . . vj s vij d
Rd the 18 of febreary 1598 . . . . viij s
Rd the 25 of febrearye 1598 . . . . x s
Rd the 4. of marche 1598 . . . . xiij s]

This some was payd backe agayne
vnto the companey of my lord admeralles
players the 8 of marche 1598 & they shared
yt a monste them I saye pd backe a gayne
the some of iij li

[3 *inches blank*]

[36v] **20065**

A Juste a cownte of all Suche monye
as I haue Receued of my lord [of]
admeralles & my lord of penbrocke. men
as foloweth be gynynge the 21 of octob3 1597

Rd the 21 of octob3 1597 . . . . *v*^li^ j s xj d
Rd the 2*8* of octob3 1597 . . . . iij^li^ xj s x d
Rd the [2]30(1) of octob3 1597 . . . . iij li
Rd the 5 of novmb3 1597 . . . . lviij s x d
Rd the 12 of novmb3 1597 . . . . xxxxvij s
Rd the 19 of novmb3 1597 . . . . xxxxviij s viij d
Rd the 26 of novmb3 1597 . . . . xxxxiiij s
Rd the 3 of desemb3 1597 . . . . xxxxiiij s
Rd the 10 of desemb3 1597 . . . . xxvj s
Rd the 17 of desemb3 1597 . . . . xxxxix s
Rd the 30 of desemb3 1597 binge crysmas weacke . vij^li^ xvj s
Rd the [2]7(2) of Janewary 1597 . . . . xxx s
Rd th*e* 14 of Jenewary 1597 . . . . l s
Rd the 21 of Jenewary 1597 . . . . iij^li^ ix s

(1) [*2*]*30*] *3* altered from *2*. (2) [*2*]7] alteration.

Rd the 28 of Janewary 1598 . . . . xxviijs ixd
Rd the 4 of febreary 1598 . . . . v^li
Rd the 11 of febreary 1598 . . . . lvjs 4^d
Rd the 18 of febreary 1598 . . . . iij^li ixs
Rd the 25 of febrearye 1598 . . . . iiij^li xv^s
Rd the 4 of marche 1598 . . . . v^li xj^s iijd

li s d
so 65 – 16 – 07

[1½ *inches blank*]

[lent vnto [gabrell] Thomas dowton the 25 of ap^rell 1598 } v^s]
In Redy money the some of . . . . }
locke the 4 leaffe forwarde

[1 *inch blank*]

[37]

[Lent vnto Robarte shawe the 23 of octob3 1597 }
to by a boocke for the company of my lorde admeralls } xxxx^s
men & my lord of penbrockes the some of . . . . }
called the cobler(1) wittnes
EAlleyn

Lent vnto Robart shawe the 5 of novmb3 1597 }
to by a boocke of yonge horton for the company }
of my lord admeralles men & my lord of penbrockes } xs
the some of . . . . }
wittnes EAlleyn

lent vnto Robart shawe the 26 of novmb3 1597 }
to by viij y^rd*e* of clothe of gowld the some of }
fower pownde*e* I saye lent for(2) . . . . . . } iiij^li
the vsse of the company. . . . . }
lent vnto Robart shawe to geue the tayller to bye }
tensell for bornes womones gowne the j of desemb3 1597(3) } ixs]
[Lent Thomas dowton the 12 of novemb3 1597 }
in Redey money the some of . . . . } xs
Lent Thomas dowton the 16 of novmb3 1597 }
in Redy money the some of . . . . } v^s

(1) *called the cobler*] added in a different ink.
(2) *for*] interlined. (3) *1597*] interlined above.

Lent Thomas Dowton the *20* of novmbȝ 1597 in Redey money the some of . . . . } v[s]

Lent vnto Thomas Dowton the 24 of novmbȝ 1597 in Redey money w[ch] Robart shawe gaue his worde [his] for yt to be p*a*yd me agayne wth in one fortnyght next f*o*lowinge wittnes to the same edward alleyn . . . . } xxxx s

lent thomas Dowton to fee a cownseller the 12 of desember . . xs

Lent Thomas Dowton to featche ij clockes owt of pane the 2 of novenbȝ 1597 the some of xij[li] xs for w[ch] money thes ij clockes were leafte vnto me in pane the one wasse & embȝadered clocke of ashecolerd velluet the other a blacke velluett clock*e* layd wth sylke laces a bowt I saye lent vnto hime in Redey money . . . . } xij[li] x[s]]

[37v] **20064**

[Rd[(1)] of the companey of my lorde admeralles men in pte of payment the firste of desembȝ 1597 of Robarte shawe the some of[(1)] . . . . } xx s]

[1 *inch blank*]

[Layd owt for the company of my lord admeralls men for to by tafetie & tynsell to macke a payer of bodeyes for a womones gowne to playe allece perce for w[ch] I dellyu*e*red vnto th*e* littell tayller In Redey money the *8* of *d*esembȝ 1597 the some of . . . . . } xx[s]

wittnes EAlleyn

lad owt mor the same tyme for makynge & a payer of yeare sleavse[(2)] of th*e* bodeyes of *p*yges[(3)] gowne . } vj s vij d

Lent vnto Bengemen Johnsone the [2]3[(4)] of desembȝ 1597 vpon a Bocke w[ch] he was to writte for vs befor crysmas next after the date herof w[ch] he showed th*e* plotte vnto the company I saye lente in Redy money vnto hime the some of } xx s

(1) *Rd...of*] An unblotted cancellation mark on f. 38 has registered on this entry, and seems to delete it.

(2) *sleavse*] *sleavfe* Greg.

(3) *pyges*] presumably the boy-actor Pyg or Pyk; see Greg, *Dramatic Documents*, I, 61.

(4) [*2*]*3*] alteration.

lent vnto Robart shawe for to by cop lace
of [g*owe*] sylver(1) to lace a payer of hosse for all*es* perce } xvj s
the 10 of desemb3 1597 the some of . . . .

wittnes w^m^ Borne Jube
& gabrell spencer

Layd owt for ij gyges for shawe & his company
to ij yonge men th*e* 12 of desemb3 1597 the some of } vj s 8^d^

layde owt the 22 of desemb3 1597 for A boocke called
mother Readcape to antony monday & m^r^ drayton . } iij^li^

Layd owt th*e* 28 of desemb3 1597 to antoney m*o*nday
to*w*ard his boocke wch I delyvered to thomas
dowton . . . . } v^s^]

[38]

[ano(2) do 1595 the xxviij^th^ of nove*m*bere
Reseved of m^r^ henslow the day and yer*e* a bov written
Th*e* Som of syx pound*e* of curant mony of England
and is in part of a mor som [yf he the sayd] by Twyxt
the sayd phillyp henslow(3) and me consaring a bargen of the beargarden
I say. Reseved. . . . . vj.^li^ / by me John mavlthouse /(2)
wittnes I EAlley(4)]

Layd owt at Sundrey tymes(5) of my owne Readey money(6) a bowt
the changinge of ower comysion as ffoloweth 1597

layd owt for goinge to the corte to the m^r^ of the Requeastes . . xij d
layd owt for goinge to corte ij . . . . ij s
[l]geuen(7) vnto the clarcke of the senetes man Edward . . . . v s
layd owt for goinge to the corte to th*e* senet . . . . xij d
Itm pd for goinge vp & downe to the corte to grenwiche . . . viij d
Itm pd for goinge vp & downe to caylleng cr*o*sse to the clarke. . vj d
Itm pd vnto the clarke of the senette . . . . xxxx s
Itm pd vnto the clarkes mane . . . . v s
Itm pd for goinge vp & downe to sencaterens m^r^ Seser . . . . iiij d

(1) *sylver*] interlined above.
(2) *ano...mavlthouse*] in Maulthouse's hand.
(3) *henslow*] interlined with caret.
(4) Autograph signature.
(5) *tymes*] interlined above.
(6) *money*] interlined above.
(7) [*l*]*geuen*] *g* altered from *l*.

[lent vnto w^m^ Borne the 12 of desemb3 1597 In Redey money to be pd vnto me a gayne at crysmas eve next comynge the some of twenty shyllyngs I saye lent . } xxs

wittnes Robart shawe
Thomas dowton
& EAlleyn

lent vnto w^m^ Borne the 19 of desemb3 1597 In Redey money to be payd me agayen at crystmas eve next comynge the some of thirtene shillinges I saye lent } xiij s

wittnes thomas dowten biger boye
whome fecthed(1) yt fore hime

layd owt for A wascotte wraght wth sylke for w^m^ borne the 24 of febreary 1598 the some of . } xxs

locke the next leaffe folowinge]

[38v] 20063

Rd(2) the.31.of october 1597: of m^r^ Phillip Henchlowe the Sūme of xiiij s ij d, for one quarters rent, due at Michaelm^s^ last past, and is to the vse of Harry Wendover(3) I say Rd. . . . . } xiiij^s^ ij^d^

p me Ra: Carter(2)

pd vnto Thomas whittle the 2 of Jeneway 1597 the some of xxxx^s^ wch was dewe vnto the m^r^ of the Revelles for one monethe playinge wch was dewe vnto hime the 28 of desemb3 1597 I saye pd . . . . } xxxxs

pd vnto Thomas whittle the 22 of Jeneway 159[7]8(4) the some of xxxxs wch was dew vnto the m^r^ of the Revelles for one moneth playinge wch was dewe vnto hime the 21 of Jeneway 1598 I saye pd . . . . } xxxxs

pd vnto John Carnab the 23 of febreary 1598 the some of xxxxs wch dew vnto the m^r^ of the Revelles for one moneth playinge I saye pd } xxxxs

[wm borne alles birde 1598 Deatte as folowth

---

(1) *fecthed*] *sic.*

(2) *Rd...Carter*] in Carter's hand; separated by a rule from the entries below.

(3) *Wendover*] *Weadover* Greg.

(4) *159[7]8*] *8* altered from *7*.

lent wm borne the 29 of marche 1598 to descarge the areaste betwext langley & hime . } vj s viij d

lent w^m^ borne by my wiffe the 3 of aguste 1598 . v^s^

lent w^m^ borne to [desc] folowe sewt(1) agenste Thomas poope the 30 of aguste 1598 [by] by my wiffe } x^s^

lent vnto w^m^ borne the 9 of agust 1598 the some of viij s wch thomas towne feched for hime I saye . } viij^s^

Lent w^m^ borne the 27 of septmb3 1598 when he Reade to croyden to ther lorde when the quene came thether. } v^s^

lent w^m^ birde ales borne the 27 of novemb3 to bye a payer of sylke stockens to playe the gwisse in . . } xx^s^

lent w^m^ borne to bye his stockens fo^r^ the gwisse . . xx^s^]

[39]

A note what money my Brother Edmonde Hensley owes me att sevaralle times lente hime as a pereth herafter 1593

Lente my Brother when He tocke the lease of his howsse in sothwarke. . . . . } iiij^li^

more he Had of me A gowne of my wifes new . . wch coste me l s & he to geue me so muche for yt } l s

Lent my brother when He tocke the lease of his howsse on the bancke syde . . . . } xxxx^s^

Lent my brother when he tocke the lease of his howsse at lambeth mearch. . . . . } xxxx s

Lent my brother for to macke an eand wth one of his costomers dwellinge on the bryge when his ware was a tached in the fayer . . . . } xx s

lent my brother when he weant to my lorde chamberlen to searue hime & wase at that time entertayned. . . . } xxxx^s^

locke the next leafe some vij^li^ xs

[w^m^ Bornes alles birde(2) Recknynge player at severall times lent as folowethe 1597

(1) *sewt*] *the sewt* Greg.

(2) *alles birde*] interlined with caret.

lent w^m borne the 12 of desemb3 1597 in Redey money to be payde
me agayne at crysmas eve next comynge the some of twenty shyllynges wittnes Robart shawe Thomas dowton & EAlleyn . . . . xx s
lent w^m borne the 19 of desemb3 1597 in Redey money to be payd
me agayne at crysmas eve next comynge thirten shillinges wittines Thomas dowtones biger boye whome feched yt for hime . . . . xiij s
layd owt for a wraght wascotte of sylke for w^m borne the 24 of febreary 1598 the some of. . . . . xx^s
lent vnto w^m borne Thomas dowton & gabrell spencer abowt the sewt be twext marten & them the 8 of marche 1598 in Redy money the some of. . . . . xxx s
lent w^m borne the 25 of marche 1598 in Redey money at ij paymentes the some of . . . . v^s
lent w^m borne to descarge the areaste of langleyes ¶ 29 marche 1598(1) xiijs 4^d(2)]

[39v] **20062**

layd owt for edmond henslowe sonne
John henslowe as foloweth 1596

Itm bowght hime a clocke for	xvij s
Itm pd for mackenge of his aparell	xxij d
Itm [pd]lent(3) hime to bye a hatte	iiij s
Itm bowght hime ij sheartes	vs vj d
some	28^s – 4^d

w^m Borne — A Juste Recknynge what I haue Receued
of w^m borne for xx s wch I lent hime
to by a wraghte wascotte as foloweth
1598

Rd the 25 of febreary 1598	ij s vj d
Rd the 27 of febreary 1598	ij s vj d
Rd the j of marche 1598.	*ijs* vj d
Rd the 4 of marche 1598	ij s vj d

[1½ *inches blank*]

---

(1) *1598*] interlined above.
(2) *xiijs 4^d*] *4^d* squeezed into the corner of the page.
(3) [*pd*]*lent*] *le* altered from *pd*.

[Borrowde(1) of mr Phillip hinchlow the 3 of apriell 1598 the some of 3 powndes in redye monye to be payd att what time he shal Call By me William Birde ./ I say borrowed. . . . . iijli (1)]

[(2)Be it knowne vnto all men by this pesentes that I gabrell spencer dothe a knowlege my seallf*e* to owe & stande fermley in deated vnto phillipe hensley the some of fower powndes of good & lafull*e* money of Ingelande locke iiij leaues f*e*rther]

[1¾ *inches blank*]

[40]

A Note of all such carges as I phillipe Hensley Haue layd owt of my owne money In th*e* be hallfe of th*e* Chelldren of Edmond Hensley d^e^sesed 1592 as ffoloweth

laydowt when I came downe first In carges . . . . . . viijs
layd owt when I came downe laste In carges . . . . . . xijs
payd vnto goodman harttrope for threshing . . . . . . viijs 4d
lent vnto my syster marg*e*rey to fynd hear. . . . . . . vs 4d
paid for a horss*e* & his carges . . . . xxxxs
pd for beinge a myted in the spritall corte . . . . iiijs
pd for provinge the ij willes & for th*e* administracion . . xviijs
pd vnto mr doctor Ridle for his fease . . . . vjs 8d
pd vnto mr cole the Regester his fease. . . . . [iij]vjs(3) 4d
pd vnto th*e* proct*o*r his f*ee* at that time . . . . iijs 4d
pd vnto th*e* Regester for setinge downe th*e* acte . . . . ijs
pd vnto th*e* Regester for mackinge th*e* bande . . . . . xijd
pd vnto the Regester for his labour . . . . xijd
pd vnto th*e* doctor*e*s man his fee . . . . xijd
pd vnto my atorney 15 of June 1593 for dieuers maters for me . vjs viijd
06 – 13 – 08 pd vnto a sargent at lawe for his cow[s]nsell(4) th*e* 15 of June 1593 . xs
some vjli xiijs viijd

lock the 2 leafe

(1) *Borrowde...iijli*] in Bird's hand.
(2) *Be...*] This last entry is separated by a rule from those above.
(3) [*iij*]*vj*] *v* altered from *ii*.
(4) *cow*[*s*]*nsell*] *n* altered from *s*.

Gabrell spences

lent vnto gabre*ll* spencer the 10 of marche 1598 In Redey money the some of xs I saye lent . } xs

lent vnto gabrell spencer the 20 of marche 1598 In Redy money vpon a Jewell . . . . } vjs

m[r] that I gabrell spencer the 5 of ap[r]ell 1598 have borowed of Phillippe Henslow the some of Thirtie shellynges in Redy money to be payed vnto hime agayne when he shalle demande yt I saye borow*ed* . . . . } xxx[s]

Gabriell Spenser(1) [T.D](2) [Gabriell] [Spenser](1)

[40v] **20061**

Lent m[r] Richard ffuller my attorney the 24 of aguste in Readey money to be payd me agayne at mihellmase tearme next cominge after the datte herof 1594 a bove written & wittneses to the leandynge herof } xx[s]

m[r] shealden player
& m[r] fullers man

[2¾ *inches blank*]

The ij chelldren of edmond hensley mary & nanne came vp to london to me to keppe the 27 of febreary & in the yeare of o[r] lord 1595

[[Receued](3) borowed(4) of m[r] hinchlow the xx[th] of march 1598 the som of 40 shillings I say . xxxxs]

p̲ me thomas downton(3)

[lent vnto Robarte shawe player the 20 of marche 1598 in Redey money the some of . . . . . . } v[s]]

[lent vnto Thomas dowton the 25 of ap[r]ell 1598 In Readey money the some of . . . . } v[s]]

[1 *inch blank*]

---

(1) *Gabriell Spenser*] The left-hand signature is autograph; the other, as Greg notes, may be a copy by Henslowe; its initial seems to be *D* altered to *G*.

(2) *T.D*] Greg merely records a scrawl here; the initials are Downton's, but may have been written by Henslowe.

(3) *Receued...downton*] in Downton's hand; this entry is set off within rules.

(4) *borowed*] interlined with caret.

[41]

A not of alle Such charges as I haue layd o*w*t to defend the Sute A geanst edward phillipes As foloweth beginínge the 5 of maye 1593

pd for tackinge of a copey of the write	vj d
pd vnto m^{r} cheacke my atorney for his feea	iijs 4d
pd vnto m^{r} cheacke for to macke Apearence	xij d
pd for going by water s iij times	ixd
pd for goinge to m^{r} vahanes atorney farmer & caringe my Atorney wth me	iiij s
pd for going*e* vp to weastmester	ij s
pd the next time & goinge by water	xviij d
pd the 16 of maye 1593 for goinge wth my atorney . .	iij s
pd the 20 of maye 1593 & the 17 of June 1593 for goinge to my lord buckhorste a bowte the copey howld land wch weales *do*th wth howld frome vs . .	iiijs
layd owt to goo to grenstead to trey*e* an Isapryse be twext edward phillipes & me a bowt th*e* l*o*ckyeares.	l s
Itm layd owt at mihellmase tearme 1593 the terme beinge hollden a sente talbanes vnto ij cownsellers & atorneyes	xl s
Itm layd owt gooinge by water	ij s
Itm pd vnto the screuener for mackinge of a lease . xx d vnto my Brother williame hensley of th*e* barne & cra*f*te & stable	
layd owt at hellery terme in th*e* yeare of ower lorde 1594 to my cownselers for iij seuerall times.	xxx^{s}
Itm for drawinge my bell in th*e* stare chambʒ a genste cowche ma*n* & Kedder & phillipes vpon pargery . .	viij s
Itm for drawinge intergetores & ingrosynge them In ꝑchment iij seueral ones.	vij^{s} 8^{d}
Itm pd vnto the exsameners of thes iij men	xiij^{s} vj^{d}
Itm dd vnto my atorney to despatche divers maters for me In the stare cha*m*ber	xxij s
Itm pd vnto my cownseler & to my attorney to put in my declaration in to th*e* stare chamber at easter terme 1594	xiij s viij d
Itm pd vnto m^{r} ward for the copey of the corte Rowles Itm pd vnto m^{r} ffuller for diuers matters ffor mydsomer	xiij s
tearme 1594	xxx^{s}
Itm pd vnto m^{r} ffuller the 10 of July 1594	iiij s
Itm pd ffor the comisyon to send into the contrey . .	iij s 4^{d}
Itm pd ffor fechynge of a leatter ffrome my lord chamberlen .	vj s
Itm geuen vnto m^{r} ffuler for cominge vp & downe to london.	ij s

	Itm geuen my cownseler (1) to draw my Intergretoryes to my comisyon the 19 of desemb3 1594	xs
li s d 14 – *oo* – oo	Itm geuen m[r] ffuller his feese	iijs

[41 v] 20060

this was when I sowld the howsse for the chylldren w[ch] howsse wasse. sowld vnto m[r] arture langworth for iiij score pownd wittnes edward allen	Itm geuen vnto Richard cvcks*o*n & is wiffe to a knowlege the fyne the 3 of June 1595	xxxx[s] (2)
	Itm for bringinge vp the ij chylldren to london .	iiij s
	Itm geuen vnto John hensleyes m[r] when he tock*e* hime prentes to m[r] newman dier. . .	xxxx[s]
	Itm geuen vnto John gryges when I put mary hensley to hime to prentes for vij yeares w[ch] was the 5 of June 1595 th*e* some of . .	iij[li]

Layd owt at severall tymes as maye a pere by my boocke befor wth this for edmond henslow & his iij chelldren the some of – 78[li]– 1[s] – 6[d]	Itm pd for Ingrosynge of the Inventory . .	xvj s vj d
	Itm pd vnto th*e* paretore his fese	ix s
	pd vnto cvxsone & his wiffe to Releace ther Righte in the howss*e* as maye apere by writinge fortie pownd*e* & then they a knowlege A fyne I saye pay*d*	40[li]

I never had any thinge of his but the howse w[ch] I s*o*w*ld* some 48[li] – 9[s] – 6[d]

ther mother had all ther good*e* to kepe them tyll they came to me some ttotales 78[li]– 1[s] – 6[d]	[Sowld vnto Thomas downton A payer] [of longe sylke stockenes of crymsone coller] [to be payd for them xxiiij s Redey money] [w*ch* he yet owes vnto me I saye]	xxiiij[s]
	[w*ch* he had of me th*e* 3 of marche] 1598	
	bowght for Joh*n* henslow A boote w[ch] coste me of Jemes Russell	v[li]
	layd owt in mony to (3) bye nanne A gowne when her syster turned her a waye	xxviij s

[Lent vnto w[m] B[o]*i*rde (4) als borne the 23 of oct*o*b3 1598 vpon A longe taney clocke of clothe of his owe the some of thirtishillinges I saye lent vnto hime	xxx[s]

(1) *cownseler*] *cownsele* Greg. (2) *xxxx[s]*] *xx[s]xx* Greg.

(3) *mony to*] the space is filled by a blot which has registered from the opposite page.

(4) *B*[*o*]*irde*] *i* altered from *o*.

Lent vnto wm Borne the 19 of novemb3 1598 vpon a longe taney clocke of clothe the some of xijs wch he sayd yt was to Imbrader his hatte for the gwisse . . . . } xijs

Lent vnto wm Birde ales borne the 22 of desemb3 1598 when the widow came to mrs Reues to super In Redey money the some of . . . . } xs

Dd vnto wm Birde ales borne ij gewells of gowld wch he layd to me to pane for xs wch I dd to hime agayne wth owt money wch he owes me . . . . } xs]

[42]

[2¾ *inches blank*]

[Be yt knowne vnto all men by this pesents that I williame Birde & gabrell spencer & Thomas dowton dothe a knowlege our seallues to owe & stande fermly in deatted vnto phillippe Henslow the some of syxe powndes of good & lafulle money of Ingland(1) wch(2) we borowed of hime & to be payed vnto the sayd phillippe his heires(3) execut or assignes at St Jhon Baptist next ensuing the date here of at his howsse(4) & for [witt] the wich payment wee bind vs or heirs executors and assignes by these prsence in wittnes whereof wee haue to this bill sett or hands the ixth of Aprill 1598(3) I say vj li(5)]

William Birde(6)
Gabriell Spenser(6)
Thomas Downton(6)

Be it knowne vnto all men by this pesentes that I gabrell spencer of london player doth a knowlege my seallfe to owe & stand fermley in deated vnto phillippe hensley the some of fower powndes of good & lafulle money of Inglande & for the trewe payment herof I bynde me my eares exsecutors & adminystratores by this pesence In wittnes here to I haue seatte my } iiijli
hande the 20 of aprell 1598 ageanste(7) sent gorges daye

Gabriell Spenser(7)

---

(1) *of Ingland* interlined with caret. (2) *wch*] omitted Greg.
(3) *his heires. . . 1598*] in Downton's hand. (4) *at his howsse*] interlined with caret.
(5) I *say vj li*] added by Henslowe. (6) Autograph signatures.
(7) *ageanste. . . Spenser*] added in a different ink from the rest of this entry; Greg is probably right in suggesting that the signature is a copy by Henslowe.

lent vnto gabrell spencer the 24 of ap^r^ell 1598 . . . . xs

Lent vnto gabrell spence[s]r(1) the 19 of maye 1598 to
bye a plume of feathers wch his mane bradshawe
feched of me xs I saye lente . . . . } xs

[42v] 20059

Lent w^m^ Birde alles Borne the 22 of ap^r^ell 1599
in Redey money wch his mane william felle Rd
[*his*(2)] yt of me for hime the some of fortishilling*s*
I say . . . . } xxxx^s^

Wittnes E Alleyn(3)

Lent vnto m^rs^ Birde alles Borne the 26
of novmb3 1600 in Redye monye to descarge
her husband owt of the kyng*e* benche when
he laye vpon my lord Jeffe Justes warant
for hurtinge of a felowe wch browght his
wiffe a leatter some of threepownd*e* I say*e* } iij^li^

[1¼ *inches blank*]

M^r^s Keyes

A not what I haue payd for
m^r^s keayes sence the 22 of ap^r^ell 1599

pd vnto Su^r^ thomas [ff*u*l] fflude for a q*ters*
Rent dew by whitt & hugson to th*e* Quene for
the howsse at grynwige the 27 of ap^r^ell 1599 . } xxxxj^s^ 8^d^

Lent vnto m^r^s keayes the 15 of maye 1599 by my
wiffe in Redy money . . . . } xx^s^

Dd vnto m^r^s keyes goodman pare Rent . . . . xs

Dd vnto m^r^s keyes fotherbeyes Rent . . . . . xvj s

[2 *inches blank*]

[43]

A not of all suche goods as I haue Bowght for
playnge sence my sonne edward allen leafte laynge(4)
1597

---

(1) *spence*[*s*]*r*] *r* altered from *s*.

(2) *his*] *hit* Greg; the word is smudged.

(3) Autograph signature.

(4) *laynge*] *sic.*

Bowght the 29 of desemb3 1597 j short vealluet clocke ymbradered wth bugelles & a hoode cape . } iij^li

Bowght the 18 of ap^rell 1598 xvj ownces of copelace brad wth sylver & gowld cop at vjij d[1] ownce . . . } xs viij d

Itm for mackynge of the gercken & threed . . . . iij s iiij d

Bowght th*e* 8 of novemb3 1598 xiiij ownces of cope lace wraght wth opene worcke for xiiij^d & ownce } xvj s

Mrs Keayes

A not what I haue Receud of m^rs
Keayes Reant of her howsses at westmester
sence I gathered the Reant & haue Kepte
in my hand sence th*e* 22 of ap^rell 1599

[Rd of m^r wa*y*ghte[2] his qters Rent . . . . xxv^s
Rd of m^r whitte his qters Rent . . . . xs
Rd of m^r downes his hallfe years Rent . . . . xx^s
Rd of the pore owld womon for qters Rent . . . . v^s
Rd of goodman pare . . . . x^s
Rd of goody fotherbe for hallfe a yeare . . . . xvj s]

lent Mrs Keayes as followeth

[Lent m^rs keyes to macke vp the l*s*[3] Rent for the college Rent*e* at westmestters some of . . . . . . } vjs viij d]

[2½ *inches blank*]

[43 v] **20058**

A Juste a cownt of All suche money as I haue
layd owt for my lord admeralles [men] players begynyng
the xi of octob3 whose names ar as foloweth
borne gabrell shaw Jonnes dowten Jube towne
synger & the ij geffes 1597

layd owt vnto Robarte shawe to by a boocke for the companey the 21 of oc*to*b3 1597 the some of . . . } xxxx^s
called the cobler wittnes EAlleyn

(1) *vjij*] Henslowe first wrote *vj*, then added *ij*. (2) *wayghte*] *wagghte* Greg.
(3) *ls*] omitted Greg.

lent vnto Robarte shaw to by a boocke of yonge harton
the 5 of novmb3 1597 the some of . . . . } xs
wittnes EAlleyn

lent vnto Robarte shaw for the company to bye viij
y^r^des of clothe of gow[e]lde(1) for the womones gowne in bran } iiij li
howlte the 26 of novmb3 1597 the some of . . . .

lent vnto Robart shawe to geue the tayller to by tynssell
for bornes gowne the j of desemb3 1597. . . . . . . } ixs

layd owt for the companye to by tafetie & tynssell
for the bodeyes of a wom*o*nes gowne to playe allce perce } xxs
wch I dd vnto the littell tayller the 8 of desemb3 1597 . .
wittnes EAlleyn

layd owt for mackynge allce perces bodeyes & A payer
of yeare sleaues th*e* some of . . . . } vjs vijd

lent vnto Bengemen Johnson the 3 of desemb3 1597
vpon a boocke wch he showed the plotte vnto th*e*
company wch he promysed to dd vnto the company } xxs
at cryssmas next the some of. . . . .

lent vnto Robart shawe to by cop^r^ lace of sylver for
a payer hosse(2) in alls perce th*e* 10 of desemb3 1597. . } xvjs
wittnes w^m^ borne Jube & gabrell spenser

layd owt for ij gyges for the companey to ij yonge
men the *1* 12(3) of desemb3 1597 the some of . . } vjs 8^d^

layd owt th*e* 22 of desemb3 1597 for a boocke called
mother Read cape to antony monday & drayton . } iij^li^

layd owt the 28 of desemb3 1597 for the boocke called
mother Read cape to antony mondaye . . . . . . } v^s^

[lent the company to bye a flame coler satten
dublett th*e* 5 of Janewary 1597 the some of . . } xxxxv^s^]

---

(1) *gow*[*e*]*lde*] *l* altered from *e*. (2) *payer hosse*] *payer of hosse* Greg.
(3) *1 12*] the first *1* is partly obscured by the tail of *f* in the line above, and Henslowe wrote another.

[44]

layd owt for my lord admeralles mean*e* a*s* foloweth 1597

1597

pd vnto antony monday & drayton for the laste payment of the Boocke of mother Readcape the 5 of Jenewary 1597 the some of	lv^{s}
Layd [of] owte[(1)] for cop^{r} lace for th*e* littell boye[(2)] & for a valle for the boye A geanste the playe of dido & enevs the 3 of Jenew*a*ry 1597	[xxix s]
Lent vnto thomas dowton the 8 of Jenewary 1597 twentyshillinges to by a boockes of m^{r} dickers lent	[xx s]
lent vnto the company when they fyrst played dido at nyght the some of thirtishillynges wch wasse the 8 of Jenewary 1597 I saye	xxx s
lent vnto the company the 15 of Jenewary 1597 to bye a boocke of m^{r} dicker called fay*e*ton fower pownde I saye lent	iiij^{li}
lent vnto Thomas dowton for the company to paye the m^{r} of the Reuells for lysensynge of ij boockes xiiij s a bated to dowton v^{s} so Reaste	ix s
lent vnto Thomas dowton for the company to bye a sewte for phayeton & ij Rebat*es* & j fardengalle the 26 of Jenewary 1598 the some of three pownde I saye lent	iij^{li}
lent vnto Thomas dowton the 28 of Janeway 1598 to bye a whitte satten dublette for phayeton forty shyllenges I saye lent	xxxx^{s}
lent vnto the companey the 4 of febreary 1598 to dise charge m^{r} dicker owt of the cownter in the powltrey the some of fortie shillinges I saye dd to thomas dowton	xxxx^{s}
layd owt vnto antony monday the 15 of febreary 1598 for a playe boocke called the firste parte of Robyne Hoode	v*^{li}*

(1) *owte*] interlined above.

(2) *for the littell boye*] interlined with caret.

lent vnto Robarte shawe the 18 of febreary 1598 to paye vnto harton for a comodey called A womon will haue her wille the some of . . . } xx[s]

lent vnto thomas dowton the 20 of febreary 1598 to lende vnto antony mondaye vpon his seconde parte of the downefall of earlle huntyngton surnamed Roben Hoode I saye lent the some of . . . . } xs

Layd owt vnto Robarte lee the 22 of febreary 1598 for a boocke called the myller some of . . . . . } xx[s]

lent vnto thomas dowton the 25 of febreary 1598 to geue vnto chettell in pt of paymente of the seconde pte of Robart hoode I saye lent . . . . } xxs

Lent vnto antony mondaye the 28 of febreary 1598 in pte of paymente of the second pte of Roben Hoode } v[s]

edwarde[(1)] [w[m]] + lent vnto Thomas dowten & Robart [Jube] shaw & Jewebey the j of marche 1598 to bye a boocke of m[r] dickers called the treplesetie of cockowlles the some of fyve powndes I say lent . . . . . . } v[li]

Lent vnto Robart shawe the 8 of marche 1598 in full paymente of the seconde pte of the booke called the downfall of Roben hoode the some of } iij[li] v[s]

li s d
some [3]46[(2)] – 07 – 03

[JSinger][(3)]
[P me Thomas Downton[(3)]
P me william Birde[(3)]
Robt Shaa[(3)] Richard Jones[(2)]
Gabriell Spenser[(3)]
Thomas towne[(3)]
Humfry Jeffes[(3)]]
[Charles massye[(3)]
Samuell Rowlye[(3)]]

Thes men dothe aknowlege this deat to be dewe by them[(4)] by seatynge of ther handes to yette

(1) *edwarde*] interlined above.
(2) [*3*]*46*] *4* altered from *3*.
(3) Autograph signatures.
(4) *by them*] interlined, with caret.

[45]

Lent vnto drayton & cheatell the 13 of marche 1598 in pte of(1) paymente of a boocke wher in is a pte of a weallche man written wch they haue promysed to delyuer by the xx day next folowinge I saye lent R money . . . } xxxx s

lent vnto the company to paye drayton & dyckers & chetell ther full payment for the boocke called the famos wares of henry the fyrste & the prynce of walles the some of . . . . } iiijli vs(2)

lent at that tyme vnto the company for to spend at the Readynge of that boocke at the sonne in new fyshstreate. . . . . } vs +

pd vnto the carman for caryinge & bryngyn of the stufe backe agayne when they played [as]in(3) fleatstreat pryuat(4) & then owr stufe was loste . . . . } iij s +

layd owt for the company to bye a boocke of mr drayton & mr dickers mr chettell & mr willsone wch is called goodwine & iij sones fower(5) powndes in pte of paymet the 25 of marche 1598 in Redy mony I saye . . . . } iiij li

layd owt the same tyme at the tavarne in fyshstreate for good cheare the some of . . . . } vs

Layd owt the 28 of marche 1598 for the licencynge of ij boocke to the mr of the Revelles called the ij ptes of Robart hoode . . . . } xiiij s

lent vnto the companey the 30 of marche 1598 in full payment for the boocke of goodwine & his iij sonnes I saye lent . . . . } xxxxs

Lent vnto the company to geue mr willsone dickers drayton & cheattell in pte of payment of a boocke called perce of exstone the some of . . . . . . } xxxx s

Lent vnto the company to by a damaske [g(6)]casocke garded wth velluet the 7 of aprell 1598 the some . . } xxs

---

(1) *pte of*] *pte* Greg. (2) *vs*] added in a different ink.

(3) [*as*]*in*] alteration (from *ab*, Greg); a doubtful reading.

(4) *pryuat*] doubtful, as Greg notes; there are too many minims, and the word appears as *prymat*.

(5) *sones fower*] *es* written over *fo*; Henslowe had left too little space for the title which he added later. (6) *g*] *ge* Greg; the second letter is incomplete.

Lent vnto thomas dowton the 11 of ap^{r}ell 1598 to bye tafitie to macke a Rochet for the beshoppe in earlle goodwine	xxiiij s
Lent vnto the co^{m}pany the 12 of ap^{r}ell 1598 to paye m^{r} hathway*e* in fulle payment for his boocke of kynge arthore the some of fower pownde I saye . . .	iiij^{li}
lent vnto the companey th*e* 29 of ap^{r}ell 1598 to bye a bvgell dvblett & a payer of paned hoosse of bugell panes drane owt wth cloth*e* of sylver & cangones (1) of the same	xxxxvj s viij d
lent vnto Thomas Dowton 2 of [*a*]maye (2) 1598 to bye a Robe for the playe of th*e* lyfe of arthure in money the some of.	[iij^{li}] pd
Lent vnto cheattell vpon the playe called black*e* batmone of the northe th*e* some of . wittnes thom*as* dowton	xx s
Lente vnto dowton to paye *v*nto horton in ꝑte of paymente of his boocke called a womon will haue her wille	xx s
lent vnto m^{r} cheattell & m^{r} dickers the 6 of ap^{r}ell 1598 vpon ther boock*e* of goodwine the 2 ꝑt th*e* some of	xx s
Lent vnto th*e* companey the 9 of maye 1598 to bye A dvblett & a payer of hooss*e* layd thicke wth gowld lac*es* (3) the some of . . .	vij^{li}
Lent vnto m^{r} Chapmane th*e* 16 of maye 1598 in earneste of a boocke for th*e* companye wittnes w^{m} Birde.	xxxx s
Lente vnto the company th*e* 16 of maye 1598 to bye v boockes of martine slather called ij ꝑtes of hercolus & focas & pethagores & elyxander & lodick*e* wch laste boocke he hath not yet delyuerd th*e* some of. . . .	vij^{li}

(1) *cangones*] i.e. canions; *canyones* Greg, but *g* is clear.

(2) [*a*]*maye*] *m* altered from *a*.

(3) *laces*] *lace* Greg.

[46]

the[1] *x*i[th] of Aprill

Rd of Phillipp Hinchlow twenty shillings in earnesst of abooke cald the Lyfe of Artur king of England to be deliuered one thursday next following after the datte [he]herof[2] I saye Rd xxs by me Ri: Hathwaye[1] } xx[s]

Bowght of m[r] willsones drayton & dickers & cheattell for the companey a boocke called blacke battmane of the northe the 22 of maye 1598 w[ch] coste sixe powndę I saye layd owt for them . . . . } vj[li]

lent vnto w[m] birde the 23 of maye 1598 w[ch] he lent vnto m[r] chappman vpon his boock w[ch] he promised vs . . . . } xxs

lent vnto the company the 30 of maye 1598 tho[3] by A boocke called love prevented the some of fower powndes dd to thomas dowton } iiij[li]
m[r] porter[4]

lent vnto thomas dowton the 6 of June 1598 to leand vnto drayton I saye leante . . . . for the 2 p̷t of goodwine . . } xs

lent vnto the companey the 10 of June 1598 to lend vnto m[r] chapman . . . . } xs

lent vnto the companey th*e* 10 of June 1598 to paye vnto m[r] drayton willson dickers & cheattell in full paymente of the second p̷te of goodwine ls as foloweth drayton 30[s] &. willson x[s] & cheattell xs some is . . . . . } ls

lent vnto m[r] willsone the 13 of June 1598 [called] vpon A bock*e* called Richard cordelion funeralle . . . . . } v[s]

lent vnto thomas dowton the 13 of June 1598 to bye divers thinges for black batmane of the northe the some of fyve pownd I saye lent . . . . } v[li]

---

(1) *the...Hathwaye*] in Downton's hand, except for Hathaway's autograph signature.

(2) [*he*]*herof*] a faint *he* is overwritten.

(3) *tho*] *sic*; *to* Greg.

(4) *m[r] porter*] perhaps a forgery; it is in a different ink from the rest of the entry, and written in heavy and clumsy strokes. Greg accepts as genuine.

lent vnto thomas dowton the 14 of June 1598 to bye divers thinges for blacke batmane of the northe the some } iij^{li}

lent vnto cheattell the 14 of June 1598 in earneste of A boock called Richard cordeliones funeralle . . . } v^{s}

[46v] 20054

Lent vnto Robart shawe & edward Jube the 15 of June 1595 to geve m^{r} Chapman in earneste of his boocke called the ⟨.⟩ylle(1) of A womon . . } xx^{s}

lent vnto Cheattell the 15 of June 1598 in earneste of ther boocke called the funerall of Richard cvrdelion . . . . } v^{s}

lent vnto cheattell willsone & mondaye the 17 of June 1598 vpon earneste of ther boocke called the funerall of Richard cordelion . . . . } xv^{s}

Lent vnto m^{r} cheattell the 21 of June 1598 in earneste of a boocke called the fenerall of Richard cvrdelion the some of . . . . } x[x]v^{s}(2)
I saye xxv^{s} wittnes w^{m} birde . . . . . .

lent vnto antony mvnday the 23 of June 1598 in earneste of a boocke called the fenerall of Richard cvrdelion the some of . . . . . . } xx^{s}

lent vnto m^{r} drayton the 24 of June 1598 in earneste of a boocke called the funerall of Richard cordelion the some of . . . . . . } xxx s

lent vnto m^{r} cheattell the 24 of June 1598 the some of xs I saye . . . . } xs

all(3) his pte of boockes to this place are payde wch weare(4) dew vnto hime [is payd] & he Reastes be syddes in my Deatte the some of xxx^{s}(3)

---

(1) ⟨.⟩*ylle*] *iylle* Greg; Malone and Collier read *wyll(e)*; two smudges before *y* may conceal a letter (*i*, but hardly *w*), but nothing can be seen, and they may well be meaningless.

(2) *x[x]v^{s}*] *v* altered from *x*; *xxv^{s}* Greg.

(3) *all*. . .*xxx^{s}*] Henslowe uses a different form of bracket here from his normal usage; there is no marginal entry.

(4) *wch weare*] interlined with caret.

Lent vnto m^r willson the 26 of June 1598 the some of xxs wch is in full paymente of of his pte of the bo*ocke* called Richard cordelion funerall . . . . xxs

& so m^r willson Reasteth in my deate al*b*einge pay*de* [xxv^s] [pd xs Rest to paye xs] (1)

lent vnto Thomas dowton the 26 of June 1598 to by satten to macke ij dubleattes for the 2 pte of goodwine the some of . . . . v^li

[47]

Lent vnto Cheattell the 26 of June 1598 in earneste of A boocke called the 2 pte of blacke battman of the north & m^r harey porter hath geven me his worde for th*e* performance of th*e* same & all so for my money . . . . . xx^s

lent vnto Thomas dowton the 27 of June 1598 to bye dyvers thinges for th*e* 2 pte of goodwin*e* xxx^s

lent vnto m^r willson m^r drayton & m^r dickers the 31 of June 1598 in earneste of A boocke called the made manes mores the some of . . . . iij^li

Lent vnto m^r Cheattell the 8 of July 1598 vpon A Boocke called the 2 pte of blacke battman the some of . . . . iij^li

Lent vnto m^r drayton the 9 of July 1598 vpon a Boocke of called the mad manes mores the some of . . . . xx^s

pd vnto m^r willsone & m^r deckers in fulle payme*nt* of A boocke called the mad manes moris the 10 of July 1598 th*e* some of . . . . xxxx^s

Lent vnto m^r willsones the 13 of July 1598 in pt of payment of a boocke called the 2 pt of blacke battman the some of . . . . xs

---

(1) *xxv^s . . . x^s*] interlined.

lent vnto m^r^ wilso*ne* the 14 of July 1598 in pt of payme*nt* of a boock called the 2 pt of black battman th*e* some of. . . . . . . } xv^s^

pd vnto m^r^ cheattell the 14 of July 1598 in fulle paymet of a boock called th*e* 2 pt of black battmane the some of . . . . . . } xv^s^

[47v] **20053**

Lent vnto H*a*rey Cheattell the 14 of July 1598 vpon a boock*e* called the playe of A womon^s^ (1) Tragedye th*e* some of v^li^ wch Robart shawe willed me to delyuer hime I saye . . . . . . } v^li^
eath*er* to dd th*e* playe or els to paye th*e* mony wth in one forthnyght. . . . .

lent vnto w^m^ borne th*e* 14 of July 1598 for to geue th*e* paynter in earneste of his pictor th*e* some of (2) . . . . } v^s^

lent vnto Thomas dowton the 16 of July 1598 for to bye A Robe to playe hercolas in the some of . . . . } xxxx^s^

lent vnto m^r^ willsone the 17 of July 1598 in earneste of a comodye called haneballe & hearmes the some of . . . . } xs

pd vnto marteyne slawghter the 18 of July for a boocke called elexsander & lodwicke the some of . . . . } xx^s^

li	s	d	
104 (3) –	12	– 8	lent vnto m^r^ willson m^r^ drayton & m^r^ dickers the 17 of July 1598 for A Boock*e* called Haneballe & hermes the some of. . . . . } iij^li^

lent vnto Robarte shaw (4) & Jewbey the 19 of July 1598 for A Boocke called Vallentyne & orsen in fulle paymente the some of v^li^ to paye hathe waye & mondaye . . . . } v^li^

(1) *womon^s^*] *womon* Greg.

(2) The words *Tassos Picture* are written in the left margin in a late hand, perhaps Malone's.

(3) *104*] *101* Greg. The figures are heavily deleted.

(4) *shaw*] interlined with caret.

pd vnto the m^r of the Revelles man for the licensynge of iij boockes the 24 of July 1598 the some of	xxj s

[48]

Lent vnto w^m borne the 25 of July 1598 to by A sewte of satten for the playe of the made manes moris the some of	iiij^li xiij^s 4^d
lent vnto m^r willsone the 26 of July 1598 vpon A Boocke called Haneballe & hermes the some of	xx s
Lent vnto m^r [willso] drayton & m^r dickers the 27 of July 1598 in pt of a Boocke called Haneballe & Hermes the some of.	xxx^s
Lent vnto the company the 28 of July 1598 to by a payer of sceartes of whitte satten for A womons gowne layd wth whitte lace the some of	xxxiij^s 4^d
pd vnto m^r drayton & m^r deckers the 28 of July 1598 in full payment of a boocke called haneball & hermes other wisse called worsse feared then hurte	x^s
15 - 17 - 8 lent vnto m^r deckers the same time vpon the next boock called perce of winschester . . .	x^s

120^li - 15^s - 4^d

li s d
[160 - 15 - 4]
[135](1)

Here I Begyne to [th] Receue the wholle gallereys frome this daye beinge the 29 of July 1598

1[46]57(2)

Rd the 29 of July 1598	x^li xiiij s
Rd the 6 of aguste 1598	vij^li x s
Rd the 13 of aguste 1598	ix^li ix s
Rd the 19 of aguste 1598	viij^li xij s
Rd the 26 of aguste 1598	viij^li ij s
Rd the 2 of [aguste] septembʒ(3) 1598	viij^li xiiij s
Rd the 10 of septmbʒ 1598	ix^li iij s
Rd the 17 of septmbʒ 1598	vj^li xviij s
Rd the 24 of septmbʒ 1598	viij^li ij s
Rd the 29 of septmbʒ 1598	v^li xiiij s

(1) *135*] *13ʳ* Greg.

(2) *1[46]57*] *57* altered from *46*.

(3) *septembʒ*] interlined above.

Rd the 7 of octob3 1598 . . . . vj^{li} iij s
Rd the 14 of octob3 1598 . . . . vij^{li} xv^{s}
Rd the 21 of octob3 1598 . . . . x^{li} xiiij s

[48v] **20052**

Rd the 28 of octob3 1598 . . . . v^{li} xix^{s}
Rd the 5 of novmb3 1598 . . . . viij^{li} ij s
Rd the 12 of novmb3 1598 . . . . v^{li} iij^{s}
Rd the 19 of novemb3 1598 . . . . vj^{li} xvj^{s}
Rd the 24 of novemb3 1598 . . . . iiij^{li} xvj^{s}
Rd the 2 of desemb3 1598 . . . . vj^{li} xvj^{s}
li s d Rd the 9 of desemb3 1598 . . . . vij^{li} xvj s
[157 - 00 - 00] Rd the 16 of desemb3 1598 . . . . iiij^{li} iij s
Rd the 23 of desemb3 1598 . . . . iiij^{li} v^{s}
Rd the 30 of desemb3 1598 . . . . xij^{li} x s
Rd the 7 of Janewary 1598 . . . . vij^{li} xvij^{s}
li s d Rd the 14 of Janewary 1598 . . . . viij^{li} xj s
[198 - 17 - 00] Rd the 21 of Janewary 1598 . . . . viij^{li} xiij s
Rd the 28 of Janewary 1598 . . . . vij^{li} vj s
Rd the 4 of ffebreary 1598 . . . . x^{li} xvij s
Rd the 11 of ffebreary 1598 . . . . vij^{li} x s
Rd the 18 of ffebreary 1598 . . . . vij^{li} x s
[247 - 03 -] 00 Rd the 24 of ffebreary 1598 . . . . xv^{li} iij s
Rd the 26 of marche 1598 dew 233^{li} – 17^{s} – 17^{d} (1) . . . iij^{li} xviij s
Rd the j of Ap^{r}ell 1598 . . . . ij^{li} ij s
Rd the 8 of Ap^{r}ell 1598 . . . . iij^{li} viij^{s}
Rd the 15 of Ap^{r}ell 159[8]9 (2) . . . . xiij^{li} vij s
Rd the 22 of Ap^{r}ell 159[8]9 (2) . . . . xiij^{li} xvj s
Rd the 29 of ap^{r}ell 1599 . . . . xj^{li} v^{s}
Rd the 6 of maye 1599 . . . . viij^{li} x s
Rd the 13 of maye 1599 . . . . ix^{li}
[324 - 00 - 00] Rd the 20 of maye 1599 . . . . xj^{li} xj s
li s d Rd the 27 of maye 1599 . . . . x li viij s
[351 - 00 - 00] Rd the 3 of June 1599 . . . . xvj^{li} xij s
Rd the 6 of octob3 1599 . . . . v^{li} iij s
358 - 03 - 00 Rd the 13 of octob3 1599 . . . . ij^{li}

(1) *dew 233^{li} – 17^{s} – 17^{d}*] interlined; the last *7* runs into the line connecting date and sum, and may be simply a bracket.
(2) *159[8]9*] *9* altered from *8*.

Reconed(1) wth the company of my lord of notinga*me* men to this place beinge th*e* 13 of octob3 1599 & yt doth a peare that I haue Receued of th*e* deate wch they owe vnto me iij hunder*d* fiftie & eyght pownds

[1½ *inches blank*]

[49]

Lent the companey the 30 of July 1598 to bye A Boocke of John daye called the con queste of brute wth the firste fyndinge of the bathe th*e* some of . . . . } xxxx^{s}

Lent vnto the company the 8 of aguste 1598 to paye m^{r} drayton willsone & dickers in ꝑte of payment of A boocke called perce of winschester th*e* some of . . . . } ls

[lent vnto antony monday th*e* 9 of aguste 1598 in earneste of A comodey for th*e* corte called the some of . . . . } m^{r} drayton hath ge*u*en his worde for [yt]the(2) boocke to be done wth *in* one fortnyght wittnes Thomas dowton] } [x^{s}]

Lent vnto th*e* company the 10 of aguste 1598 to paye m^{r} drayton willsone & dickers in fulle payment for a boock*e* called perce of winschester the some of . . . . } ls

lent vnto th*e* company th*e* 18 of aguste 1598 to bye a Boocke called hoote anger sone cowld of m^{r} porter m^{r} cheattell & bengemen Johnson in full payment the some of . . . . } vj^{li}

Lent vnto th*e* company the 19 of aguste 1598 to paye vnto m^{r} willson monday & deckers in ꝑte of payment of A boock called chance medley the some of iiij^{li} v^{s} in this mane^{r} willson xxx^{s} cheattell xxxs mondy xxv^{s} I saye . . . . } iiij^{li} v^{s}

[1 *inch blank*]

---

(1) *Reconed*] *Receved* Greg. (2) [*yt*]*the*] alteration.

Lent vnto Thomas dowton th*e* 21 of aguste
1598 to by A sewte & a gowne for vayvode } x^{li}
the some of tene pownde I saye lent . . .
wittnes m^{r} willsone

Lent m^{r} willsone the 21 of aguste 1598 in e
earnest of A Boocke called cattelyn some of . } x^{s}

Lent vnto Thomas dowton th*e* 22 of aguste
1598 to by diuers thinges for vayvode } xxxxvj^{s}
the some of . . . .

Lent vnto thomas dowton the 24 of aguste
1598 to by*e* diuers thinges for vayvode } xiiij s
th*e* some of . . . .

pd vnto m^{r} drayton the 24 of aguste 1598
in fulle payment of A Boocke called chance } xxxv^{s}
medley [or worse a feared then hurte the]⁽¹⁾ some of .

lent vnto Robart shaw the 25 of aguste
1598 to paye the lace manes byll ij^{li} xvj^{s} vj d } iiij^{li} v^{s}
& th*e* tayllers bylle xxviij s vj d some is . . .
for vayvode .

Lent vnto harey cheattell th*e* 26 of aguste
1598 in earneste of A Boock called } v^{s}
cattelanes consperesey th*e* some of . . .

Lent vnto hary cheattell th*e* 29 of aguste
1598 at the apoyntment of thomas dowton } xx^{s}
ffor his playe of vayvode th*e* some of . .

Lent vnto m^{r} willsone the 29 of aguste
1598 at th*e* Request of hary cheattell in } x^{s}
earneste of cattelyne the some of . .

[50]

Lent vnto th*e* company th*e* 30 of aguste 1598
to geue in earneste of A boock*e* called [bad]
[may a me*n*de] worse⁽²⁾ a feard then hurte⁽²⁾ vnto m^{r} drayton & dickers } l s
the some of . . . .

(1) Henslowe left too little space for the second title, added later, and *hurte* was interlined; when this title was then deleted, the word *the* was crossed out by accident.

(2) *worse...hurte*] interlined above.

Lent vnto the company the 4 of agust 1598 to paye in fulle payment for A Boocke called worse A feared then hurte vnto mr drayton & mr dickers the some of . . . . } ls

Lent vnto hary cheattell the 8 of [aguste](1) 1598 in earneste of A Boocke called Brute(2) the some of . . . . } ixs

Lent vnto hary cheattell the 9 of [aguste] septmb3(3) 1598 in earneste of A Bocke called Brute(2) at the A poyntment of Johne synger the some of . . . . } xxs

Lent vnto hary cheattell the 16 of septmb3 1598 in earneste of A Boocke called Brute . . . . } vs

Hary cheattell vntell this place owes vs viijli ixs dew al his boockes & Recknynges payd

Lent vnto the company the 19 of septmb3 1598 in Redy money A bowt the agrement betwext langley & them the some of . . . . } xxxvli

Lent vnto the company the the 23 of septmb3 1598 to bye diuers thinges for perce of winchester the some of xli dd vnto thomas dowton I saye. . . . } xli

Lent vnto thomas dowton the 28 of septmb3 1598 to bye diuers thinges for pearce of winchester the some of . . . . } xxxxs

[50v] 20049

Lent vnto thomas dowton the 29 of septmb3 1598 to [feche home a Riche clocke wch they had] [of mr langleyes the some of] to bye divers thinges for perce of winchester(4) } xijli

Lent vnto the companey the 29 of septmb3 1598 to by A boocke of mr drayton & mr dickers called the firste syvell wares in france . . . . . } vjli

---

(1) *aguste*] deleted, but nothing substituted.
(2) *Brute*] added later in spaces which it does not fill.
(3) *septmb3*] interlined above.
(4) *to . . . winchester*] squeezed in after the deletion, and partly interlined.

	Lent vnto the company the 31 of septmbȝ 1598 to by A Boocke of m[r] chapman called the ffounte of new facianes pd in pte	iij[li]
	Bowght of m[r] Jewbey the 28 of septmbȝ 1598 A blacke velluet gercken & a payer of harcoler clothe of sylver hoosse for	iiij[li]
	Bowght for the company the 1 of octobȝ 1598 A whitte saten womanes dublett & A blacke tynsell valle for	xx[s]
	Lent vnto the company the 3 of octobȝ 1598 to by A boocke of m[r] Ranckenes called mvl mvtius donwallow the some of.	iij[li]
	Lay[d]*te*(1) *vnto* the(2) company the 4 of octobȝ 1598 to by a Riche clocke of m[r] langley w[ch] they had at ther a grement the some of	xix[li]
li s d 152 - 14 - 00	Lent vnto Thomas dowton to feache ij clockes owt of pane the 2 of novembȝ 1597 [to feche ij] the some of xij[li] xs the one clocke was & ashecolerd velluet embradered wth gowld the other a longe black velluet clock*e* layd wth sylke lace w[ch] they *e*xsepted into the stocke th*e* 28 of septmbȝ 1598 some	xij[li] *x*[s]
	Lent vnto thomas dowton the 8 of octobȝ 1598 to bye divers thinges for the playe called the firste sevelle warres of france the some of	vj[li]

[51]

Lent vnto Thomas dowton the 11 of octobȝ 1598 to bye diuers thinges for the play called the first syvell wares of france the some of	iiij[li]
Lent vnto th*e* companey the 12 of octobȝ 1598 to paye vnto m[r] chapmane in fulle payment for his playe called th*e* fowntayne of new faciones .	xx[s](3)

(1) *Lay[d]te*] *Layde* incompletely altered to *Lente*. (2) *vnto the*] *vnto to* Greg.
(3) *xx[s]*] *xx* Greg.

Lent vnto the company the 12 of octob3 1598 to geve harey cheattell in pte of payment for for his playe called Brutte some of } x^s

payd for the company the 12 of octob3 1598 vnto the lace man for the playe of perce of winchester the some of . . . . } v^li ij s

[L]payd(1) vnto m^r drayton & m^r dickers the 16 of octob3 1598 in pt of payment for A boocke called [the] connan prince of cornwellthe(2) some of Bradeshaw(3) . } xxx^s

pd vnto Bradshaw at the Requeste of m^r drayton & m^r dickers in pte of payment of ther Boocke called the connan prince of(4) cornwellsome(2) of . . . } x^s

Layde owt for the company the 18 of octob3 1598 for A boocke called Brutte the some of . . to harey chettell(5) . . . . . . } iij^li

Layd owt for the companey the 20 of octob3 1598 vnto m^r drayton & m^r dickers for A Boocke called connan prince of Cornwell the some of . . . . } iiij^li

Lent vnto the company the 22 of octob3 1598 to . . . . paye harey cheattell for his boocke called Brute in fulle payment the some of . . . . } ls

[51 v] **20048**

Lent vnto Robart shawe & Jewbey the 23 of octob3 1598 to lend vnto m^r Chapmane one his playe boocke & ij ectes of A tragedie of bengemens plotte the some of . . . . } iij^li

lent h Cett^s(6) v^s & ij^s & ij^s & v^s ij d & ij s vj^d for to areste one wth lord lester

Layd owt for the company the 3 of novmb3 1598 to m^r drayton & m^r dickers for A Boocke called the second pte of the syvell wares of france the some of . . . . } vj^li

---

(1) [*L*]*payd*] *p* altered from *L*.

(2) Henslowe left too little space for the title, added later; it runs into and partly over the words *the* and *some*.

(3) *Bradeshaw*] interlined.

(4) *of*] interlined.

(5) *to . . . chettell*] interlined.

(6) *Cett^s*] *Cett* Greg.

lent h Cet – js 8^d^ Lent vnto Jube & Thomas dowton the 8 of novmbȝ 1598 to bye dyvers thinges for the playe called the fownte of new faciones some } v^li^

Lent vnto thomas dowton the 10 of novmbȝ 1598 to bye a sackebute of marke antoney for . . . . } xxxx^s^

Lent vnto Robart shawe the 13 of novembȝ 1598 to bye wemenes gownd & other thinges for the fowntayne of newe faciones the some of } vij^[s]li^ (1)

lent vnto thomas dowton the 14 of novmbȝ 1598 to bye dyvers thinges for the playe called the fowntayne of newe faciones the some of } v^li^

[Lent vnto Robart shawe & Thomas dowton the 15 of novmbȝ 1598 to lend to m^r^ haslett the some of xx^s^ wch w^m^ whitte hathe geuen his word for yt . . . . } xx^s^ (2)]

[Lent vnto Robart shawe & Thomas dowton the 16 of novmbȝ 1598 to lend to m^r^ haslette A gaynest his valtinge (3) wch w^m^ whitte hathe geuen his word for yt the some of . . . . . } xx^s^]

James cranwigge the 4 of novembȝ 1598 playd his callenge in my howsse & I sholde haue hade for my pte xxxxs wch the company hath Rd (4) & oweth yt to me . . . . } xxxx^s^

[52]

Lent vnto Robarte shawe the 18 of novmbȝ 1598 to lend vnto m^r^ dickers in earneste of A boocke called the 3 pte of the syvell wares of france some } xx^s^

Lent vnto Robarte shawe the 18 of novmbȝ 1598 to lend vnto m^r^ Cheattell vpon the mendynge of the firste pt of Robart hoode the some of . . } x^s^

Lent vnto Robart shaw & Jewbey the 19 of novmbȝ 1598 to bye diuers thinges for the playe called the 2 pt of the syvelle wares of france } x^li^

---

(1) *vij[s]li*] *li* altered from *s*.

(2) *xx^s^*] *xx* Greg.

(3) *valtinge*] *vattinge* Greg.

(4) *Rd*] the second letter retraced.

li s d		
[080 – 12 – 00][(1)]	Lent vnto Jewby the 24 of novembz 1598 to bye divers thinges for the playe [of the] called the 2 pte of the syvell wares of france the some of	x[li]
	Lent vnto harey Chettell at the Requeste of Robart shawe the 25 of novembz 1598 in earneste of his comodey called tys no deseayt to deseue the deseuer for[(2)] mendinge of Roben hood. for the corte[(2)]	x[s]
	Lent vnto Robart shawe the 27 of novembz 1598 to bye a [*se*] dublett & A payer of hosse of clothe of gowld layd thick wth blacke sylk lace some of	lviij s
	ssowld vnto the company the 28 of novembz 1598 A shorte velluett clocke wraght wth bugell & A gearcken of velluet layd wth brade cop sylver lace for	iiij[li]
	lent vnto the company the 28 of novembz 1598 to geue harey cheattell in earneste of hes boocke called tis no desayt to deseaue the deseuer the some	xx[s]
	Lent vnto Robart shawe the j of novembz 1598 to lend vnto m[r] chapman the some of. . . .	x[s]

li s d
Some – 88 – 10 – 00 –

[52v] 20047

Lent vnto Robarte shawe the 6 of desembz 1598 to bye A Boocke called ware wth owt blowes & love wth owt sewte of Thomas hawodes some of	iij[li]
Dd vnto same Rowley the 12 of desembz 1598 to bye divers thinges for to macke cottes for gyantes in brvtte the some of	xxiiij[s]
Lent vnto Richard Jonnes the 22 of desembz 1598 to bye a basse viall & other enstrementes for the companey	xxxx[s]
Lent vnto thomas dowton the 22 of desembz 1598 to bye A boocke of harey poorter called the 2 pte of the 2 angrey wemen of abengton . . .	v[li]

(1) *12 – 00*] *12 – 0* Greg.

(2) *for...corte*] interlined.

Pd vnto m^r drayton & m^r dickers the 30 of desemb3 1598 for A Boocke called the 3 p̱te of the syvell wares of france the some of . . . . } v^li

Lent vnto m^r chapman the 4 of Jeneway 1598 vpon iij ackes of A tragedie wch thomas dowton bad me dd hime the some of . . . } iij^li
called

Lent vnto Robarte Shawe the 8 of Janewary 1598 to paye m^r chapman in fulle payment for his tragedie the some of . . . . . . } iij^li
called

Lent vnto Thomas downton the xvij of Janewary 1598 to lend vnto harey chettell to [s] paye his charges in the marshallsey the some of. . . . . } xxx^s

Lent vnto thomas downton the 20 of Janewary 1598 to lend vnto m^r drayton in earneste of his [l]playe(1) called w^m longserd(2) the some of. } xxxx^s

Lent vnto w^m Jube the 20 of Janewary 1598 to lend m^r dickers in earneste of his playe called the firste Intreducyon of the syvell wares of france the some of . . . . } iij^li .

[53]

pd vnto my sonne Edward alleyn the 21 of Janeway for the playe of vayvod for the company the some of xxxx^s I saye pd . . . . 1598(3). . . } xxxx^s

Lent vnto thomas downton the 22 of Janewary 1598 to Leand vnto m^r Chapman in earneste of A Boocke called the world Rones A whelles the some of . . . . } iij^li

li s d
[42 – 12 – 00](4)

(1) [*l*]*playe*] *p* altered from *l*.

(2) *longserd*] *longberd* Greg; *s* is blotted, and the smudge may conceal another letter (? *w*, cf. f. 31). Greg thought *s* was altered to *b*, a possible reading.

(3) *1598*] interlined.

(4) The marginal entry is difficult to read; the shillings may be *12* or *10*.

Lent vnto Robart shawe the 26 of Janewary 1598
to paye Thomas hawode in full payment for his
boocke called ware wth owt blowes & loue wthowt
stryfe the some of . . . . } xxxx^{s}

Lent vnto Thomas downton the 26 of Janewary 1598
to bye the skyrtes of A womones gowne of sylver
chamlett the some of . . . . } lv^{s}

Lent vnto Thomas downton the 30 of Janewary 1598
to descarge Thomas dickers frome the a reaste of
my lord chamberlenes men I saye lent. . . . . . . } iij^{li} xs

Lent vnto Thomas dowton the 31 of Janewary 1598
to bye tafetie for ij womones gownes for the ij
angrey wemen of abengton the some of. . . . . } ix^{li}

Layd owt for the company the 1 of febreyare 1598
to bye A blacke velluet gercken layd thicke wth black
sylke lace & A payer of Rownd hosse of paynes of sylke
layd wth sylver lace & caneyanes of clothe of sylver at
the Requeste of Robart shawe the some of. . . . . . } iiij^{li} x^{s}

Lent vnto harey porter the 17 of Janewary 1598
at the Request of Richard alleyn & w^{m} Birde the
some of. . . . . } xx^{s}

[53v] **20046**

Lent vnto Thomas dowton the 10 of febreary
1598 to bye A boocke of m^{r} hewode called Jonne[1]
(as good as my ladey) the some of . . . . } iij^{li}

Lent vnto Thomas dowton & samwell Redly[2] the
10 of febreary 1598 to bye A boocke called fryer fox
& gyllen of branforde the some of . . . . } v^{li} x^{s}

Lent vnto Thomas downton the 12 of febreary
1598 to paye m^{r} hawode in full payment
for his boock called Jonne as good as my
Ladey the some of . . . . } ij^{li}

(1) *Jonne*] Henslowe left too little space for the title, added later, and all of it except this word had to go in the margin.
(2) *Redly*] *sic* (=Rowley).

Lent vnto Thomas downton the 12 of feberye 1598 to pay m^r^ poorter in fulle payment for his boock called th*e* 2 p̱te of th*e* angrey wemen of abington th*e* some of . . . . . } ij^li^

Lent vnto Thomas downton th*e* 12 of febreary 1598 to by divers thinges for th*e* play*e* called th*e* 2 p̱te of th*e* angrey wemen of abington. . } ij^li^

Lent vnto m^r^ Chapman the 13 of febre*ary* 1598 in p̱t of payment of his boocke called the world Ronnes A whelles . . . . . . } xx^s^

li s d
[*039*[1]– 00] – 00 Lent vnto samvell Rowley the 16 of febre*ary* 1598 to lend in p̱te of payment vnto hary*e* chettell vpon his boock*e* of polefemos. . . } xx^s^

Lent vnto Thomas downton the 27 of febreary 1598 to paye vnto harey cheattell in fulle payment for a playe called Troyes Revenge wth th*e* tragedy of polefeme the some of fyftye shellenges & strocken of his deatte wch he owes vnto the company fyftye shelenges more . . } ls

[54]

Lent vnto harey porter at the Requeste of th*e* company in earneste of his boocke called ij mery wemen of abenton[2] the some of fortyshellengs & for the Resayte of that money he gaue me his faythfulle promysse that I shold haue alle the boockes wch he writte ether him sellfe or wth any other wch some was dd [vpon] the 28 of febre*ary* 1598 I saye thomas downton Robart shawe[3] } xxxx^s^

Lent vnto Thomas downton the t 8 of march*e* 1598 to paye vnto th*e* m^r^ of the Reuelles for th*e* lysencenge of ij playes the some. . . . . } xiiij^s^

---

(1) *039*] Greg thought *39* was altered from *58*, as is possible.
(2) *of abenton*] interlined above. (3) *thomas...shawe*] interlined.

Lent vnto harey cheattell the 4 of marche
1598 in earneste of his boocke wch harey porter } xs
& he is a writtinge the some of. . . . . . .
called the spencers

pd vnto the mr of the Revelles the 18 of marche
1598 for the lysensynge of ij boockes some of } xiiijs

pd vnto the mr of the Reueulles(1) man for the
lysansynge of A boocke called the 4 kynges . } vijs

Lent vnto Robarte Shawe the 22 of marche 1598
to paye vnto mr porter in full paymente of his play } ⟨. .⟩(2) vli xs
called the spencers the some of . . . .

pd vnto the mr of the Revelles man for the lycensynge
of A boocke called brute grenshillde(3) the some of . } vijs

		li	s	d
lent hary chettell the 27 of march 1598 the some of . . . vs	Some –	84 –	16 –	00

[54v] 20045

Lent vnto Jewbe the 31 of marche 1598
to bye divers thinges for elexander & lode } vli
wicke the some of . . . .

Lent vnto harey porter at the apoynt
ment of Thomas downton the 7 of aprell } xxs
1599 the some of. . . . .

aprell 7 daye 1599 Lent vnto Thomas downton to lende
vnto mr dickers & harey cheattell in
earneste of ther boocke called Troyeles & } iijli
creasse daye the some of. . . . .

Aprell 7 daye 1599 Lent vnto Thomas Towne & Richard
alleyn to go to the corte vpon ester euen } xs
the some of . . . .

(1) *Reueulles*] *sic.*
(2) ⟨. .⟩] one or two figures or letters deleted and illegible.
(3) *grenshillde*] *grenshallde* Greg; Henslowe began to write *o* or *a*, but completed it as *i*.

li s d
som [032[1]-00-00] Lent vnto Thomas downton the 9 of Ap^r^ell 1599 to bye dyvers thinges as 4 clathe clockes & macke vp a womones gowne the some of . . . . x^li^
for the spencers

Lent vnto the companye the 11 of ap^r^ell 1599 to bye A frenche hoode the some of } x^s^

Lent vnto Thomas downton the 14 of Ap^r^ell 1599 to [*b*] macke divers thinges for the playe of the spencers the some of . . } xv^li^

Lent vnto harey cheattell & m^r^ dickers in pte of payment of ther boocke called Troyelles & cressed a the 16 of Ap^r^ell 1599 } xx^s^

Lent vnto the company the 17 of ap^r^ell 1599 to lend vnto edwarde my lordes pagge wch was dd vnto Robart shawe the some of . . } xxx^s^

Delyuered vnto Thomas downton boye Thomas parsones to bye dyvers thinges for the playe of the spencers the 16 of ap^r^ell 1599 the some of . . . . } v^li^

[55]

[Itm lent vnto frances the 16 of Jenewarye 159[5]3[2] vpon A peticote of Read wth iij belemen*tes* laces of A womon *d*wellinge in londitche. . . . . } viij s]

[lent vnto frances the 17 of Jeneway 1593 vpon A dublet of fuschen layd wth iiij gowld laces & A payer of hosse stryped downe wth belement lace & A womanes gowne of villet coler cloth layd w^th^ [belement lace wth a *ca*pe of velluet & a peticott*e*] } iij^li^ xs]
[[of durance wth three bellementes laces tied in a napken] & the other thinges tied in buckrome . . . .
[leafte in the Rome of this peticote the sceartes of tufed tafitie of a womones gowe . . . .] } xx^s^]

(1) *032*] *2* not clear, but confirmed, as Greg notes, by the addition.
(2) *159*[*5*]*3*] *3* altered from *5*.

[lent vnto frances th 18 of Jeneware 1593 vpon A myngelldcoler gowne wth a cape of Reased velluet lyned wth blewe bayes & a fresado peticote playne of on goody whitacarse . . . . xxviij s]

[lefe in the Rome of A brad hoope Ring the 18 of . . Jeneware 1593 A smocke wraght & a smocke skearte playne of on m^rs^ floode . . . . xij s]

vse to p

[lent vnto frances the 21 of Jeneware 1593 vpon a wenches petticote of cloth dwellinge in gardiners lane & ij diap tabell close tied in a napcken & ij peces of A veluet dublet wth xvij butons of seluer. . . . . . xs]

[lent vnto frances th 21 of Jenewarye 1593 vpon A womons gown of skie coler cloth layd wth lace an ye sleaues of goodman Baggete wth a velluet cape . . xs]

[lent vnto francis the 21 of Jenewarye vpon this Remnante of damaske & xvij y^r^ds & 3 q of belimente lase a cape of tafita a payer of covfes edged wth gowld lace & an edward angell xv^s^]

[55 v] 20041

[lent vnto frances the 21 of Jenewarye 1593 vpon A gowne of catren tenches fered wth foxe fore & A stamell peticote for . . . . xxvj s]

[lent vnto frances th 21 of Jenewarye 1593 vpon A gowne of Briget appelltres of shepes Rossete donne wth lace an the sleaues wth a cape of velluet & A peticote of cloth layd wth lace . . . . xx^s^]

[lent vnto frances the 23 of Jeneware 1593 vpon iij y^r^des of whitte saten . . . . xx^s^]

[lent vnto frances the 8 of februarey 1593 vpon A sylver goblett persell geallte . . . . xxxx^s^]

[lent vnto frances the 5 of marche 1593 vpon a casse of saten lynned wth tafitie . . . . xx^s^]

[lent vnto frances the 5 of marche 1593 vpon A payer of sylke stockenes a lyght murey coler worne of w^m^ covnde . . . . xvj s]
leafte in the

the vse pd vnto

[the 16 of desemb3 lent vnto frances 10 of marche 1593 vpon A dublet cloth of whitte saten of w^m^ harbutes . . . . xx^s^]
1593

[lent vnto frances vpon a payer of mvrey satten hosse cvtt paned & Imbrodered wth gowld of m^r^ Toogood 10 marche 1593 (1) . . . . xxxx^s^]

[lent vnto frances the 10 of marche 1593 vpon A dublett clothe of pech coller satten o w^m^ harbutes . . . . xx^s^]

[56]

[lent vnto frances the 10 of marche 1593 vpon too seluer spones on gyllte & on playne & A gowld Ringe wth this poesey vivet post funera vertus of edwardes hellodes . . . . xx^s^]

[lent vnto frances the 10 of march 1593 vpon A fyne black cloke wth A velluet cape edged wth bindinge . lace & faced wth sylke searge & A gowld wth owt a posey xx s]

[lent the 10 daye march 1593 vpon fower gowld Ringes two wth stones & ij playne of a chapmanes . . . . . . xviij s]

[lent the 10 daye of march 1593 vpon fower gowld Ringes two wraght & ij playne of m^r^s Troe . . . . xviij s]

[lent vnto frances the 10 of march 1593 vpon A wraght smock A bodeyes of A smock playne tied in A napkine of m^rs^ floodes . . . . xij s]

[lent vnto frances the 22 of march 1593 [vpon] as foloweth

Itm v elles qter corse holland	vij s vj d
Itm v elles qter halfe of cambricke	xxj s
Itm iiij elles qter of fine holland	iiij s
Itm xj elles scante measur of finer holland	xxxviij s vj d
Itm a lane aperne wraght eaged wth gowlde lace & creamson stringes	xiij s [iiij d]

---

(1) *10 marche 1593*] interlined.

Itm ix elles of cowrse lawne . . . . xviijs
Itm ix elles of corser lawne . . . . x^s
Itm ix elles of finer lawne . . . . xviijs]
Some vjli xs

[1¼ *inches blank*]

[56v] **20040**

[lent vnto frances hensley th*e* 24 of marche 1593 as foloweth

Itm j peece of Covrse lawne . . . . ixs
Itm j peece of calycoe lawne . . . . x^s
Itm v wraghte hanckerchers 3 lane two holland 3 eged
wth gowld ij wth sylke . . . . xs
Itm j black wraght stomycher . . . . ijs
Itm ⟨.⟩j[1] payer of bote hosse toopes wraght wth gowld & sylke leaft[2] in the Rome of j pare A velluet cape[2] } xs
Itm ij payer of white bothosse eged wth gowld frynge. ijs
Itm ij payer of white bothosse eged wth sylver frenge . ijs
[Itm v lawne aperens] . . . . xx[v]^s
leafte in the Rome of thes v lane aperens & this j pece of[3]
[Itm j peace of fynne lawne] . . . . xjs]
[& xxvj lane A payer of sylke stockenes grene & A movse Imbradered[3]
[& j dossen of] Rd xx peeces /// Some – iiij^{li} js
selver botens for
v^s]

[Lent vnto frances hensley th*e* 25 of march 1593 vpon
A womanes gowen of sylke grogren black wth ij gardes
of velluet & A velluet hate wth A smalle band done
wth [*bu*gells] pearlle & gowld [& A peace of lane] for the
Some of [v^{li}] iiij^{li} xs]

[lent vnto frances hensley th*e* 8 of Ap^{r}ell 1593
vpon A longe clocke of woded taney lyned
throwght wth taney bayes & A cape of velluet
of taney w*^{ch}* wase leaf*t* in the Rome of gowne
& A peticot of goody whitackers . . . . . . } xxviij^s]

---

(1) ⟨.⟩ *j*] A blot probably conceals *i*. (2) *leaft*. . .*cape*] interlined.
(3) These lines are interlined.

[Leant vpon A payer of blacke stockenes sylke woren & A geardell & A payer of hangers Im bradered wth gowld wch wase browght in the Rome of A payer of sylk stockenes the 8 of Ap^r^ell 1593 } xvj s]

[leant vnto frances the 8 of Ap^r^ell 1593 vpon A black cloke wth hangen sleaues & layd thicke wth lace . . . . } xx^s^]

[57]

[lent vnto frances the 9 of Ap^r^ell 1593 vpon Animbrodered payer of hosse of mvrey saten wth gowld for . . . . } xxx^s^]

[lent vnto frances the 9 of Ap^r^ell 1593 vpon A stamell peticote wth iij laces of A chapmanes wiffes for . . . } xs]

[lent vnto frances the 9 of Ap^r^ell 1593 vpon A payer of sylke stockens of sewater grene for . . . . } xij s]

to paye leaft in the Rome of A stamell peticote of goody [whitacakers iij gowld Ringes smalle tide to geather wch peaticot came the 5 of Jenewary 1593 . . . . } xs]

[Leant vnto frances hensley 1593 vpon A saten dvblette of m^r^ Counde the some of . . . . . wch came the 9 of Ap^r^ell . . . . } xv^s^]

[lent vnto frances the 8 of Ap^r^ell 1593 vpon A sho^r^te cloke wth a hood of the old fashen wth ij gardes of velluet Rownd A bowte for . . . . } xxv^s^]

[lent vnto frances the 9 of Ap^r^ell 1593 vpon A Reamnant of Brod cloth wch the Quene gaue A mandey thursday to A poor womon dwellnge in theveng lane for . . . . . } x^s^]

[lent vnto frances the 5 of march 1593 vpon ij hoope Ringes one of them his wiffes wch lysse in the Rome of A casse of saten lyned throwgh wth tafitie . . . . } xx^s^]

[lent vnto frances the 21 of marche 1593 vpon A womones gowne of blacke bumbassey wth A cape of velluet wch lysse in the Rome of A gown & A pettecotte of A maydes in the olld palles } xij^s^]

[lent vnto frances the 5 of marche 1593 vpon A bufen gowne wth A cape of velluet & A petticotte of brode cloth w*th* iij laces of th*e* buchers wiffe in greenes Alley in th*e* Rome of ij hoope Ringes for . . . . . . xx^s^]

[Lent vnto frances th*e* 8 of febrearye 1593 vpon A clothe petticotte of goodey whittcakers[(1)] for. . . x^s^]

[Lent vnto frances th*e* 8 of febrearye 1593 vpon A sewater grene gowne & a clothe petticote wth iij statutes laces & dewrance bodeyes of of Jane clarkes the some of . . . . xxx^s^]

[Lent vnto frances the 5 of marche 1593 vpon A Remnante of blacke satten wch lysse in th*e* Rome of of A gowne & a peticotte of a buchers wiffes in gardenares alley xx^s^]

[Lent vnto francs th*e* 9 of Ap^r^ell 1593 vpon A sade grene cloke of goodwiffe allen w*ch* lysse in the Rome of A Remnant of cloth*e* brode wch the Quene gaue on manday thursday to a poore womon dwellinge in theven lan x^s^]

Lent vnto frances the 4 of maye 1593 vpon [& *c*resse] [*co*averlet & ij Rownde hoopes Ringes of gowld] for . [xx]x^s d(2)^
leaft in th*e* Rome of one of this hoope Ringes ij smalle hoopes Ringes of gowld j playne & j wraghte . . .

[lent vnto frances th*e* 22 of maye 1593 vpon A wom*o*nes gowne of freneshe Rossette playne wth A cape of vell*u*et of good wiffe Browne for. . . . . xij s]

[lent vnto frances th*e* 9 of maye 1593 vpon A taney colerd clothe gowne wth A fugered satten cape playne of[(3)] goodwife harysones[(3)] . . . x^s^]

[lent vnto frances th*e* 9 of maye 1593 vpon A bufen gowne w*th* A velluet cape & velluet winges layde wth sylke lace of goodwife streates . . . . . . xij s]

[1 *inch blank*]

(1) *whittcakers*] *sic.* (2) *x^sd^*] *sic.* (3) *of...harysones*] interlined.

[58]

[lent vnto frances the 2 of June 1593 vpon iiij peces of A wraghte wascotte of m^{rs} northes } xs]

[lent vnto franc*es* the 2 of June 1593 vpon A peace of tafetie for A naperen of m^{rs} fflude . . . . . . } v^{s}]

[lent vnto frances th*e* 2 of June 1593 vpon A ij peces *o*f drane worke j Imbosed wth gowld & j wth owt . . . . of goody Browne . . . . . } v^{s}]

[lent vnto frances the 2 of June 1593 vpon A lockinge glasse & iiij dieper napkines & j face cloth of cambricke & j bande of la*n*ne of m^{rs} ffloodes for . . . . } xiij s]

[lent vnto frances th*e* 2 of June 1593 vpon A fanne wth A sylver handell of m^{rs} wayght. . . . . . . } viij s vj d]

[lent vnto frances the 2 of June 1593 vpon A payer of tufed tafetie breaches for . . . . } viij s]

[lent vnto frances hensley the v of June 1593 vpon A shorte cloke of sylke grogeren lyned throwghe wth velluet for . . } x^{s}]

[lent vnto frances the v of June 1593 vpon a womones gowne of bufen wth a cape of velluet & layd wth a smalle bugell lace & lyned wth taney bayes of m^{rs} palle . . . . } xs]

[lent vnto frances th*e* v of June 1593 vpon A wascotte of fyne holand wraght wth blacke worke of A buchers wrapped in a cloth . . . . } xs]

[lent vnto frances the v of June 1593 vpon A pettecotte clothe of brod cloth of stamell at . . . . } x^{s}]

[lent vnto frances th*e* v of June 1593 vpon A sade coler cloke short*e* wth sleves & playne wth a cape vnder neth of othr coler for cloth[1] . . . . } xs]

[lent vnto frances the 16 of June 1593 vpon A payer of flexen sheates & a payer of holond pelobers tied in a napken } xij^{s}]

---

(1) *cloth*] interlined.

[[v] *vse*(1) payd to the 16 [desembʒ 1593 — lent vnto frances the 16 of June 1593 vpon a hare colerd fuschen dublet & hosse lyned wth grene tafetie of w^{m} harbarte . . . . } xix^{s} vjd]

lent vnto frances the 16 of June 1593 vpon a vilote clothe gowne tied & in a chilldes mantell of elyzabeth streate . . . . } xx^{s}]

[lent vnto frances the 16 of June 1593 vpon a changable tafetie gown of goodwife williames . . . . } xx^{s}]

[lent vnto frances the 16 of June 1593 vpon a purpell gowne of m^{r} Johnes layd wth lace . . . . } viij s]

[58v] 20035

[lent vnto frances the 16 of June 1593–vpon a black cloth gowne garded wth velluet of ellen evdell . . . . } viij s]

[lent vnto frances the 16 of June 1593 vpon A black cloth gowne wth velluet cape & velluet winges of goody whittackers . . . . } xs]

[lent vnto frances the 16 of June 1593 vpon a medley colerd – cloth gowne wth a velluet cape pinked of elyzabeth stretes } xs]

[lent vnto frances the 16 of June 1593 vpon iij y^{r}des of blacke cloth tied in a napken of Katrene tenche . . . . } x^{s}]

[lent vnto frances the v of June 1593 vpon A blacke morninge cloke wth owt lynynge playne & the cape of the same cloth. . } x^{s}]

[lent vnto frances the 12 of June vpon A Rusett clothe gowne garded wth velluet wch lyse in the Rome of the sceartes of tufed tafetie wch gowne is m^{r}s Ratlefes. . . } xx^{s}]

[lent vnto frances the 16 of June 1593 vpon a Rownd hoope Ringe of gowld wch lyse in the Rome of a gowne of m^{r}s Joanes for . . . . } viij^{s}]

[lent vnto frances the 16 of June 1593 vpon A blacke bufen gowne of amayde in chanell Rowe wth a velluet cape for. . . . . } x^{s}]

[lent vnto frances the 29 of June 1593 vpon a payer of syle stockinges & a mvffe Imbradered for . . .] } xxxj s]

(1) [*v*] *vse*] the first *v* is blotted, and Henslowe began the word again.

[lent vnto frances the 29 of June 1593 vpon a velluet cape for . . . . } xs]

[lent vnto frances the 29 of June 1593 vpon xxvj sylver butens for . . . . } v^s]

[lent vnto frances the 29 of June 1593 vpon A fyne black cloth gowe wth a velluet cape & bownd wth bugell lace & tufed lace bellett wise on the sleues of m^rs fludes for . . . . } xxx^s]

[1 *inch blank*]

[59]

[lent vnto frances the 9 of maye 1593 vpon A yelowe branched damaske peticote & a forparte of myngeldcoler tafetie wch lyse in the Rome of a bufen gowe of goody streate for . . . . } xiij s]

[lent vnto frances the 9 of July 1593 vpon a clocke of grene bradcloth wth a cape of grene velluet for . . . } xiij s]

[lent vnto frances the 18 of July 1593 vpon A blacke bufen gowne layd wth belement lace of goody streates & also vpon a carpet of the old facien very thicke for . . . . . } xx^s]

[lent vnto frances the 7 of aguste 1593 vpon A hoope Ringe of gowld of his wifes for . . . } x^s]

[lent vnto frances the 7 of aguste 1593 vpon A [gowld Ringe of hande in hande for] . . } vj s]
leafte in the Rome of this Ringe wth hande in hande A hoope Ringe of gowld wth this posey hope helpeth hevenes . . . . }

[lente the 2 of [agus] septmbз 1593 vpon A foreparte of A tufed tafetie ceartell of his owne . . . . } x^s vj d]

[lent vnto frances the 7 of septmbз 1593 vpon A wraght wascotte of blacke sylke & A lane apern wraghte for . . . . } xxx^s]

lent vnto frances the 25 of septmbз 1593 vpon hangenes for a howsse of dornackes for . . . } xxxx^s [lent vnto frances the 11 of s[1] october 1593 vpon a shorte clocke of satten layd wth lace & lyned throwgh wth vell[*e*]uette[2] the some of . . . . . xx^s]

[lent vnto frances the 11 of octob3 1593 vpon A . . . womanes gowne Imbradered wth lace of sylke & gowld } xx^s]

[lent vnt*o* frances th*e* 11 of octob3 1593 vpon A pettie cotte of yelow branched tafetie & th*e* some of . . . } xs]

[lent th*e* 11 of october vpon A foreparte of branched tvfed tafetie for . . . . } xs]

[59 v] 20034

[lent vnto frances th*e* [16]11[3] of octob3 1593 vpon iiij gowld Ringes j pancey j mayes j Ringe wth a whitte ston j hoope Ringe ffor . . . . } xxs]

[lent vnto frances th*e* 11 of octob3 1593 vpon A shorte Clocke of sylke grogeren lyned throwgh wth velluett & layd wth butenes & a payer of branched velluet bre*c*hes for . . . . } xx^s]

[lent vnto frances the 11 of octob3 1593 vpon A shorte Clocke of sylke grogeren lyned throwgh wth velluet & layd wth butenes for . . . . } x^s]

o [lent vnto frances the 16 of June 1593 vpon A black*e* Clock*e* layde wth butenes [*v*]*b*ound[4] be fore & a wealte cape of velluett for . . . . } x^s]

[lent vnto frances th*e* 8 of febreary 1593 vpon A mvry colerd clocke lyned wth sa*r*ge & layd a bowt
o wth iij laces & faced wth pincked tafetie & a cape of velluet for . . . . } xs]

[lent vnto frances the 18 of July 1593 vpon A & owld carpett of turckey worcke very thicke for } x^s]
frome this
time vj d
most homble I[5]

---

(1) *s*] not deleted. (2) *vell*[*e*]*uette*] *u* altered from *e*.
(3) [*16*]*11*] blotted and doubtful; *11* interlined above. (4) [*v*]*bovnd*] *b* altered from *v*.
(5) *moste...I*] written in an Italian hand; a rule across the page below this phrase separates it from the entry of 10 December.

[lent vnto frances the 10 of desembȝ 1593 vpon A footmanes cotte of velluet wth the colysenes vpon them of syluer . . . . xx^s^]

[lent vnto frances the 10 of desembȝ 1593 vpon ij syluer spones j gylte & j playne for . . . . x^s^]

lent vnto ffrances the 10 of desembȝ 1593 vpon a blacke veluet clocke layd wth iij laces Rownd a bowt & lyned throwght wth sylke *sh*age for . ls

[lent vnto frances th*e* 18 of desembȝ 1593 vpon A stamell peticote wth ij beliment laces of good wiffe williames for . . . . viij s]

[60]

[¶ 19 of desembȝ leant vpon a womons gowne of sade colerd cloth
1593 lay*d* wth A veluet cape & a paye*r* of sheates of goodwiffe atkines for . . . . . . xiij s iiij d]

[(1)lent vpon ij hoopes Ringes of gowld one the cookes th*e* j for – xv^s^ the other m^r^s barterman for – v^s^ some is . . . . xx^s^]

[lent vpon a payer of blacke sylke stockenes of the dra*w*eres for . . . . x^s^]

[lent vpon a sea gowne of captaine swanes . . xv^s^]

Dowing you
lent vpon ij   to vnderstanding
By me John willsone Borne   Baylle(2)
Lord god saue o^r^ quene amen

[*irregular piece cut away ranging from 7 to 2 inches in width, from 3 to 7 inches in depth*]

[4 *inches blank*]

---

(1) *lent*. . .] There is a rule across the page between this entry and the one above.

(2) The names are all in Henslowe's hand.

[60 v]

[*blank*]

[*piece cut away as on recto*]

[61]

[¶ 24 of febreary 1593	o(1)	lent vpon A Rede wascotte j payer of wolen stocken*e*s j wraght falynge band j pevtter saltseller & j pewter cvpe of Robarte cadbery dwelinge in sothwarke in the iij cvpes alley for	vj s]
[¶ 18 of maye 1594		lent vnto Hecke vpon apayer of venesyons of velluet & a Doblet of Buffe & a dublet of fuschen & ij payer of venysyon of cloth & a Remnant(2) of grene cloth for	xxxx^s]

Hary cheattell hath strocken of his deate
as foloweth 1598 vnto the companye

pd of his deate in his boocke of polefeme . . . . ls
pd of his deate in his boocke of the spencers . . . . xs(3)

[antony Jeaffes & the company dothe owe
vnto me for my boye Jeames Bristo wages
from the 23 of Ap^r ell 1600 wch Robart shawe
hath geuen his word for th*e* paymente]
wittnes Richard Jonnes
Thomas Towne

[3½ *inches blank*]

[61 v] **20032**

Troyel*e*s & creasseday(4)

Receved(5) by mee thomas bris*e* scietisen & vphoulder the xxix of Jan*u*arie 1594 in fulpemente of richarde vickers the some of iiij^li xs I say receved be mee thomas bris*e*(5)	iiij^li x^s

(1) Not recorded by Greg. (2) *Remnant*] *Remment* Greg.

(3) Below this line is a modern forgery which reads:

pd of his deate in his boocke of plasidas . . xs.

(4) Probably not in Henslowe's hand (so Greg).

(5) *Receved...brise*] in Brise's hand; Greg has *bristo* for *brise*.

Lent vnto John haslette va*l*ter[1] the 27 of march*e* 1598 in Redy mony th*e* so*m*e of tenneshillinges I saye . . . . } xs

wittnes pigge
& Jemes

Lent John haslett to bye a gearte for his horsse when he t*o*mbled . . . . } *v*j d

Lent vnto John haslette valter th*e* 7 of Ap^r^ell 1599 th*e* some of . . . . . . } x^s^

wittnes EAlleyn[2]

[3¾ *inches blank*]

[62]

Beit[3] knowen to all men b*y* these presents that I henry Chettle of London Stationer doo ow vnto Philip Hinshow[4] of the parish of St Sauiours the sume of ix^li^ ix^s^. on this 22th of october 1598. In witnes whereof I haue here vnder sent[5] my hand. henry chettle ./[3]

Wytnesse Robt Shaa[6]

Borrowed[7] of phillip Henchlowe xxs the vij^th^ of Aprill ann*o* d*om* 1599

HenryPorter[7]

[1 *inch blank*]

Lent Thomas dickers & harey chettell the 2 of maye 1599 to descarge harey chettell of his A Reste frome Ingrome the some of twentyshellyngs in Redy money I saye lent . . . . } xx^s^

Lent more th*e* same time vnto m^r^ dickers in earnest of A Boock*e* called or*e*stes f[u]vres[8] . . . v^s^

---

(1) *valter*] interlined above.

(2) Below this line is a modern forgery which reads:

Lent vnto cheattell for Sir plasidas the 9 of Ap^r^ell 1599 the some of . . . } *x^s^*

Cf. the similar forgery, f. 61, n. 3, opposite.

(3) *Beit . . . chettle ./*] in Chettle's hand.

(4) *Hinshow*] *sic*; *Hinslow* Greg.

(5) *sent*] *sic*.

(6) Autograph signature.

(7) *Borrowed . . . Porter*] in Porter's hand.

(8) *f*[*u*]*vres*] *v* altered from *u*.

Lente vnto frances Henslow the 15 of desembȝ 1597 when he went to tacke his howsse one the bancksyd called the vper gro*vne*[1] the some of vj^{li} I saye Leant . . . . } vj^{li}

[2 *inches blank*]

[62 v] **20031**

[Heare I begane to Receue the gallereys agayne wch theye Receu*e*d begynynge at myhellmas wecke beinge th*e* 6 of octobȝ 1599 as foloweth

[Rd the 6 of of octobȝ 1599] . . . . [v^{li} iij^{s}]
Rd th*e* 20 of octobȝ 1599 . . . . iiij^{li} iij$^{[d]s}$[2]
Rd th*e* 27 of octobȝ 1599 . . . . iij^{li} xiiij s
Rd th*e* 3 of novmbȝ 1599 . . . . viij^{li} xvj s
Rd th*e* 10 of novmbȝ 1599 . . . . vj^{li} ix^{s}
Rd the 18 of novmbȝ 1599 . . . . ij^{li} xvij s
Rd the 25 of novmbȝ 1599 . . . . vij^{li} iiij s
Rd th*e* 1 of desembȝ 1599 . . . . v^{li} xiij s
Rd th*e* 8 of desembȝ 1599 . . . . iiij^{li}
li s d Rd th*e* 16 of desembȝ 1599 . . . . ij^{li} xvij s
[59 - 14 - 00] Rd th*e* 23 of desembȝ 1599 . . . . iij^{li} iij s
Rd the 30 of desembȝ 1599 . . . . x^{li} viij^{s}
Rd the 6 of Janewary 1599 . . . . ixli ixs
Rd the 13 of Janew*a*ry 1599 . . . . vj^{li} x[iij] vj s[3]
Rd the 20 of Janewary 1599 . . . . iij^{li} ij^{s}
li s d Rd the 27 of Janeway 1599 . . . . j^{li} xvj s
[0*8*8 - 01 - 00] Rd the 3 of febrea*r*y 1599 . . . . vij^{li} xiiij s
Rd th 10 of febreary 1599 . . . . vij^{li} xiij s
Rd th*e* 9 of march 1599 . . . . iij^{li} xiij s
li s d Rd the 16 of march 1599 . . . . vj li
[110 - 04 - 00] Rd the 23 of march 1599 . . . . iiij^{li} xvij s
Rd the 30 of march 1599 . . . . xj^{li} xiiij s
Rd th*e* *6* of Aprell 1600 . . . . vj^{li} ij s
Rd the 14 of ap^{r}ell 1600 . . . . v^{li} x s
Rd the 21 of ap^{r}ell 1600 . . . . vj^{li} xiiij s
Rd th*e* 29 of ap^{r}ell 1600 . . . . iiij^{li} x s

---

(1) *grovne*] *growne* Greg; a doubtful reading: perhaps = ground (so Collier), but Greg's first suggestion *growue* (= grove) is possible.

(2) *iij*$^{[d]s}$] *s* altered from *d*.

(3) *x*[*iij*]*vj s*] *vj* altered from *iij*.

Rd the 4 of maye 1600 . . . . iiij^{li} vij s
Rd the 11 of maye 1600 . . . . iiij^{li} xv[*ij*] s
Rd th 18 of maye 1600 . . . . xij^{li} iiij s
Rd th 25 of maye 1600 . . . . iiij^{li} vij s
Rd the 1 of June 1600. . . . . iiij^{li} xvij s
Rd the 8 of June 1600. . . . . vj^{li} xj s
Rd th 15 of June 1600 . . . . iij^{li} xiij s
Rd th 22 of June 1600 . . . . vij^{li} ij s
Rd the 1 of Julye 1600 . . . . v^{li} viij s
li
Rd th 6 of Julye 1600 . . . . iiij^{li} xij s
[〈..〉[1] – 02 – 00] Rd the 13 of July 1600 . . . . . li s d . . iiij^{li} x*j*j s[2]

207[3] – 02 – 00]

[63]

39 Layde owt for the company of m^{r} lord of
[notingame men frome the 26 of maye 1599
as ffoloweth 1599

pd vnto the lace man at the apoyntment of the company the 26 of maye 1599 in pte of payment to hime for lace the some of. . } v^{li}

Lent vnto m^{r} dickers & m^{r} chettell the 26 of maye 1599 in earneste of A Boocke called [troylles & creseda] the[4] tragede of Agamemnon[5] the some of . } xxx^{s}

Lent vnto Robart shawe the 30 of maye 1599 in fulle payment of ther Boocke called the tragedie of Agamemnone the some of . } iij^{li} v^{s}
to m^{r} dickers & hary chettell

pd vnto the m^{r} of Revelles man for lycensynge of A Boocke called the tragedie of agamemnon the 3 of [m]June[6] 1599. . . . . } vij s

pd vnto the lace man the 2 of June 1599 in pte of paymente to hime for cope lace the some of . . . . } v^{li}

---

(1) 〈..〉] figures illegible; perhaps *55* or *65*.
(2) *xjj s*] Henslowe wrote *xj*, and altered to *xjj*.
(3) *207*] *7* blotted, and altered from another figure (so Greg).
(4) *the*] interlined with caret.
(5) *of Agamemnon*] interlined above.
(6) [*m*]*June*] *J* altered from *m*.

Lent vnto Robarte shawe th*e* 2 of June 1599 }
to paye vnto m^r chapman for his Bo*o*cke } xx^s
called the worlde Runes a whelles some of }

pd vnto th*e* lace man the 8 of June 1599 }
at the ap*o*yntment of the company in p*t* } v^{li}
of payme*nt* to hime for cope lac*e* some of }

	li	s	d		li	s	d
ttottales –	[586(1) –	1[7]2(2) –	7]	some	21 –	02 –	00
Reste dewe –	[262 –	12 –	7]				

Lent vnto w^m Borne & Jewbey the 21 of }
June 1599 to lend vnto m^r chapman }
vpon his Boock called th*e* world Ronnes } xxxx^s
a whelles the some of . . . . }

Lent vnto thomas dowton th*e* 2 of July 1599 }
to paye m^r chapman in full payment for }
his Boock*e* called th*e* world Rones a whell*es* } xxx^s]
& now all foolles but the foolle some of }

[63 v] 20030

[Lent thomas dowton the 5 of Julye 1599 }
to bye cope lace the some of . . . . . } xij^s 4^d

Lent vnto Thomas dowton the 13 }
of July 1599 to bye enstrumentes for } xxx^s
th*e* company the some of . . . . }

Lent vnto Samewell Rowley & Thomas }
downton th*e* 15 of July 1599 t[h]*o*(3) bye A } iij^{li}
Boock*e* of thomas dickers Called the gentle Craft(4) the som of }

Lent vnto Thomas downton th*e* 17 of }
July 1599 [in ear] to lend vnto m^r chapman }
in earneste of A pastrall tragedie th*e* } xxxx^s
some of . . . . }

---

(1) *586*] *386* Greg.
(2) *1*[*7*]*2*] *2* altered from *7*; *17* Greg.
(3) *t*[*h*]*o*] *o* altered from *h*.
(4) *Called...Craft*] interlined above.

pd Lent vnto Thomas deckyers the 24 of July 1599 at the Requeste of Samvell Rowly & Thomas downton in earneste of A Boock*e* called stepmothers tragedy . . } [x[s]]

Lent vnto Robarte shawe th*e* 1 of aguste 1599 to paye m[r] deck*ers* for a boock*e* called [better latte then never] beare a braine(1) the some of xxxx[s] in fulle payme*n*t lent vnto m[r] deckers at that time xx[s] so all is . . . . } iij[li]

Lent vnto w[m] Borne alles birde the 10 of agust*e* 1599 to Lend vnto bengemyne Johnsone & thomas *d*eckers in earneste of ther boocke w[ch] they *be*(2) awritt*e*nge calle*d* pagge of pl*e*m*o*th(3) the some } xxxx[s]

Lent vnto Thomas downton the 20 of aguste 1599 to lend vnto hawghton in earnest*e* of A Boock*e* called th*e* poore manes paradice the some of } xiij[s]]

[1 *inch blank*]

[64]

[Lent vnto harey Chettell & Th[d] the 23 of aguste 1599 in earneste of his playe Called the stepmothers tragedie the some of . . . } xx[s]

Lent vnto Thomas downton th*e* 25 of ag*u*ste 1599 to paye [harey chettell] Thomas hawton(4) for his Boock*e* called the poore manes paradice the s*o*me of } xvij s

Lent vnto w[m] Birde Thomas downton & Jewbey the 25 of agust*e* 1599 to paye harye Chettell for his Boocke called the stepmothers tragedie some } xx[s]

Lent vnto w[m] Birde Thomas dowton w[m] Jube th*e* 2 of Septmb3 1599 to paye in full*e* payme*n*t for A Boock*e* called th*e* lamentable tragedie of pagge of plemoth th*e* some of . . . . . . } vj li

---

(1) *bear a braine*] interlined above. (2) *be*] *are* Greg.

(3) Too little space was left for the title, added later, and *oth* was interlined.

(4) *Thomas hawton*] interlined above.

Lent vnto Thomas downton the 3 of Sep^{tmb3} (1) 1599 to lend vnto Thomas deckers Bengemen Johnson hary Chettell & other Jentellman in earneste of A playe calle Robart the second Kinge of scottes tragedie the some of . . . . xxxx^{s}

Lent vnto Jewbey & thomas towne the 12 of Septmb3 1599 to bye wemen gownes for page of plemoth the some of . . . . x^{li}

Lent vnto Samwell Rowley & Robart shawe the 15 of septmb3 1599 to lend in earneste of A Boocke called the scottes tragedi vnto Thomas dickers & harey chettell the some of . . . . xx^{s}

Lent hary chettell the 16 of septmb3 1599 in earneste of A Boocke called the scottes tragedie the some of . . . . xs]

[64v] 20029

[Lent vnto w^{m} Borne the 27 of Setmb3 1599 to lend vnto Bengemen Johnsone in earneste of A Boocke called the scottes tragedie the some of . . . xx^{s}

Lent vnto w^{m} Borne the 28 of septmb3 1599 to Lent vnto m^{r} maxton the new poete m^{r} mastone (2) in earneste of A Boocke called (3) the some of. . . . . xxxx^{s}

li	s	d		
[so61 –	04 –	04]	Lent vnto the littell tayller the 4 of octob3 1599 to bye diuers for the play of polefeme the some of	viij^{s}
li	s	d		
some 41 –	12 –	04		

the (4) 13th of october 1599
Lent vnto Thomas Do[n]wnton (5) for the Booke of Trystram de lyons (4) . . . . 3^{li}

---

(1) *Sep^{tmb3}*] *tmb3* interlined above.

(2) *m^{r} mastone*] interlined with caret. Greg regards this as a modern forgery; we think it was inserted by Henslowe.

(3) A space was left for the author's name and title of the play, but only the first was filled in.

(4) *the...lyons*] in Downton's hand. (5) *Do[n]wnton*] *w* altered from *n*.

lent h chettell some of – v^s | Reckned wth the company tof(1) my lorde [*of*] the(2) earlle of notingames men to this place & I haue layd owte for them the some of vj hunderd & thirtie two pownds & they haue payd vnto me of this deatte iij hunderd & fiftie & eyghte powndes to this day beinge th*e* 13 of [novmb] octobȝ 1599

Lent h chettell some – v^s

lent h chettell some v^s

lent – iij s
lent – ij s
27[3]4(3) – *oo* – oo]

[2½ *inches blank*]

[65]

[this(4) 14th of October 1599
Receaued by me Robt Shaa of phillip Henslowe to pay H. Chettle [f] in full paiment of a booke Called the stepmothers tragedy for the vs*e* of the Company iiij li I say Receaued(4) . . . } 4^li

this(5) 16^th(6) of october 99
Receued by me Thomas downton of p*h*illipp Henchlow to pay m^r *m*onday m^r drayton & m^r wilsson & haythway for the first pte of the lyfe of Sr Jhon Ouldcasstell & in earnest of the Second pte for the vse of the compayny ten pownd I say receued(5) . . . . } 10^li

Receved(7) by me Samuell Rowlye of phyllyp henchloe for harrye chettell in Earneste of the playe of patient Gryssell for the Vse of the Comepanye(7) . . . . } xx^s

Lent vnto Robarte shaw th*e* 1 of novmbȝ 1599 to lent vnto m^r willsones the some of . . . . } xs

Lent vnto Robart shaw th*e* 1 of novmbȝ 1599 to Lend vnto w^m harton in earneste of A Boocke called th*e* tragedie of John cox some of } xx^s

---

(1) *tof*] *sic.* Henslowe altered *to* to *of*, but did not delete *t*.
(2) [*of*] *the*] alteration.
(3) *27*[*3*]*4*] *4* altered from *3*.
(4) *this*. . .*Receaued*] in Shaa's hand.
(5) *this*. . .*receued*] in Downton's hand.
(6) *16*^th] *16* Greg.
(7) *Receved*. . .*Comepanye*] in Rowley's hand.

as A gefte Receved(1) of M[r] hincheloe for M[r] Mundaye & the Reste of the poets at the playnge of S[r] John oldcastell the ferste tyme(1) . . . . . . } x[s]

Receaued(2) of m[r] Ph: Hinchlow by a note vnder the hand of m[r] Rob: Shaw in full payment for the second pt of Henrye Richmond sold to him & his Companye the some of eight pownde Current moneye the viij[t] daye of November 1599 . . . . . } viij[li]

By me RWilson(2)

li s d
some 25 – 00 – 00]

[65 v] 20028

[Lent vnto w[m] harton & John daye at . . . the Apoyntment of Thomas dowton in earnest of A Boocke called the tragedie of cox of collinste[r] the some of . . . . } xx[s]

the(3) ix[th](4) of november
Receued of phillipp Hinchlow to pay Thomas Deckker in earnest of abooke cald the hole hystory of ffortunatus xxxx[s] by me Thomas downton(3) . . } xxxx[s]

Lent vnto Thomas dowton the 10 of novmb3 1599 to lend vnto harey chettell in earneste of his boocke called(5) the some of tenne shellenge I saye . . } x[s]

the(6) xiiij[th] of nouember 1599
Receued of M[r] phillipp Hinchlow to pay to william hauton & Jhon day for the tragedy of Cox of Collomton the som of three pownd receued(6) in full(7) . . . . } iij[li]]

(1) *Receved...tyme*] in Rowley's hand, except for the side-note, added by Henslowe.
(2) *Receaued...Wilson*] in Wilson's hand.
(3) *the...downton*] in Downton's hand.
(4) *ix[th]*] *ix* Greg.
(5) Play-title not entered.
(6) *the...receued*] in Downton's hand.
(7) *in full*] interlined below.

Lent vnto w^m Harton the 21 of novmb3 in earneste of her(1) boocke called merie(2) the some of . . . . x^s

Lent vnto Thomas dickers th*e* 24 of. . . . novmb3 1599 in earneste of his Boock*e* called the wholl*e* history of fortewnatus the some of wittnes John: Shaa.(3) iij^li

Lent vnto w^m harton & John day*e* th*e* 27 of novmb3 1599 in earneste of A tragedie called mereie the some of . . . as may a pere(4) . . . xx^s

Lent vnto harey chettell the 27 of novmb3 1599 in earnest of A Boock*e* called th*e* tragedie of orphenes(5) the some of . . . x^s
as maye a pere li s d

some – 11 – 10 – 00

[66]

[Receaued(6) of Mr Henshlowe this xxx^th of novemb^r 1599 to pay M^r deckers in full payment of his booke of fortunatu*s* xx^s
By me Robt Shaa(6)

Receaed(7) of m^r Henshlow this xxxi^th of novem 1599 ffor the vse of the Com ten pownd ffor wemenes gowns(8) . . x^li
By me Thomas Downton(7)

Lent vnto Thomas dickers. at the A poynt ment of Robart shawe th*e* 31 of novmb3 1599 wch I borowed of m^r greffen for th*e* altrenge of th*e* boock*e* of th*e* wholl history of fortewnatus th*e* some of xx^s

---

(1) *her*] i.e. their, cf. f. 3v (note 1, p. 9).
(2) Too much space was left for the title, added later.
(3) Autograph signature.
(4) *as may a pere*] interlined below.
(5) *orphenes*] i.e. orphan's; cf. f. 29, l. 6.
(6) *Receaued...Shaa*] in Shaa's hand.
(7) *Receaed...Downton*] in Downton's hand.
(8) *ffor...gowns*] interlined.

Lent vnto w^m^ hawton & John day the 5 of desemb3 1599 in earneste of ther boocke called mereye at the a poyntment of Robart shawe the some of . . . . xx^s^
as may a pere

Lent vnto John daye the 6 of desemb3 1599 in earneste [called] of A Boocke called merye [the] as maye a pere . . . . . . x^s^

pd vnto w^m^ hawgton & John daye the 6 of desemb3 1599 in full payment of ther boocke called the tragedie of merie the some of xxxx^s^

Receued(1) of Mr Hinchlow for the vse of the Company x^li^ ffor to by thinges for ffortunatus . . . . .x^li^

By me Thomas Downton(1)

li s d
some – 25 – 10 – 00]

[66v] 20027

[pd vnto m^r^ deckers the 12 of desemb3 1599 for the eande of fortewnatus for the corte at the a poyntment of Robarte shawe the some of . . . . . xxxx^s^

Lent vnto harey chettell & w^m^ harton the 13 of desemb3 1599 in earneste of his Boocke called ar[d]keadian(2) virgen the some of. . . . x^s^

Lent vnto hary chettell & w^m^ harton the 17 of desemb3 1599 in earneste of ther boocke called arkedian virgen the some v^s^

Lent vnto thomas dickkers harey chettell w^m^ harton in earneste of A Boocke called patient grissell at the a poyntment of Robart shawe by his letter the some of three pownde the 19 of desemb3 1599 . . . . iij^li^

---

(1) *Receued. . . Downton*] in Downton's hand. (2) *ar[d]keadian*] *k* altered from *d*.

Receaued(1) of m[r] Henshlowe to pay to the(2) taylor xxv[s] & to the m[r] of the Revells man xiiij s for the lycensinge of 2 bookes . . } xxxix[s]
by me RobtShaa(1)

Receued(3) of m[r] Henchlow for the vse of the Company to pay m[r] drayton for the second pte of S[r] Jhon ould Casell foure pownd I say receud . . } iiij[li]
p me Thomas Downton(3)

Receaued(1) of m[r] Henshlowe the 26th of decemb[r] 1599 to pay Tho: Deckers: H. Chettle: & Will: Hawton for pacient Grissill vj[li] I say Receaued . . . . } vj[li]
by me RobtShaa(1)

Lent vnto thomas deckers the 28 of desembȝ 1599 in earneste of a playe called pacyent gresell the some of . . . . } v[s]

li s d
some – 1[6]7(4) – 19 – 00]

[67]

[Lent vnto w[m] harton the 29 of desembȝ 1599 in earnest of patient gresell some of. . . } v[s]

Receaued(5) this ix[th] of January 1599 in behalfe of the Company to pay the laceman v[li] I say Receaued . . . . } v[li]
RobtShaa(5)

li s d
[87 – 4 – o] Lent vnto John daye the 10 of Jenewary 1599 in earnest of his Boocke called the etalyan tragedie of(6) the some of. at the apoyntment of Robart shawe . . } xxxx[s]

Lent vnto mihell drayton antony monday m[r] hathwaye & m[r] willsone at the apoyntment of Thomas downton in earneste of A playe Boocke called owen teder the some of . . } iiij[li]

---

(1) *Receaued...Shaa*] in Shaa's hand.
(2) *pay to the*] *pay the* Greg.
(3) *Receued...Downton*] in Downton's hand.
(4) *1*[*6*]*7*] *7* altered from *6*.
(5) *Receaued...Shaa*] in Shaa's hand.
(6) A space was left, apparently for a name.

pd vnto the m^{r} of the Revelles man for
lycen[c]synge(1) of A Boocke called Beches } vij s
tragedie the some of . . . .

Lent vnto Thomas towne the 18 of Janewary 1599
to lend thomas dickers in earneste of A playe Boocke } xx^{s}
called trewghtę [c]suplication(2) to candelighte some of
as may a pere

Receaued(3) of Mr Henshlowe this 26th of January
1599 xx^{s} to geue vnto the tayler to buy a grey } xx^{s}
gowne for gryssell I say Receaued . . . . . .
by me RobtShaa(3)

pd vnto the Lace man the 28 of Janeway
1599 at the apoyntment of [the] Robart shawe } iij^{li}
& Thomas downton the some of . . . . . .

Lent vnto Thomas dickers at the apoyntment . .
li s d of the company the 30 of Janewary 1599 in erneste
17 - 12 - 00 of A Boocke called trewth suplicaton to candelithe } xx^{s}]
Rd by w^{m} harton for hime . . . .

[67v] 20026

[Lent vnto the company the 6 of febreary 1599
for to by a drome [f]*wh*en(4) to go into the contry } xj^{s} vj d

li s d Receaued(3) of Mr Henshlowe this 7th of february
[099 - 04 - 06] 1599 the some of xxijs to buy 2 trumpettę . . } xxij^{s}
RobtShaa(3)

pd vnto the lace man the 9 of febreary 1599
at the apoyntmen(5) of the company the some of } iij^{li}

Lent vnto the company the 9 of febreary 1599
to paye the cootch man symes the some of. . } iij^{li}

lent(6) vnto me Wbirde the 9 of februarye to paye
for a new booke to will: Boyle.cald Jugurth xxx^{s} } xxx^{s}
w^{c} if yo^{u} dislike Ile repaye it back(6) . . . . .

---

(1) *lycen[c]synge*] *s* altered from *c*.
(2) *[c]suplication*] *s* altered from *c*.
(3) *Receaued...Shaa*] in Shaa's hand.
(4) [*f*]*when*] *wh* altered from *f*.
(5) *apoyntmen*] *sic*; the pen failed to register the final *t*.
(6) *lent...back*] in Bird's hand.

Lent vnto Thomas dowton 10 of febreary 1599 for the company to geue *v*nto father ogell & other thinges . . . . } xs

sence we left play ing — Layd owt for the company the 13 of febrearye 1599 for a boocke called the spaneshe mores tragedie(1) vnto thomas deckers w^m^ harton John daye in pte of payment the some of . . . . } iij^li^

Layd owt for the company the 16 of febreary 1599 in earnest of A Boocke called damon & pethy*as* as maye a peare some is. . . . . } xxs
to hary chettell

Receavd(2) of m^r^ hinchlow the 1 of march to paye to harry chettell Thomas decker william hawton & Jhon daye for a boocke calld the 7 wise m^rs^ the some of . . . . . } xl^s^
Wbirde ·(2)

Lent vnto Samewell Rowly the 8 of marche 1599 to paye vnto harey chettell & John daye in fulle payment for A boocke called the vij wisse masters the some of . . . . } ls]

Samuell Rowlye(3)

	li	s	d
some	18	03	06

[68]

[Lent vnto hary chettell the 2 of march*e* 1599 in earnest of A Boocke called the 7 wisse masters th*e* some of. . . . . } xxxs

Lent vnto w^m^ Birde the 10 of marche 1599 to geue harey chettell in earneste of his Boocke called damon & pethias the some of . . . } xxvjs

Lent vnto Robarte shaw th*e* 10 of march*e* 1599 to Lend w^m^ harton to Releace hime owt of th*e* clyncke th*e* some of. . . . . } xs

(1) Too little space was left for the title, added later, and *tragedie* was interlined with a caret.
(2) *Receavd . . . Wbirde* ·] in Bird's hand. (3) Autograph signature.

Dd vnto the littell tayller at the apoyntment
of Robart shawe the 12 of marche 1599 to macke
thinges for the 2 pte of owld castell some of . . } xxx^{s}

Lent vnto w^{m} harton the 18 of march 1599
in earneste of A Boocke called ferex & porex
the some of . . . . } xx^{s}

[william haughton[1]]

Lent vnto [the c] Robarte shawe the 18 of march
1599 to geue vnto the printer to staye the printinge
of patient gresell the some of. . . . . } xxxx^{s}

by me Robt Shaa[2]

Lent vnto w^{m} harton the 25 of march 1599
in earneste of his Boocke called ferex &
porexe the some of . . . . } v^{s}

Receaued[3] of Mr Henslowe to lay out for the play of
the 7 wise M^{r}s in taffataes & sattyns the some of } xx^{li}
in behalfe of the Company . . . . by me Robt Shaa

Receaued more of m^{r} Henshlowe to lay out
for the play of the 7 wise Maisters in behalfe
of the Company . . . . } x^{li}

Receaued more of Mr Henshlowe [l]to[4] lay out
for the play of the 7 wyse maisters in behalf
of the Company . . . . } viij^{li}

by me Robt Shaa[3]

li s d
some 46 – 01 – 00]

[68 v] 20025

[Lent vnto Robarte shaw the 2 of ap^{r}ell 1600 for
to by a Robe for tyme some of. . . . . . . } xxxx^{s}

li s d
[0[64]76[5]–18–00] Lent w^{m} harton at the apoyntment of Robart shawe
the 3 of march 1600 in earneste of a Boocke called
ferex & porex the some of . . . . } vij^{s}

(1) Haughton's signature is not autograph; forged perhaps by Henslowe, or, Greg thinks, by Shaa.

(2) Autograph signature.

(3) *Receaued...Shaa*] in Shaa's hand.

(4) [*l*]*to*] *t* altered from *l*.

(5) *o*[*64*]*76*] *76* altered from *64*.

Receaued[1] of Mr Henshlowe in behalfe of the Company to pay Will: Haulton in full payment of his play of ferrex & Porrex iij li [vs I] iij s. . . . . } iij li iij s

by me RobtShaa[1]

Receaued of Mr Henshlowe to pay for [.]x li [2] of Copper lace in behalfe of the Company . . . . } xxxx vs [3]

by me RobtShaa

pd vnto the sylke man the 13 of aprell 1600 at the apoyntment of Robart shawe fortie shellings I say lent . . . . } xxxx s

Lent[4] vnto wm harton the 16 of aprell 1600 in earneste of A Boocke called the Ingleshe fegetives the some of . . . . } xs

wt Haughton.[4]

Item receiued more of mr Henchelowe in earnest of ye englishe fugitiues on the 24th of Aprill. by me receiued . . . . . } 20s

wt Haughton

Lent vnto harey chettell the 26 of aprell 16[9]00[5] in pte of payment of A Boocke called damon & pethias at the a poyntment of Robart shawe the some of . . . . } xxx s

henry Chettle[6]./

Lent vnto the company to goo to winswarth to the installinge the 27. of aprell 1600. . . } ls

Receaued[1] of mr Henshlowe in behalfe of the Company to geue Tho: Deckers & Jhon Day in earnest of a booke Called The golden Ass & Cupid & Psiches. . . . } xxx s

by me RobtShaa[1]

[16 - 07 - 00] payd to Harry Chettle in full payment of vj li for his booke of Damon & Pithias xxxxiiij s . . . . } xxxxiiij s

li s d

some 18 - 14 - 00]

---

(1) *Receaued...Shaa*] in Shaa's hand.

(2) [.]*x li*] [*i*]*x li* Greg; no letter is now legible.

(3) *xxxx vs*] *xxx s x s* Greg; *v* is written above the last *x*, and is smudged, perhaps deleted.

(4) *Lent...Haughton.*] in Haughton's hand.

(5) *16*[*9*]*00*] *1*[*59*]*600* Greg; the first *o* altered from *6*, which itself had been altered from *9*.

(6) Autograph signature.

[69]

[Receaued(1) by me Henry Chettle of Mr Henshlowe in earnest of a booke Called the wooinge of deathe(1) } xxs
By me henry chettle(2) ./

pd at the apoyntement of Robart shawe to one for cope lace the 6 of maye 1600 some of . . } viijs

Lent vnto Richard alleyne the 6 of maye 1600 to lende vnto hary cheattell the some of. . . . . } vs

[Lent vnto wm harton the 6 of maye] 1600 in earneste [of a Boocke] wch he wold calle the devell & his dame } [vs]

pd for licencynge of A Boocke to the mr . . . of the Revelles called ferex & porex. . . . . . } vijs

Lent at the apoyntment of Robart shawe to Thomas deckers & John daye & harye chetell the 10 of maye 1600 in pte of payment of A Bocke called the gowlden asse cuped & siches some of . . . . . } iijli

by(3) John day to the vse of Th Dekker Harry Chettle and himselfe(3)

pd at the apoyntment of Robert shawe the 14 daye of maye 1600 in fulle payment of a Boocke called the gowlden asse cuped & siches to thomas deckers & hary chettell John daye some of. . . . } xxxs

pd vnto the mr of the Revelles man for licensynge of A Boocke called damon & pethias the 16 of maye 1600 some of. . . . . } vijs

Receaued(4) of Mr Henshlowe the 17th of May 1600 [to]in(5) behalfe of the Company to pay Will: Haulton & mr pett [fo] in full payment of a play Called straunge newes out of poland(4) . . . . . . } vjli

---

(1) *Receaued...deathe*] in Shaa's hand. (2) Autograph signature.
(3) *by...himselfe*] in the hands of Henslowe (*by...of*), and Dekker; Greg thinks both lines are 'possibly' in Day's hand.
(4) *Receaued...poland*] in Shaa's hand. (5) [*to*]*in*] alteration.

Receaued(1) of Mr Henshlowe the 26th of May 1600 in behalfe of the Company to pay H. Chettle & Jhon Day in full payment of a booke Called the blynd begger of bednall greene the some of(1) . } vli xs

li s d
some 18 – 07 – 00]

[69 v] 20024

[Lent vnto wm harton the 27 of maye 1600 in earneste of A Boocke called Judas the some of . . . . } xs

wt Haughton. (2)

li s d
[21 – 07 – 00] Dd vnto the littell tayller at the apoyntement of Robart shaw the 25 of maye 1600 for to macke sewte for the playe called strange newes owt of powland } iijli

Receaued(1) of Mr Henshlowe th[e]ys(3) 3th of June 1600 in behalfe of the Company to An: Munday & the rest in pte of payment for a booke Called the fayre Constance of Roome the some of(1) } iijli vs

Lent vnto Thomas dowton the 5 of June 1[59]600(4) to bye a sewt for his boye in the playe of cvped & siches the some of . . . } xxxxs

lent to wm hawton . ij s lent mor ij s — pd vnto drayton hathway monday & deckers at the a poyntment of Robart shawe in full payment of A Boocke called the fayer constance of of Rome the 14 of June 1600 some of } xxxxiiijs

Dd vnto Robart shawe the 19 of June 1600 for to lend vnto hary chettell & J daye in earneste of A boocke called(5) } xs

---

(1) *Receaued...of*] in Shaa's hand. (2) Autograph signature.
(3) *th*[*e*]*ys*] *y* altered from *e*.
(4) *1*[*59*]*600*] *60* altered from *59*.
(5) The next line was left blank for a title never added.

li s d		
12 – o[o]9[1] – oo	Lent vnto Robart shawe the 20 of June 1600 to lend them hathway in earneste of ther second ꝑte of constance of Rome the some of	xx^s

[The full some of our debt] [ꝑ] payd[2] to Mr Allen by m^r Henshlowe in behalfe of the Company the some of xj li wch is the remainder of a debt of l^li for the payment of wch we stood bound in a C^li	xj^li
So that the full some of all the debtę wch we owe Mr Henshlowe this x^th of July 1600] comethe to Just the some of ⟨.⟩[3] three hundred poundę[2]	CCC^li

[70]

[Whiche[4] some of three hundred poundę we whose names are here vnder written, doe acknowledge our dewe debt & doe promyse payment: [out of our ꝑt][4]

JSingger[5]

Robt Shaa[5]

Thomas Downton[5]

Thomas towne[5]

Wbirde.[5]

Humfry Jeffes[5]

Edward Jubye[5]

Anthony Jeffes[5] Richard Jones[5]

Charles massye[5]

Samuell Rowlye[5]]

[5 *inches blank*]

[70v] **200[29]23[6]**

[Lent vnto Robart shawe iij^li[7] the 14 of aguste 1600 to bye A dublet & hosse of sewate[8] grene satten some of	iij^li

(1) *o[o]9*] *9* altered from *o*

(2) *payd...poundę*] in Shaa's hand.

(3) ⟨.⟩] a blot may conceal a letter.

(4) *whiche...ꝑt*] in Shaa's hand.

(5) Autograph signatures.

(6) *23*] altered from *29*.

(7) *iij^li*] interlined above.

(8) *sewate*] *sic*; *sewatr* Greg.

pd at th*e* apoyntment*e* of th*e* company
th*e* 16 of aguste 1600 for viij yardę of mvry
satten th*e* some of . . . . — iij^{li} xij s

Lent vnto Robart shawe th*e* 29 of aguste
1600 the some of fower powndę I saye . . . — iiij^{li}

pd vnto Robart shawe th*e* 2 of aguste
1600 th*e* some of . . . . — viij s

Lent vnto Robarte shawe the 6 of septmbʒ
1600 to pay*e* vnto Thomas deckers for
his boock*e* called th*e* fortewn te*n*es some of — xx^{s}

Lent vnto Robart shawe[(1)] the 12 of septmbʒ
1600 the some of three powndę I saye — iij^{li}

Lent vnto the company the 11 of novmbʒ
1600 to paye vnto my sonne EAlleyn A
bowt ther composicion th*e* some of fower
powndę I saye lent . . . . — iiij^{li}

pd vnto my sonne alleyn for th*e* firste
weckes playe the xj parte of xvij^{li} ixs
wch came to therti & ij shellengę I saye pd — xxxij s

Lent vnto Samwel*l* Rowley the 14 of
desembʒ 1600 to geue vnto thomas dickers
for his paynes in fay^{e}ton some of . . . . — x s
for the corte

Lent vnto Samwell Rowley the 20 of desembʒ
1600 to lend vnto w^{m} harton in earneste
of A Boocke called Roben hoodę penerthes — xx s

li s d
some 22 – 02 – 00]

[71]

[pd vnto the littell tayller at the A poyntment
of the companye th*e* 20 of desembʒ 1600 some — xx^{s}

Lent vnto Samwell Rowley the 22 of
desembʒ 1600 to geue vnto Thomas deckers
for alterynge of fayton for the corte . . — xxx s

(1) *shawe*] interlined with caret.

pd at the A poyntement of the company vnto th*e* littell tayller in full paymente[1] v*p*on his bille some of xixs th*e* 23 of desembз 1600 I say*e* pd . . . . . . } xixs

Lent vnto willia*m* ha*w*ghton the 27 of desembз 1600 in earnest*e* of his Boock*e* called Roben hoodeę penerthes. . . } xs

Lent vnto w^{m} Bird the 2 of Janeway 1600 for diuers thingeę A bowt A bowt[2] the playe of fayeton for th*e* corte some of . . . . . . } xx^{s}

Lent vnto m^{r} Ranckens & hathway in earnest of A Boock*e* called hanyball & sepius th*e* 3 of Janew*ar*y 1600 some of. } xxxx^{s}

Lent vnto w^{m} ha*w*ghton[3] the 4 of Jenew*ar*y 1600 in ꝑt of payment of A Boock*e* called Roben hoodę penerth some of . . . . . . } xs

Lent vnto m^{r} hathway & Ranckens th*e* 11 of Janewary *1600*[4] in ꝑt*e* of payment of A play called haneball & sepius. . . . . . } v^{s}

pd vnto m^{r} Ranckene & m^{r} hathway*e* the 12 day*e* of Janewary in full*e* payment of A Bock*e* called haneball & sepies some of } iij^{li} xv^{s}

pd at the A poyntment of w^{m} Birde [t*o*] vnto w^{m} harton for his play*e* of Roben hoodes penerth*e* the 13 of Janew*ar*y 1600 } xxxx^{s}

Lent vnto m^{r} hathway*e* & m^{r} Rancken th*e* 23 of Janeway 1600 in earnest*e* of A Boocke wherin is skogen & scellton some of. . . . } xs

li s d

wittnes EAlleyn some – 13 – 19 – 00]

---

(1) *paymente*] interlined with caret.

(2) *A bowt A bowt*] *sic.*

(3) *hawghton*] *harvghton* Greg.

(4) *1600*] smudged; Greg thinks this date has been altered.

li s d
033 – 00 – 04

lent vnto my sonne edwarde allen as ffoloweth for the company 1596 — li s d [21 – 13 – 04]

[Itm lent the 2 of maye 1596	xj li
Itm lent the 10 of maye 1596.	liijs iiijd
Itm lent the 13 of maye 1596	iij li
Itm lent the 15 of maye 1596.	xxxs
Itm lent the 16 of maye 1596	xxxx s
Itm lent the 25 of maye 1596 to paye marcvm	xxxs]
	21 – 13 – 04

[lent vnto my sonne for the company to by a new sewte of a parell . . . . } vij li xs
lent vnto my sonne to feneshe vp the blacke veluet gowne iij li
Tvrned over frome my sonne the some of. . . . . vij li vjs viijd]

li s d
39(1)– [ ](2)– 00 Receued agayne of my sonne EA(3) of this
10 deate abowe written as foloweth

Rd the 10 of maye 1596	xxx s
Rd the 11 of maye 1596	xx s
Rd the 12 of maye 159[5]6(4)	xxxxvjs
Rd the 13 of maye 159[5]6(4)	xxxxvjs
Rd the 14 of maye 1596	xxvjs
Rd the 15 of maye 159[5]6(4)	xxiiijs
Rd the 16 of maye 1596	xxxvjs
Rd the 17 of maye 1596	ls
Rd the 18 of maye 1596	liijs
Rd the 22 of maye 1596	xxviijs
Rd the 23 of maye 1596	xxxxs
Rd the 24 of maye 1596	xxijs
li s d Rd the 25 of maye 1596	xxv s (5)
025 – 10 – 00 Rd the 11 of June 1596	iij li iiijs
Rd the 23 of June 1596	iij li xiijs

(1) *39*] *3* retraced, and *9* perhaps altered from *o*.
(2) [ ] a blot may conceal figures
(3) *EA*] interlined with caret.
(4) *159[5]6*] *6* altered from *5*.
(5) A short rule is drawn on the left between the entries of 25 May and 11 June.

	Rd the 25 of June 1596	xxjs
	Rd the 26 of June 1596	xxx[s]
	Rd the 27 of June 1596	xxjs
li s ds	Rd the 1 of July 1596	xxxxvijs
36 – 07 – 00	Rd the 2 of July 1596	xxv[s]
	Rd the 5 of July 1596	xxiijs
	Rd the 6 of July 1596	xvijs
	Rd the 8 of July 1596	xxijs

[72]

M[r] Vahan I haue often seante vnto you to leat you
vnderstand that I haue ben therepened to be sued by on
edward phillipes consernynge the state w[ch] I haue of a
platte of grownd & barnes & stables belongine vnto the howsse
ther called the corner howsse w[ch] I haue in the behallffe of the
Chilldren of edmond hensley I being exsextor to the sayd edmonde
the treweth is the sayd phillipes hath mad a Reentrey & beinge
wth stoode hath poote the sayd parties in sute to treye the
sayd state & hath broth yt to a exsegente therfor I desyer
you to locke vnto yt & forther more wolde advise you because
you stand bownd to conferme the state to be goode yf not vpon
your perell beit for I promes you yf I be forced to spende
aney money In the sute of yt w[ch] I[(1)] speack vnto youe abowt [to asure
me][(1)] [youe ar] youe are[(2)] & to locke vnto & to conferme I wishe youe to aKnowlege your seallfe that I haue geuen
you to vnderstand of yt & that you will conferme me the
state quietley & dfend me from sute & trubell a bowt yt
or I promes youe yf I sustayne aney damages by the sute
of yt I will put you[r] band in sute [therfor] & this a sure
you[r] seallfe & this I Reast comitinge you to [to] god from
london the ix of febreary 1593
[therfor I praye youe locke vnto yt the]
[nexte terme or ells I will put your]
[band in sutte] Yours as youe vse hime
Phillipe Henslowe

(1) *I...me*] interlined with caret before the deleted *youe ar*.
(2) *youe are*] interlined below.

this is a trewe copeye of a leater
seant downe in to susex*e* vnto th*e* partie
a bowffe named wittneses to th*e* same

[07	- o[3]5[1]-	00]
[033	- 00	- 4]
2[2]5[2]-	[o]10[2]-	00
[08		4]

willi̅am Hensley[3]
Edwarde Alleyn[3]

[1¼ *inches blank*]

[72v] **20020**

[S^r^ I praye you cause suche monye as is dew to me]
[ffor my quarters fee [d]dew[4] to be payde at our[4] to be delyuered vnto this]

S^r^ I praye you cause suche mony as is dew vnto me
ffor my quarters fee dew to be payd at o^r^ ladye
daye laste past*e* to be delyuered vnto this bearer
& this shalbe you^r^ suficyante descarge frome
grenweche this xvij of ap^r^ell 1596
Raiffe[5] Bowes[6]

to ou^r^ lovinge frende m^r^
william kelegraye esquye^r^

memorandum that I the sayd phillipe
Henslow did demand of widowe valle
the 8 daye of July 1597 her hallfe yeares
Reant wch was dew vnto me by my leasse
from the quene vnder the great sealle of
Ingland bowght of m^r^s keyes wch Rente wasse
to be payd at midsomer in this yeare 1597 or
wth in xiiij dayes after this Rent was by me lafulye
demanded at the qter & at the 14 daye after[7] wch was
the laste daye & not payd nor tendered for w^ch^
cause I saye heare leasse is forfette wittnese
to th*e* demand
hewe davis

[3 *inches blank*]

(1) *o*[*3*]*5*] *5* altered from *3*, or perhaps from *o*.
(2) *2*[*2*]*5* – [*o*]*10*] *5* altered from *2*; *1* altered from *o*.
(3) Probably autograph signatures.
(4) [*d*]*dew*...*our*] interlined with caret.
(5) *Raiffe*] *Raffe* Greg.
(6) Autograph signature, but see Introduction, p. li.
(7) *after*] interlined with caret.

[73]

38 – 10 – 00
17

[¶ 10 of desembȝ 1593	lent vnto frances the 10 desembȝ 1593 vpon A foot manes cotte of velluet wth the colyseme vpon of syluer for	xxx[s]
¶ 10 of desembȝ 1593	lent vnto frances vpon ij syluer pones j gyllte & j playne for.	xs
¶ 10 of desembȝ 1593	lent vnto frances vpon a blacke velluet clocke layd wth iij [gardes of] laces Rownd a bowt & layned throwghe wth sylke sage(1) for	iijli [ls]
¶ 11 of desembȝ 1593	lent vnto frances vpon A wraght wascotte in iiiij peces & vpon a payer of wraght sleues Imbosed w[th] gowld & vpon iij grene tafitie curtenes & A holland towell all tied in a pece of tafitie	xxxx[s]
¶ 11 of desembȝ 1593	lent vpon iij yardes & a hallfe of blacke saten & [ix y[r]des of whitte fuschen & a pece of blacke] [tafitie]	xx[s] [xxxx[s]]
¶ 11 of desembȝ 1593	&.iij lane aperens & ij payer of bothose eged w[th] sylver & gowld frenge for	xx[s]
¶ 16 of desembȝ 1593	lent vpon A payer of blacke sylcke stockens for	xv[s]
¶ 16 of desembȝ 1593	lent vpon A stamell colerd clocke bownd a bowt w[th] sylver lace for.	xv[s]
¶ 16 of desembȝ 1593	lent vpon a whitte tafitie dublet cute & the lynynge of a clocke of shage [cors]for(2). . .	xv[s]
¶ 16 of desembȝ 1593	lent vpon a sylk mockeado gowne layd w[th] lace & a veluet cape of m[r]s northe for	xvs
¶ 16 of desembȝ 1593	lent vpon a Ridinge clock & a safgard of mvrey layd w[th] blacke sylke lace for	xv[s]
¶ 16 of desembȝ 1593	lent vpon a bufen gowne of a taylers wife in tutell strete for	xv[s]
¶ 16 of desembȝ 1593	lent vpon a payer of blacke sylke stockenes wraght in the clokes licke a flower deluce for	xijs

(1) *sage*] *sic*; ? error for *saye* or *shage*. (2) [*cors*] *for*] alteration.

¶ 16 of desemb3 1593	lent vpon a gerdell & a pay*e*r of hangers wth seluer hockes & buckelles for	viij s
¶ 16 of desemb3 1593	lent vpon a bufen gowne black*e* layd wth bugell lace & a velu*e*t cape *l*yned wth purpell bayes of goodwife william*e*s for	xij s
¶ 16 of desemb3 1593	lent vpon a manes gowne of frenshe R*u*set layd wth belyment lace f*o*red wth coney of m^{r}s spencer	xl s **]**

[73 v] **20019**

[¶ 16 of desemb3 1593	lent vpon a womones gowne of black*e* cloth garded wth velluet of m^{r}s palles for	xxx^{s}
¶ 16 of desemb3 1593	lent vpon a gowne & a peticote & a clock*e* of murey grene for	xxx^{s}
¶ 16 of desemb3 1593	lent vpon a payer of black veluet hoss*e* layd wth sylver lace & sylver panes for. . . .	xxxx^{s}
¶ 16 of desemb3 1593	lent vpon a manes gowne faced wth buge & a wraght wascotte for	[*x*]xxx^{s}
¶ 17 of desemb3 1593	lent vpon a leasse of m^{r} doringtones . . . .x^{li}	
¶ 18 of desemb3 1593	lent vpon a stamell peticote th*e* 18 of desemb3 1593 wth ij belyment l*a*ces of goodwiffe williames . . .	viij s
¶ 10 of desemb3 1593	lent vpon a black*e* dublet of bufen . . . . .x^{s}	
¶ 1[0]9[(1)] of desemb3 1593	lent vpon a Read cloth peticot wth durance bodyes layd wth iij laces of m^{r}s bedell for	xij^{s}
¶ 19 of desemb3 1593	lent vpon ij laune sheates & a fyne holand [sheat] curtine & this course sheat of m^{r}s floodes	x^{s}
¶ 1[0]9[(1)] of desemb3 1593	lent vpon ij y^{r}des & a halfe of sadcolerd clothe of elysabeth streate for	x^{s}
¶ 1[1]9[(2)] of desemb3 1593	lent vpon a tany gowne wth a tafitie cape layd wth lace of goody streate for. . .	x[ij]^{s}

---

(1) *1*[*0*]*9*] *9* altered from *0*. (2) *1*[*1*]*9*] *9* altered from *1*.

¶ 19 of desembʒ 1593 — lent vpon a blacke saten dublet pincked . . x[ˢiij]

¶ [19] 21[1] of desembʒ 1593 — lent vpon a fuschen dublet garded wᵗʰ veluet for . . . . } xˢ

¶ 21 of desembʒ 1593 — lent vpon a bufen gowne wᵗʰ a cape of veluet & lyned wᵗʰ purpell bayes of mʳs palles . . } xxˢ

¶ 6 of Jenewary 1593 — lent vpon a mvry colerd clocke lyned wᵗʰ sarge & layd a bowt wᵗʰ iij laces & faced wᵗʰ pincked tafitie wᵗʰ a cape of velluet & a Remnant of a *no*ʳthen dossen black [f]of[2] mʳs tenches for. . . . . } xxˢ

¶ 6 of Jenewary 1593 — lent vpon a womones gowne playne of villete coler of goody streates for. } xxˢ]

[74]

[¶ 6 of Jenewary 1593 — lent vpon a grene caʳpette of brad clothe for . . xxˢ

¶ 8 of Jenewary 1593 — lent vpon a Read velluet coope & a longe dieper cloth the some of. . . .mother Kempe[3] . . . . } xˢ

¶ 8 of Jenewarye 1593 — lent vpon this blacke gowne wᵗʰ a velluet of leanard Boro[w]des[4] for . . . . } xˢ

¶ 8 of Jenewarye 1593 — lent vpon A womones gowne of shepes Rossette & A petticotte & A certell of goody whitacakers for } xxxxˢ

¶ 10 of Jenewarye 1593 — lent vpon a blewe cotte & a cloth gowne wᵗʰ a velluet cape tied in a cvrten of goodman allens } xvˢ

¶ 10 of Jenewarye 1593 — lent vpon a gowne & a petticote tied in a pelleber of goody whittacares for. . . } xvˢ

¶ 10 of Jenewary 1593 — lent vpon a morninge gowne of A womones done wᵗʰ Ribbines of goody Tenches for . } xˢ

¶ 14 of Jenewary 1593 — lent vpon a petticote sceartes of durance wᵗʰ iij belimentes laces & a old grene satten dublete of mʳs Huntes the some of . . . . } xˢ

(1) *21*] interlined.
(2) [*f*]*of*] *o* altered from *f*.
(3) *mother Kempe*] interlined.
(4) *Boro*[*w*]*des*] *d* altered from *w*.

¶ 14 of Jeneway*r*y 1593	lent vpon a womones gowne of black cloth garded wth velluet tyed in a carpet of of goodwiffe Buterman for	xs
¶ 14 of Jeneway*r*y 1593	lent vpon a sewater grene clocke wthowt lynynge for	x^s
¶ 14 of Jeneway*r*y 1593	lent vpon a dieper tabell cloth & a dossen of holland napkenes for	xv^s
¶ 16 of Jeneway*r*y 1593	lent vpon a[l]womones(1) gowne of black*e* bufen wth A velluet cape of goodwife williames for	x^s
¶ 16 of Jeneway*r*y 1593	lent vpon a blacke buffen gowne of a maydes in chanell Rowe th*e* some of.	x^s
¶ 16 of Jeneway*r*ye 1593	lent vpon a sade tany clocke wthowt lynynge & a tany cape of velluet for	x^s]

[74 v] **20017**

[¶ 17 of Jeneway*r*y 1593	lent vpon a payer of sylke stockens of fleashe coler ffor	xx^s
¶ 17 of Jeneway*r*y 1593	lent vpon a payer of sylke stockenes of yelow coler ffor.	xx^s
¶ 17 of Jeneway*r*y 1593	lent vpon a sylver spone gylte for . . .	x^s
¶ 17 of Jenewarye 1593 [S]OD vnto frances mayde [t]he 18 of maye my lordes [c]locke & his payer of [s]yluer hosse	lent vpon a payer of hosse & dublet of oreng coler satte*n* & j payer of Rownd hosse of syluer lace panes & canyens of clothe of sylver & j payer of hosse of black whitt pte wth lace vpon velluet & a fayer black*e* clo*c*ke wth iiij brode laces Rownd a bowte & faced wth branched velluett for	viij^{li}
[¶] 1[7]9(2) of Jenewarye [1]593	lent vpon a Remnant of cremson grogren of goody newbereyes for.	xx^s

(1) [*l*]*womones*] *w* altered from *l*.

(2) *1*[*7*]*9*] *9* altered from *7*.

¶ 19 of Jeneway 1593	lent vpon a petticotte clothe of stamell of A y^{r}de & qter & xvj y^{r}des of sylke lace & a cape of tuffed tafitie of m^{r}s martens . . .	x^{s}
¶ 19 of Jenewary*e* 1593	lent vpon this new buffen gowne wth a velluet cape & a payer of fyne holand sheates & a payer of cloth breaches tied in this sheate of m^{r}s barterman for	xxx^{s}
¶ 20 of Jenewary*e* 1593	lent vpon v grene saye Curtenes for	xij s
¶ 20 of Jeneway 1593	lent vpon a dubell wraght Rebat*ue* new & a lane quayffe & a crosse clothe & a gilte box wher in is a lockinglasse a new combe a paier of siseres & 3 eare pickers & a payer of smalle compasies of the midwiffes dawt*er* for . . .	xij^{s}
¶ 20 of Jeneway 1593	lent vpon v sheates ij tabell [closs*e*] napkenes a new blew cotte wth th*e* parett for th*e* colysem*es* of m^{r}s fflvdes for	xx^{s}]
¶ 20 of Jeneway 1593	lent vpon ij yrdes & iij qters of sade colerd clothe of m^{r} prisses for	xij s
[¶ 20 of Jeneway 1593	lent vpon a cvberd cloth eaged wth bone lace a flexen tabell cloth & iiij flexen napkines of Ketren [ten] prisse for	xij s]

[75]

[¶ 20 of Jenewary*e* 1593	lent vpon this crane colerd fus*ch*en dublette layd downe on eche syd wth iij laces of blacke sylke & gowld of good wiffe allenes for	xij s
¶ 22 of Jeneway 1593	lent vpon a mvrey satten dublet & a payer of velluet vensyones layd wth sylke & gowld lace & a velluet hatte for	xxv^{s}
¶ 22 of Jeneway 1593	lent vpon a gowld Ringe wth th*e* death*es* heade . .	xv^{s}
ooo ¶ 22 of Jeneway	lefe in the Rome of j of this Ringes vnder *n*ethe A mvry colerd clocke of ales Hames for . . .	xv^{s}

¶ 22 of Jeneway*r*y 1593	lent vpon j[*ij*] [gowld ringes j the *co*okes for xv^{s}] the other m^{r}s barterman for – [v^{s}] some is . + . the*e* possey feare god	v^{s} [xx^{s}]
¶ 22 of Jewary 1593	lent vpon a payer of blacke sylke stock*e*nes of the drawers for	x^{s}
¶ 22 of Jeneway*r*y 1593	lent vpon a seea gowne of Capten swanes . .	xv^{s}
¶ 22 of Jeneway*r*y 1593 dd vnto frances wth owt money	lent vpon ij paier of fyne holland sheates & xiij fine diaper napkines & a diaper towell of tied in a cloth of captayne hamames for .	iij^{li}
¶ 22 of Jeneway*r*y 1593	lent vpon a stamell pettycote of beasse buchers .	xij s
¶ 22 of Jeneway*r*y 1593	lent vpon ij ceartelles of the strangers wiffes.	xij s
¶ 22 of Jeneway*r*y 1593	lent vpon a vilet colerd cloth Keartell[es] of elysabeth streates for	xj s
¶ 22 of Jeneway*r*y 1593	lent vpon v yrdes & a halfe of stracolerd fuschen perfumed & this mornynge gowne for a woman of good wife allen for . . .	xx^{s}
¶ 25 of Jeneway*r*y*e* 1593	lent vpon ij newe clockes j sewater grene & the*e* other a sade coler for	xxxx^{s}
¶ 25 of Jeneway*r*y 1593	lent vpon a blacke clothe gowne layd wth lace & a cloth petticotte layd wth lace & a payer of large holland sheates in this buck rome bage for	xxxx^{s}
¶ 25 of Jeneway*r*y 1593	lent vpon a vilett clothe gowne layd wth belliment lace on the sleves of mary adames	xxxx^{s}]

[¶ 25 of Jenewary*e* 1593	lent vpon a tany clothe mandilion layd thick*e* wth black*e* sylke lace & ij payer of fine sheates & a table clothe & a towell of dieper sewed in this clothe of Johen pettett for	xxx^{s}
¶ 26 of Jenewarye 1593	lent vpon a tany clothe gowne garded wth velluet of m^{r}s Ratlyffe for	xx^{s}

¶ 26 of Jenewary 1593	lent vpon a sewater grene clock new. . . .	xx^{s}
¶ 26 of Jenewary 1593	lent vpon this blacke cloth gowne fured & layd wth sylke lace for a man of charles williames for	xx^{s}
¶ 31 of Jenewary 1593	lent vpon a frenche grene clocke wth sleues & done a bowt wth [g]A(1) lace of sylke & gowld A forepte for a woman of branched velluet Imbradered a pone wth agleates of m^{r}s spensers	iij^{li}
¶ 31 of Jenewarye 1593	lent vpon iiij gowld Ringes j [a sealle Ringe] wth the [gryfen] sarsenes heade(2) vpon yt & j deathes head & ij hoope Ringes j biger then the other for	xxxx^{s}
¶ 4 of ffebreary 1593	lent vpon a buffen gowne wth a velluet cape edged wth bugell lace in a table cloth of m^{r}s Palles for	x^{s}
¶ 4 of ffebreary 1593	lent vpon a pucke colered clocke lyned wth ashe colerd bayes & layd a bowt wth A blacke sylke lace of m^{rs} newbery . .	xx^{s}
¶ 6 of febreary 1593	lent vpon a wraght wascotte & A [payer of selver colerd sylke stockenes] for	[30^{s}] [*x*]xxx^{s}
¶ 6 of febreary 1593	lent vpon A new blacke clocke wth A velluet cape of goody streates for	xv^{s}
¶ 6 of febreary 1593	lent vpon a blacke clocke wth a veluet cape & faced befor wth sylke bumbasye of good wife Brownes for	xv^{s}
¶ 9 of febearye 1593	lent vpon A payer of crymson colerd sylke stocke^{n}s for . . . . eged in the clockes wth gowld. . . .	xx^{s}]

[76]

[¶ 9 of febreary 1593	lent vpon A shorte velluet clocke fugerred & a whitte saten clocke fured throwghe & eged wth gowld lace & a sylke damaske Kerttell wth a brode gard of velluet Imbradered tide in a napken of good wiffe williames the	xxx^{s}

(1) [*g*]*A*] alteration.

(2) *sarsenes head*] interlined above.

¶ 9 of febreary 1593	lent vpon iij y[r]des of fyne mvrey clothe tied in this dubell cloth of thomas lewknore for .	xxvj s
¶ 9 of febreary 1593	lent vpon iij pare of sheates j dossen of napkenes A fy*ne* mvrnynge gowne for a womon & a Rownd Keartell of buffen pinkte w[th] iij gardes of saten & [A corsse petticot w[th] iij laces of sylke tide in A] [new table clothe of good] wiffe williames for lefte[(1)] in the Rome A shorte clocke[(1)] for a womon & v peces of lynnen	xxxx[s]
¶ 9 of febrearye 1593	lent vpon a womones gowne of frenshe Ruset w[th] a velluet cape & do*ne* A but w[th] ij laces of m[r]s northes for	xxi*i*ij s
¶ 14 of febreary 1593	lent vpon a pece of dieper as fran*c*es sayes yt is xxx yardes for	xxxx[s]
¶ 13 of febreary 1593	lent vpon a vilet colerd cloth clocke w[th] A velluet cape & faced w[th] searge of good wiffe whitacares for	xs
¶ 13 of febreary 1593	lent vpon A Ruset gowne for A womon w[th] A fvrred cape lyned w[th] lane tide in &[(2)] old table cloth*e* of m[r]s neler for	xs
¶ 13 of febrearye 1593	lent vpon ij payer of sheates j holland table clothe & A towell of captayne Hanames for	xx[s]
¶ 24 of febreary 1593	lent vpon a longe tany clocke [*of*] done w[th] sylke buttenes of lyon tany of good wiffe allenes for	xxxx[s]
¶ 24 of febreary 1593	lent vpon a velluatte cappe	xs
¶ 25 of ffebreary 1593	lent vpon A payer of hollande sheates & a dossen of dieper napkines & a pettycote tyed in &[(2)] old dieper napken for of angiell goodyere[(3)]	xx[s]
¶ 25 of ffebreary 1593	lent vpon clothe for a petycote & lace & a pece of tufed tafitte of m[r]s marten . .	xs**]**

(1) *lefte...clocke*] *lefte...A* interlined above; *shorte clocke* added in the left margin.
(2) *in &*] *sic.*
(3) *of...goodyere*] interlined.

[¶ 25 of ffebreary 1593	lent vpon A womones gowne of pucke colerd cloth layd wth lace on the sleues tide in a cloth of a womones dwellinge by the cocke in tuttell streate for	x^s^
¶ 25 of ffebreary 1593 pucke(1)	lent vpon a Remnant of brode clothe wch lisse in the Rome of a petticotte & ij payer of holland sheates & a dossen of dieper napkines	xx^s^
¶ 28 of febreary 159[4]3(2)	lent vpon a pece of hollande	x^s^
¶ 28 of febrearye 159[4]3(2)	lent vpon a pece of canvas	xxx^s^
¶ 31 of Jeneway 159[4]3(2)	lent vpon iij gowld Ringes j wth a sersens head vpon yt & [ij]the(3) other ij hoope Ringes j biger then the other for	xxx^s^
¶ [11]9(4) of marche 159[4]3(2)	lent vpon a clocke of fryers graye layd a bowt wth iij laces for . . .	xx^s^
¶ 7 of marche 1593	lent vpon A yellow ssatten dublett branched of my lorde Burtes man	xx^s^
¶ 7 of marche 1593	lent vpon a womones gowne of buffen [layd] wth a velluet cape layd wth bugell lace & trymd on the *w*inges wth sylke lace of williame davies for	xv^s^
¶ 13 of marche 1593	lent vpon A Dublet & Rownd hosse of blacke satten of m^r^ hvsseyes for	xx^s^
¶ 14 of marche 1593 000	lent vpon iiij Hoope Ringes & j sealle Ringe wth a grefenes head of gowld & A grogren gowne garded of the old facien & a chamblet certell & a Remnant of brod cloth Read for	v^li^

(1) *pucke*] added at left of entry.
(2) *159*[*4*]*3*] *3* altered from *4*.
(3) [*ij*]*the*] alteration.
(4) [*11*]*9*] alteration.

¶ 15 of marche 1593	lent vpon a frenshe grene clocke layd wth 4 or 5 laces of harye ssheffelde for	xxxv^{s}
¶ 15 of marche 1593	lent vpon a fyne blacke clothe clocke sleued layd wth wreathed sylke lace & lyned wth blacke cotten of Jonne Boothe	xxx^{s}]

[77]

[¶ 23 of marche 1593	lent vpon A Remnant of cremsone grogren of goody newberys for	xx^{s}
¶ 23 of marche 1593	lent vpon a buffen gowne playne wth A cape of velluet & j payer of holland sheates & j canuas sheat wch they ar wraped in of . . . . [& a payer of breaches in yt] leaft a cvshen & a morter & pesell(1)	xxx s
¶ 25 of marche 1593	lent vpon a lynynge of shage for A clocke	vj s
¶ 1 of ap^{r}ell 1593	lent vpon a fresadow gowne of Ketren powell for	x s
¶ 1 of ap^{r}ell 1593	lent vpon a payer of blacke sylke stockenes of goody streates for . . .	x s
¶ 1 of ap^{r}ell 1593	lent vpon a saten clocke layd wth lace & lyned wth squerell of m^{r} hvssey not feched	xxx s
¶ 1 of ap^{r}ell 159[3]4(2)	lent vpon this bufen gowne tied in A cloth of m^{r}s palle for	x^{s}iiij s vj d
¶ 7 of ap^{r}ell 159[3]4(2)	lent vpon a bell salte dubell persell gylte of a copers in theuenglane at. .	l s
¶ 7 of ap^{r}ell 1594	lent vpon a gowld Ringe wth a sarsenes head vpon of m^{r}s atkinsones & a Ringe wth hand in hand for . . .	[x^{s}] xv^{s}
¶ 9 of ap^{r}ell 1594	lent vpon a grene clocke wth owt lynynge & a grene velluet cape for	x s

(1) *leaft...pesell*] crowded in, and partly interlined. (2) *159[3]4*] *4* altered from *3*.

¶ 13 of ap^{r}ell 1594	lent vpon a gowne of black*e* clothe layd wth lace & j ceartell of de*w*rance layd wth belement lace of anne nockes	xxx^{s}
¶ 13 of ap^{r}ell 1594	lent vpon a littell hoope Ringe of . . . . gowld wth this posey hope healpeth heuenes	v^{s}
¶ 17 of ap^{r}ell 1594	lent vpon a cambricke face clothe eaged wth gowld lace A fyne hollande sheate & A payer of new flexen sheates sewed in A clothe of m^{r}s spensers for.	xxv^{s}
¶ 18 of ap^{r}ell 1594	lent vpon a payer of whitte sylke stockenes.	v^{s}]

[77v] 20014

[¶ 20 of ap^{r}ell 1594	lent vpon A payer of crymson velluet venysyones :	xij s
¶ 24 of ap^{r}ell 1594	lent [vpon A Dubell sufer*en*] & ij hoope Ringes of gowlde posey let vertu be thy th*e* othe*r* posey as thow haste vowed vnto me so ame I thine vntell I die of good buterman	[xx] xx^{s}
¶ 26 of ap^{r}ell 159[3]4(1)	lent vpon A Remnante of blacke satten & and A longe blacke Clocke vn made vp stricked on wth waffes of my lord Burtes for	v^{li}
¶ 28 of ap^{r}ell 1594	lent vpon a genger colerd saten dublet & A payre of grene veluet Rownd hosse & A payer of sylke stockenes of watshet for	iij^{li} iiij s
maye 1 1594	lent vpon A mvre*y* savegarde layd wth grene sylke lace of Jonne Boothe for	v^{s}
maye 2 1594	lent vpon A payer of sylke stockines genger coler for	xij s
++		
¶ 13 of maye 1594	lent vpon A sylke grogren gowne garded wth velluet & lyned wth saye of m^{r}. Burdes for	iij^{li} x s

(1) *159[3]4* *4* altered from *3*.

¶ 14 of maye 1594	lent vpon a forparte of Branched velluet & done wth Bugelles for	xx^s^
15 of maye 1594	lent vpon a manes gowne vn lined of brode cloth blacke for	xiij s]
15 of maye 1594	lente vpon a cotte of blacke clothe & a corten of goody streates for.	xvj d
[sence frances went ¶ 18 of maye 1594	lent vpon a payer of sheates & a tabell clothe the some of [thes ar her stylle] (1)	vj s
¶ 18 of maye 1594	lent vpon [a]ij (2) yard & a hallfe of fresadowe the some of.	v^s^
¶ 23 of maye 1594	lent vpon a belle salte gelte & ij sylver spones gylte for	iij^li^]

[78]

[¶ 23 of maye 1594	lent vpon a forepte of changable tuffed tafitie of m^r^ Burdes for	x^s^
¶ 26 of maye 1594	lent vpon A frenshe grene clocke wth sleves & done A bowt wth a lace of sylke & gowld & eged wth watchet tafetey of m^r^ spencers for	xxx^s^
¶ 27 of maye 1594	lent vpon halfe a dossen of dieper napkines . .	iiij s
¶ 27 of maye 1594	lent vpon iij canves shetes la*pe*t in a napkine for.	v^s^
¶ 6 of June 1594	lent vpon A payer of sylver spores.	xx s
¶ 7 of [maye]June (3) 1594	lent vpon A payer of blacke sylke stockens .	x s
¶ 8 of June 1594	lent vpon vj Ringes of gowld for	xxx^s^

(1) *thes...stylle*] interlined. (2) [*a*]*ij*] alteration.
(3) [*maye*] *June*] alteration.

¶ 8 of June 1594 + + +	lent vpon A womanes gowne of villet in grayne wth a veluet cape Imbrodered wth bugelles for	xxxvj^{s}
¶ 9 of June 1594	lent vpon iiij gowld Ringes j hande in hand ij smalle Ringes wth stones & a littell hoope Ringe amelld for	xvj s
¶ 10 of June 1594	Lent vpon A payer of sylke stockenes of syluercoler for	v^{s}
¶ 10 of June 1594	lent vpon a payer of sylke stockenes of orangcoler for	xs
¶ 10 of June 1594	lent vpon A womones gowne of blacke clothe playne wth a cape of velluet for	xs
¶ 11 of June 1594	lent vpon ij gowld Ringes j pansey & the other wth ij stones for	vjs
¶ 12 of [maye]June(1) 1594	lent vpon A manes gowne of sewatr grene layd wth Lace & fored throwghe wth lambe & faced wth graye fore for	xxx^{s}
¶ 14 of June 1594	lent vpon A buffen gowne wth a velluet cape donne wth bugell lace & layd wth bellement lace on the sleves & lyned wth taney of of cattren tenches for	xxx^{s}]

[78v] 20012

[¶ 14 of June 1594	lent vpon A payer of mvrey velluet hoosse & a fyne holand shearte wth sleves of blacke worke pind in a napken of elysabeth marnar for	xxs
¶ 17 of June 1594	lent vpon A manes gowne & A blacke Clocke tied in A clothe of goody watsones	xxxx^{s}
¶ 20 of June 1594	lent vpon iij gowld Ringes j wyth A sarsentes head & j wth ij stones & the other hande in hand for	xx^{s}

(1) [*maye*]*June*] alteration.

¶ 25 of June 1594	lent vpon A payer of sylke stockenes . . of sewatr grene & A payer of Botthosse toopes wraght wth blacke worke for	xx^{s}
¶ 25 of June 1594	lent vpon A sylke grogren gowne ffor A womon wth A cape of wraght velluet & Im bradered wth bugell & a troncke sleue layd thicke wth tu*f*ted lace & Rownd A bowt wth the same & lyned wth purpell bayes for. .	iij^{li} xs
¶ 3 of July 1594	lent vpon A xj peces of lynnen of m^{r} ha*re*s	xx^{s}
¶ 4 of July 1594	lent vpon sylke frenge & bellement lace & A Remnant of mingelcoler bufen of m^{r}s adyses for	vij s
¶ 4 of July 1594	lent vpon A canvas sheate & ij pelle bers of goody haryson for . . .	ij s
¶ 4 of July 1594	lent vpon A velluet hatte for A womon wth A band of pearlle & gowld for .	xx^{s}
¶ 8 of July 1594	lent vpon A payer of Rownd hosse of clothe of gowld & blacke saten panes & A payer of Rownd hosse of velluet wth sylver panes & layd thicke wth sylver lace for.	xxxx^{s}
¶ 12 of July 1594	lent vpon A s[ce]*k*yecoler (1) clocke wthowt lynynge & A cape of velluet layd wth lace of goody whitta*ca*res	xs
¶ 15 of July 1594	lent vpon A manes gowne of lyned throwghe wth la*une* & faced wth grey fore	xxx^{s}
¶ 15 of July 1594	lent vpon A Dublett & A payer of venysyones of whitt taffyttie cvtte for . .	xs]

[79]

[¶ 17 of July 1594	lent vpon A Remnante of brode clothe blacke & a Remnante of brode bayes of m^{r}s martenes	xx^{s}
¶ 22 of July 1594	lent vpon a manes gowne of brode clothe ffaced wth buge & lyned wth whitte cotten of goody whittacares ffor	xs

(1) *s[ce]kyecoler] k* altered from *ce*.

¶ 26 of July 1594	lent vpon ij gowld Ringes j wth a sarsenes head & the other wth ij stones for	xiiij s
¶ 27 of July 1594 30 – 00 – 00 00 –[*09*]12(1)– 00 [00 – 15 – 00]	lent vpon iij gowld Ringes j wth a per*ell* & j wth a whitte stone & a littell hoope Ringe ingraven for	xs
¶ 28 of July 1594	lent vpon A clocke of ssade myngeld coler for cloth*e* brode(2)	xv^s
¶ 28 of July 1594	lent vpon a dublett of yelow satten & a payer Rownd hosse of blacke satten ffor	xxx^s
¶ 9 of septmbȝ 1594	lent vpon [*a*]ij(3) payer of fyne sheates & a tabell cloth & a towell & a sylke quyllte for.	iiij^li]
¶ 16 of septmbȝ 1594 at 8^d 00	lent vpon A xj peces of chyldbedlynen of goody harysones for	xxs
¶ 16 of septmbȝ 1594 – 8^d 0000000	lent vpon a bybell & x peces of lynen tyde in & a*p*kine of goody haryson at. . Receued xv^d more	xs
[¶ 16 of septmbȝ 1594 – 8^d	lent vpon ij corsse smockes of goody harysones for	ijs vjd]
¶ 16 of septmbȝ 1594 – [8^d]at(4) 14^d a moneth	lent vpon a womones gowne of Blacke clothe playne wth a cape of velluet & a cvbe*r*d cloth of turckey work*e* & A vij peces(5) of calecow & a peleber wch they be put in of goody harysones for. . . .	xxxiijs ijd
[¶ 16 of septmbȝ 1594 – 9^d month	lent vpon a womones gowne of ffrenshe Rossett playne wth a cape of velluet & lyned wth ashc*o*ler bayes for . . . . . goody harysones	xxijs viijd
¶ 16 of septmbȝ 1594 – 8^d	lent vpon a manes gowne ffaced wth blacke lane(6) & lyned wth whitte cotten of goody whittlocke for.	x^s]

(1) [*09*]*12*] alteration.
(2) *clothe brode*] interlined.
(3) [*a*]*ij*] alteration.
(4) [8^d] *at*] alteration.
(5) *peces*] interlined above.
(6) *lane*] written *lame*.

[¶ 17 of septmbȝ 1594	lent vpon a manes gowne playne & a Roset clocke a coverlet a face clothe of dieper & the Intreste of goody watsones for	xxxxij[s] [xiiij s *ij*[d]]
¶ 17 of septmbȝ 1594	lent vpon ij petycotes of goody watsones . .	xiiij s ij[d]
¶ 17 of septmbȝ 1594 ooo	lent vpon a manes gowne faced wth buge [& a blacke clocke] of goody watsones Intreste & al for lefte[(1)] in the Rome a gowld Ringe to to tvrne wth a deathes heade[(1)]	42[s] – 8[d]
¶ 17 of septmbȝ 1594	lent vpon a playne gowne for a womon ffvred & Intres . . . . goody watsones . . .	vj s vj d
¶ 17 of septmbȝ 1594	lent vpon a sampler & a owld tafetie aperen & two bandes of goody watsones	v[s]]
¶ 18 of septmbȝ 1594 15 8[d]	lent vpon A payer of venesyones of Rasshe of goody harysones . . . . not pd	[v[s] 4[d]] v[s] 4[*d*]
[¶ 22 of septmbȝ 1594 pd o i	lent vpon A womones gowne wth A cape of velluet & cvtt one the sleves of goody watsones for	x[s]
¶ 24 of septmbȝ 1594	lent vpon A womones gowne of blacke clothe playne w[th] a fuschen & apes cape the 24 of septmbȝ 1594 of goody watsones for	x[s]
¶ 25 of septmbȝ 1594	lent vpon a fyne damaske tableclothe & a dossen of damaske napkines & i payer of holande sheates w[th]owt seame [a]&[(2)] a coberd clothe for a corte cvbard of damaske & ij payer of peleberes wraped in a clothe of goody tenshe for	iij[li]]

(1) *lefte . . . heade*] interlined. (2) [*a*] &] alteration.

¶ 29 of septmbȝ 1594	lent vpon a blacke fresado gowne . . & a peticote of stamell fresado & a ceattell of brase of goodye s[1] Tvcke for . . .	xvj s
[¶ 2 of october 1594	lent vpon a payer of sheates & A dieper tabell clothe & a dieper towell & a dossen of dieper napkenes & a dieper cvberd clothe of goody tenche	xxxs
	lent goody watson the 4 of octobȝ 1594 In Redy money to be payd at crys*t*mas next. xxs to be payd xxij s]	

[80]

[¶ 9 of octobȝ 1594	lent goody watsone vpon a womones gowne [*p*]*of*[2] blacke cloth playne wth a fvred cape for	vij s
¶ 13 of octobȝ 1594	lent vpon A dublet & A payer of breches ffor A chylld	vj s
¶ 14 of octobȝ 1594 oo	lent vnto goody watsones vpon A payer of sheates & a Read ma*nt*ell of brode clothe for	x s]
¶ 16 of octobȝ 1594	lent goody watsones vpon ij bybes for A Chylld & ther falles	iij s
[¶ 17 of octobȝ 1594	lent goody watsone vpon A womones gowne of brode cloth blacke & ij smockes & ij necktchers & a whitte aperen wraped in a Read sceartes of A petycotte for & a wascotte for[3]	xxj s
¶ 17 of octobȝ 1594	lent goody watson vpon a ceartell of purpell cloth wthowt lace for	iiij s
¶ 20 of octobȝ 1594	lent goody watsone vpon a blacke satten dublett of his owne for	iiij s
¶ 20 of octobȝ 1594	lent goodman hvlle vpon a womones gowne of new coller laped in a ca*ne*s[4] sheatte for .	xxs

(1) *s*] *sic.*

(2) [*p*]*of*] *o* altered from *p*.

(3) *&*. . .*for*] interlined.

(4) *canes*] or *caues* (?=canvas).

¶ 22 of octob3 1594	lent goody watson vpon a hatt for A man vnderlyned wth velluet for	v^{s}]
¶ 27 of octob3 1594 o	lent goody watsone vpon A fuschen dublet cvt vpon gren & a keartell of purpell wth bodeyes & ij peleberes wraght in the semes for	xxx^{s}
[¶ 28 of octob3 1594	lent goody watson vpon a felte hatte for for a womon faced wth tafetey for. . .	v^{s}]
¶ 30 of octob3 1594	lent goody watsone vpon A fetherbeade & A bowlster & A Rooge for	xxxv^{s}
[¶ 25 of octob3 1594	lent goody watsone vpon a pursevantes boxe of slever(1) & gylte for	xij s]
¶ 5 of novemb3 1594 A 6^{d}	lent goody watsone vpon a womones gowne of fresado wth a branched cape for	xvj s
[¶ 15 of novmb3 1594	lent goody watsone vpon ij smockes & ij nececheres & a whitt wascot & a whitte aperen for	vij s]
¶ 16 of novmb3 1594	lent vnto m^{r} Crowche vpon his wiffes gowne the some of	iij^{li} xs

[80v] **20010**

[¶ 22 of novmb3 1 5 9 4 o	lent goody watsone vpon A womones gowne of frenshe Rossett layd wth lace for	x^{s}
¶ 22 of novmb3 1594	lent goody watson vpon A womones gowne of blacke buffen layd one the sleves wth lace & spotted wth bugles for	x^{s}
¶ 22 of novmb3 1594	lent goody watson vpon A payer of tonges & A fyershovell for	xviij d]
¶ 25 of novmb3 1594	lent goody watson for A lyttell clocke of pettchcoler for	iij s 4^{d}

(1) *slever*] *sic.*

[¶ 26 of novmbȝ	lent m^{r}s combers vpon her wedynge Ringe wch hath this posey god hath A poynted I ame content	x s]
¶ 29 of novmbȝ 1594	lent goody watsone vpon A payer of ffuschen breches paned & layd vpon wth a gowld lace for	iij s
[¶ 2 of desembȝ 1594	lent goody watsone vpon A clocke of whitte Rusett for	vj s
¶ 5 of desemebȝ 1594 for – vj d A m	lent goody watsone vpon A skeye colerd clocke wth sylver hoockes for .	xij s
¶ 9 of desembȝ 1594	lent goody watsone vpon A ceartell of kearsey dyed purpell in grayne & layd wth ij statutes laces for	vj s]
¶ 16 of desembȝ 1594	lent goody watson vpon A payer of venesyones of brode cloth blacke layd wth ij bellement laces for.	xij^{s}
[¶ 20 of desembȝ 1594	lent goody watsone the 20 of desembȝ 1594 In Redey money to be payde at ower ladey daye next the some of. .	xxiij s
¶ 21 of desembȝ 1594	lent goody watson vpon a ceartell of Rossett Kearsey wth j gard of velluet & a corsse smocke for	iiij s
¶ 22 of desembȝ 1594	lent goody watsone vpon A corsse canves sheat & ij pellebers for . .	iiij s
¶ 22 of desembȝ 1594	lent goody watson vpon A wascot & ij peleber & j cornercercher & j croscloth	xviij d]

[81]

[¶ 22 of desembȝ 1594	lent goody watson vpon A dieper towell wraght wth blewe ffor	ij^{s} vj^{d}]
¶ 22 of desembȝ 1594	lent [vp] goody watson vpon A payer of owld fuschen breches for	xviij d

[¶ 2 of Jenewary 1594	lent goody watson vpon A womones gowne of buffen layd wth lace & spotted wth bugelles for	xx s
¶ 3 of Jenewarye 1594	lent goody w*a*tson vpon & owld [f]taffettie(1) cvrten for	xviij d]
¶ 7 of Jeneway 1594	lent goody watson vpon a tafetie hatt wth a bugell band for . . .	viij s
[¶ 7 of Jenew*a*ry 1594	lent goody watson vpon A Kearttell of [viellett] Rossett for	iiij^s^
¶ 7 of Jeneway 1594	lent goody watson vpon iij platters & a bassen & ij pewtter candellstyckes & j qt pott & j pint pot for	vj s
¶ 8 of Jeneway 159[5]4(2)	lent goody watson vpon A dublett of brod cloth ffrenshe Rossett & A manes hatt vnderlyned wth velluett for	vj s
¶ 14 of Jeneway 1594	lent goody watson vpon A Ceartell of . . of Rossett buffen layd wth iij belement laces	vj s]
¶ 15 of Jene*wa*ry 1594	lent goodman watson vpon A pece & A flaske	xviij d
[¶ 17 of Jenew*a*ry 1594 put in a clockbagge	lent goodman watson vpon A whitte clocke & A white saten dublet honge wth ij poyntes & A payer of crymson velluet venesyons layd thicke wth gowld lace . .	iij^li^]
[¶ 21 of Jeneway 1594	lent goody watson vpon A pettycote skearte of stufe Imbradered wth grene lace of france hensley	x s
¶ 22 of Jeneway 1594	lent vpon iij gowld Ringes wth stones . . . to goody watson j of the*m* wth iij littell white stones for	xx^s^

(1) [*f*]*taffettie*] initial *t* altered from *f*. (2) *159*[*5*]*4*] *4* altered from *5*.

¶ 22 of Jeneway*r*y 1594 — lent goody watson vpon a blacke fealte hate vnderlyned wth tafety & a womones gowne of blacke bufen for . . . . vij s]

[81 v] 2009

[m^d^ (1) that I Robert Wilson do owe vnto m^r^ Phillippe Hensloe the so*m*e of twentie shilling*e* Current moneye of England to be payde vnto hym his Executo^r^s & Assignes att hys or theyr will & pleasure wyttnes my hand the second daye of June 1598 A Regni R^ine^ nunc quadragesimo
By me]
RWilson (1)

xxv^th^ (2) daie of October 1599.
Rec the daie aforesaid for the vse of my m^r^ Edmond Tylney Esquier of m^r^ Henslowe the some of . . . . iij^li^
p me Rich: veale:/

xx^o^ die Novembr 1599
Rec ye daie aforesaid for ye vse of my m^r^ Edmond Tylney Esquier of m^r^ Henslowe the some of . . . . iij^li^
p me Rich: veale: (2)

the (3) ix^th^ daye (4) Januarye 1600
Rec ye daye aforesayde for ye vse of my m^r^ Edmond Tyllney Esquire m^r^ of the reuells of m^r^ Henslowe the Som . . . . iij^li^
p m*ei* Willm Playstowe

*ix^th^* ix^th^ daye feabruarye 1600/
Rec ye daye & yeare abouewritten for the vse of my m^r^ Edmond Tyllney m^r^ of the revelles of m^r^ Henshlowe the som of . . iij^li^
p me Willm Playstowe (3)

---

(1) *m^d^ . . . Wilson*] in Wilson's hand.
(2) *xxv^th^ . . . veale*:] in Veale's hand.
(3) *the . . . Playstowe*] in Playstowe's hand.
(4) *daye*] *daye of* Greg.

Robart Johnson of letherhed in
S[1] Sury m^r Revells man
the[2] xx[i]viij^th[3] of Aprill 1600 /
Receaued the daye & yeare aboue written for the vse of my m^r Edmond Tylney esquire of phillip Hinslowe[4] the som of iij^li of good & lawefull mony of England I say Rd the some of } iij^li
p mei
Willm Playstowe

the xxiiij^th of maye ano 1600 /
Receaued the daye & yeare aboue written for the vse of my m^r Edmonde Tyllneye esquire of Phillip Hynslowe the som of three poundes of good & lawefull monye of England I say Rd . } iij^li
p mei Willm Playstowe[2]

Receiud of m^r Henchlowe in ernest of the second parte of the blind begger of Bednall Greene the Sum of . . . . 40^s.
29 of January. W^t . Haughton
1600 J Day

Lent vnto Nicolas Bickers the 10 of June 1601 at the Requeste of the lorde of notengams players the some of thirtishillenge to be payd me agayne by ij s a wecke begenenge at the daye aboue written I saye lent . . . . . } xxx s

Rd the 24 of June 1601 in pte . . . . ij s
Rd the 28 of June 1601 in pt . . . . ij s
Rd the 11 of July 1601 in pt . . . . ij s
Rd the 18 of July 1601 in pt . . . . ij s
Rd the 8 of agust 1601 in pt . . . . ij s
Rd the 15 of agust 1601 in pt . . . . ij s
Rd the 22 of agust 1601 in pt . . . . ij s
Rd the 3 of septmb3 1601 in pt. . . . . ij s
Rd the 10 of septmb3 1601 in pt . . . . ij s
Rd the 17 of septmb3 1601 in pt . . . . ij s

---

(1) *S*] *sic.*
(2) *the...Playstowe*] in Playstowe's hand.
(3) *xx*[*i*]*viij^th*] *xxviij* altered from *xxiiij*.
(4) *Hinslowe*] interlined with caret.

I begine to Receue of antony Jeaffes
for the weackes w^n^ he[1] is behind & owes
vnto me for my boyes Jeames wages w^ch^
begines the 8 of agust 1600 as foloweth

Rd the 8 of aguste of antony Jeffes . . . . iijs
Rd the 16 of aguste of antonye Jeffes . . . . iijs

[9 *inches blank*]

[83]

[my]My[2] Lordę of penbrockes men begane to playe
at the Rosse the 28 of octob3 1600 as foloweth

[Rd at]	Rd at the [devell] licke vnto licke . . .	xj^s^ 6^d^
octob3 28	Rd at RadeRicke[3]	v^s^
29		

[5¾ *inches blank*]

[4 *inches cut out*]

[83v]

July[4] 31 1601 /

Rd from m^r^ Henslowe by me willm . .
Plaistowe to the vse of my m^r^ m^r^ Edmond
Tylney m^r^ of hir m^aties^ Revellę for one } iij^li^
monthes paye due vnto him the daie and
yeare aboue written the som of 3^li^ I say

p mei Willm Playstowe[4]

Receiued[5] of m^r^ Hinchlo ye xxix^th^ of Agust
iijl for this last moneths pay for
the ffortune./

Robert Hassard./[5]

(1) *w^n^ he*] *w^m^ hie* Greg, who thinks Henslowe intended *w^cb^*; perhaps a contraction for *when*. A stroke after *h* might be read as *i*.

(2) [*my*]*My*] alteration. (3) *RadeRicke*] *RodeRicke* Greg.

(4) *July...Playstowe*] in Playstowe's hand.

(5) *Receiued...Hassard./*] in Hassard's hand.

The[1] i and twentie daie of scepttem*b*er
dvke a thousand six houndard [too]I[2] borrowd
player of mr hinchl*aw*[3] in Redie monie the som
of fortie shillings to be paid the
twentie daie of october next
folleinge th*e* date her of in witnes
her of I set to my ha*n*d
John duke[1]

[4 *inches cut out as on recto*]

[84]

[*Blank*]

[84v] **2005**

[*Blank*]

[85]

[Sowld vnto Richard Bradsh*a*we player the 15
of desemb3 1600 j pownd & ij owences of coope lace
to be payde at to his Retorne a gayne to london
next after th*e* datte herof some of xiiij s & for th*e*
A knowelegement of this th*e* sayd Bradshaw hath
h*er*vnto seat his hand . . . . } xiiij s]
Richard Bradshawe[4]
Wittnes Ed Alleyn[4]

[lent more vnto Richard Bradshawe player
th*e* 29 *of* aprell 1601 in mony to be payd at
his next Retorne to london th*e* some of } vs]

June[5] 13th. 1[5]60[2]1[6]
Borrowed of mr Phillip Hinsloe by me Anthon*ie*
wadeson the sum of xxs in earnest of a booke
cald the honorable lyfe of the Humorous Earle
of Gloster wth his conquest of Portugall . . . . } xxs

wittnes Thomas Downton Ant Wadeson.[5]

[5 *inches blank*]

(1) *The...duke*] in Duke's hand, with side-note by Henslowe.
(2) [*too*]*I*] alteration. (3) *hinchlaw*] *law* an alteration, or retraced.
(4) Autograph signatures.
(5) *June... Wadeson.*] in Wadeson's hand, except for Downton's autograph signature.
(6) *1*[*5*]*60*[*2*]*1*] Wadeson began to write *15*, altered to *16*, added *02*, and then revised to *01*.

[85 v] 2004

[the earlle of nothengames players [as foloweth]
deatte as 1600 folowethe

Lent at the Apoyntment of samwell Rowley
& thomas towne vnto m[r] Ranckens & m[r]
hathway*e* the[(1)] 26 of Janew*ar*y 1600 in earneste
of A Boocke called wherin is skogen & skelton
th*e* some of . . . . xxx s

Lent vnto w[m] Harton & J daye at th*e*
apoyntme*n*t of Samwell Rowly th*e* 29
of Janeway 1600 in earnest of A Boocke
called th*e* second p*te* of th*e* blinde beager
of bednowl*e* grene wth tho*mm*e strowde[(2)] some of . . . xxxx s

Lent vnto m[r] hathway*e* & m[r] Ranckens
vpon A Boocke wherin is skogen &
skelton at th*e* a poyntment of samwell
Rowley th*e* 5 of febreary 1600 some of . . . xx[s]

Lent vnto m[r] Ran*c*kens th*e* 8 of febre*ar*y
1600 in eareste[(3)] . . . . ij s

Lent vnto w[m] harton & John daye
in earnest of A Boo*c*ke called th*e*
2 p*t* of tthome str*o*wde th*e* 10 daye
of febreary 1600 some of . . . . xxx[s]

Lent vnto m[r] hathwaye the 25 of febreary*e*
1600 [in p*te* of] for A Boocke[(4)] wherin is skelton & skogen at
the A poyntmente of Samwell Rowley*e*
in p*te* of payment th*e* some of . . . . xxxx[s]

Samuell Rowlye[(5)]

Lent vnto the company th*e* 6 of m[r]ch
1600 to pay m[r] three heren & his wiffe
& m[r] hares screuener some of . . . xxvij s vj d

(1) *the*] *this* Greg.
(2) *w*[*th*] *thomme strowde*] interlined with caret.
(3) *eareste*] *sic.*
(4) *for A Boocke*] interlined above.
(5) Autograph signature of Rowley.

the company dothe owe vnto me for my boye Jemes bristoes wages frome the 23 of ap^r^ell 1600 vnto the xv of febreary 1600 nexte after the Ratte of iijs A wecke some } vj^li^ ix^s^]

li s d
some – 15 – 18 – 06

layd owt for the company frome the 14 of Aguste 1600 at seuerall tymes as maye Apere – 51^li^– 19^s^ – 06^d^

[86]

[1600

pd vnto m^r^ Ranckens & m^r^ hathwaye at the apoyntment of the company the 8 of m^r^ch 1600 in full payment of A Boocke wherin is skogen & skelton some of . . . . } xviijs

pd at the apoyntment of Samell Rowley vnto John daye & w^m^ harton for A boock called the second pte of thome strowd the 10 of m^r^ch 1600 the some of . . . . } xxx^s^

Lent vnto m^r^ hathwaye & m^r^ Ranckens the 24 of m^r^ch 1600 in earneste of A Boocke called conqueste of spayne some of . . . . at the A poyntment of Samewell Rowly . . . } xs

Layd owte at the A poyntment of Samwell Rowly vnto harey chettell in pte of paymente for A Boocke called al is not gowld y^t^ glesters the laste of m^r^che 1601 some of . . . . . . } xxxx^s^

+ Lent vnto John daye & w^m^ hawghton the 4 of . ap^r^ell 1601 in earnest of playe called the conqueste of the weste enges at the apoyntment of Samwell Rowlye the some of . . . . } xxxxs

Lent vnto m^r^ hathwaye & m^r^ Ranckens the 4 of Ap^r^ell 1601 in earneste of A playe called the conqueste of spayne the some of . . . . } v^s^

pd vnto harey chettell the 6 of ap^{r}ell
1601 in full payment of A Boock*e* called
al is not gowld that glysters at th*e* A
poyntment of Samwell Rowley some of } iiij^{li}

Lent vnto m^{r} hathway & m^{r} Ranckens th*e*
xj of Ap^{r}ell in earneste of A Boocke called th*e*
conqueste of spayne by John a gant some . . } xx^{s}

Lent vnto m^{r} smyth & w^{m} hawghton th*e* xj
\+ of Ap^{r}ell 1601 in earnest of A Boocke called the
conquest of th*e* west*e* enges at th*e* apoyntment
of samwell Rowly th*e* some of . . . . } xx s

some – 13 – 03 – 00]

[86v] 2003

[Lent vnto m^{r} hathwaye & m^{r} Ranckens th*e* 16
of ap^{r}ell 1601 in p̱te of payeme*nt* for A Boocke
called the conques*t*e of spayne some of . . . . } iiij s

Lent vnto Jubey the 18 of Ap^{r}ell 1601 to lend
vnto Thomas deckers & hary chettell in earneste
of A Boocke called kinge sebastiane of portingal*le*
th*e* some of. . . . . } xx s

\+ Lent vnto th*e* companye th*e* 20 of Ap^{r}ell 1601
to bye A blacke satten dublette the some of } xvj s

lent m^{r} Ranckens
& m^{r} hathwaye } iiij s

dd vnto the littell tayler th*e* 27 of ap^{r}ell
1601 for th*e* yousse of th*e* company*e* to bye
\+ A sutte [f]&[(1)] lace for the 2 p̱te of strowde
th*e* some of. . . . . } xxx s

pd vnto John daye at th*e* apoyntment of
th*e* company 1601 after th*e* playnge of the
2 p̱t of strowde th*e* some of. . . . . . } x s

---

(1) [*f*]& alteration.

+ dd vnto the littell tayller at the apoyntment of the companye the 2 of maye 1601 to bye divers thing*e* for the playe of [skelton & skogen] the[1] blind begger of elexsandrea[1] } iij[li]

+ Lent w[m] haughton in earneste of the playe called the conquest of the west enges the 2 of maye 1601 the some of . . . . } v[s]

pd vnto John daye & w[m] hawghton in fulle payment of A playe called the 2 pte of strowde the 5 of maye 1601 some at the apoyntment of Samwell Rowlye . . . } xs

63 18 6[2] + dd vnto Radford[3] the littell tayller the 5 of maye 1601 at the apoyntment of the companye to bye dyvers thing*e* for the playe of the blind begger of elex sandrea the some of . . . . } xxxx[s]]

l s d

some – 09 – 15 – 00

Layd owt for the company to geatte the boye into the ospetalle w[ch] was hurt at the fortewne . . . } xs

[87]

[Lent vnto the littell tayller the 8 of maye 1601 at the apoyntment of the company to bye thing*e* for the blind begger of elexsandrea some } xs +

pd vnto the cope lace man at the apoynt ment of the companye the 8 of maye 1601 for coper lace the some of . . . . } v[s] +

pd vnto m[r] heath merser the 13 of may 1601 at the a poyntment of the company & for ther deat in pt the some of tenne pownd*e* I saye } x[li]

Lent vnto the company the 16 of maye 1601 to paye vnto Thomas deckers & harye chettell in pte of payment of A playe called kynge sebastion of portingall the some of . . . . } xxxx[s]

(1) *the...elexsandrea*] interlined above. (2) *63 18 6*] *63 18 5* Greg.
(3) *Radford*] *f* retraced.

Lent vnto Robart shawe & m^{r}[1] Jube th*e* 19 of maye 1601 to bye divers thing*e* for th*e* Jewe of malta th*e* some of . . . . v^{li} +

lent mor *to* th*e* littell tayller the same daye for more thing*e* for th*e* Jewe of malta some of . . . xs +

Lent vnto w^{m} hawghton th*e* 20 of maye 1601 in earnest of th*e* vj yemon of th*e* weast*e* the some of. . . xs
.Lent[2] more vnto w^{m} hawghton[2] . . . v^{s}

Lent vnto John daye the 21 of maye 1601 in earnest of A Boock*e* called th*e* [vj yemen] of the[3] west*e* [enges] enges[4] th*e* some of . . . . xxs +
at th*e* a poyntme*n*t of Samwell Rowley

Lent vnto John daye at th*e* apoyntment of Samwell Rowley th*e* 21 of maye 1601 in earnest of A Bock*e* called th*e* 3 p*t* of thome strowde th*e* some of . . . . xs

pd at th*e* a poyntment of EAlleyn th*e* 22 of may 1601 vnto Thomas deckers in fulle payment of a boocke[5] called kynge sebastian of portyngall th*e* some of. . . . . iij^{li}

li s d
some – 23 – 10 – 00]

[87v] 2002

+ [pd vnto the cop*e* lace man for iiij score ownce of cop*e* lace at x d & ownce for th*e* manes gowne & A sewt*e* for th*e* blind begger of elexsandria th*e* some of . . . . iij^{li} $xiij^{s}$ 4^{d}

Lent at th*e* a poyntment of Samwell Rowlye the 4 daye of June 1601 vnto John daye in p*t* of payment of A Boocke called th*e* vj yemon of the weast*e* th*e* some of . . . . xxxx^{s}

---

(1) *m^{r}*] interlined. (2) *Lent...hawghton*] interlined.

(3) [*vj yemen*] *of the*] interlined with caret; in restoring the first title, Henslowe omitted to delete *of the*.

(4) *enges*] interlined above; in the MS. this word is at the beginning of a line.

(5) *boocke*] interlined with caret.

pd vnto m^r^ Richard Hethe sylckman the 5 of June 1601 at the apoyntment of the company & for theyer deate the some of forten powndę & fyftenshellengę & sevenpence in fulle paye mente of the[r]some(2) of 24^li^ – xv^s^ – vij d pd by me Phillippe henslow̄ some of . . . . } xiiij^li^–[5]15^s^(1)–7^d^

+ Lent vnto Samwell Rowlye 1601 to paye vnto harye [S] chettell for writtinge the Boocke of carnalle wolseye lyfe(3) the 5 of June some of. . . } xxs

pd vnto the cope Lace man the 6 of June 1601 at the A poyntment of the companye for ther(4) dete for cope lace the some of sixe pownds in pte of payment I saye pd . . . . } vjli

pd at the A poyntment of Samell Rowlye vnto w^m^ hawghton in pte of paymente of A Boocke called the vj yemon of the weste the 6 of June 1601 the some of . . . . . } xv^s^

Lent vnto Samwell Rowleye the 8 of June 1601 to paye vnto w^m^ howghton in fulle paymente of A Boocke called the vj yemon of the weste the some of . . . . } xxx^s^

Lent at the A poyntment of Thomas downton the 13 of June 1601 vnto Antony wadeson in earneste of A Boocke called the life of the humeros earlle of gloster wth his conquest of portingalle some of . . . . } xxs
as maye apere]

	li	s	d
locke vj leaves forward some	– 30 –	13 –	11

[88]

[. . . . . . .orth(5)

Be(6) it knowen vnto all men by thes p^r^ntę that I Arthur Langworth of Ringmer w^th^in the County of Sussex

(1) [5]15] 1 altered from 5.
(2) the[r]some] r overwritten s.
(3) lyfe] interlined with caret.
(4) ther] er perhaps an alteration (so Greg).
(5) Greg read only an initial B, which may be there; the whole scrawl is heavily smudged.
(6) Be...Langworth] in Langworth's hand.

gent haue borrowed of m[r] phillip henslowe of london the some of two hundred and six pounde of lawfull money of England to be repaid vnto the said phillip or his assignes at or befor the twelf day of this p[r]sent moneth [now next] In witnes wherof I haue setto(1) my hand the vij[th] of december 1594

[Arthur Langworth(2)]

paid and quitt(3)]

[5½ *inches cut out*]

[**88v**]

lente m[r] arture Langworth the 9 of June 1595 In Redy money the some of tennepownde to be payd Agayne the 17 of the same moneth wittnes his kinsman beaste(4) w[ch] feched yt frome my dawghter m[r]s allen wittnes [m] I saye lent . . . . } x[li]

m[r]s allen

[Rd of m[r] EAlleyn the 4 of maye 1601 the some of twentyeyght pownde & tenneshellenge w[ch] he Receued at the corte for ther cort mony for playnge ther at cryssmas w[ch] was dewe vnto the earlle of nothingames players & I Receued yt in pt of A more some I say Rd . . . . } xxviij[li] x s

pd for the company the 10 of ap[r]ell 1601 vnto m[r] treheren vpon A band w[ch] they stode bownd vnto him to paye w[ch] Band I *payd*(5) w[ch] came to twentie pownde & } xxj[li] x s]

[5½ *inches cut out as on recto*]

---

(1) *setto*] *sic*; *sette* Greg.

(2) *Be...Langworth*] in Langworth's hand.

(3) Quittance in Henslowe's hand, we think; in Langworth's hand according to Greg.

(4) *beaste*] added in a space left for the name.

(5) *payd*] partially cut away.

[89]

Lent vnto m^{r} arture Langworth the 20 of June 1604 wch was delyuered vnto his man mathew the some of . . . . } xs

Lent vnto m^{r} arture Langworth the 29 of June 1604 in Redye mony wch was delyuered vnto his man mathew at the Corte at whithalle the some of . . } ls

[8½ *inches blank*]

[89v] 2001

[Lent vnto m^{r} paschall th*e* 28 of desembʒ 1599 vpon the lickinge of his horse th*e* some of fyfti*e* & five shilling*es* wch hors*e* I licked not so he is to pay me agayne my. . . . . } lv^{s}]

[1 *inch blank*]

Be it knowne vnto all men by this presentę that I williame Birde [servante vnto] beinge one of[1] the earlle of nothingam player^{s} dothe A knowlege my seallfe to owe & stand firmly in deatted vnto phillipp*e* Henslow of the peshe of Sent saver*es* in sothwarke genttellman the some of twenti [po] & three powndę of good & lawfull*e* mony*e* of Ingland to be payd vnto the sayd phillipp or his ears exseqetors adminestrators or a synes at such*e* tymes as he the sayd phillipp or his a synes shall thinck mette & convenyent & for wch mony*e* well & trewly*e* to be payd I bind me my ers exsetors administr*a*tors & a synes by this presence in wittnes wherof I haue her vnto seatte my hand + / + + + even the 11 daye of Julye 1601

Wbirde.[2]

Rd in pte of payment the 29 of octobʒ 1601 of this bill a bowe written of w^{m} birde the some of . . . } xxv^{s}

dd backe agayne to w^{m} birde of this . . . . xxs

(1) *beinge one of*] interlined with caret. (2) Autograph signature.

M[d] (1) that the 12th daie of Marche 1602. W[m] Bird hath paid*d* to me Phillipp Henslowe the some of xviij[li] (2) xs. in pte of paiem[t]. of the said debte of xxiij[li] Soe that theare rest*e* due by him to me pticulerlie, this daie iiij[li] xs as the remaynder of this debte and another debte of vj[li] or theareabout*e*. vppo*n* a bond. And he is cle*e*re of all debt*e* & demaundes *e*xcept theis debt*e* and suche stocke & coven[e]nt*e* as I maie clayme & challendge of him by reason of his coniunction w[th] the Companie :/ (1) Phillippe Henslow (3)

Witnes me. w[m] Harris (3)

pubscr (4)

[90]

Be (5) it knowen vnto all men by thes present*e*
that I George Chapman of London gentleman
doe owe vnto m[r] phillip Henshlowe of the
pishe of S[t] Saviours gentleman the some
of x[li] x[s] of lawfull money of England. In
wittnesse whereof I haue herevnto sett my
hand this [present] xxiiij[th] of october 1598 (5) } x[li] x[s]

Geo: Chapman. (6)

[2 *inches blank*]

[Be (7) it knowne vnto all men by thes presents that
I william Paschall on of her mai*s* gentlemen
Sewers doe owe vnto m[r] phillip henshlowe of the
pishe of S[t] Saviours gentleman the sume of vli
of la*w*full mony of England, In witnesse wh
eareof I haue herevnto sett my hand this
xiiij of June. 1599 to be payed vpon y[e]/ iiij/ of July nexte

William Paschall (7)] v[li]

wittnes (8)

Ed Alleyn (8)

[1½ *inches blank*]

(1) *M[d]...Companie :/*] in an unknown hand, which Greg thinks might be Dekker's.

(2) *xviij[li]*] *xviiij[li]* Greg.

(3) Autograph signatures.

(4) *pubscr*] *puker* Greg.

(5) *Be...1598*] in Chapman's hand.

(6) Signature presumed to be autograph; in an Italian hand.

(7) *Be...Paschall*] in Paschall's hand.

(8) In Alleyn's hand.

[90v]

Receyued[(1)] by me william Paschall at the apoyntment of my lord Chamberlen at ye hands of m^{r} Phillip henselow the sum of [x]ten[(2)] pōudes, in part of twenty, vpon the / xxviij / day of marche 1[9]600[(3)]

William Paschall[(1)]

Lent vnto frances Henslōw [the]to[(4)] descharge hime seallfe owt of the whitte Lion from a hatmacker in barmsey strette a bowt his horsse wch was stolen frome hime & he sewed my kynsman at the syes for hime & to macke & end betwext he payd hime fyve pownd wch I lent hime I saye . . . . . } v^{li}

Lent vnto frances henslow the same tyme to geue vnto the knyghtes mane wch sewed them for Robinge of his master threepownds & syxshellynges & eyght pence & promesed hime iij^{li} more wch saverey mvste paye his parte I saye . . . . } iij^{li} vj^{s} 8^{d}

[3½ *inches blank*]

[91]

[Layd owt at the A poyntment of my sonne & the company vnto harey cheattell for the altrynge of the boocke of carnowlle wollsey the 28 of June 1601 the some of . . . . } xx s +

Lent vnto the company the j of July 1601 to bye divers thinges for the vj yemen of the weaste the some of fortye shellenges . . } xxxx^{s} +

pd vnto the cope lace man the j of July 1[5]601[(5)] for cope lace the some of . . } vj s +

---

(1) *Receyued...Paschall*] in Paschall's hand. (2) [*x*]*ten*] *t* altered from *x*.
(3) *1*[*9*]*600*] *6* altered from *9*. (4) [*the*]*to*] alteration.
(5) *1*[*5*]*601*] *1600* Greg; *6* altered from *5*.

Lent vnto the littell tayller at the A poynt ment of the 2 of July 1601 to bye divers thing*e* of the vj[1] yemen of the weste some of. . } xxs +

pd vnto the cope lace man the 2 of July 1601 at the A poyntment of the company for cope lace for the vj yemen of the weaste som . . . } [*x*] ixs +

pd at the A poyntment of the company the 3 of Julye 1601 to the cope lace man for owld deate*e* the some of . . . . } iiij li

pd at the A *po*yntment of the company the 3 of Julye 1601 vnto the cope lace man for [d*ie*] lace for the vj yemon of the weaste some of . . . } vj s +

vmfry geffes sewte

Lent vnto John daye & wm hawghton at the A poyntme*n*te of Robart shawe in earneste [A]of[2] A Boocke called fryer Rushe & the prowde womon the some of . . . the 4 daye of Julye[3] . . . . . } xx s

Lent vnto Robart shawe the t[4] 4 of Julye 1601 to paye vnto harey cheattell for the Boocke of carnowlle wollsey in fulle pay ment the some of. . . . . } xxxx s +

pd vnto the cope lace man for cop lace for the vj ye*m*en of the west the 4 of July 1601 the some of. . 10 A ownc 36 onces[5] } vj s +

li s d
some – 12 – 07 – 00]

[91 v] **10098**

+ [Lent vnto Robart shawe the 6 of July 1601 to paye vnto the tayller for mackynge of vmfry Jeaffes sewt in the vj yemen the some of . . . } xviij s [xvj[s]jj s[6]]

---

(1) *of the vj*] *sic*; *for the vj* Greg.

(2) [*A*]*of*] alteration.

(3) *the...Julye*] interlined.

(4) *t*] not crossed or deleted.

(5) *10...onces*] interlined.

(6) *xvj*[*s*]*jjs*] Henslowe wrote *xvjs*, deleted *s* and added *jjs*, then deleted the whole, and inserted *xviijs* above.

	pd at the A poyntment of Robart shawe the 6 of Julye 1601 vnto the littell tayller for mackynge of sewtes for the vj yemen the some of	xxij s
	pd vnto the cope lace man the 10 of July 1601 (1) at the A poyntment of the company in fulle payment the some of.	lijs xd [xxxxjs xd (2)]
	the wholle deat was xij li ij s xd	
	Lent vnto Robart shawe the 14 of July 1[5]601 to geue vnto wm hawgton & John daye in earneste of A Boocke called the prowde womon of anwarpe frier Rushe (3) the some of . .	xxxs
lent h Chettel j s lent h chettell ij s	lent vnto wm hawghton the 18 of July 1601 in pte of payment of the 3 pt of Thome strowde . . .	xs
	lent mor the same time vnto John daye in earnest of A Boocke called the 3 pt of Thome strowde some of . .	vs
lent Jo daye ij s lent Jo day ij s	Lent vnto the companye the 17 of July 1601 to geue vnto hary chettell for the Boock of the carnawlle wollsey to paye vnto mr Bromffelld the some of	xxs
+	Lent vnto the company the 23 of July 1601 to paye for viij pownde of cope lace the some of	xxiiijs
	Lent vnto antony wadsone (4) at the apoynt ment of A boocke called the onarable lyfe] of the hewmerus earlle of gloster some of	xs
	li s d some is – 9 – 11 – 10	

(1) *1601*] interlined with caret.
(2) *xxxxjs xd*] *xxxxs xd* Greg; heavily deleted and doubtful.
(3) *frier Rushe*] interlined with caret. (4) *wadsone*] *wasone* Greg.

[92]

[Lent vnto Samwell Rowley 1601 the 25 of July to lend vnto John daye & w^m^ hawghton in pt of payment of A Boocke called the thirde pt of Thome strowde the some of . . . . } 40^s^

Lent vnto Samwell Rowley the 30 of July 1601 to paye vnto John daye & w^m^ hawghton in fulle paymente of A Boocke called the third pt of thome strowde the some of . . . . } iij^li^ v^s^

lent vnto John daye the same time [vpon] in earnest of(1) A Boocke called the 2 pt of thome dowghe(2) the some of } xs

Layd owt at the A poyntment of the company the 2 of agust 1601 for A parell for mahewmet the some of . . . . . } + xs iiij d

Layd owt at the A poyntment of the company toward ther supe to m^r^ mason at the quenes head the some of. . . . . the 3 of agust . . . . } xxs

pd at the A poyntment of the company for mackynge of diuers thing*e* for mahewmett vnto dover the tayller. . . . . } + xij^s^

pd [*vn*]at(3) the apoyntment of the company vnto w^m^ whitte for mackynge of crowne*e* & other thing*e* for mahewmet the 4 of agust 1601 the some of . . . . } + ls

Lent vnto Samwell Rowley the 5 of agust 1601 to lend in pte of payment vnto John daye & w^m^ hawghton of A Boocke called the weaste enges some of . . . . } + xs]

	li	s	d
some –	10 –	i3 –	4

---

(1) *in earnest of*] interlined above.

(2) Not enough space was left for the title, added later, and *dowghe* was interlined.

(3) [*vn*]*at*] alteration.

+ [Lent vnto Robart shawe the 7 of aguste 1601 to bye diuers thinge tanye cottes[1] for the playe of carnowle wollsey the some of . . . . } xxx^s

+ Lent the same tymes vnto the littell tayller[2] for the same playe of carnowlle wollsey some of } vij s

+ Bowght of m^r stonne merser the 10 of aguste 1601 ij pylle velluet of carnardyn at xx^s y^{r}d & sattenes at xij s & tafeties at xij s & vj d wch I layd owt for the company some is for the playe of carnawll wollsey . . . . . } xxj^{li}

+ Layd owt more for the playe of carnowlle wollsey for tynsell & tyffeney & lynynge & other thinge the same tyme dd vnto Jewby the some of . . . . } iij^{li} xs

+ pd vnto the cope lace man for whit cope sylluer lace the same tyme the some of } v^s vj d

+ Lent vnto Robart shawe the 11 of aguste to bye cotte for the playe of carnowlle wollsey the some of . . . . } xx s

+ Lent vnto w^m hawghton & John daye the 11 of aguste 1601 in pt of payment of ther playe called the west enges some of } xx s

+ Lent vnto Robart shawe the 12 of aguste 1601 to bye diuers thinge for the playe of carnowlle wollsey the some of . . . . } xx^s

+ Lent vnto the littell tayller the 12 of agust to bye diuers thinge for the playe of carnowlle wollsey at the apoyntment of my sonne the some of . . . . } x s

+ Layd owt at the A poyntment of the company the 13 of agust 1601 for ij tayllers billes & w^m whittes bille after the playe of carnowells wollsey the some of. . . . . . . } viij^{li} 4^s

---

(1) *tanye cottes*] interlined above. (2) *tayller*] interlined above.

pd vnto the tyer man the 14 of aguste 1601 for mony wch he layd owt to bye teffeny for the playe of carnowlle wollsey some of } xiiij d +

some – 38 – 7s – 8d]

[93]

[Lent vnto Robart shawe the 18 of aguste 1601 to paye vnto harey chettell for his Boocke of(1) carnowlle wollsey the some of } xxs +

Lent vnto the companye the 20 of agust 1601 to bye A docters gowne for the play of carnowlle wollsey the some of . . . dd to Radford . . . . } xs +

Lent vnto Robart shawe the 21 of aguste 1601 for velluet & mackynge of the docters gowne in carnowlle wollsey the some of } xxs +

pd vnto edward alleyn at the a poyntment of the company the 22 of aguste 1601 for the Boocke of mahemett the some of. . . . . } xxxxs +

Lent vnto Robart shaw the 24 of aguste 1601 to lend vnto harey chettell in earenest of A play called j pt of carnall wollsey(2) the som *of* } xxs +

Lent vnto John daye the 26 of agust 1601 in pt of payment of A Boocke called the weast enges the some of. . . . . } xs +

Lent at the a poyntment of the company the 27 of aguste 1601 vnto(3) dover the tayller to bye dyvers thinge for the 3 pte of thome strowd the some of. . . . . } xxxs +

Lent vnto the company the 29 of aguste 1601 to paye the Jewrey xvj s & the clarke of the syes xj s viij d & ower diner viij s 4 d some . } xxxvj s

---

(1) *Boocke of*] *Boocke for* Greg.

(2) Title added later, and cramped into the space left for it.

(3) *1601 vnto*] The space is occupied by the huge tail of *y* in the line above.

Lent vnto the company the 1 of sep^t mb3 to Lend John daye in pt of payment of A Boocke called the weaste enges some of . . } + x s

Lent vnto the company the 1 of sep^t mb3 1601 to bye blacke buckrome to macke a sewte for a fyer drack in the 3 pt of thome strowde the some of . . . . } + iij s vj d

li s d
some is – 09 – 19 – 06]

[93 v] 10094

+ [Lent vnto the companey the 3 of septmb3 1601 to paye the tayller dover for mackenge of diuers thinges for the third pte of tome stro[de]wde(1) the some of . . . . . } l s

Lente vnto the company the 3 of septmb3 1601 to paye vnto John daye & w^m hawghton in pt of payment of A Boocke called the 2 pte of thome dowghe } iij^li

Lent vnto the company the 3 of septmb3 1601 to paye vnto the m^r of the Revelles for licensynge of [A Bo]the(2) 3 pte of thome strowde & the Remaynder of carnowlle wollsey . . . . } x s

Lent vnto the company the 10 of septmb3 1601 wch them sellfes mvst paye for to paye vnto dover the tayller vpon his bill for the 3 pt of thome strowde the some of . . . . . . } xiij^s 4^d

Lent at the Apoyntment of Robart shawe the 11 of septmb3 1601 to lend vnto w^m hawghton in pt of payment of the 2 pt of thome dowghe some of . . . . } x^s

+ pd at the Apoyntment of the 19 of septmb3 1601 for the playe of the wysman of weschester vnto my sonne EAlleyn the some of . . . . } xxxx^s

---

(1) *stro[de]wde*] *w* altered from *de*. (2) [*A Bo*]*the*] *the* altered from *A*; *Bo* deleted.

Layd owt for the company the 21 of septmbȝ 1601 for ower metynge at the tavern when we did eatte ower vensone the some of . . } iij[li] xij[s] 9[d]

+ pd at the apoyntment of the company 1601 the 23 of septmbȝ vnto m[r] bramfelld for v y[r]de of Roset brode cloth the some of. . . . . . for the [&[3 pt of thome strowd[(1)] . . . . . } xxx[s]

Lent vnto Samwell Rowley the 24 of septmbȝ 1601 to paye vnto hary chettell in pt of payment for A Boocke called the orfenes tragedy some of } xs

li s d
Some. . . 14 – 16 – 1]

[94]

Lent vnto m[r] alleyn the 25 of septmbȝ 1601 to lend vnto Bengemen Johnson vpon hn[(2)] writtinge of his adicians in geronymo the some of . . . . } + xxxx[s]

[*L*]dd[(3)] vnto w[m] hawghton at the Apoyntment of Samwell Rowlley the 31 of septmbȝ 1601 in pt of payment of A Boocke called the prowde womon of anwarpe the some of . . . . . . } xs

Lent vnto my sonne & w[m] Jube the 31 of Septmbȝ[(4)] 1601 to bye divers thinges & sewttes & stockenes for the playe of the weaste enges the some of . . . . } + x[li] xs

pd more vnto the lace man for cope lace some . . + iij[s] ix[d]

pd mor for cope lace for this playe . . . . + vij s

pd the tayllers bille Radford & w[m] whittes bell at the apoyntment of Robart shawe & Jube the 10 of octobȝ 1601 for the playe of the weaste enges the some of . . . . } + lvij s

---

(1) *strowd*] *strowe* Greg; *d* attenuated.

(2) *hn*] *sic*; *his* Greg, which may have been Henslowe's meaning.

(3) [*L*]*dd*] alteration. (4) *31 of Septmbȝ*] *sic*.

Lent vnto Robarte shawe to lend vnto hary chettell
& antony monday*e* & mihell drayton in earneste of A
Boocke called th*e* Rissenge of carnowlle wolsey th*e* 10
of octob3 1601 . . . . } + xxxx^s

Lent at th*e* apoyntment of Samwell Rowley the
12 of octob3 1601 to [len] m^r hathwaye & wenworte
smyth & w^m hawghton in earnest*e* of A playe called
th*e* vj clothers the some of. . . . . } xxxx^s

Lent at the apoyntment of samwell Rowlley
the 22[(1)] of octob3 1601 vnto m^r hathwaye &
wentworthe smyth & w^m hawghton in p̱t of
paym*en*te of A Boocke called th*e* vj clothers some } iij^li

Lent vnto w^m Jube th*e* 3 of novmb3 1601 to
bye stamell cllath for A clocke for th*e* gwisse[(2)]
th*e* some of . . . . } iij^li

li s d
some 26 – o[10]07[(3)]– 9

[94v] 10093

\+ Lent vnto the company to lend
the littell tayller to bye fuschen and
lynynge for th*e* clockes for the masaker
of france th*e* some of . . . . } xxx^s

Lent vnto Samelle Rowley & Rob3t
shawe to paye[(4)] vnto m^r hathwaye &
m^r smyth & w^m hawghton for A Boock*e*
called the 2 p̱te of th*e* vj clothers . . . } xxxx^s

\+ Lent vnto the company the 8 of novmb3 1601 to
paye vnto the littell tayller vpon his bell for
mackeynge of sewtę for th*e* gwess*e* the some of } xx^s

---

(1) *22*] retraced, and perhaps altered.

(2) *gwisse*] followed by a caret mark, and the name *Webster* interlined above; both seem to be modern forgeries.

(3) *o*[*10*]*07*] *07* altered, probably from *10*.

(4) *paye*] *p* is written over a line which may be, as Greg thinks, an incipient *l*.

Lent vnto Samwell Rowley by th*e* apoyntment
of the companye the 9 of novmbз 1601 to paye vnto
w^{m} hawghton for his boocke of the prowd
womon of Anwarppe the some of . . . . xx^{s}

\+ Layd owt for the company for the mend*ing*
of hew daves tanye cotte the some of . . .
wch was eatten wth the Rattes . . . . . vij s vj^{d}

\+ Lent vnto harey chettell by the company at
the eagell & th*e* chillde in ꝑt of payment of A
Boocke called th*e* Rissynge of carnoll wollsey
th*e* some of . . ¶ 6 of novmbз 1601[1] . . . x s

\+ Lent vnto th*e* company th*e* 9 of novmbз 1601
to paye vnto m^{r} monday & hary chettell in
ꝑt of payment of A Boock*e* called th*e*
Rissynge of carnowlle wollsey th*e* some of x s

\+ Lent vnto the company the 12 of novmbз
1601 to paye vnto antony monday & harye
chettell mihell drayton & smythe in fulle
payment of the firste ꝑt of carnowll wollsey
th*e* some of . . . . iij^{li}

some is ix li xvij s vj d

[95]

Lent vnto th*e* companye the 13 of novmbз 1601 +
to paye th*e* littell tayller Radford vpon his bill
for the gwiss*e* the some of . . . . xx s

Lent at th*e* apoyntment of th*e* company & my
son*ne* vnto hary chettell in earnest of a playe
called to good to be trewe[2] th*e* some of
the 14 of novmbз 1[5]601[3] . . . . v^{s}

pd at th*e* Apoyntment of the company vnto +
my sonne EAlleyn for A Boocke called [m]vorti[m]ger[4]
th*e* 20 of november th*e* 1[5]601 the some of . . . . . . xxxx^{s}

(1) ¶ . . . *1601*] interlined.

(2) *trewe*] followed by a caret mark, and the words *or northern Man* interlined above; these are modern forgeries.

(3) *1[5]601*] *6* altered from *5*.

(4) *[m]vorti[m]ger*] *vortiger* altered from *mortimer*.

pd at the apoyntme*n*te of th*e* company vnto the littell tayller in fulle payme*n*t of his Bille for the gwisse the 26 of novmb3 1601 so*m*e } xxiiij[s] 6[d] +

Lent vnto Samwell Rowlley the 29 of nvmb3 1601 to paye w[m] hawghton in fulle paye for his playe called th*e* prowd womon of anwarpe the some of . . . . } xx[s]

Layd owt for the company to bye buckerom for A sewt for the playe of th*e* nvtte to th*e* littell tayller th*e* 4 of desemb3 1601 th*e* some of } v[s] +

dd vnto th*e* littell tayller to bye . . . . . . for the play of he[c]rcollas(1) the 14 of desemb3 1601 the some of . . . . } xxs +

pd vnto th*e* littell tayller 18 of desemb3 1601 for diuers thinges for th*e* playe of hercolas th*e* some of . . . . } v[s] +

pd vnto w[m] Borne at th*e* apoyntment of [A Boocke] company th*e* 20 of desemb3 1601 In earnest of A Boock*e* called Judas w[ch] samewell Rowly & he is a writting*e* so*m*e of } xxs +

some vij[li] xixs vjd

[95 v] 10092

+ pd at the apoyntment of the company*e* vnto m[rs] gosen(2) for a head tyer th*e* 21 of desemb3 1601 th*e* some of . . . . } xijs

+ pd at the apoyntment of the company vnto h*i*m at the eagell & chylld for holberd*e* the 21 of desemb3 1601 th*e* some of . . . . } xviij[s]

+ pd at th*e* apoyntment of the company [1601] in fulle payment for A Boocke called Judas vnto w[m] Borne & Samvvelle Rowley th*e* 24 of desemb3 1601 th*e* some of } v[li]

---

(1) *he*[*c*]*rcollas*] *r* altered from *c*.

(2) *gosen*] *goson* Greg.

+	Le*n*tte at th*e* apoyntment of th*e* company vnto th*e* lettell tayller to taffty sasenet to macke a payer of hosse for nycke to tvmbell in be fore th*e* quen the 25 of desmb3 1601 some of	xiiij s
+	pd vnto Robart shaw th*e* 26 of desemb3 1601 to descarge his Recknynge at th*e* sone th*e* some of	xvij^s 3^d
+	pd for th*e* company vnto m^r hewettes for mony wch they borowed of hime for to bye xj yard*e* of velluett th*e* 1 of Janewary 1601 wch Robart shawe borowed the some	iij^li ij^s vj^d
+	pd at the apoyntment of th*e* compan*y*e vnto th*e* sylkdier for dienge of th*e* Imbradered klock*e* th*e* 2 of Janewary 1601 th*e* some of	x s
+	Lent vnto antony Jaffes the 3 of Janew*ar*y 1601 to bye cloth for th*e* play*e* of Judas th*e* some of	xxx^s
	pd at the apoyntment of Robart shawe & thomas towne vnto m^r Hathwaye & m^r smythe in ꝑte of payment of A Boocke called to goode to be trewe the 6 of Janewary 1601 the some of	l s
	some	xv^li xiij s ix d

[96]

Rde(1) by me kenri*c*ke williams ye 2 the of July 1601 in *f*ull ꝑ pament the so*m*e of .7^li..0^s. 0^d in full pament of all Recking the so*m*e of	07.3.01

I say Rde ꝑ me KenricKe Willās(1)

(1) *Rde*... *Willās*] in Williams's hand; as Greg notes, the last letter of *Willās* is an elaborate scrawl.

pd at the apoyntment of EAlleyn the 6 of Janeway 1601 in pte of payment of A Boocke called the spaneshe fygge the some of . . . . } iij^{li} +

pd at the apoyntment of Robart shawe the 7 of Janeway 1601 vnto hary cheattell & m^{r} hathawaye & m^{r} smyth in fulle payment for A Boocke called to good to be trewe the some of . . . . } iij^{li} xs

pd vnto Thomas deckers at the apoyntmente of the company for A prologe & a epiloge for the playe of ponescioues[1] pillet the 12 of Janeway 1601 the some of . . . . } + xs ⟨. .⟩[2]

Lent vnto Thomas deckers at the A poyntment of the company the 16 of Janeway 1601 toward the alterynge of tasso the some of . . . . } + xxs

pd at the Apoyntment of the companye the 18 of Janeway 1601 vnto EAlleyn for iij boockes wch wer played called the french docter the massaker of france & the nvtte the some of } + vj li + + +

pd for x dossen of lace to lace the harecolerd clocke the some of xs & vj dossen more vjs some } xvjs
locke the 8 leafe forward some xiiij^{li} xvjs

[96v] 1009I

Rde[3] by me kenricke williams y^{e}.2. of Augste 1600 of m^{r} alline the some of twenty pound in p of pament of A mo^{r}e some I say Rde } li s d 020.0.0
p me KenricKe Williams

---

(1) *ponescioues*] *ponesciones* Greg (=Pontius).
(2) ⟨. .⟩] a scrawl; perhaps tests of a pen.
(3) *Rde*. . .*Rde*] in Williams's hand.

Rde by me kenricke williams y^e 20 of Auguste 1[5]600(1) of alline the *some* of ten pound in part of pament of mo^re *some* of I say Rde . . . . } li s d 010 – 0 – 0

p me KenricKe William*s*

Rde by me kenricke williams ye 3 of Sep*t*ember 1600 in p pament of mo^re *some* of I [R]say(2) Rde the fife poundes } li s d 05 – 0 – 0

in p p me KenricKe William*s*

Rde by me kenricke williams ye 20 th of September 1600. of m^r henslowe in p pament the *some* of ten poundes in p of mo^re *some* I say Rde } li s d 10 . 0 . 0

KenricKe William*s*

Rde by me kenricke williams ye 10 th of OCtober 1600. of m^r henslowe in p pament the *some* of ten pounds I say Rde p me KenricKe William*s* } li 010 . 0 . 0

Rde by^e me kenricke williams ye firste of november 1600. in p of pament the *some* of xli I . . say Rde the *some* of . . . . . } li s d 10 – 0 – 0

p me KenricKe William*s*

Rde(3)

pd vnto kenrecke williamese the 26 of . . . novmbʒ 1600 in fulle payment of all Recknengs from the begynge of th*e* world vnto the day*e* of th*e* datte herof some of thertieshelling*e* I } xxx^s

[97]

what we owe abowt ou^r howsse
as foloweth 1600

Itm frome dickensone j lode of dubell quarte*rs*
Itm frome dick*en*son hallfe A lode of syngell qters
Itm norththu*m*berland cort ij hunderd of delles at. . . . . xij^li v^s

---

(1) *1[5]600*] *6* altered from *5*. (2) *[R]say*] *s* altered from *R*.
(3) *Rde...Rde*] in Williams's hand.

Itm more from hime j hunderd of delle at . . . . v^{li} xs

Itm more from hime ij hunderd of furepowlles. . . . . .

Itm more fore clape bordꝭ . . . .

Itm from dickenson ij lode of dubell qters . . . .

Itm from dickensone j lode of dubell qters. . . . .

Itm from dickenson j lod of Rafters. . . . .

Itm from northumberland[1] cort j hunde*r*d of delborde . . vj^{li} ij s vj^{d}

Itm from northumberland[1] coret j hunderd of delborde . vj li

Itm for one powle for th*e* stayer casse . . . .

Itm frome dickenson j lode of Rafters . . . .

Itm frome dickenson j lode of dubell qters. . . . .

Itm frome dickenson j lode of singell & dubel qtes . . . .

Itm frome duckenson j lode of dubell qters . . . .

Itm frome duckenson hallfe a lode of syngell qters . . . .

Itm frome no^{r}thmberland[1] cort*e* j hunderd of delbordꝭ . vj^{li} 2[2]

Itm frome dickensone j lode of duble qte*r*s . . . .

Itm from no^{r}thumberland[1] cort*e* hallfe a hunderd of delbordꝭ

Itm from dickenson j lode of qurters . . . .

Itm from dickenson halfe a lode of Rafters. . . . .

Itm f*rom* dickenson j lode of sorted qters . . . .

Itm mor vj gystes . . . .

at C[3]

Itm fr*om* no^{r}thumberland[1] corte hallfe A hunded of dealle iiij^{li} xs

Itm from no^{r}thumberland corte hallf*e* A hunderd of dealle

Itm from dickensone hallfe A lode of dubell qtes hallfe }
A lode of singell qters half*e* a lod of gystes. . . . . }

Itm from no^{r}thomberland[1] cort*e* j qter of lod of sly*te* dealles

Itm from no^{r}thomberland[1] cort j qter of lode of slette dealles

It*m* from no^{r}thumberland corte j qter of delbordeꝭ . . . .

Itm from dickenson ii of agust 1600 hallfe a lode of syngell qters

Itm fōr[4] no^{r}thomberland[1] corte xv [delbordes] fv^{r}powlls[5] & vj
[f*v*rpowlles] delbords[6]. .

Itm[7] from dickenson vj dubbel & vj syngell qters[7]

Itm from dickenson Inche bordeꝭ

Itm from no^{r}thomberland[1] cort*e* vj furpowlls & viij delbordeꝭ

---

(1) *northumberland*] *northumberlane* Greg; *d* is here indistinguishable from *e*.

(2) *2*] not read by Greg, who noted a mark here.

(3) *at C*] interlined above; *at d* Greg; the letter is similar to the odd *C* (100) used in accounts on f. 5, etc., and looks like a *D* with a stroke through it (so Greg, in his note).

(4) *for*] *sic* (? frō; cf. f. 35; n. 1, p. 70). (5) *fv^{r}powlls*] interlined above.

(6) *delbords*] interlined above.

(7) *Itm. . qters*] There is a short rule on the left between this entry and the one above.

Itm from m^r^ dickenson j qter of A hunderd of syngell qters at . . . .

Itm from northumberland(1) corte xx delbordẹ & x slete dealles at . . . .

Itm from northumberland(1) corte vj dealles . . .

Jemes Rosse goyner & gorge dixson(2) hath geuen his
worde for A Biche of wm dixson [&]
[gorge dixson] that she shalbe forthe
cominge to se^r^ve the Quen when I shall
send for her(3) & vpon this promisse hath tackn
of me A jd one a asumsette to forfette v^li^
yf she be not browght when I shall
send for her [in wittnes] &(4) for the performance of v^li^(4) wherof they haue
sett to ther handẹ the 29 of septmbȝ 1601

Jemes X Rosses mark
Gorge ⌣ dixson

wittnes to this abowe(5)
written

John ſolfelld

[3½ *inches blank*]

[98]

[m^rd^ that m^r^ arture Langworthe Hathe absolutly sayd]
[w^th^]

m^r^dm that m^r^ arture Langworth hath promysed the 16.
daye of maye 1595 to paye vnto me phillipe Henslow
the some of j hundreth powndẹ ffor a howsse & land [w^ch^] &
goodẹ w^ch^(6) he bargened wth me wth owt any condicion but absolut
ly to paye me so mvche mony & to tacke suche a surence
as I haue at this time wittneses to this promes
of payement

EAlleyn(7) edward [mark] allenes wiffes marke(8)

Rd in pte of payment the 3 of June 1595 – the some of fiftie pownd I saye Rd . . . . . – 50^li^ – 0^s^ – 0^d^

(1) *northumberland*] *northumberlane* Greg.
(2) *& gorge dixson*] interlined with caret.
(3) *her*] interlined above.
(4) *&...v^li^*] interlined above.
(5) *this abowe*] *the above* Greg.
(6) *good^e^ w^ch^*] added in left margin.
(7) Autograph signature of Alleyn.
(8) Greg interprets Joan Alleyn's mark as *J A*.

lent vnto m^r artur lengworth In Redey money the x of June 1595 the some of tenne powndes wch was delyuered vnto hime by the hands of my dawghter edwardes allenes wiffe I saye . . . . } xli

[4½ *inches blank*]

[98v] **10089**

Rd[1] the Last daye of August 1595 of— m^r phillipp henslowe the some of three pownde of Currant mony of England & is in full discharge of a psell of wares delyvered to Ryc vycars wherto his hand is to our booke I saye Rd for Ryc calverley & my selfe. . . . . for all accownte betwene vs I saye } iij^li

By me w^m Lyngar*d*[1]

John[2] Grigge wittnese vnto the same /[2]

[1 *inch blank*]

A not what I haue layd owte sence we went a bowt ower new howsse as foloweth 1600

pd for th*e* Removinge of the donge wth th*e* car*te*	xs
pd for goinge at grenwich*e* wth Robart shawe	xviij d
pd for a bracke fas*te* at that time wth shawe	xij d
pd for drincke when we payd wages	vd
pd at the Rede[3] crosse for brackfas*te* when we sowght strete . .	ij s
geuen to th*e* worckmen to drincke	vj d
pd for a brackefas*te* for streate	xij d
geuen vnto th*e* wor*k*men[4] to drin*c*ke th*e* 24 maye	vj d
geuen strete to his brackfas*te*	ix d
geuen the worckmen for drinck*e*	vj d

(1) *Rd*. . .*Lyngard*] in Lyngard's hand; Greg reads *Lyngare*.

(2) *John*. . .*same*] probably in Griggs's hand.

(3) *Rede*] interlined with caret.

(4) *workmen*] *wortmen* Greg; *k* incomplete.

payd the waterman for goinge throwe Brige frō blackfreyrs . . iiij d
pd the 2 of June 1600 for stretę diner & myne . . . . xij d
pd the 3 of June for stretę diner & myne . . . . viij d
pd the 4 of June for stretę diner & myne . . . . xij d
pd the 5 of June for stretę & estes & myne . . . . xvj d
pd for drincke for the worckmen . . . . iiij d
pd for goinge by watr wth the m[r] of the Revelles . . . . xij d
pd for cominge by watr my sonne & I . . . . xviij d
pd for stretę & gelberd eastes diners & myne . . . . xiiij d
pd for ower diner & by watr . . . . xviij d
pd for ou[r] diner the 13 of June 1600 . . . . xv[d]
pd for diner the 14 of June . . . . x d

[99]

pd the 16 of June for diner for strete & my seallfe . . . . . . xiij d
pd the 18 of June for strete easte & my sellfe diner . . . . . . xviij d
pd the 19 of June for strete easte & my seallfe . . . . ij s
geuen the worcke men to drincke . . . . iiij d
pd for petter easte & my seallfe for diner . . . . xj d
pd the 22 for diner . . . . x d
pd the 24 of June for diner for p[tr] est sellfe . . . . xv d
pd the 25 of June for workmen & ou[r] sellfs diner . . . . xviij d
pd the 27 of Jne 1600 for [. . . . g the] diner[(1)] stret easte my sellfe . xviij d
pd the [2]1[(2)] of July 1600 for diner for strete east my seallfe . . xvj d
pd the [3]2[(2)] of July 1600 for diner for strete easte my sellf . . xx[d]
pd the [4]3[(2)] of July 1600 for dine[(3)] for strete east my sellfe . . xviij[d]
pd for stretę easte & my sellfe . . . . xiiij d
pd the 4 of July for dener for east strete & my sellfe . . . . . xvj d
pd the 5 of July for diner for east strete & my sellfe . . . . . . xviij d
pd for whipcorde & goinge by watr . . . . vj d
pd the 6 of July for diner for peter easte & my sellfe . . . . . xviij d
pd the 7 of July for diner for peter easte & my sellfe . . . . . xij d
pd the 8 of July for diner for peter easte & my sellfe . . . . . xvj d
pd the 10 of July for diner for peter easte & my sellfe . . . . . xv d
pd the 12 of July for diner for peter east & my sellfe . . . . . xviij d
pd the 14 of July for diner for pter east & my sellfe . . . . . . xviij d
pd the 15 of July for diner for pter east & my sellfe . . . . . . xviij d

---

(1) [. . . . *g the*] *diner*] *diner* an alteration; *the* deleted.
(2) [*2*]*1* . . . [*3*]*2* . . . [*4*]*3*] alterations. (3) *dine*] *sic.*

pd the 16 of July for diner for pter east & my sellfe . . . . . xiij d
pd the 18 of Julye for diner for pter easte & my sellfe . . . . . xij d
the the 20 of July for diner for pter east & my sellfe. . . . . . xv d
pd the 22 of July for diner for pter easte & my sellfe . . . . . xj d
pd the 23 of July for diner for pter easte & my sellfe . . . . . viij d
pd the 25 of July for diner for ptr & my sellfe . . . . xij d
pd the 28 of July for diner for pter east & my sellfe . . . . . . xvj d
pd the 29 of July for diner for pter east & my sellfe . . . . . . xviij d
pd the j of agust for diner for ptr east & my sellfe . . . . . . xiij d
pd the 2 of agust for diner for strete & my sellfe . . . . xij d
pd the 4 of agust for diner for easte stret my sellf. . . . . . . xv[d]
pd the 5 of agust for diner for stret & my sellfe . . . . xj d
pd the 6 of agust for diner for easte stret my sellfe . . . . . . viij d
pd the 7 of agust for diner for easte strete my sellfe . . . . . . xv d
pd the 8 of agust for diner for easte strete my sellfe . . . . . . xiij d

03[li] – 15[s] – 09[d]

[99 v] **10087**

[*Blank*]

[100]

[Brother william I comend me vnto you the cause of my writinge vnto you is to leat youe vnderstand that I haue Receued your leatter the wch you sente vnto me wher in youe seartifi me that m[r] wealles]

Rd of m[r] henslow the 6 of maye 1601 for the vsse of my m[r] Richard walles in pte of payment the some of fyve pownde } v[li]
I saye Rd by me

Robert Clyfton (1)

Receaved (2) by vs Ri· Hathway; wenworth Smyth & willīā Haughton of M[r] Hinslye the sūme of forty shillinge in earneste of the play called the second pte of the sixe clothyers.

Ri: Hathwaye (2)
W: Smyth. (3)

---

(1) Autograph signature. (2) *Receaved...Hathwaye*] in Hathaway's hand.
(3) Smyth's signature may be in Hathaway's hand; Greg thinks it is autograph.

Receyved(1) of mr Hynchloe ye 9th of June iijli wch he is to paye for ye moneths paye for ye ffortune, and due vnto ye mr of ye Revellę . . .

Robte Hassard. /(1)

Lent vnto frances henslow to goyne(2) wth owld garlland & symcockes & sauerey when they played in the duckes nam at ther laste goinge owt the some of vijli I saye Lent	vijli

[3½ *inches blank*]

[100v] **10084**

Receiued(3) of(4) mr Philip Hinchloes(4) in earnest of the Booke of Shoare, now newly to be written for the Earle of worcesters players at the Rose of mr Henchloes xls. I say receiued(3) . . . .

[10½ *inches blank*]

[101]

30(5). die Januarij. 1598.

Receaued by mee Thomas Dekker of Mr Phillip Hynchlow the some of Three Powndes Ten shillings to bee repayd [vpo] vnto Him or his Assignes vpon the last of February next ensuing. for payment whereof I bynd mee my Heyres executors, and Administrators,. /

Thomas Dekker. /(5)

Wittnes EAlleyn(6)
Samuell Rowlye(6)

[1½ *inches blank*]

(1) *Receyved...Hassard./*] in Hassard's hand. (2) *goyne*] *sic.*

(3) *Receiued...receiued*] Greg thinks this is in Chettle's hand, but the writing differs in some respects from other examples of his hand.

(4) *of...Hinchloes*] interlined with caret.

(5) *30...Dekker. /*] in Dekker's hand. (6) Autograph signatures.

Rd[1] of m^r Henslowe the viij^th of July 1602
for one months pay due the third of July being
this p^r sent month the som of 3^li to the vse of my
m^r m^r Edmond Tylney esquire I say Rd the som of } iij^li

p mei Will Playstowe[1]

[3¾ *inches blank*]

[101 v] 10083

[*Blank*]

[102]

memorandū[2] I doe owe vnto m^r phillip

[1¼ *inches blank*]

[Be it knowne vnto all men by thes presentę that I william
Paschall of Maplesteade in ye Coūtey of Essex Esquire
doe owe and stand indebeted vnto Phillip henslowe of Saīt
Saviers nere londen Gentleman, in ye sum of ten poundes of
good and lawfull money of [E]Ingland,[3] to be payed vnto him the
sayde Phillip henslowe or his assignes, at or vpon the firste
daye of Nouembar nexte cum̄inge, at ye nowe dwellinge house
of ye sayde Phillip henslowe, vnto ye whitche payment well
and truley to be payed I bynde me my heyers, executors, and
administrators, firmeley by thes presents, In witnes whereof
I haue her vnto put my hand the xxviij / day of Septembar
1599..

William Paschall[2]

Wittnes EAlleyn[4]]

[4¾ *inches blank*]

---

(1) *Rd...Playstowe*] in Playstowe's hand.
(2) *memorandū...Paschall*] in Paschall's hand.
(3) [*E*]*Ingland*] *I* altered from *E*.
(4) Autograph signature.

william Birde

[Rd th*e* 30 of June 1601 in pt*e* . . . . xvij s 8^{d}
Rd th*e* 4 of Julye 1601 in pt . . . . xiiij s
pd him backe a gayne this mony]

[1 *inch blank*]

Lent vnto w^{m} Kempe the 10 of marche . . .
1602 in Redy mony*e* [the][1] twentye shellengℯ } xx^{s}
for his necesary*e* vsses the some of[2] . . . .

[ ]

[3 *inches blank*]

Robarte shawe

Rd th*e* 30 of June 1601 in pt . . . . xvij s[3] 8^{d}
Rd th*e* 4 of July 1601 in pt . . . . xiiij s
Rd th*e* 11 of July 1601 in pt . . . . xiij s 4^{d}
Rd th*e* 18 of July 1601 in pt . . . . xvj s
Rd th*e* 25 of July 1601 in pt . . . . xvj s j d
Rd the j of agust 1601 in pt . . . . v^{s} viij d
Rd th*e* 8 of agust 1601 in pt . . . . xs vij s[4]
Rd the 15 of aguste 1601 in pte . . . . xv s iiij d

[1 *inch blank*]

[103]

Begininge to Receue of thes meane ther privet
deatℯ wch they owe vnto me acordinge to the
dayes wch foloweth 1601

Richard Jonnes

[Rd the 30 of June 1601 in pte . . . . xvij s 8^{d}
Rd th*e* 4 of July 1601 in pt*e* . . . . xiiij s
Rd th*e* 11 of July 1601 in pt*e* . . . . xiij s 4^{d}
Rd th*e* 18 of Julye 1601 in pte . . . . x*v*j s[5]
Rd th*e* 25 of July 1601 in pte . . . . xvj s j d

(1) *the*] heavily deleted; not read by Greg.

(2) *some of*] below these words something (a signature?) has been erased, perhaps, Greg suggests, an unsuccessful forgery.

(3) *xvijs*] above and to the left are some smudged pen-strokes, perhaps made to test a pen.

(4) *vijs*] *sic*; *vijd* Greg.

(5) *xvjs*] *v* an alteration.

Rd the j of aguste 1601 in pt . . . . vs viij
Rd the 8 of aguste 1601 in pt. . . . . xs vij d
Rd the 15 of aguste 1601 in pt . . . . xvs iiij d
Rd the 22 of aguste 1601 in pt . . . . xvs vj d
Rd the 29 of aguste 1601 in pt . . . . xxs]

[1 *inch blank*]

[Thomas downton

[Rd the 30 of June 1601 in pte]. . . . . [xvij s 8d]
Rd the 4 of July 1601 in pt . . . . xiiij s
Rd the 11 of July 1601 in pte. . . . . xiij s 4d
Rd the 18 of July 1601 in pte . . . . xvj s
Rd the 25 of Julye 1601 in pt . . . . xvj s j d
Rd the j [p]*of*(1) agust 1601 in pt . . . . vs viij d
Rd the 8 of aguste 1601 in pt. . . . . xs vij d
Rd th 15 of aguste 1601 in pt . . . . xvs iiij d
Rd the 22 of aguste 1601 in pt . . . . xvs vj d
Rd the 29 of aguste 1601 in pte . . . . xxs
Rd the 5 of Septmbз 1601 in pt . . . . xiiij s]

[2½ *inches blank*]

[103 v] **10079**

Lent Wm Birde alles borne the some of. . . . . } vli

Rd in pte . . . . xs
Rd in pte . . . . xs
Rd in pte . . . . viij s
Rd in pt the 18 of octobз 1601 . . . . iij s 8d
Rd in pt the [18]25(2) of octobз 1601 . . . . ij s 4d
Rd in pt the 1 of novmbз 1601. . . . . iij s 4 d

[2 *inches blank*]

[Lent vnto mr Jonnes the 2 of octobз.
1601 & Receued as folowethe some xxxxs

Rd in pte [of]the(3) 3 of octobз 1601 . . . . vs
Rd in pt the 11 of octobз 1601 . . . . viij s

(1) [*p*]*of*] alteration. (2) [*18*]*25*] alteration.
(3) [*of*]*the*] alteration.

Rd in pt the 18 of octob3 1601 . . . . iijs 8d
Rd in pt the 25 of octob3 1601 . . . . ijs 4d
Rd in pt the 1 of novmb3 1601 . . . . iijs 4d
pd & quite]

[3¾ *inches blank*]

[104]

[pd the 21 of Janeway for xij oz of lace . . .
for Indies–xs & pd to spencer for twiste
ij s vj d pd for ij tiers–xs & pd for v oz
& lacynge ye sleues–vs vj d(1) to EAleyn the some of } + xxviijs

Lent vnto Robart shawe the 21 of
Janewarye 1601 to geue vnto harey
cheattell for mendinge of the Boocke
called the prowde womon the some of } xs

pd at the a poyntmente of EAlleyn for the
companye vnto the cope lace man for lace
the 25 of Janewary 1601 the some of . . } + xxxvs

pd at the a poyntmente of the company
to mrs goossen for a headtyer the [1]7(2) of
febreary 1601 the some of . . . . } + xijs]

		li s d
ttotalles frome ther	Some	4 – 5 – 0
handes before in the	211 – 9 – 0.	
yeare 1600 frome the	Jhon(4) Singer	
x of July is 3[1]08li(3) 16–04d	Thomas Dounton	
	William Byrd	
	[Jhon Singer]	
	Edward Juby	
	Thomas Towne	
	Humphrey Jeffs	
	Anthony Jeffs	
	Samuell Rowley	
	Charles Massy(4)	

(1) – *vs vjd*] interlined with caret. (2) [*1*]7] alteration.

(3) *3*[*1*]*08*] *08* altered from *1*; a difficult reading, as Greg notes; he prints *31*.

(4) *Jhon...Massy*] signatures probably in Downton's hand; Greg thinks they are in Shaa's hand. Singer's name was apparently written within the list, deleted, and afterwards added again above Downton's.

frome ther handes to this place is 30[8]4^{li} (1) – [1]06^{s} (1) – 04^{d}
dewe vnto me & *w*th the three hunderd of owld is –60[8]4 (1) – [1]0*6* (1) – 04^{d}

Lent vnto th*e* company to geve vnto m^{r} Jonnes & m^{r} shaw at ther goinge A waye fyftye powndes wch is not in this Recknynge I saye . . . . [*l*] 50^{li}

[104v] **10078**

[*Blank*]

[105]

Begininge wth A new Recknyng wth my lord of nothingames men the 23 daye of febreary 1601 as foloweth

Itm pd vnto my sonne EAlleyn wch was after we had Reckneyd to geath*er* th*e* company & I wch after ou^{r} cas*tyng* dew (2) to my sone owt of th*e* gallery mony th*e* some of . . . . xxvij s vj d

Lent vnto harey cheattell march*e* 25 (3) at the a . . . poyntmente Thomas (4) dowton & my son*ne* EAlleyn at the sealleynge of h Chettells band to writte for them the some of iij^{li}

pd at th*e* apoyntment of the companye the 18 of ap^{r}ell 1602 vnto charlles massey for a playe Boock*e* called malcolm Kynge of scott*e* (5) the some of . . . . v^{li}
\+ \+

pd at the apoyntment of my sonne the 21 of ap^{r}elle 1602 for a scertes of clath of sylver for a womons gowne th*e* some of . . . . \+ xxxx s

---

(1) *30[8]4* – [*1*]*06*. . .*60*[*8*]*4* – [*1*]*06*] figures altered; Greg reads *30*[*4*]*8* and *60*[*4*]*8*.
(2) *dew*] *d* an alteration, Greg thinks from *v*.
(3) *marche 25*] interlined above. (4) *poyntmente Thomas*] *sic*.
(5) Title added in a space left for it.

Lent vnto Thomas downton the 27 of ap[r]ell 1602 to bye a sewt of motley for the scotchman for the playe called the malcolm Kynge of scotes th*e* some of . . . . } + xxx s + +

Lent vnto Thomas downton the 4 of maye 1602 to bye A Boocke of harye cheattell & m[r] smyth called the love ptes frenship[(1)] the some of . . . . } vj li

Lent at th*e* a poyntment of Samewell Rowlye vnto John daye the 4 of maye 1602 in earneste of A play called bristo traged*i*[(1)] as maye a pere th*e* some of . . . . . . } xx s

written by hime sellfe

Some 19 – 17 – 06

[105 v] **10074**

+ Lent vnto th*e* companye the 5 of maye 1602 to geue vnto antony monday & thomas deckers [f]I[(2)] earnest of a Booke called Jeff*ae*[(3)] As may apere the some of . . . . } v[li]

+ Lent vnto thomas downton the 15 of maye 1602 to paye harey chettell for the mendynge of the fyrste pt*e* of carnowlle wollsey th*e* some of . . . . } xx[s]

Lent vnto thomas downton the 16 of maye 1602 to geue harey cheattell in earneste of a playe called Tobyas the some of . . } xx s

+ Layd owt for the companye the 16 of maye 1602 for to bye a dublett & a p*a*yer of venesyons of clothe of sylver wraght wth Read sylke the some of fower pownd & ten shellenge I saye . . . . } iiij[li] xs

---

(1) Titles added in a different ink. (2) [*f*]*I*] alteration.

(3) *Jeffae*] added in a space left; the last two letters are not clear.

Layd owt for th*e* companye when they
\+ + Read th*e* playe of Jeffa for wine at ij s
the tavern dd vnto thomas downton

Lent vnto Thomas ⟨.⟩[1] downton th*e* 18 of
\+ + maij to bye maskyngsewt*e* antycke[2] for th*e* 2 pte iij^{li} v^{s}
of carnowlle wollsey the some of. . . . . . .

Lent vnto Thomas downton the 20
1602 of maij to by a grene sewt & wou*o*n[3] l s
\+ + sleves th*e* some of for wollsey*e*[4] . .

Lent vnto the company th*e* 22 of majj
1602 to geue vnto antoney monday &
mihell drayton webester & th*e* Rest mydelton[5] *in* v^{li}
earneste of A Boocke called sesers *ff*alle[6]
the some of . . . .

Some 22^{li} – 07^{s} – 00^{d}

[**106**]

pd vnto John daye at the apoyntmente
of w^{m} Jube & the Reste of the companye for xxxx s
A Boocke called Bristo tragedi[7] the 23 of maij
1602 the some of. . . . .
written by hi*m*e sellfe

Lent vnto thomas downton the 27 of maij
1602 to bye w^{m} someres cotte & other thinges iij^{li}
for th*e* 2 pt of wollsey th*e* some of . . . . . +

dd at the apoyntment of Thomas towne
the 28 of maye 1602 vnto John daye in xxxx s
fulle payment for his playe written by hime
sellfe called bristo tragedie[7] the some of . .

Lent vnto Thomas downton the 27 of maye
1602 to by Rebatous & other thing*e* for th*e* xxv^{s}
2 pt of carnowlle wollsey the some of. . . . +

---

(1) ⟨.⟩] a blot may conceal a letter.
(2) *antycke*] interlined above.
(3) *wouon*] *womon* Greg.
(4) *for wollseye*] interlined.
(5) *mydelton*] interlined above *Rest*.
(6) Title added in a different ink.
(7) Title added in a different ink.

Lent vnto Thomas downton the 29 of maye 1602 to paye Thomas dickers drayton mydellton & webester & mondaye in fulle paymente for ther playe called too shapes(1) the some of } iij li

Lent vnto Thomas downton the 31 of maye 1602 to paye vnto the coper lace in pt of paymente the some of . . . } xx s +

Lent vnto Thomas downton the 31 of maye 1602 to bye a sewt for ther playe called love partes frenshippe } l s +

Lent vnto thomas downton the 2 of June 1602 to paye vnto the cope lace mane in fulle payment for [the](2) lace for the 2 pt of wollsey } + xxvj s

Lent vnto thomas downton the 2 of June 1602 to geue harey cheattell vpon his Boocke of tobyas the some of . . . . } xx s

s d
17 2(3) – 00

[*triangular piece torn out*]

[106 v] **10073**

\+ Lent vnto Thomas downton the 8 of maye(4) 1602 to bye cottes for the playe of Jeffa the some of . . . . } vj li

\+ Lent vnto thomas downton the 12 of June 1602 to by Rebatous & other thinge for the playe of Jeffa the some of. . . . . } iiij li

(1) *too shapes*] added in a space left; not in Henslowe's hand. Greg thinks it may be in Downton's.

(2) *the*] deletion not recorded by Greg.

(3) *17 2*] A small triangular piece is torn from the bottom of the leaf between *17* and *2*.

(4) *maye*] *sic*; error for *June*?

++ Lent vnto bengemy Johnsone(1) at the A poyntment of EAlleyn & w^m^ birde the 22 of June 1602 in earneste of A Boocke called Richard crockbacke & for new adicyons for Jeronymo the some of . . . . x^li^

+ [L]pd(2) at the apoynt of thomas downton vnto the tayller for mackynge of sewte for Jeffa the 25 of June 1602 some of xxx^s^

Lent vnto Thomas downton the 26 of [Jene] June 1602 to paye vnto harey chettell in pt of payment of A Boocke called tobyas the some of . . . . . . iij^li^

Lent vnto thomas downton the 27 of June 1602 to paye vnto harey chettell in fulle payment of his Boocke called tobias the some of . . . . xxv^s^

+ Lent vnto the company 1602 the 27 of June to paye vnto hime wch made ther propertyes for Jeffa the some of . . . xxv^s^

+ Lent vnto thomas downton the 5 of July 1602 to paye the cvter for the play of Jeffa the some of. xxij^s^

Some xxviij^li^ ij s

[107]

Lent vnto thomas downton the 7 of July 1602 to [Lend] geue vnto harye chettell in earneste of A tragedye called A danyshe tragedy(3) the some of . . . . xx s +

Lent vnto thomas downton the 9 of July 1602 to Lend vnto antony the poyete in earneste of(4) A comody called the widowes cherme(5) the some of . . xs

(1) *vnto bengemy Johnsone*] interlined with caret.

(2) [*L*]*pd*] *p* altered from *L*.

(3) *tragedy*] interlined below.

(4) *of*] retraced.

(5) Title added in space left.

steate(1) [pd at the a poyntment of EAlleyn the 16 of July 1602 to mr stonnes man for A payer of crymsen satten venysyons wth a strype of gowld lace the some of . . . . . } xxxs] +

stete(1) [Lent vnto Thomas downton & edwarde Jewbe to geue vnto Thomas deckers in earnest of A comody called A medysen for A cvrste wiffe. 19 of July 1602(2) . . . . . } xxxxs]

Lent to h chettell. vs Lent vnto [Thom] Samwell Rowley & edwarde Jewbe to paye for the Boocke of Samson the 29 of July 1602 the some of . . . . } vjli +

stete(1) [Lent vnto thomas downton the 31 of July 1602 to paye vnto [hary chettell] Thomas deckers in pte of payment of his comody called a medyssen for a cvrste wiffe . . . . the some of . . . . } xxxxs]

pd vnto my sone EA for ij bocke called phillipe of spayne & Longshanckes the 8 of agust 1602 the some of . . . . . . } iiijli +

Lent vnto antony the poyet in pt of payment of A comody called widowes [..]*Ch*arme(3) the 26 of agust 1602 the some of . . . . } vs

Some – 1[3]7li(4) – 05s(5) – 00d

[107v] **10072**

Lent vnto wm Birde & wm Jube the 2 of septmb3 1602 to paye vnto antonye the poyet in pte of payment of A comody called A widowes Charme the some of } xs

Lent vnto wm Bird & Thomas towne & [wm] edward(6) Jube the 8 of septmb3 1602 to paye vnto wm haughton for A playe [called]of(7) wm cartwryght some of . . . . } [iiijli] ls

---

(1) *ste(a)te*] interlined above. (2) *19...1602*] interlined.

(3) [..]*Charme*] two letters, perhaps *dr*, are concealed by *Ch*; title added in a different ink.

(4) *1[3]7*] *7* altered from *3*. (5) *05*] *o* dotted, perhaps altered from *1*.

(6) *edward*] interlined above.

(7) [*called*]*of*] *of* altered from *ca*; *lled* deleted; *of called* Greg.

Lent vnto vmfrey Jeaffes the 9 of septmbȝ 1602 in pt of payment vnto m^r Roben sone for A tragedie called felmel*an*co the some of . . . . iij li

Lent vnto edward Jube the 10 of septmbȝ to + macke ij *sewt*es a licke for the playe of mortymore the some of . . . . . . vj li
more for the same sewtę at the play howse. . xviij s

Lent vnto antony the poet the 11 of septmbȝ 1602 in pte of payment of A comody called the widowes charme some of. . . . v s

Lent vnto thomas downton the 15 of septmbȝ 1602 to paye vnto harey chettell in pte of payment for his tragedie of felmel*an*co the some of. . . . . xs

totalles
718 li – 12 s – 10 d Lent vnto the company 1*6*02 to . . paye ther bil*les* for tayllers & others + for the new play*e* of the earlle of *h*arfurd the some of . . . . . . xxxij s

pd at the a poyntment of thomas downton to harey chettell in fulle payment of his tragedie called felmelanco some of ls

Some xvij li xv s

[108]

pd vnto Samwell Rowley the 27 *of* septmbȝ 1602 for his play*e* of Jhosua in fulle payment the some of. . . + vij li

pd vnto my sonne EAlleyn at the A poynt ment of the company [of the] for his Boocke of tambercam the 2 of octobȝ 1602 the some of + xxxx s

p*d* at the apoynt of w^m Jube the 21 of octobȝ 1602 vnto m^r medelton in pt*e* of payment ffor his playe called [felmel*anco*] Chester (1) tragedie the some of . . . . iiij li

(1) This title seems to be in the hand of Downton; Greg thinks it is in Shaa's hand. *Chester* is interlined below.

[*p*d vnt*o* my sonne EAlleyn th*e* 22 of octob3 1602 at the apoyntmente of th*e* companye for A grogren clock*e* ij velluet gerk*ens* & ij dublet*s*(1) & ij hedtyers j payer of hosse the some of } [xx^{li}]]

Lent vnto my so*ne* EAlleyn the 3 of novmb3 1602 to geue vnto thomas deckers for mendinge of th*e* playe of tasso th*e* some of . . . . } + xxxx s

Lent vnto Edward Jube th*e* 5(2) of novmb3 1602 . . . to geue vnto John daye in earnest*e* of A Boock*e* called mery *as* may be(3) for th*e* cort the some of . . . } xxxx^{s}

Lent vnto Edward Jube the 9 of novmb3 1602 to paye vnto m^{r} mydelton in full*e* paymente of his pla*ye* called Randowlle earlle of chester th*e* some of . . . . } xxxx s

Len*t* vnto Thomas downton the 17 of novmb3 1602 to paye vnto Johne daye & m^{r} smythe & hathwaye in fulle paymente for A Boocke called as merey as may be the some of . . . . } vj^{li}

Some xxv^{li} – oo –

[108 v] 10071

++ Lent vnto the companye the 22 of novmb3 1602 to paye vnto w^{m} Bvrde & Samwell Rowle(4) for ther adicyones in docter fostes the some of } iiij^{li}

+ Lent vnto Edwarde Jube th*e* 2 of desemb3 1602 to paye vnto antony mondaye in fulle payment for a play*e* called th*e* seeat at tenes some is . . } iij^{li}

+ Lent vnto w^{m} birde the 4 of desemb3 1602 to paye vnto thomas deckers in ꝑt of pay ment for tasso the some of . . . . . } xx^{s}

---

(1) *dublets*] *dublet* Greg; *s* concealed by the bracket.

(2) *5*] *9* Greg; blotted, perhaps an alteration.

(3) This title seems to be in the hand of Downton; Greg thinks it is in Shaa's hand.

(4) *Rowle*] *sic.*

+ +	Lent vnto Thomas downton the 14 of desembȝ 1602 to paye vnto mr mydelton for a prologe & A epeloge for the playe of bacon for the corte the some of	vs
+	pd at the apoyntmente of the company the 18 of desembȝ vnto mr stone merser in fulle paymente of all Recknynge to this daye as maye a per by his quitiance the some of	viijli xviijs
+	Lent vnto Thomas downton the 17 of desembȝ 1602 to paye vnto harey chettell in earneste of A playe called london florenten the some of . . .	xs
+ +	pd at the apoyntment of the company the 20 of desembȝ 1602 vnto Thomas hewode in pt for his playe called london florentyn the some of .	xxxxs
+	Lent vnto Thomas downton the 22 of desembȝ 1602 to paye vnto harey chettell in fulle payment for his playe called the London florentyn the some	iijli

Some is xxijli xiij s

caste vp my a cowntes to this place now at cryssmas 1602
all Reckneng{e} a bated & they owe vnto me wth fyftie pownde
wch I lent them to geue Jones & shawe 226li – 16s – 8d

[109]

Lent vnto Thomas downton the 29 of desembȝ 1602 to paye vnto harey chettell for a prologe & a epyloge for the corte the some of	vs	+ +
Lent vnto Thomas downton the 29 of desembȝ 1602 to geue vnto harey chettell in pte of paymente [o]for(1) A tragedie called Hawghman the some of.	vs	
pd for the company the 7 of Janewary 1602 vnton(2) [t]Thomas(3) hawode in full paymente for his playe called the London florantyn the some of	+ xxs	

(1) [*o*]*for*] Henslowe wrote *of*, deleted *o* and altered to *for*.

(2) *vnton*] *sic.*

(3) [*t*]*Thomas*] *T* altered from a faint *t*.

pd at the apoyntment of the companye 1602
the 13 of Janewarye vnto John Syngger for his
playe called Syngers vallentarey the some of } + v^{li}

[Layd owt at the apoyntment of thomas
Hewode in earneste of A playe called[1]
vnto m^{r} harey chettell & thomas
Hewode the 14 of Janewary 1602 some of } [xxxx s]]

Layd owt for the company*e* the 10 of desemb3 1602
vnto Robarte shawe for A boocke of the 4 sonnes
of amon the some of . . . . } + xl s

\+

Lent vnto Jube th*e* 1 of march*e* 1602 to geue vnto
John daye & hathway*e* in earneste of A playe
called[2] the bosse of bellengesgat*e* the some of . . . } + xxxx^{s}

Lent th*e* 7 of marche 1602 in p*te* of paymente
for th*e* playe called th*e* bosse of bellen*s*gate vnto
John daye & hathwaye th*e* some of . . . . . } + xxxx^{s}

Some is xij^{li} – xs

[109 v] **10070**

Lent vnto Edward Jube the 7 of marche 1602
to geue vnto Charles massey*e* in eareneste of
A playe called the sedge of doncerke wth
alleyn th*e* pyrete th*e* some of. . . . . . } xxxx^{s}

pd at th*e* apoyntment of th*e* company*e* the 7th
of marche 1602 vnto m^{r} bromflde[3] for th*e* play*e*
wch harey chettell Layd vnto hime to pane for } xx s

pd th*e* 12 of march*e* 1602 for th*e* company
vnto John day*e* & his felowe poetes in fulle
payment for his play*e* called th*e* bosse[4] of
bellei*n*gesgate th*e* some of . . . . } + xxxx^{s}

---

(1) The space left for a title is filled by a modern forgery, *Like quits Like.*

(2) *called*] heavily blotted, perhaps deleted.

(3) *bromflde*] *sic.*

(4) *bosse*] *bossce* Greg.

pd at the apoyntmen*t*e o*f* thomas dowton the 12 of marche 1602 vnto hary chettell in earneste of the 2 p͞te of the florentyn the some of . . . . } xx^s

18[8]9^li (1) – [1]01^s (1) – 6^d

	li	s	d
			d
Some is vj^li / Some vpon band	211	– 9	– 0
	188	– 11	– 6
	400	– 00	– 6

ttottalles – 193^li – 10^s – 06^d besydes the 50^li wch m^r Jonnes & Robart shawe hade

be sydes the band wch they ow*e* vnto me as may*e* apere by band & bo*o*cke the some as foloweth dew

Ther Reastethe dew vnto me to this daye beinge the v daye of maye 1603 when we leafte of playe *n*ow at the kynges co*m*inge all Recknynge*ꝭ* abated the some of A hundred fowerscore & sevntenepownd*ꝭ* & thirteneshellyng*ꝭ* & fowerpence I saye dew – 197^li – 13^s – 4^d the fyftye pownd*ꝭ* wch Jonnes & shawe had at ther goinge a way not Reconed [*as* I tacke y*t*]

Layd owt for facynge of A blacke grogren Clocke wth taffytye . . . . } ixs

[110]

Lent vnto the Company to geue vnto Thomas deckers & midelton in earneste of ther playe Called the pasyent man & the onest hore th*e* some of 1604(2) } v^li

	li	s	d
ttotalles from ther hand*ꝭ* is –	194	– 10	– 06

Caste vp all the acowntes frome the begininge of the world vntell this daye beinge the 14 daye of march*e* 1604 by Thomas dowghton & edward Jube for the company of th*e* princes men & I

(1) [*8*]*9* – [*1*]*01*] *9* altered from *8*, *0* from *1*.
(2) *1604*] interlined.

Phillipe henslow so th[r] Reastethe dew vnto me
P henslow the some of xxiiij[li] all Reconynge*ꝭ* con
sernynge the company in stocke generall descarged
& my sealfe descarged to them of al deat*ꝭ*

[6 *inches blank*]

[110 v] **10069**

[*Blank*]

[111]

[*Blank*]

[5 *inches cut away*]

[111 v] **10066**

The[(1)] ꝑticular of all that her ins[(2)] fferme *in* [s][(3)]hampenet nere *n*orth. *e*letche[(4)]
in y[e] Countey of Gloscester
Inprimis it maketh / lxxx / Acres of ffallowe euerey yeare.
Item it soweth / lxxx / Acres of Corne euerey yeare.
Item it pastureth / 200 / sheepe vpon y[e] dounes.
Item it pastureth / xv / keayne, vpon y[e] Cowe leas.
Item it pastureth / v / horses vpon y[e] horse leas.
Item it hath / xvij / Acres of inclosure for medowe.
besides y[e] hous, Barnes, stables, doue house, and on quarrey of stone,
theare vnto belonginge,
An Estate to be had in y[e] same for / iij / lyues in ꝑsent,
and in Reuercion for / xxxxj / yeares after y[e] iij liues

The price is vj hundered poundes

The rent to y[e] Q*ue̅* xxxix s vj[d (1)]

[1 *inch blank*]

[5 *inches cut away as on recto*]

---

(1) *The...vj[d]*] entry made with book reversed; probably in Paschall's hand.
(2) *her ins*] *sic*; the name of the farm?
(3) *s*] smudged, and presumed to be deleted; as Greg notes, Hampnett is a village a mile north-west of Northleach.
(4) *eletche*] interlined with caret.

[112]

Lent vnto John ockey the 4 of febreary
1601 in Redye m*o*nye the some of

[1 *inch blank*]

memorandom that I John ockeye do owe
and ame in deatted vnto Phillippe henslow
& EAlleyn the some of fyve pownd*e* wch I
borowed of the*m* in mony & to [p]be(1) paye a
gayne at th*e* sayll*e* of the*r* starce in wittnes
wheof I haue herto sette my hande th*e*
4 of febreary 1601
the mark*e* of † John ockey
wittnes to this
nycolas + dame

Mem*o*randum(2) that I Rob*e*rt Sha*a*
haue receaued of m^r^ Phillip Henshlowe
the some of forty shilling*e* vpon a booke
Called the fow*er* sones of Aymon wch booke
if it be not playd by the company of the
fortune nor no[r]e(3) other company by my [*copy*] *lea*⟨..⟩(4)
I doe then bynd my selfe by theis p^r^sent*e* to
repay the sayd some of forty shilling*e*
vpon the deliuery of *m*y booke att Cristmas
next wch shall be in the yeare of our Lord
god 1603 & in the xlvj^th^ yeare of th*e*
Raigne of the queene
p me Robt Shaa(2)

[112v] 10065

[*Blank*]

[113]

[*Blank*]

(1) [*p*]*be*] *b* altered from *p*.
(2) *Memorandum...Shaa*] in Shaa's hand; the signature partly covers the figures *58* and *85*, apparently in Henslowe's hand.
(3) *no*[*r*]*e*] *e* altered from *r*.
(4) *lea*⟨..⟩] interlined above, and heavily blotted; Greg reads *leave*.

Menses[1] Jenewary 20 Ao Rē Elizabeth xl 1597
Richard Connesbey one of the ordenary gentlmen vshers
asketh the allowance for hime sealfe and a grome of the
chamber and a grome of the wardropp for makinge Redey
and attending of the cowntis of darbe debitie for the [Q]
Quenes ma^tie^ at the Crystenyng of my lord winsers chillde
att is [the] howsse in london by the space of two dayes wher
fore they praye to be allowed for ther botheyer and other
Charges two and frowe and to be ra*t*ed and payed them by
the Tresoerer of her ma^tie^ moste honorable chamber .[1]

[4 *inches blank*]

Lent th*e* 12 of marche 1602[2] vnto Thomas blackwode
when he Ride into the *c*ontrey wth his company
to playe in Redy mony the some of . . . . } x^s^

Lent vnto John lowyn th*e* 12 of marche 1602 .
when h*e* went into th*e* contrey wth th*e* company
to playe in Redy mony th*e* some of. . . . . } v^s^

[2¼ *inches blank*]

[114]

Quinto[3] die Maij . 1602 .

Bee it knowne vnto all men by
theis pn̄tę that wee Anthony
Mundy & Thom^a^s Dekker doe
owe vnto Phillip Hynchl*a*y gent
the Som̄e of five powndes of
lawfull mony of Englan*d* to bee
payd vnto him his executo^r^s or
assignes vppon the xth of June
next ensuing the date hereof
In wittnes hereof herevnto
wee haue Sett o^r^ handes
dated the day & yere above
written /[3]

(1) *Menses...chamber.*] written vertically up the left-hand side of the page; in an unidentified hand; perhaps, as Greg suggests, Henslowe taking pains to write neatly.

(2) *1602*] *2* retraced, perhaps, as Greg thinks, altered from *1*.

(3) *Quinto...written /*] in Dekker's hand; signatures of Dekker and Munday, presumably cut from below this entry, are pasted into books in the Bodleian Library; see p. 265.

[2 *inches cut out*]

[Lent vnto Thomas hewode th*e* 1 of septmbȝ to bye hime A payer of sylke garters th*e* some of . . . . } ij s vj d]

Lent vnto Richard perckens th*e* 4 of septmbȝ 1602 to bye thing*e* for thomas hewode playe & to Lend vnto dick syfer weste to Ride downe to his felowes some of } xv[s]

Lent *vn*to Rychard perckyns the 12 of marche 1602[(1)] when he Rid wth th*e* company to playe in th*e* con trey in Redy mony th*e* some of . . . . } x[s]

[1½ *inches blank*]

[114v] 10063

Memorandom that the 25 of June 1603 I talked wth m[r] *P*ope at the scryveners shope wher he lisse consernynge the [l*ea*[(2)]] tackynge of th*e* leace a new of the littell Roosse & he showed me a wrytynge betwext the pareshe & hime seallfe w[ch] was to paye twenty pownd a yeare Rent & to bestowe a hunderd marckes vpon billdinge w[ch] I sayd I wold *R*ather pulledowne the play*e*howse then I wold do so & [b] he beade me do & sayd he gaue me leaue & wold beare me owt for yt wasse [*h*] in hime to do yt

[2 *inches cut out*]

[6 *inches blank*]

[115]

Lent vnto my Lorde of worsters players
as foloweth begynynge the 17 daye of aguste
1602

Lent vnto the companye the 17 of aguste 1602 to pay*e* vnto thomas deckers for new A dicyons in owldcastelle the some of . . . . . } xxxx s

(1) *1602*] interlined above. (2) *lea*] *ta* Greg.

Lent vnto John dewcke th*e* 18 of aguste 1602 to bye Rebatose & fardingalls the some of . } xxxx s

Lent vnto thomas blackwode & John dewcke . to bye tafetie & other stuffe to macke ij wemens gownes the 19 of aguste 1602 the some of . . } ix li

Layd owt for the company at th*e* mermayd when we weare at owre a grement the 21 of aguste 1602 [s]toward(1) ou^r^ sup*e* th*e* some of. } ix s

Lent vnto w^m^ kempe th*e* 22 of aguste 1602 to bye buckram to mack*e*(2) a payer of gyent*e* hosse th*e* some of } v^s^

Lent vnto John ducke & John [thare]thayer(3) the 21 of aguste 1602 to bye A sewt for owld castell & A sewt & A dublet of satten the some of . . . . } xij^li^

Lent vnto John duck*e* to paye for the tvrckes head & ij wemens gownes mackenge & fresh wat*r* for owld castell & th*e* merser bill & harey chettell i*n* eareneste of a tragedie called(4) . . . . ye 24 of aguste 1602 } 3^li^ xs

Layd owt for th*e* company the 25 of aguste 1602 for A clocke of chamllett lined wth crymsen tafetie pincked the some of . . } iiij^li^

Lent vnto John ducke the 27 of aguste 1602 to paye th*e* merser for [saye] layce(5) for th*e* clocke . . . } xiiij s

Layd owt more for the company in p*te* of payment for A Boocke called medsen for a cvrst wiffe(6) the some of. vnto thomas deckers . . . . } xs

li s d
some is – 34 – [7]8(7) – 00

---

(1) [*s*]*toward*] *t* altered from *s*.
(2) *buckram to macke*] interlined with caret.
(3) [*thare*]*thayer*] alteration.
(4) Space was left for a title never entered.
(5) [*saye*] *layce*] alteration.
(6) *wiffe*] interlined above.
(7) [*7*]*8*] alteration.

Lent vnto John ducke the 28 of aguste 1602 to paye vnto xpofer[1] bestone for A manes gowne of Branshed velluet & A dublet for the some of . . . . . } vj^{li}

Lent vnto John ducke the 28 of aguste 1602 to paye vnto the tayllor for stuffe & mackynge of ij wemens gownes the some of . . . . . . } xxxiiij^{s}

pd at the A poyntment of the company the 1 of septmbȝ 1602 in pte of payment for A comody called *A* medysen for A cvrste wiffe to thomas deckers some of } iiij li

pd at the A poyntment the [2 o]*of*[2] comp*any* the 2 of septmbȝ 1602 in fulle payme*nt* for A comody called A medysen for A cvrste wiffe to thomas deckers the some of } xxx^{s}

Lent vnto the company the 3 of septmbȝ 1602 to bye A sewte for wm kem*p*e the some of . . . . } xxx^{s}

Layd owt for the company the 3 of septmbȝ 1602 to bye iiij Lances for the comody of thomas hewedes & m^{r} smythes some of } viij^{s}

Layd owt for the company the 4 of septmbȝ 1602 to bye A flage of sylke the *so*me of } xxvj^{s} 8^{d}

pd at the A poyntment of the company the 4 of septmbȝ 1602 vnto Thomas hewod & m^{r} smyth in fulle payment for A Boocke called al*be*[*l*]re galles[3] some of } vj^{li}

pd vnto you^{r} tyer man for mackynge of w^{m} kempes sewt & the b*o*yes the 4 of septmbȝ 1602 some of . . . . } viij^{s} 8^{d}

some xxij^{li} – xvij s – iiij d

---

(1) *xpofer*] *sic.*

(2) [*2 o*] *of*] Henslowe wrote *2 of*, and altered by scrawling a large *o* over *2 o*.

(3) *albe*[*l*]*re galles*] *r* altered from *l* (from *t*, Greg); the title was added in a space left.

[116]

Lente vnto John thare the 7 of septmb3 1602
to geue vnto Thomas deck*er*s for his adicions } x s
in owld castell th*e* some of . . . .

Lent vnto harey chettell th*e* 7 of septmb3 1602
at th*e* apoyntment [to l*end*] in earenest of A } x^{s}
tragedie called (1) so*me* of

Lent vnto John thare th*e* 8 of septmb3 1602 } x^{s}
to geue vnto harey chettell th*e* so*me* of . .

Lent vnto harey chettell th*e* 9 of septmb3
1602 in p*t* of payme*nt* of A tragedie } x s
called (1) some of

Lent vnto John thare th*e* 10 of septmb3
1602 to paye vnto th*e* merser in p*t* for } lvj s iiij d
sylke for Robes th*e* some of . . . .

Lent vnto thomas blackwode th*e* 19 of
septmb3 1602 to paye vnto Robarte shawe } xvj s
th*e* some of . . . .

Lent vnto th*e* companye the 20 of septmb3 1602
to paye vnto m^{r} smythe in p*te* of payment } iij^{li}
of of A Boocke called marshalle oserecke some of

pd vnto Thomas hewode th*e* 20 of septmb3 } xx s
for the new a dicyons of cvttyng dicke some of

Lent vnto Johen (2) thare the 21 of septmb3 1602 } xx s
to paye for targates the some of . . . . . .

Lent vnto John ducke the 25 of septmb3 1602
to bye A blacke sewt of satten for th*e* playe } vl^{i}
of burone the some of . . . .

pd vnto thomas deckers the 27 of septmb3 1602
over & a bove his price of his boocke called A } x s
medysen for A cvrste wiffe some of. . . . .

Some – 16^{li} – 2^{s} – 3^{d}

---

(1) A modern forger has filled in the title *Robin hoodfellowe* (*goodfellowe* in the second entry), in each case deleting the word *tragedie*, and adding *playe*, interlined in the second entry (so Greg).

(2) *Johen*] *hen* retraced; *John* Greg.

pd vnto Thomas hewode the 30 of septmb3 1602 in fulle payment for his Boocke of oserecke the some of . . . . } iij[li]

Lent vnto John thare the 30 of septmb3 1602 to paye vnto the armerer for targattes in full payment the some of . . . . } xx s

pd at the Apoyntment of the company the 1 of octob3 1602 [*in*]to(1) m[r] smythe in pte of payment for A tragedie called the ij brothers the some of . . . . } xxxx s

[pd vnto my sonne EAlleyn at the A poyntment of the company for his Boocke of tambercame the 2 of octob3 1602 the some of . . . . } [xxxx s]]

Layd owt at the apoyntmente of the companye to macke A scafowld & bare for the playe of Berowne [t]&(2) carpenters wages . . . . } xiij[s]

Lent at the a poyntment of John ducke in earneste of A playe called(3) the some of . . 3 of octob3 1602(4) . to m[r] mydellton . . . . } xx[s]

pd for poleyes & worckmanshipp for to hange absolome . . . . } x*i*iij d

pd at the A poyntment of John dewcke vnto m[r] smythe in pte of payment of his Boocke called the ij brothers tragedie the 11 of octob3 1602 the some of . . } xxxx[s]

pd vnto vnderell at the apoyntmente of the company for wages w[ch] they owght hime the 11 of octob3 1602 the some of . } x s

Some is x[li] iiij s ij d

---

(1) [*in*]*to*] *t* altered from *in* (from *m*, Greg). (2) [*t*]&] alteration.
(3) Space was left for a title never entered. (4) *3 of...1602*] interlined.

[117]

pd at the apoyntmente of John ducke to m^r^ smyth in fulle payment of his Boocke called the ij brothers the 15 of octob3 1602 the *e* some of . . . . } xxxx^s^

Lent vnto John thare the 15 of octob3 1602 to geue vnto harey chettell Thomas deckers thomas hewode & m^r^ smyth*e* & m^r^ webster in earneste of A playe called Ladey Jane the some of . . . . } l s

Le*n*t at the apoyntment of the company to th*e* tyerman to by s*o*wtedge to make devells sewtes for th*e* new playe of the ij brothers tragedie the some of . . . } viij^s^

Lent at the apoyntment of the company vnto the tyerman to bye saye for th*e* playe of th*e* ij brethers (1) to macke a wiches gowne th*e* some of . . . . } [*18*^s^] 18^s^

Lent vnto thomas hewode the 21 of octob3 1602 to paye vnto m^r^ deckers chettell smythe webester & hewode in fulle payme*n*t of ther playe of ladye Jane th*e* some of . . . . . } v^li^ xs

pd vnto EAlleyn the 22 of octob3 1602 at th*e* a poyntme*n*t of the company for a grogren clock*e* ij veluet gerkens ij du*b*letes ij hedtyers the some of . . . . } xx li

pd for bordes & quarters & naylles for to mack*e* a tabell & a coffen for th*e* play*e* of th*e* iij brothes (2) th*e* 22 of octob3 1602 so*m*e of } xij s iij d

some xxxj^li^ xviij s iij d

[117v] **10060**

Lent vnto John thare the 23 of octob3 1602 to paye vnto the paynter of the properties for the playe of the iij *b*rothers th*e* some of . . . . } xx s

---

(1) *brethers*] *brothers* Greg. (2) *brothes*] *sic.*

pd vnto the tyer man for mackynge of the devells sute & sperethes & for the witche for the playe of the iij brothers the 23 of octob3 1602 some of } xs ixd

pd vnto [p]xpofer(1) beston the 26 of octob3 1602 in pte of paymente for the Jerken wch the company had of hime the some of. . } xxs

Lent vnto John ducke the 27 of octob3 1602 to [l]geue(2) vnto thomas deckers in earneste of the 2 pte of Lady Jane the some of } v^s^

Lent vnto Thomas hewode & John webster the 2 of novmb3 1602 in earneste of A playe called cryssmas comes but once ayeare the some of. . . . . } iij^li^

pd for vj yardes of tynsell for the company the 2 of novmb3 1602 the some of . . . . } iij^s^

pd at the apoynttment of the companye the 3 of novmb3 1602 vnto the tayller for the mackynge of the sewte of oserocke the some } xxvj s

Layd owt for the compayne(3) the 6 of novmb3 1602 for xiiij ownces of cope Lace the some of . . . . } ixs 4^d^

more the same tyme vj ownces & ½ of coplace iiij s 4^d^

Lent vnto John dewcke the 6 of novmb3 1602 for to macke a sewt of satten of for the playe of the overthrowe of Rebelles the some of . . . . } v^li^

some xij^li^ 18^s^ x[i]viij s(4) [j]v d(5)

[118]

pd at the a poyntment of the company the 12 of novmb3 1602 vnto the cop lace man in pt of payment for his lace . . . . } xxs

---

(1) [*p*]*xpofer*] *x* altered from *p*.
(2) [*l*]*geue*] *g* altered from *l*.
(3) *compayne*] *sic*.
(4) *x*[*i*]*viijs*] *xviij* altered from *xiiij*.
(5) [*j*]*vd*] *v* altered from *j*.

pd at th*e* a poyntment of John lowen the 12 of
novmbȝ 1602 vnto m^{r} smyth th*e* some of . . . xs

pd at th*e* a poyntment of John lewen th*e* 12 of
novmbȝ 1602 vnto harey chettell th*e* some of. iij s

*L*ent vnto John dewcke the 23 of novmbȝ 1602
to paye vnto hareye chettell & thomas deckers
in p*te* of paymente of A playe called crysmas
comes but once A yeare the some of . . . . xxxx s

pd at the A poyntment of John ducke the
24 of novmbȝ 160[3]2 (1) to m^{r} hathwaye in earneste
of A playe called [John dayes comodye] the blacke doge of newgate (2) some of. . . . . xxxx^{s}

pd vnto Thomas hewode the 24 of novmbȝ
160[3]2 (1) in p*te* of payment of his playe called
th*e* blinde eates many A flye the some of . . iij^{li}

pd at the A poyntment of Thomas hawode the
26 of novmbȝ 16*0*2 [in f*u*] harey chettell in
fulle payment*e* of A playe called cryssmas
comes but once A year*e* th*e* some of . . . . xxxx^{s}

Lent vnto xpofer beston & Robart palante the
26 of novmbȝ 1602 to paye vnto John day m^{r} smyth*e*
m^{r} hathway & th*e* other poet*e* in p*te* of payment
of th*e* playe called [John dayes com*o*dy] the some of
the blacke dogge of newgate (3) xxxx^{s}

Bowght for the company of Robart shawe the 6 of
desembȝ 1602 iiij clothe clockes layd wth cope lace
for iiij^{li} a clocke & for my forberance of my mony to
a lowe me v^{s} vpon euery clocke some is. . . . . . xvij^{li}

some – xxix^{li} xiij s – *00*

---

(1) *160[3]2] 2* altered from *3*.

(2) Not enough space was left for the title, added later, and the word *comodye* had to be written below *John dayes*; this was then deleted, and the full title interlined.

(3) Title interlined below.

Layed owt for the companye the 9 of novmbȝ 1602 to by ij calleco sewtes & ij buckerom sewtę for the playe of cryssmas comes but once a yeare the some of . . . . } xxxviij^s 8^d

[L]Sowld(1) vnto the company the 9 of desembȝ 1602 ij peces of cangable taffetie to macke A womones gowne & a Robe some of . . . } iij^li(2) x^s
for the play of crysmas comes but once a year

Lent vnto the companye the 15 of desembȝ 1602 to paye vnto Thomas hewode [fo]In(3) pte of payment for his playe called the blind eates many A fley the some of . . . . . . } xxx^s

pd at the apoyntment of John dewcte(4) the 18 of desembȝ 1602 vnto ij tayllers for mackyn of gowns & thingę for them j xxs the other xixs the some . . . . } xxxixs

pd at the apoyntment of the company the 20 of desembȝ 1602 vnto m^r hatheway m^r smythe & John daye & the other poyet in fulle payment for A playe called the blacke dogge of newgat some of } xxxx^s

Lent vnto John thare the 1 of Janewary 1602 to geue vnto m^rs calle for ij cvrenetę for hed tyers for the corte the some of . . . . . . } xs

Lent vnto the company the 7 of Janewary 1602 to paye vnt(5) m^r hawode in fulle payment for his playe called the blinde eates many a flye the some of . . . . } xxx^s

Lent vnto Crystofer beston & John ducke the 7 of Janewary 1602 to geue vnto m^r hathwaye & m^r smyth in earneste of A playe called vnfortunat(6) Jenerall frenshe hestorey the some of . . } xxx^s

Some xiiij^li vijs viijd

---

(1) [*L*]*Sowld*] *S* altered from *L*. (2) *iij^li*] *iiij^li* Greg.

(3) [*fo*]*In*] alteration.

(4) *dewcte*] *sic*; *dewcke* Greg; cf. f. 123v, 'Kacke'. (5) *vnt*] *sic*.

(6) *vnfortunat*] title added in insufficient space, and Henslowe began in the margin.

[119]

Lent vnto John dewcke the 10 of Janewarye 1602 to by Lame skenes for the blacke dogge of newgate the some of . . . . . . } xs

pd at the apoyntment of the company the 10 of Janewary 1602 [in]vnto(1) mr hathway & mr smythe in pte of paymente for ther(2) playe called vnfortunat Jeneralle(3) the frenshe hestoreye the some of . . . . } xxxs

Layd owt for the company the 10 of Janewary 1602 to bye cope lace x owners at 10d & ownce the some of . . . . } viijs 4d

pd at the apoyntment of thomas hewod the 14 of Janewary 1602 in earneste of A playe called(4) vnto harey chettell & thomas hewod the some of . . . . } xxxxs

the tayller xviijs pd for the company the 16 of Janewarye 1602 vnto the tayller in the borowghe wch they owght vnto hime the some of . . . . . . } xviijs

pd for the company the 16 of Janewary 1602 vnto the cope lace man in pt of paymente for cope lace the some of . . . . } xxxxs

pd more for the company the 16 of Janewarye 1602 vnto goodman freshwatr for [c]A(5) canves sewt & skenes for the black doge of newgate } xijs

pd at the apoyntment of the company the 16 of Janewarye 1602 vnto mr hathway mr smythe & John daye in pte of payment for ther boocke called the vnfortunat generall frenshe hestorey some of } 40s

Some ixli xviijs iiijd

---

(1) [*in*]*vnto*] *v* altered from *in*. (2) *for ther*] *of ther* Greg.

(3) Not enough space was left for the title, added later, and *Jeneralle* had to be interlined below.

(4) Space left for a title never entered. (5) [*c*]*A*] alteration.

pd at th*e* apoyntment of John ducke & th*e* company th*e* 19 of Janew*a*r*y*e 1602 vnto m^r hathway & m^r smyth & John daye & the other poyet in fulle payment for ther playe called the frenshe hestorye some of . . xxxx^s
vnfortunat Jenerall[1]

Lent vnto John Le*w*en & catte*r*nes[2] the 24 of Janewary 1602 to by a sytyzen cotte & sleves for the playe of the vnfortunat Jenerall the some of . . . . l s

pd at th*e* apoyntment of the compan*y*e the 24 of Janewary 1602 vnto the coꝑ lace man in ꝑte of paymente the some of . . . . xx^s

Lent vnto John Lewen vpon John duckes noote of his hande the 29 of Janewar*y*e 1602 to geue in earneste of th*e* second ꝑt of the boocke called th*e* blacke dooge of newgate vnto m^r hathwa*y*e & John daye & m^r smyth & the other poete the some of . . . . iij^{li}

pd at the apoyntment of John ducke th*e* 3 of febre*a*r*y* 1602 vnto m^r hathwa*y*e m^r smythe John daye & th*e* other poet in fulle payment for *the* boocke called th*e* seco*n*de ꝑt of th*e* blacke dooge the some of . . . . iiij^{li}

pd at the a poyntment of the companye the 4 of febreary 1602 vnto the tayller for velluet & satten for the womon gowne of black velluet wth th*e* other lynenges belonging*e* to yt the some of . xxij s

pd vnto Thomas hewode th*e* 5 of fe*b*reary 1602 for A womones gowne of black velluett for the play*e* of A womon kylld wth kyndnes some of vj^{li} 13^s

pd vnto th*e* cop*e*lace man in ꝑte of payment th*e* 7 of febreary 1602 for th*e* com*pany* the some of . . . . xx s

Som xxj^{li} v^s oo d

---

(1) Title interlined below. (2) *catternes*] *cattanes* Greg; *er* blotted.

pd at the A poyntment of the company the 12 of febreary 1602 [in]vnto[1] thomas Hewwod in pt of payment for his playe called A womon kylled wth kyndnes the some of	iij li
dd vnto the tyerman for the companye 1602 to bye viij yrdes & A hallfe of blacke satten at xij s a y^{r}de to macke a sewt for the 2 pte of the blacke dogge the some of	v^{li} ij s
¶ 15 of febrearye	
pd at the apoyntmente of the companye the 16 of febreary 1602 vnto the cope lace man in pte of payment the some of	xx s
Lent vnto Thomas blacke wode the 21 of febreary 1602 to geue vnto the 4 poetes in earneste of ther adicyones for the 2 pte of the blacke dog the some of	x s
Lent vnto Thomas blacke wode the 24 of febreary 1602 to geue vnto the 4 poetes in pte of paymente for ther adycyons in the 2 pte of the blacke doge .	x s
Lent vnto John dewcke the 26 of febreary 1602 to paye the poetes in fulle payment for ther adycyones for the 2 pte of the blacke doge the some of	xx s
pd vnto the cop lace man the 4 of marche 1602 in pte of payment the some of	xx s
pd at the apoyntment of the company the 6 of marche 1602 vnto Thomas Hewode in fulle p payment for his playe called a womon kyld wth kyndnes the some of	iij li
pd at the apoyntment of thomas blackewod & John Lewen the 7 of marche 1602 vnto m^{r} smythe in earneste of & etalleyon tragedie the some of	xxxx^{s}

ttotalles – 220^{li} – 13^{s} – 3^{d} Some is – xvij^{li} – ij s Reste dew – 131^{li} – 12^{s} – 04^{d}

---

(1) [*in*]*vnto*] *v* altered from *in*.

pd at the apoyntmente of Thomas blackwode
the 7 of marche 1602 vnto the tayller wch made
the blacke satten sewt for the womon kyld wth kyndnes } xs
the some of . . . .

pd at the a poyntment of John Lowine the 12 of
marche 1602 vnto m^{r} smythe in fulle payment for } iiij^{li}
his tragedie called the etallyan tragedie . . . .
the some of . . . .

pd for the company the 16 of marche 1602 vnto
the mercers man w^{m} Pvl^{e}ston for his m^{r} [deatte]
John willett deate the some of eighte pownde } viij^{li} x^{s}
& xs wch they owght hime for satten & charges
in the clyncke for arestynge John ducke I say
as maye apere

Some – 140^{li} – 1 – 00^{d}

Mem̄ that the fulle some of all the deatbtes
wch we owe vnto m^{r} Henslow̄ to this xvj of m^{r}che
1603 comethe to Juste the some of 140^{li} – 1 s – 00 d
wch some of 140^{li} – 01^{s} – 00^{d} we w[o]hosse[1] names
are here vnder wrytten do a knowledge ower dew
deatte & promysse trewe payment
Thomas Blackwod[2]

pd the cope lace man is to be[3] payed iiij^{li}
pd more the cope lace the some of – vj^{li} iiij s

[2¼ *inches blank*]

[121]

In the name of god Amen

Begininge to playe Agayne by the kynges licence
& Layd owt sence for my lord of worsters men
as folowethe 1603 9 of maye

(1) *w[o]hosse*] *h* altered from *o*.
(2) The signature seems to be autograph.
(3) *be*] interlined.

Lent at the apoyntment of Thomas hewode & John ducke vnto harey chettell & John daye in earneste of A playe wherin shores wiffe is writen the some of . . . . . . } xxxx^{s}

[8¼ *inches blank*]

[121 v] **10053**

[*Blank*]

[122]

[*Blank*]

[122 v] **10049**

A Juste note what I haue Lent
vnto edmond Henslow in mony & Layd
owt in the be hallfe of his iij Chelldren
as folowethe 1593

Lent vnto my brother when he tocke the Leace of his Howsse in sothwarke the some of . . . } iiij li

more he hade of me A new gowne for his wiffe wch coste me Redy mony the some of. . . . } l s

Lent vnto my brother when he tocke the Leace of his howsse on the bancksyd th*e* some of . . . . } xxxx^{s}

Lent vnto my brother when he tocke the Leace of his howsse in Lambeth marche the some of . . } xxxx s

Lent vnto my brother to macke & eand wth one of his credytores wch did a tache his ware in soth fayer the some of . . . . } xx s

Lent vnto my brother when he went vnto my lorde chamberlens to searve hime & was at that tyme entertayned } xxxx^{s}

Layd owt when I came downe firste when my brother Laye sycke in carges to them ther wch kepte hime . } viij s

Layd owt when I came downe Laste in carges to them wch kept hime . . . . } xij s

pd vnto goodman Hartrope for threshinge. . . . . viij s 4 d

Lent vnto my syster margery to fynd heare . . . . v^s 4d
pd for a horsse & his charges to Ride vp & downe . . . . . xxxx^s
pd for beinge a myted in the sprytiall(1) corte . . . . iiij s
pd for provinge the ij willes & for the admynystracyon . . . $xviij^s$
pd vnto m^r docter Ridley for his fee . . . . vj s 8^d
pd vnto m^r cole for his fee . . . . vj s 4d
pd vnto the procter his fee . . . . iij s 4^d
pd vnto the Regester for seatyng downe the acte . . . . . . ij s
pd vnto the Regester for mackynge the bande . . . . xij d
pd vnto the docters mane & the Regester for ther(2) Labur . . ij s
pd vnto the sargent at Lawe for his cownsell . . . . x s
pd vnto my atorny for diues(3) tyme goinge wth me h*i*s fee . vj s 8^d
pd for a copey of th*e* wryte . . . . vj d
pd m^r checke my atorney his fee . . . . iij s 4^d
pd m^r checke for mackynge a pearance & goinge by wat^r . . xxj^d
pd for goinge vp to westmester diuers tymes. . . . . ij s

[123]

pd for goinge to m^r vahanes atorny fermer & arynge(4) my a torney wth me . . . . } iiij s
pd vnto my atorney & goinge by water . . . . iiij s vj d
pd the 20 of maye 1593 for goinge wth my atorney to my Lord of buckhurst*e* a bowt the copey hold Land wch welles doeth wth howld frome vs. . . . . } iiij s
Layd owt to goo to grensted to trye & Isapryse(5) betwxt edward phillipes & me for the Land called the Lockyears . . . . } l s
pd vnto ij cownselers & my atorney to go to the tearme beinge howlden at senttalbones 1593 myhelmas terme } xxxx^s
pd vnto the screuener for mackynge of a Leace my brother w^m henslow of the barne & stable & crafte. . . . . . . } iiij s
Layd owt at helery terme in the yeare 1594 to my cownselers for iij several tyme . . . . } xxx s
pd for draynge my bylle to put into the starechambȝ a geanste cowchman keder & phillipes vpon pargerey } viij s
pd for drainge of intargreytoreys & Ingrosynge them in pchment iij severall ones . . . . } vij s 8^d

---

(1) *sprytiall*] *sic*; *sprytrall* Greg.
(2) *ther*] *the* Greg.
(3) *diues*] *sic*; *diuers* Greg.
(4) *arynge*] *sic*.
(5) *& Isapryse*] *sic*; *Isaprys*t Greg; cf. f. 41.

pd vnto hime wch dide exsamen thes iij men . . . . xiij s vj d

pd vnto my atorny fuller to despatche diuers matters for me in the starechamb3 . . . . } xxij s

pd vnto my cownseler & my atorney for putinge in of — my declaration into the stare chamb3 at easter tearme 1594 } 13^s^ 8^d^

pd vnto m^r^ ward for the copey of the corte Rowles . . . . xiij s

pd vnto m^r^ fuller for diuers matters for mydsomer terme a bowt this sewtes . . . . } xxx^s^

pd vnto fuller for fetchinge the comysyon & his fee to carey downe into the contrey . . . . } vij s 4^d^

pd m^r^ fuller for Ridinge into the contrey & comynge vp agayne to London . . . . } v^s^

geuen my cownseler for drawinge my Intergretoreys to my comysyon the 19 of desemb3 1594 . . . . } x s

geuen vnto Richard cvxson & his wife to a knowlege A fyne a bowt the howsse & Land the 3 of June 1595 . } xxxx s

pd for bringinge vp the ij chelldren to London. . . . . iiij s

pd vnto John gryges when I put mary henslow to him to Learne to sowe al maner of workes & to Lerne bonelace wch was the 5 daye of June 1595 the some of. . . . . . } v^li^

pd vnto Richard skeppe at the apoyntment of my brother edmonde henslow wch he owght hime . . . . } xx s

[123 v] **10048**

pd for the Ingrosynge of the Inventarye . . . . xvj s vj d

pd vnto the pareter his fee . . . . ix s

pd vnto cvxson(1) & his wiffe to Releace [his]ther(2) Righte in the howsse as maye apeare by wrytynge forty powndeȩ & then they a knoleged a fyne I saye pd. . . . . } 40^li^

Layd owt in mony to by nane a gowne when her syster turned her awaye . . . . } xxviij^s^

[*83*]84^li^(3) – 15^s^ – 5^d^

pd vnto Richard Cuxen for the copiholld landes & mackynge the writingeȩ & sewt(4) . . . . } xxxv^li^ x s

pd vnto w^m^ henslow his mony wch he Layd owt for berynge of my brother edmond hensley . . . . } xxxx^s^

(1) *cvxson*] *cvxton* Greg.
(2) [*his*]*ther*] alteration.
(3) [*83*]*84*] alteration.
(4) *& sewt*] interlined.

pd vnto John walters the 23 of maye 1592 for my systers Legassey when he mareyd her . } 060li – 0s – 0d

pd John walters for the vsse of the mony the some of . . . . . . } xli [97 – 10 – 00d]

li s d

107 – 10 – 00

Layd owt to defend the sewt ageanste
John henslow sonne of edmond henslow
to defend his fathers(1) will as foloweth 1604

pd for searchinge the Recordes for the aregenall will & for the procters paynes . . . . } iiij s

Itm pd vnto my docter his fee . . . . xs

Itm pd vnto the exsamener of my wetneses . . . . xs

Itm pd for my brother williames carges Lyghinge — in towne with his horsse to be exsamened for the wille } xxvj s

pd & John henslow to Kacke(2) his syster marey home to his howsse [w]after(3) she was fallen Lame . . . . } xxxxs

besyddes her aperell

Bowght a gowne & a certtell the 20 of maye 1607
for nane henslow wch coste . . . . xxxxs

goody glover hathe payd vnto nane henslow for a boote wch she had of hichenson wch I gaue my word for [h]vnto(4) hime the 20 of July 1607 the some of . . . . } 27s

dd vnto nane henslow more a bedsteade standinge. . . . . . xs

[124]

Sowld vnto mr arthur Langworth the howsse wch my brother dwelte in after the deseace of my syster margery his wiffe wth the trashe therin for the some of . . . . iiij score pownd℮ wittnes EAlleyn I saye . . . . . . } 80li

Rd of mr Thomas Chalener vpon a band 100li

This margrey(5) the wife of edmond henslow deseaced ded desyer
to haue the bordinge & bringyn vp of her owne iij chelldren
after al the good weare praysed wch the one halfe was to
her sealfe & the other halfe vnto John & mary wch was
valewed to 30li (6) & for that halfe she was contented

(1) *fathers*] interlined with caret.
(2) *Kacke*] *sic.*
(3) [*w*]*after*] *a* altered from *w*.
(4) [*h*]*vnto*] *v* altered from *h*.
(5) *margrey*] *sic*; *margery* Greg.
(6) *30li*] added later.

to bord them & scolle them & so did for the space of iij
yeares w[ch]hyll(1) she liued & after her deseace they came al vp to
me to London to kepe the 27 of febreary 1595 & hathe bene
euer sence at my carges & as I haue payd for ther borde to
ther mother I locke a cordynge to the will to be(2) a lowed yt agayn*e*

Layd owt at Severall tyme for John
Henslow the sonne of edmond Henslow
as foloweth 1596

Layd owt money to by hime a clocke. . . . . xvij s
Layd owt for mackynge his a parell . . . . xxij d
Lent hime in mony to by a hatte . . . . iiij s
Lent hime to by ij shertes . . . . v^s^ vj d
Layd owt for hime to m^r^ newman dier when he tocke hime prenteys th*e* some of. . . . . xxxx s
Lent vnto John henslow by my wiffe . . . . v^s^
Lent vnto hime more by my wiffe when he was sycke . . . vij s
Lent vnto hime by my wiffe when he Leafte his clocke . . . xv^s^
Layd owt vnto Jeames Rusell for a botte for hime . . . . . v^li^
Layd owt the 28 of septmb*3* 1605 to bye the kyng*e* water manes place[*f*]&(3) for his Leatters wch he weare*e* 14^li^ – 16

marey Henslow felle sicke of a dead pallsey in th*e*
yeare 1605 & liued after in that deasease ij yeares
al wch time I payd for her kepinge ij s a weeke
besydes that wch she coste at surgerey & docters
wch ij yeares comes to – x^li^ the Reast I leue

[124 v] **10046**

1609

Layd owt a bowt nane henslow to m^r^ gryffen wch folowed ther sewte in the spirtuall corte for her & w^m^ parsones a genste goodmane fo[*l*]rlonge(4) Son*ne* wch wold a mareyd her wch was at one tyme – xxvj s & at & other tyme – l s wch was in th*e* yeare 1609 some is . . . . 04^li^ – 06^s^ – 00^d^

[9½ *inches blank*]

(1) *w[ch]hyll*] *h* altered from *ch*.
(2) *be*] added later, and squeezed into the line.
(3) [*f*]&] alteration.
(4) *fo*[*l*]*rlonge*] *r* altered from *l*.

[125]

[*Blank*]

[125 v] 10045

A Juste note what wm henslow owes vnto me
Phillype henslow as foloweth

Lent vnto w^{m} henslew at severall tymes In Redy
money th*e* some of . . . . } xv^{s}

my brother w^{m} doth owe vnto me 13^{li} – 10^{s} – 0 wch wase
dew vnto my Brother edmond by the gy*f*te of
John henslow by his will vpon a band dew by
m^{r} Car[*ew*]alle(1) knyght wch band was a hunderd
& fyve powd℮ wch hunderd w^{m} was to haue
& the 5^{li} & th*e* vsse is dew vnto me Phillipe hensl*owe*
wch v^{li} w^{m} sayes the knyght hath payd yt to my
broth*er* John so Restet. . . . . } 09^{li} – 10^{s}

Lent vnto w^{m} Hensley th*e* 3 of ap^{r}ell 1593 to do his
besynes when he went to my Lord chamberlens
In Redy mony th*e* some of . . . . } xxxx^{s}

Lent w^{m} more th*e* 20 of ap^{r}ell 1593 a bowt my lord
chamberlens service In Redy mony some of . . . } xx^{s}

Lent vnto w^{m} henslow the 29 of ap^{r}ell 1593 when he
bowght goody*e* mowshurste a hatte & to Ride
home into th*e* contrey ij s & ij s some is . . . . . } iiij s

Lent more vnto w^{m} henslow the 29 of maye 1593 in
Redy mony when he wanted th*e* some of . . . . } iiij^{s}

w^{m} henslow hath Receued of goodman hartrop for
a cowlte wch was myne th*e* some of. . . . . . . } xvj s

Lent vnto w^{m} hensl*o*w at severall tymes as he
nedeth in Redy mony. . . . . } viij s

Lent vnto w^{m} henslow when he feched owt his writ℮
for his witneses at grensteade In Redy mony . . . . } v^{s}

[1½ *inches blank*]

(1) *Car*[*ew*]*alle*] *al* altered from *ew*.

3. ENTRIES BY PHILIP HENSLOWE MADE WITH THE BOOK REVERSED, FF. 238–126 v

[238]

A not what edward allen hath layd owt
as foloweth

Itm pd for ij thowsen & halfe of bryckes . . . . xxvij s vj d
Itm pd for a mantell tre . . . . xij d
Itm pd for tylle penes . . . . viij d
Itm pd ij d for bryngen of the leade . . . . ij d
Itm pd for a lode of bryckes . . . . vsj vj d
Itm pd for hallfe a lode of lathes . . . . xij s vj d
Itm pd for makenge and eande of the chemnese . . . . . v s
Itm pd vnto the brycklayer for tyllenge . . . . iij s viij d
Itm pd vnto the laberer for ij dayes . . . . xx d
Itm pd vnto R laberer for iiij dayes . . . . iij s [4]6d (1)
Itm pd vnto gorg for bryngen of bordes . . . . ij d
Itm pd for a thowsand of tylles . . . . xj s
Itm pd vnto the tyller & the laberer . . . . iiij s 4d
Itm pd vnto bolocke the laborer . . . . xviij d
Itm pd for Rige tilles . . . . xviij d
Itm pd vnto Robart for his wages . . . . ij s
Itm pd vnto the baraman (2) . . . . vj d
Itm pd vnto J gryges man John the 24 of novemb3 1592 (3). xxxxs
Itm pd vnto mr draper for deall bordes . . . . l s
Itm pd for A lode of Rafters . . . . xxij s
Itm pd vnto the plomer for 4–1–22 of lead at j d & qli. . . l s
Itm pd vnto the glaser the 24 of novmb3 1592 . . . . . . xxs
Itm pd vnto R Rogers toward his bargen In pte . . . . . viij s
Itm pd for ij lode of sande . . . . ij s
Itm pd for xij bushelles of heare . . . . vijs ij d

(1) [4]6] alteration.
(2) *baraman*] a doubtful reading.
(3) *1592*] interlined above.

Itm pd for j lode of lome . . . . xij d
Itm pd for xxj longe dealle bordes . . . . lij s
Itm lente vnto R Rogers . . . . ij s vj d
Itm pd for bryngen of the dell bordes by water . . . . . xviij d
Itm lent vnto R Rogers . . . . ix s vj d
Itm pd for lome . . . . xij d
Itm pd for iiiij bundell of lathes . . . . v s
Itm lent R Rogers . . . . xij d
Itm pd vnto the Joyner for his worke . . . . vj s
Itm pd vnto R Rogers . . . . to by coler . . . . iij[s] 4[d]

[1 *inch blank*]

[237v]

	2	11 –	
30	01 – 18 – 00		
	. 6 – 02		
	13 – 04 02		

[237]

the A cownte of Suche Carges as hathe bene
layd owt a bowt edward alenes howsse as foloweth
1592

novemb3 4 1592 Itm pd vnto John gryges In pt . . . . v[s]li (1)
Itm pd vnto the Bricklayer his wages . . . . xij s
Itm pd vnto the laborer his wages . . . . v s
Itm pd vnto a laborer . . . . viij d
Itm pd vnto the smyth for Iorne bares for the windo . . . v s
Itm pd vnto the smyth for a doge of Iorne . . . . j s vj d
Itm pd for halfe a lode of lathes . . . . xiij s
Itm pd for a bundell of lathes & tillepenes . . . . xvj[d]
novemb3 11 Itm pd for j hundered of vj d naylles . . . . vj d
Itm pd vnto the bricklayer y[t] makes the chemnes . . . . . xx s
Itm pd vnto Robart . . . . x[s]
Itm pd vnto the labourer . . . . iij s vj d
Itm pd for sande & lome . . . . x[s]
Itm pd for bryngen of tylles & bryngen of lathes . . . . . xij d
Itm pd for bryngen of bordes . . . . vj d

(1) v[s]li] *l* altered from *s*.

Itm pd for a hunderd of lath naylls . . . . iij d
Itm pd for a packe of tyle pennes . . . . iiij d
Itm pd for ij thowsen of tylles . . . . xxij s
[Itm(1) pd vnto J gryges man John the 24 novembʒ 1592 . xxxx^s
Itm pd vnto m^r draper for dealle bordes . . . . l s
Itm pd for a lode of Rafters . . . . xxij s
Itm pd vnto the plomer for 4–1–22 of lead at j^d & q^li . . . l s
Itm pd vnto the glaser the 24 of novmbʒ 1592 In pt . . . . xx^s(1)]
Itm pd for vj payer of sheates & a coverlet . . . . v^li
pd vnto John grygges in fulle payment of all Recknynges . xxxx^s
Itm pd vnto Robart Rogers In pte ye 22 desembʒ . . . . . ix s
Itm pd vnto Robart Rogers In pt . . . . iij s 4^d
Itm pd vnto the lyme man the 23 of desembʒ 1592 . . . . xxiiij s vj^d
Itm pd vnto Robart rogers to worde his bargen . . . . . . [v]x s(2)
Itm lent R Rogers to by coler . . . . iij s 4^d
Itm lent Ro Rogers to by coler . . . . x[v]x d(3)
Itm lent R Rogers to by Roset coler . . . . ij s
Itm pd vnto the naylle man at the fringpane In fulle. } lj s
locke the next leafe folowinge but one [pd vnto the] [Joyner ix s vj d] payment the 19 of Jeneway 1593 the some of . . . }
Itm pd for a bundell of lathes . . . . xij d
Itm pd R Rogers in full payment the 20 Jenewarye . . . . xij^s
Itm pd for mackinge of ij Iorne cassementes . . . . iij s
Itm pd vnto the Joyner . . . . iij s
Itm pd for hallfe a hunderd of lyme . . . . ij s x d
Itm pd vnto the Joynner in pte . . . . xx s

[236]

Layd owt for my Lorde Admeralle seruantes . . . . . .
as ffoloweth 1594

layd owt for gowinge & cominge to somerset }
howe for iiij tymes . . . . } j s 4^d
layd owt for mackinge of o^r leater twise . . . . xij d
layd owt for drinckinge wth the Jentellmen . . . . iiij s 8^d
layd owt at a nother time for drinckinge . . . . xij[s]d(4)
s d – 2 – 08(5) layd owt goinge vp & downe to corte twise . . . . j s 4^d

[8½ *inches torn out*]

---

(1) *Itm...xx^s*] cancelled; these entries are duplicated from f. 238.
(2) [*v*]*xs*] *x* altered from *v*. (3) *x*[*v*]*xd*] *x* altered from *v*.
(4) *xij*[*s*]*d*] *d* altered from *s*. (5) Part of the sum is torn away.

[235v]

300–	[1]02 (1)	–03
132–	19	–02
167–	[00]3 (2)	01
300	*02*	03

143 –	02 –	08
020 –	00 –	00
120 –	02 –	08
033 –	00 –	00
020 –	00 –	00
173	02	08

050 –	00 –	00
007 –	00 –	00
009 –	09 –	00
002 –	13 –	08
027 –	14 –	02
087	16	10

362 –	19 –	03
239 –	17 –	04
123	01	11
362	19	03

173 –	02 –	08
087 –	16 –	10
085	05	10
173	02	08

5 –	6 –	8
6 –	0 –	0
2 –	0 –	0
2 –	13 –	4
9 –	10 –	0
4 –	0 –	0
2 –	13 –	4
2 –	13 –	4
2 –	0 –	0
6 –	13 –	0
4 –	0 –	0
6 –	3 –	4
1 –	10 –	0
55	1	0

for (3) z° in
in

Booke (3)

(1) [*1*]*02*] *o* altered from *1*. (2) [*oo*]*3*] *oo* smudged and probably deleted.
(3) *for*...*Booke*] possibly not in Henslowe's hand.

[235]

// edwarde allenes Recknynge(1)

Itm pd vnto the Joyner . . . . ix^s vj^d

Itm pd for iiij new quarters & ij ynche bordes . . . . xix d

Itm pd for iiij old pece of tymbȝ for th*e* chem̅ . . . . xviij ds

Itm pd vnto th*e* Joyner In p̱te . . . . xxxx s

Itm pd vnto steven th*e* carpenter for his wages . . . . iiij s

Itm pd vnto the gardener for diginge th*e* garden . . . . . . xvj d

Itm pd vnto th*e* Joyner in fulle payment*e* . . . . xx^s vj d

Itm pd vnto th*e* lymman for hallfe a hunde*r*d of lyme. . . . ij s x d

Itm pd for j bundell of lathe & 1 q̱ter & bryngynge. . . . . ij s

Itm pd for A lod of lyme . . . . xiij d

Itm pd for small*e* spertelles grene . . . . xx d

Itm pd for halfe a hund*er*d of square tylles . . . . iiij s v d

Itm pd vnto th*e* glaser in fulle paymente . . . . xvij s

Itm pd for cheacker tylles . . . . iij s 4 d

Itm pd for other tylles . . . . vj d

Itm pd vnto steuen th*e* carpent*er* . . . . xij d

Itm pd vnto brader for v^{li} & a hallfe of Iorne . . . . xij d

Itm pd vnt*o* edward allen j carpet of dornex*e* . . . . ix^s

Itm lent edward allen to paye the Joyner ¶ 9 of febreary 1593(2) xxxx^s

Itm pd vnto the nayllman th*e* 29 of febreary 1594 . . . . . vj s viij d

Itm pd for the leasse to Robartes . . . . xxij^{li}

Itm pd for makinge th*e* writtinges . . . . v^s

Itm pd vnto eadward allen the 5 of July in mony. . . . . . x^{li}

edward allen had of me Russett to make h*im* a clock*e* . . . . xij s

Itm pd vnto edward allen th*e* 9 of septmbȝ 1594 money . . . xx^{li}

Itm pd vnto frances hensley for a Keverynge. . . . . xviij s

Itm sowld vnto my sonne A fether bead for . . . . xxx s

Itm pd vnto m^r langworthe for my sonne . . . . xxvij^{li} x s

Itm pd vnto m^r langworthe the same time. . . . . x s

li s d Itm pd for makinge of wr*i*tinges for my sones p̱te . . . . . xx s

148 - 12 - 00 Itm pd vnto m^r langworthe in ffulle payment . . . . xxxj^{li}

Itm pd toward the [death] beringe of ardnold . . . . ij^{li} x s

li s d Itm pd hime in exchange of his clocke for saten & a clocke of mine . l s

154 - 12 - 00 Itm tvrned over frome the tayller to my sonne . . . . xx s

\+ Itm lent vnto my sone edward alen to leand vnto edward dvtten the 14 of marche 1597 the some of . . . . } iij^{li}

\+ at ther laste comynge Itm lent vnto my sonne edward alen to lend vnto John synger & thomas towne when they went into the contrey some } xxxx^s

(1) Greg thinks that this heading was added later. (2) *1593*] interlined above.

	154	12	
	46		
Reste	45	8	dewe
		15 – 12	

Some is my moste homble

	li	s	ds	
[owinge vnto my sonne . .	045 –	08 –	00	
my sonne owes me	060 –	00 –	00	
&	100 –	00 –	00	
&	002 –	10 –	00	
lent m^r langworth	002 –	00 –	00	
for m^r ffuller	001 –	02 –	00	
lent m^r langworth at my lordes . .		02 –	06	
+ lent m^r langworth	[024 –	00 –	00]	
lent m^r langworth	003 –	00 –	00	in the marshallse]

[234]

A note what money I owe vnto my Sonne edward allenne as ffolowethe & a notte what my sonne edward allen owes vnto me

	li	s	d
[Itm I owe vnto my sonne	o[2]45 (1) –	08 –	00
Itm my sonne owes vnto me.	[o]060 –	00 –	00
Itm lent my sonne to paye m^r langworth .	100 –	00 –	00
Itm lent more vnto m^r langworth	002 –	10 –	00
Itm lent mor vnto m^r langworth sonne (2) .	002 –	00 –	00
Itm turned to m^r langworth frome m^r fuler	001 –	00 –	00
Itm lent m^r langworth at my lordes . . .	000 –	02 –	06
Itm lent m^r langworth in presen	003 –	00 –	00]

(1) *o[2]45*] *4* altered from *2*. (2) *sonne*] *some* Greg, who conjectures *sonne* in his notes.

[Itm layd owt for edward alleyn the 9 of June 1597 for
to descarge hime of his preue sealle the some of . . . } xx^{s}
Itm pd vnto the clarke of the senette for my sonne
edward alleyn for a lowenge of the pattiyne . . . . } xx^{s}]

lent vnto edward dutten the 18 of July 1597 in
Redey money to be payd me wth in one forth } xx^{s}
nyght agayene wittnes EAlleyn & m^{r}s Gryges(1)
lent hime more in money . . . . . [ij s]

[Itm lent vnto my sonne edward allen for synger . . . . xx s
Itm lent vnto my sonne to bye a gowne for his wiffe . . . xxxx^{s}
Itm lent vnto my sonne for to geue the tayller . . . . . . xxxx s]

lent vnto Bengemen Johnson player the 28 of
July 1597 in Redey mony the some of fower powndes
to be payd yt agayne when so euer ether I or any
for me shall demande yt I saye . . . . } $iiij^{li}$
wittnes EAlleyn & John synger

[233 v] **10**

1[0]23(2)– 04 – 06
3

126 – 04 – 06

[Receued of my sonne for John synger in pte of payment . . . . x s

lent Bengemyne Johnson the 5 of Jeneway 1597
I(3) Redy mony the some of . . . . v^{s}

[233]

M^{r}andom that the 27 of Jeuley 1597 I heayred
Thomas hearne wth ij^{d} pence for to searve me ij yeares
in the qualetie of playenge for fyue shellynges
a weacke for one yeare & vj^{s} viij d for the other
yeare wch he hath couenanted hime seallfe

---

(1) *Gryges*] interlined below.
(2) *1[0]23*] *2* altered from *0*.
(3) *I*] *sic.*

to searue me & not to departe frome my companey
tyll this ij yeares be eanded wittnes to this
John synger
Jeames donston
thomas towne

lent vnto John synger the 25 of July 1597 in Redey money to be payd me wth in one fortnyght next after the date herof . . . } xx^s^
lent[1] more the 9 of aguste 1597 Redey money. . . x^s^[1]
wittnes EAlleyn

[lent vnto Richard alleyn at severalle
tymes in Redey money as foloweth this yeare 1597
lent hime the 27 of maye 1597 . . . . v^s^
lent hime the 19 of June 1597 . . . . v^s^
lent hime the 4 of July 1597 . . . . vj d
lent hime the 23 of July 1597 . . . . xij d
lent hime the 1 of agust 1597 . . . . xij d
Lent hime vpon a payer of sylke stockens . . . . xiij s
payd for the dienge of them sylke stockens . . . . xvj d]

[lent John Helle the clowne the 3 of aguste 1597 in Redey money the some of. . . . . } x^s^
at that tyme I bownd hime by ane a sumsett of ij d
to contenew wth me at my howsse in playnge tylle
srafte tyd next after the date a boue written yf not
to forfytte vnto me fortipowndes wittneses to the same
EAlleyn John synger Jeames donstall
edward Jubey samewell Rowley]

[1 *inch blank*]

[232v] 11

M^r^andom that the 6 of aguste 1597 I bownd Richard Jones
by & a sumsett of ij d to contenew & playe wth the company
of my lord admeralles players frome mi[x]helmase[2] next after the
daye a bowe w^r^itten vntell the eand & tearme of iij yeares
emediatly folowinge & to playe[3] in my howsse only knowne by the name
of the Rosse & in no other howse a bowt london publicke & yf

(1) *lent...x^s^*] interlined.
(2) *mi*[*x*]*helmase*] *h* altered from *x*.
(3) *& to playe*] interlined with caret.

Restraynte be granted then to go for th*e* tyme into th*e* contrey & af*t*er to retorne agayne to london yf he breacke this a sumsett then to forfett vnto me for the same a hundreth markes of lafull money of Ingland wittnes to this EAlleyn & John midelton

(1)more over Richard Jones at that tyme hathe tacken one other ij d of me vpon & asumset to forfet vnto me one hundrethe [*m*] markes yf one Robart shaee do not playe wth my lordes admeralles men as he hath covenanted be fore in euery thinge & tyme to th*e* oter meste wittnes / EAlleyn / John midellton /

[232]

M^r^dom that the 10 of aguste 1597 w^m^ borne came & *o*fered hime sealfe to come and playe wth my lord admeralles mean at my howsse called by the name of the Rosse setewate one th*e* back(2) after this order folowinge he hathe Receued of me iij d vpon & A sumsette to forfette vnto me a hundrethe marckes of lafull money of Ingland yf he do not performe thes thinges folowing*e* that is presentley after libertie beinge granted for playinge to come & to playe wth my lorde*s* admeralle*s* men at my howss*e* aforsayd & not in any other howsse publick*e* a bowt london for th*e* space of iij yeares beginynge Imediatly after this Re straynt is Recaled by the lordes of the cownsell wch Restraynt is by the menes of playinge the Ieylle of dooges yf he do not then he forfettes this asumset afore or ells not wittnes to this EAlleyn & Robsone

M^r^dom that the 6 of octob3 1597 Thomas dowten came & bownd hime seallfe vnto me in xxxx^li^ in [covenante] & a s*o*mesett(3) by the Rec*e*uing of iij d of me before wittnes the covenant is this that he shold frome th*e* daye a bove written vntell sra*ft*id next come ij yeares to playe [wth me] in my howsse [. .]&(4) in no other a bowte London pvblickeley yf he do wth owt my consent to forfet vnto me this some of money a bove writte*n* wittnes to this EAlleyn Robarte shawe w^m^ borne John synger dick*e* Jonnes

---

(1) *more over*...] separated from the entry above by a rule.

(2) *back*] *sic* (=bank).

(3) *& a somesett*] interlined above.

(4) [. .]&] alteration.

Bowght my boye Jeames brystow of william agusten
player the 18 of desemb3 1597 for viij li

[2½ *inches blank*]

[231]

[5 × 7½ *inches cut out*]

me^{r}d that this 25 of marche 1598[(1)] Richard alleyne[(1)] came & bownde hime seallfe vnto me for ij yeares in & asumsette as a hiered servante wth ij [d] syngell pence & to contenew frome the daye aboue written vnto th*e* eand & tearme of ij yeares yf he do not performe this couenant then he to forfette for the breache of yt fortye powndes & wittnes to this

w^{m} borne
Thomas dowton
gabrell spencer
Robart shawe
Richard Jonnes

m^{do}r that this 25 of marche 1598 Thomas hawoode came & hiered hime seallfe wth me as a covenante searvante for ij yeares by th*e* Receuenge of ij syngell pence acordinge to th*e* statute of winshester & to begin*ne* at th*e* daye aboue written & not to playe any wher publicke a bowt london not whille thes ij yeares be exspired but in my howsse yf he do then he doth*e* forfett vnto me th*e* Receuinge of thes ij d fortie powndes & wittnes to this

Antony monday	w^{m} Borne
gabrell spencer	Thomas dowton
Robart shawe	Richard Jonnes
Richard alleyn	

[230v] 13

M^{r}dm that this 16 of novmb3 1598 I hired as my covenente Servantes Charlles massey & samewell Rowley for A yeare & as mvche as to sra*f*tide begeninge at th*e* daye A bove written after the statute of winchester wth ij syngell pence & for them they haue covenanted wth me to

---

(1) *1598...alleyne*] partially cut away.

playe in my howes & in no other howsse dewringe the thime(1) publeck but in mine yf they dooe wth owt my consent [to for] yf they dooe to forfett vnto me xxxx^li^ a pece wittnes thomas dowton Robart shawe w^m^ borne(2) Jubey Richard Jonnes

[230]

Lent vnto Richard alleyn this yeare a 1597
at severall tymes in Redey money as foloweth

	lent hime the 27 of maye 1597	v^s^
	Lent hime the 19 of June 1597	v^s^
	Lent hime the 4 of July 1597	vj d
	Lent hime the 23 of July 1597.	xij d
	Lent hime the 1 of aguste 1597	xij d
	Lent hime vpon a payer of sylke stockens.	vj^s^ vj d
	Lent hime the 9 of aguste 1598 to geue the atorney ceachen for the bande wch he hade in his hande the some of	viij^s^ iiij^d^
	Layd owt for hime the same time to m^r^ ceatchen & Receued his bande frome hime some of . .	l s
	Lent vnto m^rs^ alleyn widow the 18 of septemb3 1602 in Redy mony the some of	xxxx^s^
[this goodes be dd back agayne & I Rd my mony [iiij^li^] v^li^ v^s^	Lent vnto m^r^s alleyn widow the 19 of septmb3 1602 to fetche her mantell & shette & fascloth from m^r^ colles the some of . .	v^li^ x s]

[4¾ *inches blank*]

[229 v] **14**

harey porter tocke & a somsete of me Phillip henslowe the 16 of Ap^r^ell 1599 vpon this condiōn that yf I wold geue hime xij d at that Instante for that xij d he bownd hime seallfe vnto me in x^li^ of corant Inglesh money for this cawse to paye vnto me the next daye folowinge all the money wch he(3) oweth vnto me or els to forfette

(1) *thime*] *sic.* (2) *borne*] a blot obscures the first two letters.
(3) *he*] interlined with caret.

for that xij d tenn powndes w[ch] deate wase vnto
me xxv[s] w[ch] he hath not payd acordinge to his
bond & so hathe forfetted vnto me wittnes to
this a somsette

John haslette vater
M[r] Kyngman the
elder

[*corner torn out as on recto*]

[229]

By(1) me williamson
Anis Rusell By me willsons
Thome haw.
Dm of thomas h to Johne

finis haslette

pdonomoy &

fines haslette
thomas hawode
hamb

[*irregular corner 5 × 3¼ inches torn off*]

Amen

Aamen

So Amen wth owt merrcy(1)

[221]

Doinge(2) you to vnderstand that I haue
Receued your[r] leatter the w[ch] I haue
The condicion of this oblegaticion
Lamentable Complayneth & showeth
Dowinge you to vnderstand

B By me John Willsone of(2)

[8½ *inches blank*]

(1) *By...merrcy*] partly printed by Greg, who omitted the names *Anis Russell* and *thomas hawode*. The last word is doubtful. Written with book reversed.

(2) *Doinge...of*] written with book reversed; cf. f. 215v and p. 4.

[215 v] 28

Douinge(1) you to vnderstand y^t I haue
Receued your leatter the wch you haue sent
by the berrer herof william willsone
A man wth owt mer(2) of me(1)

[204]

Itm̄(3) yt is agreed betwixt vs phillipe henslow
EAlleyn John ockley free of the larymores other wisse
called the betmakers & nycolas dame starchemacker
as foloweth
Itm̄ firste y^t phillipe henslow & EAlleyn is to previde
a howsse for to macke starche in & lickwisse to provide
grownd to keppe hogge one at ower owne charges
& the sayd John ocklye & nycolas dame to paye
vnto vs no Rente
secondlye the sayd John ockley & nycolas dame is
to provid at ther owne carges al fattes & other
vesselles [so][w](4) what so ever fytte for starch mackynge
of starce & when yt is mad & sowld the iij pte of
the gayne to be vnto the sayd p h & EA delyuered
for ther pte(3)

[6¼ *inches blank*]

[201 v]

The following words are scrawled in Henslowe's hand below mining accounts: *yovr Righte, Downg, Some is x^li, Lamentable C, Complay^neth*.

[191 v] 57

m^r hareys I wold desyer you to macke A bande for me wch all
the companye of the earlle of nothingame players mvste stand bownd
for the payment to me

M^r hares I mvste paye xx^li & ode mony to m^r treheren
for the earlle(5) of nothingames players wch they haue

(1) *Douinge...me*] cf. the entry on f. 221, and p. 4. (2) *mer*] *me* Greg.
(3) *Itm̄...pte*] written with book reversed.
(4) [*so*][*w*] *w* altered from *so* and deleted.
(5) *earlle*] perhaps *earllee*, final *e* accidentally duplicated; *earllee* Greg.

borowed of hime vpon ther bande & for the payement ther
of they will geue me ther band generall to this effeacte that
I shall haue ther corte mony wch they haue dew*e* vntto them
for playnge this crysmas af*o*re the Quene so sone as yt ca*ne* *b*e
Receued by any of them or ells by my sone wth thowt frade

[5½ *inches cut out*]

[179]

Memorandom y^{t} I Phillippe henslow made
A Reentory for none payment of Rente
by good[1] Renolles widow the 26 of novmb3
1603 wittneses

hewe davis
gilbart easte my
bayllefe

pd	[Goodman thornes owes vnto me at this day*e* beinge the 3 of ap^{r}ell 1604 wch is to ower Ladye daye the some of forty fyve shellenges	[xxxxv^{s}]
	Rd pd at mihellmas qter 1604	xx^{s}
	Rd pd at crystmas in pte 1604	xs
	Rd pd at mighellmas qter 1605	xs]
	so Resteth dew vnto me now at mighellmas qter 1605 the some of	xxxx[v]*x*v^{s} [2]

[1¼ *inches blank*]

pd	Goodman balle owes vnto me to this daye beinge the 3 of ap^{r}ell 1604 wch is ou^{r} Ladye daye qter the some of	[lij s vj^{d}] iij li
	Rd of this deat the some of.	xxx s
	Rd the 8 of octob3 1604 in pt.	xs
	Rd the 17 of desemb3 1604 in pte	xs
pd	so Reasteth dew vnto me nowe at Crystmas Laste 1604 wth xs of owlde wch they owe vnto me new & owld comes to th*e* some of	[xxv^{s}]

(1) *good*] *sic.*

(2) *xxxx*[*v*]*xv^{s}*] *x* altered from *v*, and *v* added.

so Resteth dew vnto me now at midsomer quarter 1605 the some of. . . . . } xxv^s
Rd the thirtenthe of novmb3 1605 of this. . . . xv^s
so Reaste dew vnto me at mighellmas qter 1605 the some of . . . . . . } xvij s vj^d

[178v]

A not what I paye every yeare
as foloweth 1602 for Rente

pd vnto the Quene . . . . xxvij^li 13^s 4^d
pd vnto m^r ower. . . . . xiiij^li
pd vnto St mildred℮ . . . . vij li
pd vnto the beshope . . . . ix s
pd vnto windover . . . . [xx^li xij^s 4^d] iij li xij s 4^d (1)

goodey fesey owes vnto me at meghellmas (2) quarter in the yeare of our Lorde 1605 the some of . . . } xxxx^s

pd the same tyme for one quarte . . . . x s
Reste 30^s
m
[Goody fesey Hathe payed me xxx^s the 10 of
July 1603 & hathe Leafte vnpayde xx^s
to this qter beinge midsomer 1603

Rd in pt the 21 of Janewary 1604. . . . . . . x s
Rd in pt the 24 of July 1605 . . . . x s]
I philliphe Henslow haue Confermed (3) a Leace made by widowe Renowells in the [nynetene]nyne and (4) thirtie yeare of the Quenes ma^ties Rayne for xviij[s] yeares (5) vnto M^r dard℮ the second yeare of the kynges ma^ties Rayne for the Resedew of the yeares to come of that Leace for A good fate Capone euery yeare to be payd at senttandros tyde yf defalte then to be voyde or ells to Remayne dewringe the Leace yt (6) to come

---

(1) *iijli xijs 4^d*] interlined above.
(2) *meghellmas*] *mas* interlined above.
(3) *Confermed*] *Conformed* Greg.
(4) [*nynetene*]*nyne and*] alteration.
(5) *xviij*[*s*] *yeares*] *y* altered from *s*.
(6) *yt*] *sic*.

[178]

A note of alle my tenent℮ & what they paye yearley as foloweth frome th*e* 13 of marche 1602 beginng at ou^{r} Ladye daye

Roger Jonnes ./././././././o/ . . . . xl s

M^{r} whetl*e*y[1] m^{r}s[2] keayes his leace[2] ./././ ./././././[/]o xl s

. . . . vj li 13^{s} 4^{d}[3]

M^{r} williamsone /./././././././o . . . . vj^{li} 13^{s} 4^{d}

goodman pigette[4]

[pd x^{s}[5] goody Reno*w*lles] ./././././././o . . . . [iiij^{li}][6]

thomas towne ./././././././o . . . . iij li

[Richard marbecke] ./. / . . . . [vj li]

./././././. . . . . vij li[7]

widowe watsone ././././././ . . . . ix li

M^{r}s Rockette ./././././././o . . . . xliij s[8] iiij d

Mr Haryson skner ./././././././[/]o[9] . . . . . liij^{s} iiij d

Goody spencer ./././././././o . . . . iiij li

Edward adyson ./././././././o . . . . ix^{li} x^{s}

gorge tayller owermackr ./././././././o . . . . liij s iiij d

w^{m} Tyghton ./././././././o/ . . . . xl s

Robart drewe ./././././././o . . . . v^{li} vj s 8^{d}

M^{r} malthowes Rent℮ as foloweth

1602

w^{m} glover ./././././././o. . . . . liij s iiij^{d}

EAlleyn ./././././././o . . . . x li

Simon Birde ./././././././o/ . . . . xxvj s 8^{d}

w^{m} Tyghton ./././././././o/ . . . . xxvj s 8^{d}

the Rosse Rent℮ as foloweth

ower tyerman ./././o/ . . . . . pd v^{s}[10]. . iij^{li}

goody feasey[11] ./././o/./ . . . . xl s

goody parson ./././././././o/ . . . . xxvj s 8^{d}

widow vnderher ./././././././o . . . . xxx s

goodman thornes 〈 〉[12] ././././ . . . . xl s

goodman Richardson ./././././././o . . . . xl s

---

(1) *whetley*] *whotley* Greg. (2) *m^{r}s...leace*] interlined above.

(3) This line is interlined. (4) *pigette*] *pegette* Greg.

(5) *pd x^{s}*] Greg prints outside the deletion brackets.

(6) *iiij^{li}*] *iij^{li}* Greg. (7) *vijli*] *iij^{li}* Greg; interlined.

(8) *xliijs*] *x* inserted later. (9) [/]*o*] alteration.

(10) *pd v^{s}*] interlined. (11) *feasey*] *seasey* Greg.

(12) 〈 〉] A blot may conceal writing.

goodman Balle ./././././ [2[1] q*tr*s] ows 3*o*s pd 10^{s}[1] . xxvj s 8^{d}

goodman flemynge ./././././././ . . . . xxx s

goody glover ./././././././o . . . . xl s

lytell howsse ./././././././o . . . . vj^{li}

M^{r}s whitte ./././././././o/ . . . . iij^{li} vj s

*w*indovers Rense

Hewe daves ./././././././o/ . . . . vj li

M^{r} page ./././././././o . . . . xx s

M^{r} owers Rence

M^{r} [skedmore[2]] Jubey[3] ./././././././o . . . . . . vj^{li}

[177v] **73**

The tenantes of Jemes Russ*ell*es Leace
as followeth begenynge [the]At[4] ou^{r} Ladye daye
1602

Harye sparkes ./././././././o . . . . ij li

John wode[5] ./././././././o . . . . .Lucasse[6] . . ij^{li} x s

w^{m} Smythe ./././././././o . . . . fide[7] . . . ij^{li} x s

Robarte mownte[8] ./././././././o . . . . ij li x s

John haynes ./././././././o . . . . xij s

John wayshfelld ./././././././o . . . . ij^{li} x s

20^{s}

Robarte Russell ./././././././o . . . . ij^{li} x s

mathew hunte ./././././././o . . . . ij li

John bande ./././././././o . . . . ij^{li}

John smythe ./././././././o. . . . . ij^{li}

Robart washfellde ./././././././o . . . . ij^{li}

widowe smythe ./././././././o . . . . ij^{li}

Itm iij shoppes ./././././././o. . . . . iiij^{li} x s

w^{m} corden ./././././././o . . . . xvj d[9]

Jemes Russells howss*e* & yardes. . . . . xx^{li}

Robart mownte[8] for a garden ./././././././o . . . . j^{li} iiij s

---

(1) *2 qtrs . . . 10^{s}*] interlined. (2) *skedmore*] *sledmore* Greg.

(3) *Jubey*] interlined above. (4) [*the*]*At*] alteration.

(5) *wode*] *Wade* Greg. (6) *Lucasse*] interlined.

(7) *fide*] interlined. (8) *mownte*] or *mowute.*

(9) *xvj d*] as Greg notes, perhaps a slip (? for *xvj s*).

The Bores Heade tenantℯ as foloweth
be genynge at crystmase Laste 1604

Edward Rygmayden ./../ . . . . x^li
Elizabeth Roosse ./../ . . . . xxvj^s 8^d
Lewce(1) easste ./ . . . . xx s
Thomas Hardinge ./../ . . . . xxvj^s 8^d
Raffe Haynes ./../ . . . . xxxij s
Richard sanders ./../ . . . . xxiiij s
Robart stockes ./../ . . . . xx s
ellyn foreste ./../ . . . . xxxx s
w^m Lowe ./../ . . . . xx s
Thomas dawson(2) ./../ . . . . xx s
John strete ./../ . . . . xx s
Richard Homes ./../ . . . . xx s
widow Saye ./../ . . . . xx s
Tege Lince ./../ . . . . xxxx^s

[177]

A not of them of my tenantℯ
wch are to paye me Capones
& when euery year by ther leaces
as foloweth 1604

in a Leace of widow Reno*w*els to pay j capon at senttan*d*rostyd . . . . } j Capon
good man hichenson to paye at crystmas ij capones
m^r mownt(3) to paye at shraftid ij Capones
thomas towne to paye at shraftid j Capon
goodman pigat to paye at shraftid j Capon
goodman hunte to paye at crystmas ij Capones

Thes be my tenantℯ belonginge to the
Bores head one the other sy[te]de(4) of
the Lea[c]ffe(5) as folowethe begynynge at
crystmas Last*e* 1604 al one Ren*ce*

---

(1) *Lewce*] *Lewes* Greg.
(2) *dawson*] *dowson* Greg.
(3) *mownt*] or *mowut*.
(4) *sy*[*te*]*de*] *de* altered from *te*.
(5) *Lea*[*c*]*ffe*] *f* altered from *c*.

Simon ⟨.⟩uttrell(1) . // . . . . xx s
Harey Alleyn . // . . . . xx s
Thomas Lawsson . // . . . . xx s
Hamlet Brather . // . . . . xxiiij s
John malborne . . . . xxvj s 8^d^
sarey Brewer . // . . . . xxx s
Thomas walborne . // . . . . xxxx^s^
John Hunte . // . . . . l s
John Hichensone . // . . . . vij^li^

[2¾ *inches blank*]

[168v] **84**

Recev*d*(2) the second daye of July 1601 . .
of m^r^ henslowe the some of [foretye] fyfetye(3)
[ayte] eaythe shellynges in full paymend
of all Reckn̄iges by me Richard wallys(2) . . } 02^li^ – 18^s^ – 0

[168]

Gallemenester(4)
Thomas Hamane

```
   1 2 3 4 5(5)
       1 2 3
   ---------
   3 7 0 3 5
 2 4 6 8 0          15003
1 2 3 4 5
-------------
1 5 1 8 3 3 5
-------------
```

Lordd godd
Complayneth

mony John willsones

Lamentable.
Comendations(6)
Comentabley
Dowinge yow
Lamentable(5)

---

(1) *⟨.⟩uttrell* A blot conceals a letter (? *L*).
(2) *Recevd...wallys*] in Wallis's hand, apparently. (3) [*foretye*] *fyfetye*] alteration.
(4) *Gallemenester...williamson*] printed in part by Greg in his notes; he reads *Sallemenester*. It is probably all in Henslowe's hand.
(5) *12345...Lamentable*] written with the book reversed.
(6) *Comendations*] *Somendations* Greg; see Introduction, p. xlv.

Be it knowne vnto all men by this presentes
that I williamsones carpenter of london
dothe aknowlege my sealfe to owe & stand
fermely in deated vnto williamson (1)

[5¼ *inches blank*]

[167 v] (2)

The following words in Henslowe's hand are scrawled in the margins around mining accounts: *Amen* (5 times), *and ne or que, god save, Mr willsones, Gorge chapman, md* (8 times). They are written with the book reversed.

[167] (2)

ssixtley (3) she saith that I dowe imbase her I [*torn*]
not so well Borne as she is but George Asmoll
his ffather is but A Bridell Bitt maker (3)

[162]

1598 (4)

The condicione of this obligatione is suche that yf the with
in bownden John willsone is eayeares exsecoters or adminy̅
or any of them (4)

[10¼ *inches blank*]

[159 v] **93**

Below some mining accounts is a large *M* in Henslowe's hand.

---

(1) *Gallemenester... williamson*] printed in part by Greg in his notes; he reads *Sallemenester*. It is probably all in Henslowe's hand.

(2) 167 v–167. This leaf does not belong to the original volume, and has been inserted at some time, probably before Philip Henslowe came to use it, since it contains words in his hand.

(3) *ssixtley... maker*] perhaps in Henslowe's hand; written with the book reversed. Not recorded by Greg.

(4) *1598... them*] in an unidentified hand; written with the book reversed.

[159]

289[(1)]– 14 – 2
[44]
[154 – 3]
[112 – 0 – 0]
056 – 00
47 – 04
392 – 18 – 2d[(1)]

[6½ *inches blank*]

Md that I Thomas Larance Haue sence the
tyme that EAlleyn & I bargayned for th*e* bringing
in of all th*e* tymbȝ & tallwodes of A Leventresse
haue sence browght into hewsse[(2)] wharffe al th*e*
plancke & [tallwod] tymbȝ wth i or[(3)] ij crockes for shipes
& A lod & a hallfe or ther A bowte of tallwood[(4)] & ther yt
Remayneth in the wode some other tallwode wch
shalbe browght in /
thomas lawrence[(5)]

[158 v] **94**

Below some mining accounts is written in Henslowe's hand, and smudged, *Righte welle loved & my verye good friend.*

[151]

Receued[(6)] of mr henslow the xjth daye of
aprill 1602 the some of tenpovnds d*ew*
to me at ourlady abouff wrytten for
that quarter the*n* dew to me for Rent
John dorington[(6)]

[9 *inches blank*]

---

(1) *289...2d*] written with book reversed; in Henslowe's hand; not printed by Greg.
(2) *hewsse*] *howsse* Greg.
(3) *i or*] interlined with caret.
(4) *of tallwood*] interlined with caret.
(5) Autograph signature.
(6) *Receued...dorington*] in Dorington's hand.

A good dryncke for the pestelence

\+ Take & wasse cleane A lylly Roote & boyle it in white wine tylle the one hallfe be wasted then geue yt the pacient to dryncke & he shall breack owt fulle of Bladers as he weare Burnt or scallded wth hot water & then they will drey & the parson wax hole

ffor the winde in the stomack

\+ Take Commin & bet yt to powder & myngell yt wth Reade wine & dryncke yt laste at nyght iij dayes & he shalbe hole

ffor to Restore the lyver

\+ Take a quantitie of wildtansey & stampe yt & drynck yt wth wine or ale ix dayes or more & he shall amend

ffor the dropsey

\+ Take Chyckweade & clethers ale & otmele & make potage ther w^th & vse yt ix days & euery daye freshe & he shalbe hole

[5¼ *inches blank*]

[136][(1)]

m^rs grantes Recknynge 1593

[¶ 17 of Jeneway 1593 o lent vpon a holand smocke wraght a bowt the necke & a spotted nyghcape & a holand necher & [a] ij payer of flexen shettes & a napken they be wraped in for . . . . xij s]

[¶ 8 of feberey^ary 1594 lent Goody nalle vpon [*A*][*ij*(2)] gownes j blacke clothe fored [& the other A vilet clothe gowne] [wth a velluet & layd a bowt wth ij belement lace] [of her dawghters] for . . . . xs [xxvj s]]

[¶ 11 of ap^rell 1593 leafte by her dawghter & apern of durance & a falynge band wraght for ij s]

(1) Folios 136–133 not printed by Greg.

(2) [*A*]*ij*] alteration.

[¶ 8 of febery^{ary} 1594 00000 00000 ij d	lent vpon a playne clothe petticotte layd wth ij small laces of goody nockes	x^{s}]
[¶ 8 of febreary 1594	lent vpon halfe a dossen of poryngers & a bell salt seler of ower tenentes for .	ij s]
[¶ 8 of febreary 1594	lent vpon viij peces of pewter ij brasen canstickes & j bell salt seler for . . . & a payer of andeyerns & a we^{n}shes cote of buffen	viij s]
[¶ 8 of febreary 1594	lent vpon a manes band & a pewter pinte potte & j old pewter dyshe for	xvj d]
[¶ 8 of febreary 1594	lent vpon a neckeycher & a hancher & A payer of whitte sleves of my tenent tomsones	iij s]
[¶ 8 of febreary 1594	lent vpon a greate cavderne of goody diers for	x s]
[¶ 9 of marche 1594	lent goody nalle vpon a black gowne of corsse clothe & a shearte lapte in yt for	xv^{s}]
¶ 8 of maye 1594	lent goody nalle [vpon A shearte the] [of corsse holland] for . . . . . . lefte(1) in the Rome of this thinges a payer of canvas sheates(1)	v^{s}
[¶ 14 of maye 1594	lent goodman cadman the 14 of maye vpon A womones gowne of playne cloth blacke lapt in a cloth for	viij s
¶ 22 of maye 1594	lente gooddy nalles dawghter vpon a frenshe Rosset gowne layd wth ij belyment laces Rownd A bowt for	xx^{s}]

[135 v] **10021**

[leant vnto Anne Nockes the 26 of marche 1593 vpon ij sheates & A pelober wraght wth A lace throwght the mydest of the sheates wch lyse for	vj s]

(1) *lefte...sheates*] interlined.

[leant vnto Anne nockes the [26]12(1) of Ap^r^ell 1593 vpon iij napkenes & j sheate & ij smalle gowld Ringes j pancey & amelld Ringe for . . . . viij s]

[lent vnto anne nokes the 19 of June 1593 vpon a Ringe of gowld & a sylver whesell & a corall seat in sylver for a chyllde for . . . . vj s]

pd for vsse for this A bowe . . xv^d^

[lent vnto anne nokes the 9 of desemb3 1593 vpon a clocke of frenshe Rossett & faced wth searge the some of . . . . xv^s^]

[lent the 25 of desemb3 1593 vnto anne nokes vpon A payer of canves sheates j tabell cloth & viij flexen napkenes & ij hancherchers j Red & j blacke j payer of gloves j gerdell & j peleber for . . . . x^s^]

[lent vnto anne nockes the [2.]18 18(2) of desemb3 1593 vpon a littell smale gowld Ringe & vpon A littell whisell of seluer for] . . . . iiij^s^]

[lent vnto goody nockes the 4 of Jeneway 1593 vpon a vilette colerd clocke layd befor wth buttenes & don a bowt wth lace & faced wth sarge for . . . x^s^]

[lent vnto goody nockes the 8 of Jeneway 1593 vpon a tanye clocke of brad cloth bownd a bowt wth a lace for . . . . x s]

[lent vnto anne nockes the 18 of Jeneway 1593 vpon ij smalle gowld Ringes j pancey & j hope Ringe wraght for . . . . v^s^]

[lent vnto goody nockes the 20 of Jeneway 1593 vpon a tany clocke of brad cloth bownd a bowt wth lace for . . . . xv^s^]

1578 1596

---

(1) *12*] interlined above.

(2) [*2.*]*18 18*] *18* altered, perhaps from *20*, and another *18* interlined above.

[135]

[lent vpon v grene saye Cvrtenes m^{rs} prisse . xij s

[¶ 8 of febe^{ra}ry 1593	lent anne nockes vpon A blo[1] womones gowne of blacke bufen wth A velleut[2] cape & lyned wth tany bayes & j yarde of cambricke cut owt in lenghetes[3] for	xx^{s}
¶ 19 of febreary 1593	lent anne nockes vpon a sade colerd clocke layd vpon wth Ruset sylke lace & v sylke cvrtenes & A sylke vallanes for A beade for	xxv^{s}
¶ j of marche 1594	lent anne nockes vpon j holland sheate & a cvberd cloth wraght & ij holland pelebers	x s
¶ 28 of marche 1593	lent anne nockes vpon ij table closse wone of them dieper & j dossen of napkines & a nowld carpett for.	x^{s}
¶ 4 of ap^{r}ell 1593	lent anne nockes vpon A ceartell of frenshe Rosset brodclothe wth j garde of velluet for .	x s
¶ 20 of ap^{r}ell 1594	lent anne nockes vpon A chyllde bed sheat eadged wth lace for	v^{s}
¶ 14 of maye 1594	lent anne nockes vpon [A]hallfe[4] a dossen of napkenes	ij s
¶ 11 of maye 1594	lent anne nockes vpon a clocke & a payer of sheates put in a Read buckrome clockbage for	xxxx^{s}
¶ 19 of maye 1594	lent anne nockes vpon a gowld Ringe wth a stone brocken in yt for . . .	xx^{s}
¶ 22 of maye 1594	lent anne nockes vpon iij gowld Ringes j pances & ij small hoope Ringes & a syluer whisell for	vij s
¶ 27 of maye 1594	lent anne nockes vpon a holland sheate . .	vj s
¶ 7 of maye 1594	lent goody nalle vpon A payer of canvas sheates for	v^{s}]

ffor my

---

(1) *blo*] *sic.*
(2) *velleut*] *sic.*
(3) *lenghetes*] *sic.*
(4) [*A*]*hallfe*] *h* altered from *A*.

[lent ¶ 18 of maye 1594	lent vnto goody harese vpon v powndes of fflexen yarne the some of	v^{s}]
[¶ 11 of June 1594	lent vnto goody Breaye vpon a womones gowne playne of Myngelld coler wth a cape of velluet & lyned wth taney Bayes of Johne gasken^{s} for	xx^{s}]
¶ 15 of June 1594	lent vpon A womones gowne of pucke wth A cape of wraght velluet & layd a bowt wth one lace of belement of goody Brayes for . . .	vj s
¶ 13 of June 1594	lent vpon A petticott of playne clothe stamell wth ij bellement laces for	ij s
[¶ 27 of June 1594	lent goody cadmanes mother vpon A chylldes fface cloth & ij dieper napkines for	ij s]
[¶ 29 of June 1594	lent vnto anne nockes vpon A Ceartell of villett coler clothe wth agarde of velluet for .	xj s]
[¶ 2 of July 1594	lent vnto anne nockes vpon A Ceartell of buffen of Rossett wth one bellement lace put in A peleber for.	viij s]
[¶ 5 of aguste 1594	lent anne nockes vpon a womones gowne of blacke clothe playne wth a cape of velluet & put into a pelleber ffor	xv^{s}]
[¶ 11 of aguste 1594	lent anne nockes vpon a payer of canvas[1] sheates & a holland band wraped in a clothe for	viij s vj d]
[¶ 15 of aguste 1594	lent anne nockes vpon A dublett of white canvas pincked & Read butenes for . .	v^{s} [. . . j d[2]] iiij d[3]]
[¶ 21 of aguste 1594	lent anne nockes vpon a fayer blacke clocke faced wth velluet & layd wth frenge lace & A payer of fyne sheates put in a buckrome bage	xxxxj s]

(1) *canvas*] interlined with caret. (2) . . . *j d*] heavily blotted.
(3) *iiij d*] interlined above deletion.

[¶ 25 of aguste 1594	lent anne nockes vpon a womones gowne of brode clothe of sade taney layd wth bellement lace & a cape of velluet & a certell of purpell buffen wth bellente (1) lac*e* p*in*de in a clothe	xxx^{s} vj d]

[134]

[¶ 25 of aguste 1594	lent vpon a clocke of shepes Roosset wth a seame downe the back & a cape of velluet & faced wth sarge for	vij^{s}]
¶ 6 of septmbȝ 1594	lent vpon A clocke & A payer of Reased velluet venesysyones of m^{r} doringtones .	xxxiij^{s} x^{d}
[¶ 9 of [agust]*septm*bȝ (2) 1594	lent vpon a cearttell of Ruset buffen wth j bellemente lace of goody nockes for.	viij s
¶ 9 of [ag]septmbȝ (3) 1594 at 7^{d} ꝑ Rd. . . . .iij^{li} [v^{s}] w^{m}	lent vpon a ceverynge of ores & iij payer of sheates & a pay*e*r of pelebers & a mantell sheate & a fase clothe & a longe dieper cloth*e* of m^{r}s Rysse a tayllers wiffe for	vj^{li}
¶ 11 of septmbȝ 1594 at 8 d	lent goody harese vpon A sheapes Rusett clocke wth owt lynynge & a cape of velluet .	vj s]
¶ 16 of septmbȝ 1594	lent goody nockes vpon a plater & a dyshe & a skellet for	iij s
[¶ 16 of septmbȝ 1594	lent goody nalles dawghter vpon A pettey c*o*te & a hate lefte in the Rome (4)	xiij s
¶ 18 of septmbȝ 1594 for ij monthes borowed	lent vpon a payer of black venesyon layd wth smalle lace & j payer of venesyon villet coler wth ij gardes of velluet & a payer of venesyon of leatther & j payer of veneseones of velluet & a Remnant of brode cloth*e* grene & a Remnant of brod cloth*e* blewe & a dublet of fuschen of John heckes . . .	xxxx^{s}

(1) *bellente*] *sic.*

(2) [*agust*] *septmbȝ*] alteration.

(3) [*ag*]*septmbȝ*] *se* altered from *ag*.

(4) *lefte*...*Rome*] interlined.

¶ 23 of septmbȝ 1594	lent goody nockes vpon j fyne chyllde bead sheat*e* & j fyne holand sleate(1) for	x^{s}
¶ 29 of septmbȝ 1594	lent Jude merecke vpon a womones gowne of cloth*e* garded wth velluet th*e* 29 of septmbȝ 1594 for	xj s 4^{d}
¶ 30 of septmbȝ 1594	lent goody nockes vpon v Cvrtenes of grene kearssey & the vallanes of the same tied in & owld cvrten for	xx^{s}
¶ 2 of octobȝ 1594	lent vpon a payer of blancketes & a corsse sheate of goodman cadmanes	vij s
¶ 4 of octobȝ 1594	lent anne nockes vpon a dieper table & a tvrckey cvlerd cloth & j sheate & j playne tabell cloth*e* & j damaske littell tabell cloth*e* for	xv^{s}]

[133 v] 10023

[¶ 22 of octobȝ 1594	lent anne noctes vpon [A] ij peleberes & a tabell cloth & a sheate for	xs
¶ 23 of octobȝ 1594	lent anne nockes vpon A hatte of bever for A womon wth a bande of gowld & perell for .	xvj^{s}
	lent vpon A womones gowne of branched damaske & lyned throwghe wth pincked tafetie & layd wth a lace of sylke & gowld of m^{r}s Rysses for	v^{li}
¶ 23 of octobȝ 1594	lent vpon A lynynge for a clocke of branched velluet & a changable tafitie fore pte & a petticote of scarlete garded wth velluet & a pece of weved worcke of m^{r}s Rysse for.	v^{li}
¶ 12 of novmbȝ 1594	lent anne nockes vpon a payer of corsse canvas sheattes for . . .	v^{s}
¶ 15 of novmbȝ 1594	lent anne nockes vpon a fayer blacke Cloocke wth vj frenge laces layd vpon for	xxx^{s}

(1) *sleate*] *sic.*

¶ 20 of novmb3 1594	lent the womone wch selles earbes in the market vpon A Remnant of brode clothe shepes Rossette	xij s
¶ 25 of novmb3 1594	lent anne nockes vpon A hoope Ringe of gowld for A womon for	iij s
¶ 26 of novmb3 1594	lent goody haryson vpon A villett colerd clocke lyned hallfe wth sarge for . . .	iiij s
¶ 2 of desemb3 1594	lent anne nockes vpon ij pelebers for	iij s]
¶ 9 of desemb3 1594	lent anne nockes vpon iij Ringes j of them A lyttell mayes wth a stone the other A lyttell Ringe wth a tuckey ston & A gemer of sylver gylte for	vj s
¶ 7 of Jenewary 1594	lent the womon wch sealles Reasones vpon A kearttell of buffen for	xij^{s}
¶ 7 of Jenewary 1594	lent anne nockes vpon iij sheates & A tabell clothe for.	viij s

[133]

¶ 23 of Jenewary 1594	lent m^{rs} Rysse vpon v cvrtenes of sylke stryped & ij yardes of grogeren & iij quarters of a yard of Ryche tafetie	xxxx^{s}
[¶ 4 of febreary 1594	lent m^{rs} Rysses [man] boye vpon A hoope Ringe of gowld wraghte for. .	x^{s}]
¶ 14 of febreary 1594	lent m^{rs} Rysse vpon iiij posselles spones of sylver & j littell hoope Ringe of gowld for	l s
¶ 7 of marche [1589] 1594	lent m^{rs} Rysse vpon ij pesell gylte gobelettes & j stone Juge gylte & a littell gylte cupe & j braselet of gowld & Jeate for	xiij^{li}
[¶ 5 of marche 1594	lent a Joyner vpon his dublet & hosse	x s]

[¶ 15 of ap[r]ell 159[4]5[(1)] lent goody nalles davghter vpon her owne gowne of brade clothe of villett layd w[th] ij belementes laces the 15 of ap[r]ell 1595 for . . } xixs]

[¶ 20 of maye 1595 lent m[r]s Rysse vpon a manes gowne vnmade vp & j payer of fyne sheates & j cvberdcloth & j face cloth & j beringe clothe for . . . . } iij[li]]

[¶ 25 of aguste 1595 for iij d p mōnth lent annes nockes vpon a buffen ceartell w[th] j bellement lace & put into a pelleber wraght for. . . } vij s]

[¶ 12 of septmbȝ 159[4]5[(1)] oo lent vnto goody tenche vpon a womones gowne of frenshe Rossett brodcloth & done a bowt w[th] a small lace & a cape of velluet for . . . . } xx[s]]

¶ 12 of ap[r]ell 159[5]6[(2)] Lefte in the Rome of goody tennches gowne the 12 of ap[r]ell 1595 ij payer of canvas sheattes & j ode sheate for. . . . . } xs vse and al payd to that time

[132 v] 10025

The following is written, perhaps in Shaa's hand (Greg thinks Henslowe's), at the top of the page, and heavily smudged: *T The xvij[th] day of Nov 1597.*

[131]

Be[(3)] it knowne vnto all men by thes p[r]sente that
I Charles Rose servaunt to w[m] pullforde of
pawles Churchyarde taylor[(4)] in London, haue bargained and
soulde vnto phillip Henshlowe of S[t] Saviours
in the County of Surrey gent one dublett &
a paire of rownd hose of Cloath of gould layde
thicke w[th] blacke silke lace in open markett·
In wittnes wherof I the sayd Charles Rose
haue herevnto sett my hande this xxviij[th] of

(1) *159[4]5] 5* altered from *4*.
(2) *159[5]6] 6* altered from *5*.
(3) *Be...written.*] in Shaa's hand.
(4) *taylor*] interlined with caret.

November 1598. in Consideration of lviij s in currant Englishe money by me receaued the day & yeare aboue written.(1)

By me Charles Rosse(2)

Wittnes Robt Shaa(2)

[5½ *inches blank*]

[129 v] **10029**

decimo(3) die Januarij Anno Dn̄i /
1603 /

m[d] that I ffraunc*e* Woodward do acknowledge my self to owe & to be indebtted vnto Phillipp Henslowe Citizen & Dier London in the somē of tenn pound*e* of Currant money to be payd to the said Phillipp *on* the first daye of ffebruary next Cominge after the date hereof for testimony hereof I have herevnto sett*e* my hand. } x[li]

p̱ me ffranciscū
wodward(3)

wittnes my sonne
EAlleyn & my dawther

Lent(4) vnto martyne Slawghter the 22 of July 1604 the some of fyvepowndes to be payd me a[t]gayne(5) the next moneth folowinge after the date w[ch] mony was delyuered vnto his wiffe I saye lent(4) } v[li]

wittnes EAlleyn(6)

---

(1) *Be...written.*] in Shaa's hand. (2) Autograph signatures.

(3) *decimo...wodward*] perhaps in Woodward's hand (so Greg), though the signature differs from the text. The bracket and sum were added by Henslowe.

(4) *Lent...lent*] a crossed line in the left-hand margin may be a cancellation sign.

(5) *a[t]gayne*] *g* altered from *t*. (6) Greg thinks Alleyn's signature is autograph.

[Lent vnto m^r freman of sussex the 26 of novmb3 1604 to folowe his sewt in the Corte of Requestes ageanste m^r Bande the some of twenty shellengę I saye lent } xx s]
wittnes w^m Henslōw

[128]

Rd of m^r Robarte wealles In pte of paymente the 24 of maye 1593 for Rente dewe for the Lockyers . . } xx^s
Rd of Robart wealles In the contrey for Rente . . xs

[10½ *inches blank*]

[127v] 10031

Mem^rd,(1) that yt [was] is(2) A gread betwene
m^r Robarte weles of Buxted in
the [Counted] Counte of Sussex
& m^r phillip hensly of Londone
the xxiiij^th of maye in the yere of
o^r Lorde 1593/ that the sayed
Robarte weles shall delyuer
vnto the Sayed phillip hensly
vpon o^r Ladye daye nexte
Comeng after the date herof
on serten pece of Land lyenge
in Buxted Caled Locyer*s*
qeyetly, wth owte any troble [done]
by the Sayed Robarte weles(1)
Rober*t* wellę(3)

[5 *inches blank*]

---

(1) *Mem^rd...weles*] scrawled in an unidentified hand.
(2) *is*] interlined with caret.
(3) Presumably an autograph signature.

[127]

Rd at the bergarden this yeare 1608 begini*ng*
at Chrystmas holedayes as foloweth . . . . . .

Rd one m*o*nday S^{t} steuenes daye . . . . iiij^{li}
Rd one tewesdaye St Johnes daye . . . . vj^{li}
Rd one wensday beinge Chilldermas[1] daye . . . . iij^{li} xiij s

[9½ *inches blank*]

[126v] 10034

Rd at the fortewne this yeare 1608 begenynge at
Crystmas h*o*ledayes

Rd one S^{t} steuenes daye . . . . xxv^{s}
Rd one St Johnes daye . . . . xxxxv^{s}
Rd one Chelldermas daye . . . . xxxxiiij^{s}[2] ix^{d}

[9½ *inches blank*]

---

(1) *Chilldermas*] *Shilldermas* Greg; see Introduction, p. xlvi.
(2) *xxxxiiij^{s}*] *xxxxiiij* Greg.

4. FRAGMENTS FROM THE DIARY

The major fragments that have been found are printed below in the order of their probable placing in the *Diary*. In addition to these, six signatures on scraps of paper probably cut from the *Diary* have been noted in books in the Bodleian Library. Chapman's signature may have been cut from Fragment 4; the signatures of Mundy and Dekker would seem to be those missing from f. 114; but the Drayton signatures cannot be placed, and are less certainly from the *Diary*.

The signatures are as follows: 'Geo: Chapman' in *The Blind Beggar of Alexandria* (Malone 240); 'Tho: Dekker' in *Old Fortunatus* (Malone 235); 'An. Mundy' in *The Downfall of Robert Earl of Huntingdon* (Malone 248); 'Mi: Drayton' and 'Michell Drayton' in Drayton's *Poems* of 1605 (Douce DD 136). Another signature of this poet was pasted in his *Mortimeriados* of 1596 (Malone 496), but has now disappeared. For discussion and facsimiles see W. W. Greg, *English Literary Autographs* (1932), sections viii and x, and *Collections Volume IV* (Malone Society, 1956), p. 32.

(1) Bodleian MS. Eng. misc. c. 4 (f. 15). This fragment is of the same measurements as the strip cut from the top of f. 30, and almost certainly belongs there. See W. W. Greg, *English Literary Autographs* (1932), section xii, and *Collections Volume IV* (Malone Society, 1956), pp. 29–30, for discussion and facsimiles.

(Recto)

Be[1] it knowne vnto all men by theise pntȩ That I
Henry Porter do owe and am indebted vnto
Mr Phillip Henchlowe in the some of
Twenty shillyngȩ of good and lawfull money
of England, ffor the wch true and good payment

(1) *Be...Porter*] in Porter's hand.

I bynd me my heiers and executore, where vnto I have set my hand this present seavent[h]ene(1) of January, a°. do. 1598

per me, HenryPorter(2)

(Verso)

Receued(3) of mr Phillip Hinchlow the som of thirty shillings good and Lawfull *mony* of Englond to be paid to the said Phillip his heirs or assigns on ashwensday next after the date hereof in wittnes I haue sett my hand the xvijth of Januarey 159[9]8(4) Josseph Hunt(3)

wittnes
Thomas Downton(5)

(2) British Museum MS. Add. 30262, f. 66. Chapman's signature ends in a flourish which is partly cut away from the bottom of this fragment; Greg showed that the missing part, or some of it, appears at the head of Fragment 3. These two must have belonged to the same leaf in the *Diary*, probably one of the leaves missing or mutilated between ff. 29 and 32 (20069 and 20073 in the original foliation; see Introduction, p. xiii); cf. also the headnote to Fragment 4. For discussion and facsimiles see W. W. Greg, 'A Fragment from Henslowe's Diary', *The Library*, fourth series, XIX (1938–9), 180–4.

(? Recto)

Receaued(6) by me George Chapman for a Pastorall ending in a Tragedye in part of payment the Sum̃ of fortye shillinge, this xvijth of July Anno 1599 { [*sum cut away*]

By me George Chapman(6)

(1) *seavent*[*h*]*ene*] *e* altered from *h*.
(2) *Be...Porter*] in Porter's hand.
(3) *Receued...Hunt*] in Hunt's hand.
(4) *159*[*9*]*8*] *8* altered from *9*.
(5) Autograph signature.
(6) *Receaued...Chapman*] in Chapman's hand.

(? Verso)

1.(1) August . 1599

Receaved by mee Thomas Dekker at the hands of m[r]
Phillip Hynchlow the Some of twenty Shillings. to bee
payd the last of this moneth . . . .

Thomas Dekker.(1)

(3) Fragment in the collection of the Duke of Rutland at Belvoir Castle. It was cut from the same leaf as Fragment 2; see headnote to this. For discussion and facsimiles see *The Library*, fourth series, XIX (1938–9), 180–4.

(? Recto)

y[e] 10 of Jeneware 1599(2)

Receyved(4) in pt of payment & in er[e]nest(3) of a playe called Owen Tewder the some of foure pounde wittnes o[r] hands. . . . (4) } iiij[li]
Ri: Hathwaye(5) RWilson.(5) An: Mundy(5)

(? Verso)

witnes
Robt Shaa(5)

18°.(6) die Januarij. 1599

[*1. in. square cut out*] ⟨R⟩eceaved by mee Thomas Dekker at the handes of M[r]
⟨Ph⟩illip Hynchlow the Some of twenty Shillinges in ernest
⟨of⟩ a play Called Truethes supplication to Candle-light

By mee Thomas Dekker.(6)

wittnes
thomas towne(5)

(4) Folger Shakespeare Library MS. 2068.1. Fragment probably, as Greg has suggested, from the parts of two leaves or the whole leaf missing from the *Diary* between ff. 29 and 32, and perhaps from the same leaf as Fragments 2 and 3; cf. headnotes to these. For discussion and facsimiles see J. Q. Adams, 'Another Fragment from

---

(1) *1....Dekker.*] in Dekker's hand. (2) *y[e]...1599*] in Henslowe's hand.
(3) *er[e]nest*] *n* altered from *e*.
(4) *Receyved...hands*] probably in Wilson's hand.
(5) Autograph signature.
(6) *18°...Dekker.*] in Dekker's hand.

Henslowe's Diary', *The Library*, fourth series, xx (1939–40), 154–8, and W. W. Greg, 'Fragments from Henslowe's Diary', *Collections Volume IV* (Malone Society, 1956), pp. 31–2.

(? Recto)

18°[(1)] Januarij. 1598.

Receaved by mee Thomas Dekker at the handes of Mr Phillip
Hynchlow the Some̅ of three powndes to bee repayd [the]
at thend of one Moneth next ensuing I say receaved iij^li^./
Thomas Dekker./[(1)]

[2⅛ × 1 *inch cut out*]

wittnes
Thomas Downton[(2)]

wittnes
Edward Jubye[(2)]

(? Verso)

22°[(3)] . Januarij. 1598.

[Receaved by mee George Chapman gentleman of M^r^
Phillip Hynchelow the Some̅ of three powndes in
part of payment of a Comedy Called The World ronnes
vpon Wheeles.. . . . . iij^li^]
Wittnes
Tho: Dekker[(3)] [*cut out as on recto*]
Thomas Downton[(2)]

(5) British Museum MS. Egerton 2623, f. 19. The accounts on the verso of this fragment enabled Greg to identify it as belonging to f. 231 of the *Diary*. It is not as large as the piece missing from this leaf, and a strip about 2 inches wide is lost from the inner margin. For discussion and facsimile of the recto see W. W. Greg, *Collections Volume IV* (Malone Society, 1956), pp. 27–8.

(Recto)

Md[(4)] y^t^ this 8th of december 1597 my father
philyp hinchlow hiered as A Covenauant
servant willyam kendall for ij years after
The statute of winchester w^t^ ij single penc
A to geue hym for his sayd servis everi

(1) *18°...Dekker.*] in Dekker's hand.
(2) Autograph signature.
(3) *22°...Dekker*] in Dekker's hand.
(4) *Md...EAlleyn*] in Alleyn's hand.

week of his playng in london x s & in y^e^
Cuntrie v^s^: for the wch he covenaunteth
for y^e^ space of those ij years To be redy
att all Tymes to play in y^e^ howse of
the sayd philyp & in no other during the
sayd Terme

wittnes my self the writer
of This EAlleyn[1]

---

(1) *Md*. . .*EAlleyn*] in Alleyn's hand.

APPENDICES

APPENDIX I

MANUSCRIPTS AT DULWICH RELATING TO THE DIARY

All of these except MS. III. 6 were printed by Greg in *Henslowe Papers* (1907). The texts given here are based on fresh transcriptions and will be found to differ in details from Greg's text. Some important differences are noted in head- or footnotes.

MANUSCRIPTS, VOLUME I

Article 2. Deed of Sale, dated 3 January 1588/9, by Richard Jones to Edward Alleyn of his share in theatrical property held jointly with Alleyn and others (Greg, *Henslowe Papers*, pp. 31–2). This is presumed to be the same Richard Jones who became an actor and sharer in the Admiral's Men, and figures frequently in the *Diary* from 1594 onwards. See also note below on article 8. John Alleyn, the elder brother of Edward, and also an actor, died before 4 May 1596 (see *Diary*, f. 3v); for Robert Browne, an actor with Worcester's Men, cf. article 12 below.

Be it knowē vnto all men by theis pn̄tꝭ. That I Richarde Jones of London
yoman for and in consideracon of the Some of Thirtie Seaven poundes and Tenne
shillinges of lawfull mony of Englande to me by Edwarde Allen of London
gent well and trulie paid. Haue bargayned and solde and in playne and open
Market wthin the citie of London haue delyu^{r}ed to the same Edwarde Allen
All and singuler suche Share parte and porcōn of playinge apparrellꝭ playe
Bookes, Instrumentꝭ, and other comodities whatsoeu^{r} belonginge to the same, as I
the saide Richarde Jones nowe haue or of right ought to haue Joyntlye wth the
same Edwarde Allen John Allen Citizen and Inholder of London and Roberte
Browne yoman, To haue holde and enioye All and singuler my said Share
of playinge apparell Playe bookꝭ Instrumentꝭ and other cōmodities whatsoeu^{r} aboue
Bargained and solde, to the same Edwarde Allen his Executors admstrato^{r}s
and assignes as his and theire owne goodꝭ freelie peaceablie and quyetelye foreu^{r}more

w^th^out let clayme or dysturbaunce of me the saide Richarde Jones my executo^rs^ Adm̃strato^rs^ or assignes or any of vs or of any other ꝑson or ꝑsons by o^r^ meanes consent or procurement / In witnes whereof I the saide Richarde Jones to this my pn̄t writinge haue set my hande and Seale the Thirde daie of Januarye a° dn̄ı. 1588 And in the one and Thirteethe yeare of the raigne of o^r^ sou^r^aigne Ladie Elizabethe by the grace of god Queene of England fraunce and Irelande defendo^r^ of the ffaithe &c/

By me Richard Jones

Sigillat^r^ et delibat^r^ in pn̄tia mei John̄is
Haruey appn̄tic Tho: Wrightson Scr. /

Article 8. Letter from Richard Jones to Edward Alleyn asking to borrow money preparatory to going abroad with 'm^r^ browne and the company'; this was dated in February 1592 by Warner, *Catalogue*, p. 5, and by Greg, *Papers*, p. 33, but is not reprinted here as Chambers, *E.S.* II, 273–4, 287, shows that it was probably written about 1615.

Article 9. Letter from Edward Alleyn to his wife, from Chelmsford, 2 May 1593. This and the other letters, articles 10–15, written during the year of the great plague, help to fill in gaps in the *Diary*, and to expand the entries on f. 1v. This letter was presumably written in jest; 'bess dodipoll' is Joan Alleyn's sister Elizabeth, mentioned also in several of the articles following.

My good sweett harte & loving mouse I send
the a thousand comendations wishing thee
as well as well may be & hoping thou art
in good helth w^t^ my father mother & sister
I haue no newes to send thee but y^t^ I thank god
we ar all well & in helth wch I pray god to contine⟨w⟩
w^t^ vs in the contry and w^t^ yo^u^ in london, but mouse
I littell thought to hear y^t^ wch I now hear by you
for it is well knowne they say y^t^ yo^u^ wear by
my lorde maiors officer mad to rid in a cart
yo^u^ & all yor felowes wch I ame sory to herar
but yo^u^ may thank yor ij suporters yor stronge
leges I mene y^t^ would nott cary yo^u^ away
but lett yo^u^ fall in to the handes of suche
Tarmagants but mouse when I come hom Il be
revengd on them till when mouse I bid thee fayerwell
I pre thee send me word how thou doste

& do my harty comendations to my father mother
& sister & to thy owne self and so swett hart
the lord bless thee from Chellmsford
the 2 of maye 1593

thyn ever & no bodies els by god of heaven
Edwarde Alleyn

farwell mecho mousin & mouse
& farwell bess dodipoll

[*addressed*:] To E Alline
on the bank side

Article 10. Letter from Philip Henslowe to Edward Alleyn, from London, 5 July 1593. John Griggs, carpenter, is named in muniment 16 (see below) as prospective builder of the Rose Theatre; and he was concerned in work on it, and on Edward Alleyn's house in 1592 (*Diary*, ff. 4, 4v, 237, 238).

Sonne Edward allen as your mother & I with your syster el[s]izabeth
hath in generalle or hartie comendaticions vnto you & very glade to
heare of your health wch we praye god to contenew to his wille
& pleasure & allthowge laste yet not leaste your mowse desiereth
to be Remembered vnto you & she sendeth frome her harte that
comendationes vnto you wch youe desyer of & prayeth nyght & daye for
your good health & quicke Retorne the cause of our writinge vnto you
Is to seartifie you yt the Joyner hath bene wth vs & hath broth thinges
& hath the money wch you promesed hime & all other maters thanckes be
to god ar weall & to your lickinge & thus I sease to trubell you of
forther maters but John gryges & his wife hath hartily comendations
vnto you & I praye you lyck wise doe my comendations vnto all
the Reste of your fealowes, & I praye god to seand you all that
good health yt [we] we haue as yet at london wch I hoope [yt] in god
yt will contenew frome london the 5 of July 1593

Your power mowse for euer
& your assured frendes tell
death phillipe Henslow
& ag

[*addressed*:] This be delyvered vnto my
welbeloued Husband
mr edward allen
wth speade

Article 11. Letter from Edward Alleyn to his wife, from Bristol, 1 August 1593(?). Alleyn was travelling with Strange's Men, in which company Thomas Pope was an actor; he is mentioned once in the *Diary*, f. 38v. R. Cowley and Pope are also named in the plot of *2 Seven Deadly Sins* (1592). *Harry of Cornwall* first appears in the *Diary*, f. 7, as acted on 25 February 1592.

Emanell

My good sweett mouse I comend me hartely
to yo^{u} And to my father my mother & my
sister bess hoping in god thought the siknes
beround about you yett by his mercy itt may
escape yor house wch by ye grace of god it
shall therfor vse this corse kepe yor house
fayr and clean wch I knowe you will
and every evening throwe water before yor dore
and in yor bakcsid and haue in yor windowes
good store of rwe and herbe of grace and
w^{t} all the grace of god wch must be obtaynd
by prayers and so doinge no dout but ye lord
will mercyfully defend yo^{u}: now good mouse
I haue no newse to send you but this thatt
we haue all ou^{r} helth for wch the lord be praysed
I reseved yor letter att bristo by richard couley
for the wich I thank you   I haue sent yo^{u} by this
berer Thomas popes kinsman my whit
wascote because it is a trobell to me to cary it
reseave it w^{t} this letter And lay it vp for
me till I com   if you send any mor letters
send to me by the cariers of shrowsbery or to west
chester or to york to be keptt till my lord
stranges players com and thus sweett hartt
w^{t} my harty comendā to all o^{r} frends I sess
from bristo this wensday after saynt Jams his day
being redy to begin the playe of hary of cornwall
mouse do my harty comend to m^{r} grigs his wif
and all his houshould and to my sister phillyps

Yo^{r} Loving housband E Alleyn

mouse you send me no newes of any things
you should send of yor domestycall matters

such things as hapens att home as how yo[r]
distilled watter proves or this or that or any
thing what you will

[*vertically in left-hand margin*]

and Jug I pray yo[u] lett my orayng tawny stokins of wolen
be dyed a very good blak against I com hom to wear in the
winter yo[u] sente me nott word of my garden but next tym you will
but remember this in any case that all that bed w[ch] was parsley
in the month of september you sowe itt w[t] spinage for then is the tym:
I would do it my self but we shall nott com hom till allholand tyd
and so swett mouse farwell and broke ou[r] long Jorney w[t] patienc

[*addressed*:]
This be delyvered
to m[r] hinslo on of the
gromes of hir maist
chamber dwelling
on the bank sid
right over against
the clink

Article 12. Letter from Philip Henslowe to Edward Alleyn, from London, August 1593 (?). Robert Browne, an actor with Worcester's Men, was abroad in Germany at this time. For a further note on the bedstead, see *Diary*, f. 1 v.

Welbeloved Sonne edward allen After owr hartie Comendationes bothe
I & your[r] mother & syster bease all in generall dothe hartieley comende
vs vnto you & as for your[r] mowse her comendationes comes by yt seallfe
w[ch] as she sayes comes from her harte & her sowle prainge to god day
daye & nyght for your[r] good heallth w[ch] trewley to be playne we doe soe
alle hoopinge in the lorde Jesus that we shall haue agayne a mery meting
for I thancke god we haue be flytted wth ffeare of the syckes but thanckes
be vnto god we are all at this time in good healthe in owr howsse but
Rownd a bowte vs yt hathe bene all moste in every howsse abowt vs
& wholle howsholdes deyed & yt my frend the baylle doth scape but he
smealles monstrusly for feare & dares staye no wheare for ther hathe deyed
this laste weacke in generall 1603 of the w[ch] nomber ther hathe died of
them of the plage 113[5]–0–5 w[ch] hause bene the greatest that came yet
& as for other newes of this & that I cane tealle youe none but that
Robart brownes wife in shordech & all her chelldren & howshowld be
dead & heare dores sheat vpe & as for your[r] Joyner he hath browght

you a corte coberd & hath seat vp you^{r} portowle in the chamber & sayes you shall haue a good bead stead & as for you^{r} garden yt is weall & you^{r} spenege bead not forgoten you^{r} orenge colerd stockenes died but no market at smythfylld nether to bye you^{r} cloth nor yet to sealle yor horsse for no mane wold ofer me a bove fower pownd for hime therfor I wold not sealle hime but haue seante hime in to the contrey tylle youe Retorne backe agayene this licke poore peapell Reioysinge that the lorde hath in compased vs Rownd & kepeth vs all in health we end prayinge to god to seand you all good health that yet maye pleasse god to send that we maye all merelye meat & I praye you do ower comendationes vnto them all & I wold gladley heare the licke frome them & thankes be to god you^{r} poore mowsse hath not ben seack seance you weant.

You^{r} lovinge wiffe tylle death Jone allen

You^{r} poore & a sured frend tell death Phillipe Hensley

[*addressed*:]
To my wealle loved
Sonne Edward allen one
of my lorde Stranges
Players this be
delyuered
wth spead

Article 13. Letter from Philip Henslowe to Edward Alleyn, from London, 14 August 1593; 'pet^{r}' may be the same person as 'my soger peter', for whom Henslowe paid charges in 1596 (*Diary*, ff. 20, 21).

Jesus

welbeloued Sonne edwarde allen I and you^{r} mother & your sister Beasse haue all in generalle ou^{r} hartie commendations vnto you & verey glad to heare of you^{r} good healthe wch we praye god to cone tenew longe to his will & pleassur for we hard that you weare very sycke at bathe & that one of you^{r} felowes weare fayne to playe you^{r} parte for you wch wasse no lytell greafe vnto vs to heare but thanckes be to god for a mendmente for we feared yt mvche because we had no leatter frome you when the other wifes had leatters sente wch mad you^{r} mowse not to weape a lyttell but tocke yt very greauesly thinckinge y^{t} you hade conseved some vnkindenes of her be cause you weare ever wont to write wth the firste & I praye ye do so stylle for we wold all be sorey but to heare as often frome you as others do frome ther frendes for we wold write oftener to you then we doo but we knowe not whether to sende to you therfor I

praye you for geat not you^{r} mowsse & vs for you seant in one
leatter that we Rettorned not answeare wheather we Receued y^{m}
or no for we Receued one wch you made at seant James tide
wher in mackes mensyon of you^{r} whitte wascote & you^{r} lvte bockes
& other thinges wch we haue Receued & now lastly a leater wch pet^{r}
browghte wth you^{r} horsse wch I wilbe as carfull as I cane In yt
now sonne althowge longe yt at the laste I Remember A
hundered comendations from you^{r} mowsse wch Is very glade to
heare of you^{r} health & prayeth daye & nyght to the lord to contenew
the same & lickewisse prayeth vnto the lord to seace his hand frome
punyshenge vs wth his crosse that she mowght haue you at home
wth her hopinge hopinge then that you shold be eased of this heavey
labowre & toylle & you sayd in you^{r} leater that she seant you not
worde how you^{r} garden & all you^{r} things dothe prosper very well
thanckes be to god for you^{r} beanes are growen to hey headge & well
coded & all other thinges doth very well but you^{r} tenantes weax
very power for they cane paye no Reant nor will paye no Rent
whill myhellmas next & then we shall haue yt yf we cane geat
yt & lyckewisse you^{r} Joyner comendes hime vnto you & sayes
he will mack you such good stufe and suche good peneworthes as
he hoopeth shall weall licke you & contente you wch I hope
he will do because he sayes he will prove hime seallfe ane onest man
& for you^{r} good cownsell wch you gaue vs in you^{r} leater we all thancke
you wch wasse for kepinge of ou^{r} howsse cleane & watringe of ou^{r} dores &
strainge ou^{r} windowes wth wormwode & Rewe wch I hope all this we
do & more for we strowe yt withe hartie prayers vnto the lorde
wch vnto vs Is more avaylable then all thinges eallsse in the world
for I praysse the lord god for yt we are all in very good healthe
& I praye ye sonne comend me harteley to all the Reast of you^{r}
fealowes in generall for I growe poore for lacke of them therfor haue
no geaftes to sende but as good & faythfull a harte as they shall
desyer to haue comen a mongeste them now sonne we thanck you
all for you^{r} tockenes you seant vs and as for newes of the syckness
I cane not seand you no Juste note of yt be cause there is command
ment to the contrary but as I thincke doth die wth in the sitteye
and wth owt of all syckneses to the nomber of seventen or eyghten
hundreth in one weacke & this praynge to god for you^{r} health
I ende frome london the 14 of aguste 1593

you^{r} lovinge wiffe to
comande tell death
Johne Allen

you^{r} lovinge ffather & mother
to owr powers P H . A

[*addressed*:]
Too my wealbeloued
husbande m^{r} Edwarde
Allen on of my lorde
stranges players
this be delyuered
wth speade.

Article 14. Letter from Philip Henslowe to Edward Alleyn, from London, 28 September 1593. Hudson is mentioned in the *Diary*, f. 1 v. Sister Phillips's husband may be the Edward Phillips concerned in a lawsuit with Henslow, f. 41.

Righte wealbeloved Sonne edward allen I & you^{r} mother & you^{r} sisster
beasse haue all in generall ou^{r} hartie Comendations vnto you & as for
you^{r} wiffe & mowsse she desieres to send heare Comendationes alone w^{ch}
she sayes Comes ffrome heare very harte but as ffor you^{r} wellfare
& heallth we do all Joyne to geather in Joye and ReJoysse ther att & do
all to geather wth one consent praye to god longe to contenew the same
now sonne leate vs growe to alyttell vnkindnes wth you becausse we cane
not heare from you as we wold do that is when others do & if we cold as sartenly
send to you as you maye to vs we wold not leat to vesete you often
ffor we beinge wth in the cross of the lorde you littell knowe howe we do
but by sendinge for yt hath pleassed the lorde to vesette me Rownd a
bowte & almoste alle my nebores dead of the plage & not my howsse ffree
for my two weanches haue hade the plage & yet thankes be to god leveth
& ar welle & I my wiffe & my two dawghters I thancke god ar very well
& in good heallth now to caste a waye vnkindnes & to come to owr newes
that is that we hade a very bade market at smyth fylld for no mane
wold ofer me a bove fower pownd for you^{r} horsse & therfor haue not sowld
hime but to saue carges I haue sent him downe In to the contrey ther to
be keapte tell you Retorne & as for you^{r} clocke cloth ther wasse none
sowld by Retaylle for all wasse bowght vp by wholle saylle in to dayes
so the fayer lasted but iij dayes & as for you^{r} stockings they are deyed
& yor Joyner hath seate vp you^{r} portolle in the chambȝ & hath brothe
you a corte cobert & sayes he will bringe the Reaste very shortley & we
beare wth hime because his howsse is visited & as for you^{r} garden that
is very weall you^{r} spenege bead & all sowed & as for my lorde a
penbrockes wch you desier to knowe wheare they be they are all at home
and hauffe ben t⟨his⟩ v or sixe weackes for they cane not saue ther carges
⟨w⟩th trauell as I heare & weare fayne to pane the⟨r⟩ parell for ther carge
⟨& w⟩hen I wasse in smythfell a sellyng of you^{r} h⟨orsse⟩ I meate wth owld

[*several lines are wanting at the foot of the page: the letter continues on the back*]

To aske for yt for yf we dead we wold haue sowght yt owt but we never had yt & this I eand praysinge god that it doth pleass hime of his mersey to slacke his hand frome visietinge vs & the sittie of london for ther hath abated this last two weacke of the sycknes iiij hundreth thurtie and five & hath died in all betwexte a leven and twealle hundred this laste weack wch I hoop In the lord yt will contenew in seasynge euery weacke that we maye ReJoysse agayne at owr meatinge & this wth my hartie comendation to thy own seall & lickwise to all the Reast of my felowes I genereall I praye you hartily comende me from london the 28 of [ag]septemb3 1593

you^r^ asured owne seallfe	you^r^ lovinge father & frend to my power
tell deathe Jonne allen	tell death Phillipe Henslowe
comendinge to her mvnshen	

you^r^ wiffe prayeth you to send her word in yor next leater what goodman hudson payes you yerley for his Reante for he hause the sealer and all stille in his hand & as for you^r^ tenenantes we cane geat no Rent & as for greges & his wife hath ther comendations vnto you & you^r^ sister phillipes & her husband hath bered two or thre owt of ther howsse yt they in good healt⟨h⟩ & doth hartily comend them vnto you

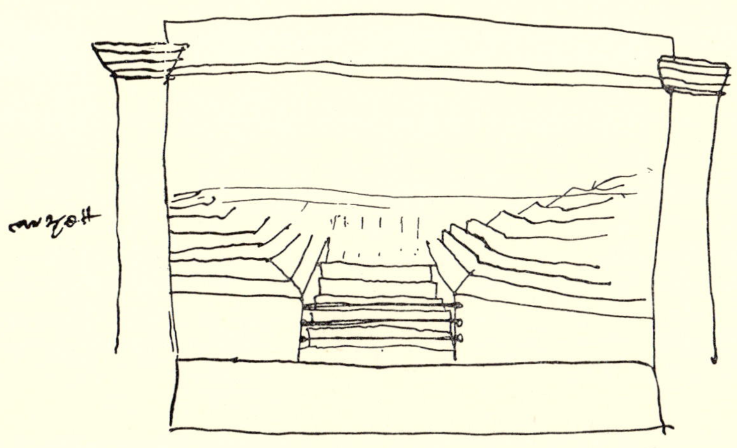

[*addressed*:]
This be delyuered vnto
my welbeloued husband
m^r edward allen one of
my lord stranges
players geue
wth spede

[*By the address are drawings of four heads, one haloed, and a full-length figure of an old man with a staff, holding out one hand; a few words are also written, including the phrase.* '*The things w^cb I Craves*'. *On the blank leaf opposite the end of the letter is written in Henslowe's hand* '*A Imbroydered carpett*', *next to a rough sketch of what appears to be a stage, reproduced above. The original measures* $5 \times 3\frac{1}{8}$ *inches.*]

Article 15. Letter from John Pyk to Mistress Alleyn, undated; John Pyk (Pyg), a boy player, is mentioned in the *Diary*, ff. 37v, 61v. The letter is in the hand of Edward Alleyn, and is evidently meant in jest. Greg thinks the signature to be autograph, but there is little to distinguish it from the rest. Thomas Downton figures frequently in the *Diary* as an important member of the Admiral's Men.

mysteris yor honest ancyent and
Loving servant pige hath his
humbell comendā to you and to my
goode master hinsley & mystiris and to
my m^rs sister bess for all her harde
delyng w^t me I send her harty
Comendā hoping to [p]be behowlding
to her agayne for the opinyng of
the coberde: and to my neyghbore
doll for calynge me vp in a mornyng
and to my wyf sara for making clean
my showes & to that ould Jentillman
mounsir pearle y^t ever fought
w^t me for the blok in the chemeney
corner & though yo^u all Look for
the redy retorne of my proper person
yett I swear to you by the fayth of a
fustyan kinge never to retorne till
fortune vs bryng w^t a Joyfull

metyng to lovly london I sesse
yor petty prety pratlyng parlyng pyg
by me John pyk

[*vertically in the left-hand margin*:]
mystiris I praye yo^u kepe this that
my mayster may se it for I gott on to
wright it m^r doutone & my m^r knowes nott of it

[*addressed*:]
To his loving m^rs
mysteris Alline
on the banck syd
over agaynst
the clynk

Article 16. Petition to the Privy Council from Lord Strange's men. The date of this and the two following documents is uncertain; Chambers, *E.S.* IV, 311, follows Greg in allotting them to July 1592. A riot in Southwark in early June led to a suspension of playing from 23 June. Plague, which increased in incidence in August and the following months (Chambers, *E.S.* IV, 347–8), probably put a stop to playing in the autumn, and Henslowe records no performance between 22 June and 29 December (f. 8). It may be that the warrant for reopening the Rose (article 18) coincided with the increase of plague, which prevented, perhaps, a resumption of playing; or possibly, as Chambers suggested, these documents relate to 1591, though there is no corroborative evidence for this year. 1593 seems hardly possible, since plague kept the theatres closed for most of the year. It is conceivable that these articles, which seem to relate to some specific closure of the Rose, may belong to the period in 1594 when the Admiral's Men, joined after a time by the Chamberlain's Men, played at Newington Butts, until mid-June, when the Admiral's Men seem to have returned to the Rose; see article 18, and *Diary*, f. 9.

To the righte honorable o^r verie good Lord*e*, the Lord*e* of her ma^ts. moste honorable privie Councell/.

Our dueties in all humblenes remembred to yor hono^rs. fforasmuche (righte honorable) oure Companie is greate, and thearbie o^r chardge intollerable, in

travellinge the Countrie, and the Contynuaunce thereof, wilbe a meane to bringe vs
to division and seperacõn, wheareby wee shall not onelie be vndone, but alsoe
vnreadie to serve her ma^{tie}, when it shall please her highenes to commaund vs, And
for that the vse of o^{r} plaiehowse on the Banckside, by reason [by reason] of the
passage to and frome the same by water, is a greate releif to the poore watermen
theare, And o^{r} dismission thence. nowe in this longe vacation, is to those
poore men. a greate hindraunce, and in manner an vndoeinge, as they gen^{r}allie
complaine, Both o^{r}, and theire humble peticõ and suite thearefore to yor good
honno^{r}s is, That yo^{u} wilbe pleased of yor speciall favo^{r}, to recall this o^{r} restrainte,
And p̱mitt vs the vse of the said Plaiehowse againe / And not onelie o^{r} selues
But alsoe a greate nomber of poore men. shalbe especiallie bounden to praie
for yor Hono^{r}s /.

Yor hono^{r}s humble supp^{ts} .
The righte honorable the Lord Straunge
his servant℮ and Plaiers / .

Article 17. Petition from the Watermen of the Bankside to Lord Howard. See note to previous article.

To the right honnorable my Lorde Haywarde Lorde highe Admirall
of Englande and one of her ma^{ties} moste honnorable previe Counsayle/
In the most hvmble manner Complayneth and sheweth vnto your good Lordeshippe, your poore suppliant℮
and dayly Orato^{r}s Phillipp Henslo, and others the poore watermen on the bancke side / whereas
yor good L. hathe derected your warrant vnto hir ma^{ties} Justices, for the restraynte of a playe
howse [beinge] belonginge vnto the saide Phillipp henslo [.] one of the groomes of her ma^{ties} Chamber
So it is if it please your good Lordshipp, that wee yor saide poore watermen have had muche helpe
and reliefe for vs oure poore wives and Children by meanes of the resorte of suche people as come
vnto the said playe howse, It maye therefore please your good L.' for godes sake and in the waye of
Charetie to respecte vs your poore water[e] men, and to give leave vnto the said Phillipp Henslo
to have playinge in his saide howse during suche tyme as others have according as it hathe byne
accustomed / And in yor honnors so doinge yo^{u} shall not onely doe a good and a Charitable dede but also

bynde vs all according to oure dewties, wth oure poore wives and Children dayly to praye for your
honnor in mvche happynes longe to lyve

Isack Towelle William dorret m^r^ of her maie[g]stes barge
Gylbart ⊥ Rockett marke on wyllm hodgy[s]ɇ quens man
of her m^ties^ wattermen
Edward ⊥ Robartes marke on of her m^ties^ wattermen Thomas + Jarmonger on of her m^ties^ wattermen
thomes toy william M Tuchenner on of her m^ties^ mean
Thomas + Edmanson marke
Edwarde + Adysson on of her m^ties^ wattermen James Russell
Henry Draper
W T Jeames + Granger fardinandoo Black
xpoffer ⊥ topen marke Parker Playne

Article 18. Copy of warrant from the Privy Council for the reopening of the Rose. See note to article 16.

Wheareas not longe since vpon some Consideracōns we did restraine the Lorde Straunge his s^r^vauntɇ
from playinge at the rose on the banckside, and enioyned them to plaie three daies at newington
Butts, Now forasmuch as wee are satisfied that by reason of the tediousnes of the waie and y^t^
of longe tyme plaies haue not there bene vsed on working daies, And for that a nomber of poore
watermen are therby releeved, Yo^u^ shall ꝑmitt and suffer them or any other there to exercise y^em^
selues in suche sorte as they haue don heretofore, And that the Rose maie be at libertie w^th^out any
restrainte, solonge as yt shalbe free from infection of sicknes, Any Comaundem^t^ from vs hereto
fore to the Contrye notw^th^standinge: ffrom

To the Justices Bayliffes
Constables and others to
whome yt shall Apperteyne:

Article 24. Letter from Philip Henslowe to Edward Alleyn, London, 26 September 1598. Gabriel Spenser appears among the lists of sharers of the Admiral's Company in 1597 and 1598 (*Diary*, ff. 43, 44v); Jonson was by this time acting (f. 234) and writing plays

(f. 37v). See note below on Manuscripts, volume II, concerning the Beargarden (p. 299).

ssonne Edward alleyn I haue Rd you^{r} leatter the wch you sent
vnto me by the careyer wher in I vnderstand of both you^{r} good
healthes wch I praye to god to contenew and forther I vnder
stand you haue considered of the wordes wch you and I had
betwen vs consernynge the beargarden & acordinge to you^{r}
wordes you and I and all over frendes shall haue as mvch
as we cane do to bring yt vnto a good eand therfore I wold
willingeley that you weare at the bancate for then wth our
losse I shold be the meryer therfore yf you thincke as I thinck
yt weare fytte that we weare both her to do what we mowgh⟨t⟩
& not as two frends but as two Joyned in one therfor ned
I love not to mack many great glosses & protestaciones to you
as others do but as a poor frend you shall comande me
as I hoope I shall do you therfore I desyer Rather to haue you^{r}
company & you^{r} wiffes then you^{r} leatters for ower laste talke w^{ch}
we had abowte m^{r} pascalle assuer you I do not for geatte now to
leat you vnderstand newes I will teall you some but yt is
for me harde & heavey sence you weare wth me I haue loste one
of my company wch hurteth me greatley that is gabrell for
he is slayen in [f]hoges den fylldes by the hands of benge⟨men⟩
Jonson bricklayer therfore I wold fayne haue alittell of you^{r}
cownsell yf I cowld thus wth hartie comendations to you &
my dawghter & lyckwise to all the Reast of our frends I eande
from london the 26 of septemb3 1598

You^{r} assured frend
to my power

Phillippe Henlowe

[*addressed*:]
To my welbeloude ssonne
m^{r} Edward alleyne at
m^{r} arthure langworthes
at the brille in
susex giue
this

[On the back also appear a drawing of a man's head, and scrawls including the names of Henslowe and Alleyn, and the sentences 'Lamentation is Ever moued to ioy', and 'Hinchlowe is my name & w^{t} my pen I writt ye same'.]

Article 25. Bond from Richard Bradshaw, Byrcot Bird and Robert Archer to William Bird for the payment of 50*s.* on 2 March 1599, and an acknowledgement of a debt of 10*s.* owed by William Bird to Edward Alleyn, with power to recover this sum from Richard Bradshaw upon the bond. Bond dated 10 October, 40 Elizabeth (1598); William Bird's note dated 8 January 1604. Extracts only are given. Bradshaw and William Bird figure as actors in the *Diary*, and Bird is associated with a Mrs Reeve on f. 41 v.

The condicion of this obligacon̄ is suche that...Richard Bradhawe
Byrcotte Byrde and Robert Archer...shall...paye vnto...william
Byrde...the some of ffyftye shillinges of good and lawfull money
of England, vpon the seconde daye of marche next comynge at the
house of Mr Reeve scituate and beinge w^th^in the pishe of S^t
Saveryes in the Countye of Surrey

Sealed and deliuered in the presens of vs wittnesses Nicholas foster	Richard Bradshaw
John Greennhill	Burckot Byrd
	Robert Archer

Be it knowne to all men by these presentę that I William
Bird of hogsdon doe owe vnto m^r Edward Allin of St Saviours
in Southwark...the some of x^s of lawfull mony of England
to be payd the five and twenteth daye of march next coming
for the wch payment I give full authoryte to m^r Edward Allin,
to recover of Richard Bradshaa vppon this his bond...to
satisfy him selfe for the x^s wch I owe him, and then
returne the remaynder to me as my due...this 8th daye of
Januarye 1604

Wbirde

Article 26. Letter from Robert Shaa to Philip Henslowe, 8 November 1599. Warner first related this note to the entry in the *Diary*, f. 65, of payment of £8 to Wilson for *2 Henry Richmond*, which fixes the date. On the back is what appears to be an outline of one act of it. 'Q. & Eliza:' in line 2 is interlined with a caret.

Mr Henshlowe we haue heard their booke and lyke yt their pryce is eight pound*e*, wch I pray pay now to m^r^ wilson, according to our promysse, I would haue Come my selfe, but that I ame troubled wth a scytation.

yo^rs^ Robt Shaa

[*on the back:*]

1. Sce Wm Wor: & Ansell & to them ye plowghmen
2. Sce: Richard Q. & Eliza: Catesbie, Louell, Rice ap tho: Blunt, Banester
3. Sce: Ansell Dauye Denys Hen: Oxf: Courtney Bou^r^chief & Grace to them Rice ap Tho: & his Soldiors
4. Sce: Mitton Ban: his wyfe & children

[6. Sce:]

5. Sce: K Rich: Catesb: Louell. Norf. Northumb: Percye

Article 27. Warrant from Charles Howard, Earl of Nottingham, for the building of the Fortune, Richmond, 12 January 1599/1600. This and the next two items, relating to the erection of the Fortune Theatre, should be compared with Muniments, article 22, given below, and *Diary*, ff. 32, 32v, 98v, 99.

Wheareas my Servant Edward Allen. in respect of the dangerous decaye of that Howse wch he and his Companye haue nowe, on the Banck, And for that the same standeth verie noysome for resorte of people in the wynter tyme) Hath thearfore nowe of late, taken a plott of grounde neere Redcrossestreete london. verie fitt and convenient) for the buildinge, of a new Howse theare, and hath prouided Tymber and other necessaries for theffectinge theareof. to his greate chardge: fforasmuche as the place. standeth verie convenient, for the ease of. People, And that her Matie. (in respect. of the acceptable Service, wch my saide Servant and his Companie. haue doen and presented before her Highenes to her greate lykeinge and Contentm^t^; aswell this last Christmas as att sondrie other tymes) ys gratiouslie moued toward*e* them. wth a speciall regarde of fauor in their proceeding*e*: Theis shalbe thearefore to praie and requier yo^w^. and. everie of yo^w^. To permitt and suffer my saide Servant to proceede in theffecting and finishinge of the saide Newhowse, w^th^out anie yor lett or molestacōn. toward*e* him or any of his woorkmen. And soe not doubtinge of yor observacōn in this behalf . I bidd yo^w^ right hartelie farewell. att the Courte. at Richmond the xij^th^ of Januarye. 1599

Notingham

To all & euery her ma^ts^ Justices & other Ministers . and Officers . w^th^in the Countye of Midds . & to euery of them . And to all others whome it shall Concerne:

Article 28. Address of the Inhabitants of Finsbury to the Privy Council, undated, but probably about January 1600.

To ye righte honorable the Lordes and others of her ma^ts^ most honorable privie Councell: /

In all humblenes: Wee the Inhabitantę of ye Lordshipp of . ffynisburye . w^th^in the parrishe of St Gyles w^th^out Creplegate London) doe certifie vnto yor honno^r^s . That wheare the Servantę of the right honorable Earle of Nottingham . haue latelie gone aboute to erect and sett vpp . a Newe Playehowse . w^th^in the said L^p^:) Wee could be contented, that the same might proceede . and be Tollerated (Soe it stande wth yor honno^r^s pleasuers) ffor the reasons and Causes followeinge/ .

First because the Place . appoynted oute for that purpose Standeth very tollerable neere vnto the ffeildes, and soe farr distant and remote frome any person or Place of accompt. As that None cann be Annoyed thearbie:

Secondlie because the Erecto^r^s of the saied howse, are contented to give a very liberall porcōn of money weekelie, towardę ye releef of our Poore, The nomber & necessity whereof, is soe greate that the same will redounde to ye contynuall comfort of ye saied Poore:

Thirdlie and lastlie wee are the rather Contented to accept this meanes of releif of o^r^ Poore, because our Parrishe is not able to releeue them . Neither hath the Justices of the Sheire taken any order, for any Supplie oute of ye Countye, As is enioyned by ye late Acte of Parliam^te^:/

hary stapleforde		
Thomas Reade	William WB Browne Constable	Edward Gateward
Anthonie marlowe	William Hewlett	John Remys
william baylle	Roger Wild	

willm̄ W G Garruld
Nycolas sherman
Thomas stapullford
Martyn W ff fforde
Stephen 卐 Abbott
Nicholas R Russell
John ꝭ Johnson
Thomas whelple
Richard Lewes

Richard goode
George Garland overseer for o^{r} poore
John Webbe
John Hitchens overseer for o^{r} poore
Awsten AG Garland
Roger: osborne.
O Nicholas Warden
Thomas T Gibbes
Thomas A Nichollꝭ

The Certificate of ye Inhabitantꝭ of ye L^{p}: of ffynisburye of theire Consent to the Tolleracōn of the Erection of the newe Plaiehowse theare:/

Article 29. Warrant from the Privy Council to the Justices of Middlesex, Richmond, 8 April 1600.

After our hartie comendacōns . Whereas . her Matie. (haveinge been well pleased heeretofore. at tymes of recreacōn. wth the services of Edward Allen and his Companie. Servantꝭ to me the Earle of Nottingham. wheareof, of late he hath made discontynuance:) Hath sondrye tymes signified her pleasuer, that he should revive the same agayne: fforasmuche as he hath bestowed a greate some of money, not onelie for the Title of a plott of grounde, scituat in averie remote and exempt place neere Goulding lane, theare to Erect a newe house but alsoe is in good forwardnes. aboute the frame and woorkmanshipp theareof. The conveniencie of wch place. for that purpose ys testified vnto us; vnder the handes of manie of the Inhabitantꝭ of the Libertie of fynisbury. wheare it is. and recomended by some of the Justices them selves. Wee thearfore haveinge informed her Matie lykewise of the decaye of the howse, wherein this Companye latelie plaied. scituate vppon the Bancke. verie noysome, for the resorte of people in the wynter tyme. haue receaued order to requier yo^{u}. to Tollerate the proceedinge of the saide New howse neere Goulding lane. And doe heerbye requier yo^{u}. and everie of yo^{u} . To permitt and suffer the said Edward Allen to proceede in theffectinge and finishinge. of the same Newehowse, wthout anie yor lett or interrupcōn, towardꝭ him, or anye of his woorkmen. the rather because an other howse is pulled downe, in steade of yt. And soe not doubtinge of yor conformitye heerein. Wee comitt yo^{u} to God, frome the Courte at Richmond the viijth of April 1600. Yo^{r} loveinge freindes

Notingham

G Hunsdon

Ro: Cecyll

To ye Justices of Peace of ye Countye of Midds
especially of St Gyles. wth out Creplegate.
And to all others. whome it shall
Concerne.

Article 30. A list of playing apparel in the hand of Edward Alleyn, with forged additions, written on one sheet in six parallel columns. The lineation of the MS is not kept, and the forgeries are omitted from this text. This inventory may, as Greg conjectured, belong to the same period as those printed by Malone from a manuscript now lost, and dated 1598 (see Appendix 2 below); but a later date, *c.* 1602, seems preferable; see Introduction, p. xliii. Whereas this is in the hand of Edward Alleyn, those Malone printed suggest Henslowe's usages and spellings. A number of items are crossed out, in a different ink from the entries, and this is indicated by a square bracket in the left-hand margin.

1 A scarlett cloke wth ij brode gould Laces: w^t gould buttens of the sam downe the sids

2 A black velvett cloke

A scarlett cloke Layd [the] downe w^t silver Lace and silver buttens

4 A short velvett cap clok embroydered w^t gould and gould spangles

5 A watshod sattins clok w^t v gould laces

6 A pur[l]pell sattin w^telted w^t velvett and silver twist

7 A bla*ck* tufted cloke cloke

8 A dama*s*k cloke garded cloke garded w^t velvett

A longe blak tafata cloke

A colored bugell for aboye

A scarlett w^t buttens of gould fact w^t blew velvett

12 A scarlett fact w^t blak velvett

13 A stamell cloke w^t [b]gould lace

14 blak bugell cloke

Gownes

[1 hary ye viij gowne

2 the blak velvett gowne w^t wight fure

3 A crimosin Robe strypt w^{t} gould fact w^{t} ermin

4 on of wrought cloth of gould

5 on of red silk w^{t} gould butt*ens*

[6 a cardinalls gowne

7 wemens gowns

8 i blak velvett embroyde[1]

9 w^{t} gould

[10 i cloth of gould candish[2] his *s*tuf

11 i blak velvett lact and drawne owt w^{t} wight sarsnett

12 A black silk w^{t} red flush

13 A cloth of silver for pan[3]

14 a yelow silk gowne

[15 a red silk gowne

[16 angels silk

17 ij blew calico gowns

Antik sutes

1 a cote of crimosen velvett cutt in payns and embryderd in gould

2 i cloth of gould cote w^{t} grene bases

3 i cloth of goul*d* cote w^{t} oraingtawny bases

4 i cloth of go⟨. .⟩ silver cott w^{t} blewe silk & tinsell[4] bases

5 i blew damask cote the more[5]

6 a red velvett hors mans cote

7 A yelow tafata pd[6]

8 cloth of gould horsmans cote

9 cloth *of* bodkin hormans cote

10 orayngtany horsmans cot of cloth lact

11 daniels gowne

12 blew embroyderde bases

13 will somers cote

14 wight embroyd bases

---

(1) *embroyde*] *embroyde^{r}* Greg.

(2) *candish*] *h* very attenuated. Presumably this is the name Cavendish, as Greg notes; he has not been identified.

(3) *pan*] *par^{r}*, Greg, who identifies him with the actor W. Parr who appears in the plot of *1 Tamar Cam* (1602).

(4) *tinsell*] *tuisell* Greg.

(5) *more*] *moro* Greg.

(6) *pd*] *ps* Greg.

15 [g]gilt lether cot
16 ij hedtirs sett w^{t} stons
17

Jerkings and
dublets

1 A crymosin velvett pd w^{t} gould buttens & lace
2 a crymasin sattin case lact w^{t} gould lace all over
[3 A velvett dublett cut di*a*mond lact w^{t} gould lace and spang
4 a dublett of blak velvett cut on sillver tinsell
5 A ginger colored dublett
6 i wight sattin cute onwight
7 blak velvett w^{t} gould lace
8 green velvett
9 blak tafata cut on blak velvett lacte w^{t} bugell
10 blak velvett playne
11 ould wight sattin
12 red velvett for a boye
13 A carnation velvett lacte w^{t} silver
14 A yelow spangled case
15 red velvett w^{t} blew sattin sleves & case
16 cloth of silver Jerkin
17 faustus Jerkin his clok

1 frenchose
blew velvett embr[1] w^{t} gould paynes blew sattin scalin
2 silver paynes lact w^{t} carnation satins[2] lact over w^{t} silver
3 the guises
[4 Rich payns w^{t} Long *sto*kins
5 gould payns w^{t} blak stript scalings of ca*nis*
6 gould payns w^{t} velvett scalings
7 gould payns w^{t} red strypt scalings[3]
8 black bugell
9 red payns for a boy w^{t} yelo scalins
10 pryams hoes
11 spangled hoes

---

(1) *embr*] *embr^{d}* Greg.
(2) *satins*] *salins* Greg.
(3) *scalings*] *scaling* Greg.

venetians

[1 A purple velvett cut in dimonds Lact & spangels

2 red velved lact w^{t} gould spanish

[3 a purpell velvet emproydored w^{t} silver cut on tinse*l*

4 green velvett lact w^{t} gould spanish

5 blake velvett

6 cloth of silver

7 gren strypt sattin

8 cloth of gould for a boye

Article 31. Letter from Robert Shaa to Philip Henslowe; the payment of 44*s.* to Drayton and others for *Fair Constance* is recorded in the *Diary*, f. 69v, on 14 June 1600. This letter is the only evidence for Wilson's share in the authorship. On the back are some numbers, the name 'Robarte Willson', and a drawing of a dog.

I praye you Mr Henshlowe deliuer vnto the bringer hereof the some
of fyue & fifty shillinges to make the 3^{li} -fyue shillingℯ wch they
receaued before, full six poundℯ in full payment of their booke
Called the fayre Constance of Roome. whereof I pray you
reserue for me Mr Willsons whole share wch is xjs. w^{ch}
I to supply his neede deliuered hime yesternight.

yor Lovinge ffrend Robt Shaa

Article 32. Letter from Samuel Rowley to Philip Henslowe, 4 April 1600 (1601); the loan is also recorded in the *Diary*, f. 86.

Mr Hinchloe I haue harde fyue shetes of a playe of the
Conqueste of the Indes & I dow not doute but It wyll
be a verye good playe tharefore I praye ye delyuer them
fortye shyllynges In earneste of yt & take the papers
Into yor one hands & on easter eue thaye promyse to make
an ende of all the Reste

lent the 4 of ap^{r}ell Samuell
160[0]1 — xxxxs. Rowlye

Article 33. Letter from Samuel Rowley to Philip Henslowe; there are entries relating to the play *The Conquest of Spain by John of Gaunt*, dated from 24 March to 16 April 1601, in the *Diary*, ff. 86, 86v. These, like all the entries on these pages except the last on f. 86v, are crossed out.

> M^r hynchlo I praye ye let M^r hathwaye haue his papars
> agayne of the playe of John a gante [f]& for the
> Repayemente of the monye backagayne he Is contente
> to gyue ye a byll of his hande to be payde at
> some cartayne tyme as In yor dyscressyon yow shall
> thinke good. wch done ye maye [dayshe I] crose It oute
> of yor boouke & [*o*p]keepe the byll. or else wele stande so muche
> indetted to yow & kepe the byll o^r selues.
>
> Samuell Rowlye

Article 34. Letter from Samuel Rowley to Philip Henslowe, 8 June 1601; the date is fixed by the entry in the *Diary*, f. 87v. Henslowe records, ff. 87, 87v, the prior payment of £4. 10*s*.

> Mr Hynchlye I praye ye dow so muche for vs If Jhon
> Daye & wyll houghton haue reseved but thre pounde ten
> shyllynges as to delyver them thurtye shyllynges more &
> take thare papers
>
> Yo^rs to commande
> Samuell Rowlye

Article 35. Letter from Samuel Rowley to Philip Henslowe; this is apparently an earlier letter than Article 34, and may refer to the payment made by Henslowe on 6 June 1601; see *Diary*, f. 87v. Warner and Greg read 'hamton sadler' for 'hauton fidler' in l. 8; the reading 'fidler' is doubtful. On the back are twelve lines in Day's hand of a speech by Hotspur(?) from an unidentified play; and at the head of the sheet some scribble beginning 'To ayde me to waylle and to mone...'.

> Mr Henchloe I praye ye delyver the Reste of the
> Monye to John daye & wyll hawton dew to them
> of the syx yemen of the weste
>
> Samuell
> Rowlye
>
> about the plott of the Indyes
> I have occasion to be absent therfore pray
> delyver it to [the] will hauton f*id*ler
>
> by me John Daye

Article 36. Letter from Robert Shaa to Philip Henslowe, 7 January 1601/2; see entries in the *Diary*, ff. 95v, 96, which fix the date. Henslowe had paid, on 14 November 1601 (f. 95) an extra 5*s.* to Chettle for this play

> I I I I I I I I I
> I pray you Mr Henslowe deliuer in behalfe of
> the Company, vnto the fifty shilling℮ wch they receaud
> the other day, three pound℮ & tenn shilling℮ more, in
> full payment of six pound℮ the pryce of their play
> Called to good to be true.
> yo^{rs} Robt Shaa

Article 37. Acquittance from William Playstowe to Philip Henslowe for one month's fees due to the Master of the Revels; dated 4 August 1602. An acquittance for July 1602 is in the *Diary*, f. 101; for *Tobias, Jephthah, Love Parts Friendship* and *Cardinal Wolsey*, see ff. 105, 105v. *Baxter's Tragedy* is not otherwise known, but may possibly, as Warner suggested, be identified with Day's *Bristol Tragedy*, which figures on ff. 105, 106.

> Receved of m^{r} Henslowe the iiijth of Agust 1602
> for one monthes paye: due vnto my m^{r} Edmund iij^{li}
> Tylney vppon the xxxj^{te} day of July last past
> the som of iij^{li} I say Rd

> bookes owinge for /5/ ꝑ mei Willplaystowe
> baxters tragedy
> Tobias Comedy
> Jepha Judg of Israel & the cardinall
> loue parts frendshipp.

Article 38. Letter from Joan Alleyn to Edward Alleyn, 21 October 1603. Imperfect; part of the postscript is lost where the paper has decayed. Robert Browne was leader of the company at the Boar's head; see C. J. Sisson, 'Mr and Mrs Browne of the Boar's Head', *Life and Letters To-day* (Winter 1936–7). 'm^{r} woodward' may be the Francis Woodward named on f. 129v of the *Diary*. Thomas Chaloner appears on ff. 19, 124. Mr Bromfield, a merchant, had a few dealings with the Admiral's Men, cf. *Diary*, ff. 91 v, 93 v, 109 v. 'Nicke' and 'Jeames' were probably, as Greg noted, boys attached to the company; for the former, see f. 95 v, and for the latter, probably James Bristow, see ff. 85 v, 232. 'm^{r} Cooke' we have not traced further.

Jhesus

My Intyre & welbeloved sweete harte still it Joyes me & longe I
pray god may I Joye to heare of yor healthe & welfare as you of ours
Allmighty god be thancked my owne selfe yor selfe, & my mother &
whole house are in good healthe & about vs the sycknes dothe Cease
& likely more & more by godꝭ healpe to Cease. All the Companyes
be Come hoame & well for ought we knowe, but that Browne of
the Boares head is dead & dyed very pore, he went not into the
Countrye at all. and all of yor owne Company ar well at theyr owne houses.
my father is at the Corte but wheare the Court ys I know not
I am of your owne mynde, that it is needles to meete my father
at Basynge the Incertayntye being as it ys & I Com̄end your
discreation it were a sore Journey to loase yor labour besyd expenses
& Change of Ayre mighte hurte you therfore you are Resolved vpon
the best Course. for yor Cominge hoame I am not to advyse you
neither will I, vse yor owne discreation yet I longe & am very
desyrous to see you & my poore & symple opinion is yf it shall please
you you maye safely Come hoame, heare is none now sycke neare vs,
vs, yet let it not be as I wyll but at yor owne best lykynge, I am
glad to heare you take delight in hauckinge, & thoughe you have
have worne your appayrell [the best ys] to Rags the best ys you knowe
wheare to have better, & as wellcome to me shall you be wth
yor rags as yf you were in Cloathe of gold or velvet, trye
& see. I have payd fyfty shillings for yor Rent for the warfe
the Lordes Rent. m^{r} woodward my Lordꝭ bayly was not in towne but poynted
his deputy who Receaved all the Rents I had witnesses wth me
at the payment of the money & have his quittance but
the quyttance cost me a groat, they sayd it was the baylives
fee, you know best whether you were wont to paye it, yf not
they made a symple woman of me. you shall Receave a letter
from the Joyner hym selfe & a prynted bill. & so wth my
humble & harty Comendations to yor owne selfe m^{r} Chaloners
& his wyfe wth thanckes for yor kynde vsage, wth my good
mothers kyndest Com̄endations wth the rest of yor houshold
⟨. . .⟩ece is well but Can not speake I ende prayenge allmighty god
s⟨ti⟩ll to blesse vs for his mercyes sacke & so swete harte

once more farwell till we meete wch I hope shall not
be longe. this xxith of octobe⟨r 1⟩603
Abovte a weeke a goe ther ⟨ ⟩ a youthe who said he was
m^{r} frauncis Chalo⟨ ⟩s man ⟨ ⟩ld have borrow⟨⟩d x⟨⟩^{s} to
have bought things for ⟨ ⟩s M^{ri} ⟨ ⟩t hym
Cominge wthout ⟨ ⟩ken ⟨ ⟩e
I would have ⟨ ⟩
⟨ ⟩I bene su⟨ ⟩
And inquire after the fellow & said he had lent hym a horse, I
feare me he gulled hym thoughe he gulled not vs the youthe
was a prety youthe & hansom in appayrell we know not what became
of hym. m^{r} Bromffeild Cōmendꝭ hym he was heare yesterdaye. Nicke
& Jeames be well & Cōmēnd them so dothe m^{r} Cooke & his weife
in the kyndest sorte & so once more in the hartiest manner
farwell

yor faithfull & lovinge weife
Joane Alleyne

[*fragment of address on back*:]
⟨ ⟩vex⟨ ⟩ Susse⟨ ⟩

Articles 40, 42. The first is a warrant from the Duke of Lennox, addressed to mayors, justices of the peace, etc., on behalf of his company of players, who had apparently been forbidden to act, and is dated 13 October 1604. The second is a bond from Francis Henslowe to Philip Henslowe in £60 to observe certain articles of agreement between Francis, John Garland and Abraham Saverie, 'his ffellowes, servantꝭ to the most noble Prince the duke of Lennox', dated 16 March 1605. These help to explain and date the entry in the *Diary*, f. 100, referring to Francis joining with 'owld garlland' and 'sauerey'; see also f. 90v.

Article 105. Letter from William Birde to Philip Henslowe, which corresponds to the entry in the *Diary*, f. 42v, dated 22 April 1599. The note underneath is in Henslowe's hand.

M^{r} henchlowe I pray let me intreate
yo^{u} to lende me forty shillingꝭ tell
the next weeke and Ile then paye it
yo^{u} agayne by the grace of god I
pray as yo^{u} loue me fayle me not,

here is one at home must receaue
it presently if yo[u] will doe me this
fauour yo[u] shall comaunde me in a
greater matter./
yo[rs] will: Birde

feched by william felle
his man

MANUSCRIPTS, VOLUME II

This collection relates to the Beargarden, and to the joint Mastership of the Royal Game of Bears, Bulls and Mastiff Dogs, which Henslowe and Alleyn obtained by purchase from Sir William Steward on 28 November 1604 (articles 5 and 6). Alleyn had bought the Beargarden in 1594 (see below, Manuscripts, volume VIII, f. 5v), and apparently operated there under licence from the Master. When Ralph Bowes, Master from 1573, was dying in or about 1598, Henslowe and Alleyn made great efforts to secure his office, and articles 1 and 2 are concerned with this attempt. Henslowe tried to enlist the aid of Dr Julius Caesar (article 1, a letter from Henslowe to Alleyn, 4 June 1598, refers to this, and cf. *Diary*, f. 38) and other important men; he says, 'I haue bene wth my lord admeralle a bowte yt', but also complains, 'I ame sure my lorde admerall will do nothinge'. They failed in their aim, and paid the next Master, John Dorington, a quarterly fee of £10 for licence to run the Beargarden, as is shown by acquittances, one in the *Diary*, f. 151, dated 11 April 1602, and one which is article 4 here, dated 1 January 1601/2.

MANUSCRIPTS, VOLUME III

Articles 1 and 2. These concern the affairs of Isabel Keys, from whom Henslowe bought a lease in 1597 (*Diary*, f. 72v), and for whom he acted on occasion as agent, paying and collecting her rents (*Diary*, ff. 42v, 43). Article 1 is a letter from Alexander White (perhaps the 'whitt' of the *Diary*, ff. 42, 42v), to Henslowe, asking him to help Isabel Keys who is about to be arrested by one Francis Chambers. Warner dated this wrongly 21 February 1576/7, misreading a scrawled 1596; the letter could not have been written before October

1592, when Alleyn married (*Diary*, f. 2), for it begins, 'm^{r} phillip henslowe I comend me vnto you and vnto your wyfe and vnto m^{r} Allen and his wyfe thanking yow for all kindnes...'. The date is of importance because Warner's misreading led Greg to think Henslowe was living in the Clink in 1577, according to the address on this letter (*Diary*, pp. 2, 4), whereas the first known reference to him is of 1584 (Muniments, article 86).

Article 5. Letter from Francis Henslowe to his uncle Philip asking for assistance; he complains of having been 'vylanously betrayed by ye Lynke who had feed a Coople of sergantę and arested me vnto ye Counter in woodstreet'. On the back is a note by Philip of expenses on behalf of Francis amounting to 16*s*. 4*d*. This letter must have been written prior to 23 May 1592, by which date Edmond Henslowe, to whom it is jointly addressed, had died. See above, Manuscripts, volume I, article 42.

Article 6. Letter from William Henslowe to Philip Henslowe, dated 7 December 1592. The quarrel concerning Lockyers, and the affairs of Margery and John Henslowe are mentioned in the *Diary*; see especially ff. 122v–124, 127v. Extracts only of the letter are given.

brother phillip / wheras yo^{u} sent me worde, by my syster, that
I shold dryue the Locyers, the truth is, I haue done so, &
powned the Cattell which I fownde ther, for the which [w]m^{r} weles
& James Burgis dothe [Suue] Sve me / in dodeles well Courte
& I have sente yo^{u} a Copye of there declarations a gaynste me /
& one saynt stevens daye next, I must pute in my Awnswer, for
there ys the Courte A gayne / other wyse I shalbe over throne /
therfor I wold wyshe yo^{u} to haue the opynyon of a Counseler
how to dele in the Actione...I praye ye for gete not, to aske
yor Counsele, whether [anybodye] my syster Cane make a forfetore
of her Copye hold, by leseng yt withoute lycence of the Lorde,
shee beyng not amyttede to yt, for my syster was never a mytted to
yt sence Rafe hogge dyed / & I haue sent yo^{u} the very true
Serender which Rafe hogge delyuered in his dethbead....Truly I
ame advised that my syster maye Recouer all here Rente, with
damegis, for weles his Rouge folk detayneng &...Kepenge her
Rytę from her, for weles hade yt iij yeres & a halfe, & never

payed Rente....m^r weles standes mvch one the Lece which shee made hem befor my Lord buchorste, & thinkes to bere yt away by that, but shee beyng not a metted that is worth nothenge...I wold have byne at London o^r this tyme if yt had note byne for this mater / & presently after saynt stefens daye I Come god willinge...my syster margery willed me to Rememb^r you of that you promeced her when shee was at London / her sonn Johne & shee canot a gree by no menes / but her is shvche a store betwen them, yt ys wonderfell / I think if ye Cold, yt were very good for y^e to profyd hem a m^r / for the world wonders at them two / in any wyse let me her from ye...thuse endying, with harty Comendations to y^e / with all o^r frendes in Jenerall / hopenge of yor good helthes from buxted the vij^th of [desemb^r] [novemb^r] 1592 desemb^r///

yor Louenge brother William Henslow

[*endorsed*:]
W: H: letter to
p: Henslo

MANUSCRIPTS, VOLUME VIII

This consists of a memorandum-book of Edward Alleyn, containing notes relating to his dealings in property between 1594 and 1616. Among the items of theatrical interest printed here, the information about his expenses on the Fortune theatre is of special relevance to the *Diary*.

f. 5v:

What The Bear garden Cost
me for my owne part
in december 1594

	li
first to m^r: burnabye	.200
Then for the patten	.250
Some is . . .	.450

I held itt 16 year &	
Rd [3]60^li p anum w^ch: is . .	.960^li
Sowld itt to my father	
Hinchloe in februarie	
1610 for	.580^li

f. 6v:

What The fortune Cost me
. . . . novemb 1599

first for ye leas to brew . . . 240^li^
then for ye building ye playhowe . . . 520^li^
for other pruat buildings of myn
owne . . . . 120^li^
so in all itt hath Cost me
for ye Leasse . . . . . 880^li^
bought the Inheritance of the land
of the gills of ye Isle of man w^ch^:
is ye fortune & all the Howses in
whight crosstrett & gowlding Lane
in June 1610 for the some
of . . . . . . 340^li^
bought in John garretts Lease
in revertion from the gills
for 21 years for . . . 100^li^
so in all itt Cost me . . . . 1320^li^

Blessed be ye Lord god
Euerlasting

MANUSCRIPTS, VOLUME XI

This listing of 'all the offices in Englande withe ther ffees' is dated by Warner *c.* 1600. It contains among its pages some notes in the hand of Henslowe relating to Worcester's Men (see *Diary*, ff. 100v, 115–21). This company is only known to have played once at Court, on 3 January 1602 (Chambers, *E.S.* IV, 114), and the first entry may relate to this. Greg suggests that the other entries may have to do with their 'warrant on becoming the Queen's men' (*Papers*, p. 108). The meaning of the figures jotted down by Henslowe on f. 30v is not known.

f. 29v:

Rd pd for my Lo^r^ worsters menes warant
10^li^ for playinge at the cort vnto the clarke of
the cownselles for geatynge the cownselles
hande to yt. . . . . vij s
pd at the Receuinge of the mony owt of the
payhowsse to m^r^ moysse for fese . . . . x^s^ vj d

f. 30:

1603

Layd owt as folowethe for sewinge at the
cort when the Kinge Laye at grenwiche

Itm pd for a petion wch m^r doryngton had . . . .xij d
Itm pd for a petion wch my Lo chamberlen hade . . .xij d
Itm pd for a peticon to dd to the cownsell table . . . . .xij d
Itm pd for mackinge of ij Lycenses in parchment . . . .iij s
Itm pd for ou^r warent for baytynge . . . . .vij s
Itm pd for goinge & comming by wat^r [3]4 tymes . .ij s
Itm pd for goinge by wat^r ij tymes in adaye . . . . . .xvj d

f. 30v:

25 – 6 – 2	22 – 1 – 6
12 –18 –10	17 – 9 – 6
11 –18 –..	
5 –.. –..	39 –11 –..
45 – 3 –..	

MANUSCRIPTS, VOLUME XVIII

Article 6. This is a rent-book of Philip Henslowe, listing names of his tenants in various holdings between 1604 and 1611. There are similar lists in the *Diary*, ff. 177–8.

Article 7. A note in the hand of Edward Alleyn of his expenditure between 1602 and 1608 on the Beargarden and the Fortune. The figures on the back are unexplained; T. W. Baldwin assumed in 'Posting Henslowe's Accounts', pp. 65–71, that they represent a year's takings at the Hope. Corrections of erroneous figures altered or overwritten are not recorded here.

	beargden			Play Howse		
	li	s	d	li	s	
1602	121 –	11 –	6	089 –	05 –	0
1603	118 –	07 –	0	004 –	02 –	0
1604	153 –	14 –	0	232 –	01 –	8
1605	092 –	12 –	4	108 –	14 –	3
	486 –	04 –	10	434 –	02 –	11

1606 1607 pd for yᵉ building		127 – 00 – 00
1608 of yᵉ Howses wᶜʰ		163 – 00 – 00
may be Counted to – 360ˡⁱ		121 – 06 – 00
some totall – 846 – 04 – 10		411 – 06 – 00
	totall	845ˡⁱ– 08 – 11

[*on the back*:]

li	s	d	
874	04	9	ob
212	02	8	ob
083	12	11	ob
019	19	9	ob
001	02	01	o
1191	02	04	

Besids yᵉ money wᶜʰ wase
Taken vp for yᵉ Reūllˢ

MUNIMENTS

Muniment no. 16. Deed of partnership in the Rose Theatre between Philip Henslowe and John Cholmley, 10 January 1586/7. Excerpts only are given here. The partnership was due to end in April 1595, but the name Cholmley appears only in the scrawl on the opening page of the *Diary*, and Henslowe's references to 'my play howse' in 1592 (f. 4) and in Lent 1595 (f. 2v) may show that the partnership was dissolved before the theatrical entries in the *Diary* commence.

This Indenture made the Tenthe daye of Januarye Anno dn̄ī 1586... betwene Phillippe Hinshley Cittizen and Dyer of London one thonne ꝑtye and John Cholmley Cittizen and grocer of London one thother ꝑtye Witneseth that the said partyes...are entrid into partnershippe in the...posessinge...of all that ꝑcell of grownde or garden plotte Contayninge in lenghe and bredthe sqare every waye ffoorescore and fourteene foote of assize little more or lesse As also...in the...beniffyttꝭ somes of moneye proffitte and Advauntage of a playe howse now in framinge and shortly to be ereckted and sett vppe vpone the same grounde or garden plotte from the Daye of the Date of these pʳsentꝭ for and duringe and vntill the ende and terme of Eighte yeares And three monethes from thence nexte ensuinge...yt is...agreed...That yt shall and maye be lawfull to and for the saide John Cholmeley...To have...The moytie or one halfe of All suche some and somes of moneye gaynes profytt and Comodytye wch shall...become due for the saide ꝑcell of grounde and playe howse when and after yt shalbe ereckted and sett vpe by reasonne of any playe or playes that shalbe showen or played there or otherwysse howsoever...And...the saide Phillippe Hinshley...To have...The other moytie...That he the saide John Cholmley shall...have...All that small tēnte or dwellinge howse scittuate and standinge at the sowthe ende or syde of the saide ꝑcell of growmde or garden plotte to keepe victualinge in or to putt to any other vse or vsses whatsoever...the same howse neare adioyninge vnto a lane there Comonly Called mayden Lane now in the tenure of the saide John Cholmley o^{r} his assignes wth free ...passage...as well by and throughe the Alleye there called Rosse Alleye leadinge from the Ryver of thames into the saide ꝑcell of growmde As allso in and by and throughe the waye leadinge into the saide mayden Lane...And...That the saide Phyllipe... shall...wth as muche expedicōn as may be ereckte fynishe and sett vpp or cause to be erected finished and sett vpe by John Gryggꝭ Carpenter his servantꝭ or assignes the saide playhouse wth all furniture thervnto belonginge...All wch premisses...ar scittuate ...on the bancke syde in the ꝑyshe of St Savoyes in Sovthworke in the County of Surr In consideracōn wherof the saide John Cholmley ...dothe...graunte to...Phillippe Hinshley...well and truly to paie for a yerlye anuytie the some of Eighte hundreth and Sixteene Poundꝭ of lawfull moneye of Englande in mann^{r} and forme followinge that is to saye One the feaste Daye of the Nativitie of St John Baptiste...Twentie five Poundꝭ and Tenne shillingꝭ... And so further after that from feaste daye to feaste daye quarter to quarter and yeare vnto yeare...quarterly one every of the like feaste dayes...Twentie five Poundꝭ and Tenne shillingꝭ vntill all the saide somme of Eighte hundreth and Sixteene Poundꝭ be so truly Contented and payde...And yf yt shall happen the saide...quarterly paymēts...to be behinde and vnpayde...by the space of twentye and one dayes...after any feaste daye...then and from thencforthe the saide Copartnershippe...shalbe voyde...And that yt shall and maye be lawfull to and for the saide Phillipe Hinshley...to renter And the saide John Cholmley...vtterly to expell...And further the saide ꝑtyes...doe...graunte eyther wth other by these p^{r}sentꝭ that yt shall and may be lawfull to and for the saide Phillype Hinshleye and John Cholmley...ioyntly to appoynte and ꝑmitte suche ꝑsonne and ꝑsonnes players to vse exersyse & playe in the saide playe howse...And...that the saide Phillype Hinshley and John Cholmley shall and wilbe there p^{r}sent them selves or appoynte theire sufficiente debutyes or assignes wth them selves or otherwysse at their Choyse to Coleckte gather and receave all such some and somes of moneye of every ꝑsonne & ꝑsonnes resortinge and Cominge to the saide playe howse to vew see and heare any playe o^{r} enterlude at any tyme or tymes to be showed and playde duringe the saide terme of Eighte yeares and three monethes excepte yt please any of the said ꝑtyes to suffer theire frendę to go in for nothinge And that all suche some and somes be equally devided...whereof the saide Phillipe Hinshleye... to have the one halfe...And...John Cholmley...to have the other... And further the saide Phillipe Hinshleye...shall...paye...All and all mann^{r} of quitte rentę and other rente Chargis due and payable to the Lorde or Lordę of the ꝑmisses...And likewayes shall... repaire and amende all the brigges and wharffes belonginge to the saide ꝑcell of grounde...at or before the xxixth daye of September nexte cominge...And likewayes the saide John Cholmleye and Phillipe Hinshleye...doe...graunte eyther wth other...That they...shall... after the saide xxixth daye of September nexte Cominge...repare amende sustayne mantayne and vpholde the saide playehowse 〈........〉 brigges wharffę and all other the wayes and brygges now leadinge... into onto and from the saide ꝑcell of grownde...when and as often as neede shall require...And further the saide Phillipe Hinshley... dothe...graunte to and wth the saide John Cholmleye...That he... will not ꝑmitte or suffer any ꝑsonne o^{r} ꝑsonnes other than the saide John Cholmley...to vtter sell o^{r} putt to sale in or aboute the saide ꝑcell of grownde...any breade o^{r} drinke other then suche as shalbe solde to and for the vse...of the saide John Cholmley...In witnes whereof the saide ꝑtyes to theis p^{r}sente Indentures Interchaungeably haue sett their Seales the day and yeres firste aboue written/

By me John Cholmley grocer

Muniment no. 22. Contract between Peter Streete and Philip Henslowe and Edward Alleyn for the erection of the Fortune at the cost of £440, dated 8 January 1599/1600. The accounts which appear on the back, and which are printed below, should be compared with those in the *Diary*, ff. 97, 97v, 98v–99. The entry on f. 70v, 'pd vnto my sonne alleyn for the first weckes playe...' which occurs between entries dated 11 November 1600 and 14 December 1600 probably relates to the first performances at the new theatre.

This Indenture made the Eighte daie of Januarye 1599 And in the Twoe and ffortyth yeare of the Reigne of our sovereigne Ladie Elizabeth by the grace of God Queene of England

ffraunce and Irelande defender of the ffaythe &cꝭ Betwene Phillipp Henslowe and Edwarde Allen of the ꝑishe of Ste Savio^{rs} in Southwark in the Countie of Surrey gentlemen on thone ꝑte And Peeter Streete

Cittizen and Carpenter of London on thother parte witnesseth That whereas the saide Phillipp Henslowe & Edward Allen the daie of the date hereof Haue bargayned Compounded & agreed

wth the saide Peter Streete ffor the erectinge buildinge & settinge upp of a newe howse and Stadge, for a Plaiehowse in and vppon a certeine plott or ꝑcell of grounde appoynted oute for that purpose

Scytuate and beinge nere Goldinge lane in the ꝑishe of Ste Giles wthoute Cripplegate of London To be by him the saide Peeter Streete or so͞me other sufficyent woorkmen of his provideinge and

appoyntem^{te} and att his propper Costes & Chardges for the consideraco͞n hereafter in theis pn͞tꝭ expressed / Made erected, builded and sett upp In manner & forme followeinge (that is to saie) The

frame of the saide howse to be sett square and to conteine ffowerscore foote of lawfull assize everye waie square wthoute and fiftie fiue foote of like assize square everye waie wthin, wth a good

suer and stronge foundaco͞n of pyles brick lyme and sand, both wthoute & wthin, to be wroughte one foote of assize att the leiste aboue the grounde And the saide fframe to conteine Three

Stories in heighth The first or lower Storie to Conteine Twelue foote of lawfull assize in heighth The second Storie Eleaven foote of lawfull assize in heighth And the Third or vpper Storie to conteine

Nyne foote of lawfull assize in height / All which Stories shall conteine Twelue foote and a half of lawfull assize in breadth througheoute besides a Juttey forwardꝭ in eyther of the saide Two

vpper Stories of Tenne ynches of lawfull assize, wth ffower convenient divisions for gentlemens roomes and other sufficient and convenient divisions for Twoe pennie roomes wth necessarie Seates to be

placed and sett Aswell in those roomes as througheoute all the rest of the galleries of the saide howse and wth suche like steares Conveyances & divisions wthoute & wthin as are made & Contryved in and to the late erected Plaiehowse On the Banck in the saide p̱ishe of Ste Savio^{rs} Called the Globe Wth a Stadge and Tyreinge howse to be made erected & settupp wthin the saide fframe, wth a shadowe or cover

over the saide Stadge, wch Stadge shalbe placed & sett As alsoe the stearecases of the saide fframe in suche sorte as is p^{r}figured in a Plott thereof drawen And wch Stadge shall conteine in length

ffortie and Three foote of lawfull assize and in breadth to extende to the middle of the yarde of the saide howse, The same Stadge to be paled in belowe wth good stronge and sufficyent newe oken

bourdes And likewise the lower Storie of the saide fframe wthinside, and the same lower storie to be alsoe laide over and fenced wth stronge yron pykes And the saide Stadge to be in all other proporco̅n̅s

Contryved and fashioned like vnto the Stadge of the saide Plaiehowse Called the Globe, Wth convenient windowes and lightꝭ glazed to the saide Tyreinge howse And the saide fframe Stadge and

Stearecases to be covered wth Tyle, and to haue a sufficient gutter of lead to Carrie & convey the water frome the Coveringe of the saide Stadge to fall backwardes And alsoe all the saide fframe and

the Stairecases thereof to be sufficyently enclosed wthoute wth lathe lyme & haire and the gentlemens roomes and Twoe pennie roomes to be seeled wth lathe lyme & haire and all the fflowers of the

saide Galleries Stories and Stadge to be bourded wth good & sufficyent newe deale bourdes of the whole thicknes wheare neede shalbe And the saide howse and other thinges beforemenco̅e̅d to be

made & doen To be in all other Contrivitions Conveyances fashions thinge and thinges effected finished and doen accordinge to the manner and fashion of the saide howse Called the Globe Saveinge only

that all the princypall and maine postes of the saide fframe and Stadge forwarde shalbe square and wroughte palasterwise wth carved proporco̅n̅s Called Satiers to be placed & sett on the Topp of

every of the same postes And saveinge alsoe that the said Peeter Streete shall not be chardged wth anie manner of pay⟨ntin⟩ge in or aboute the saide fframe howse or Stadge or anie p̱te thereof nor

Rendringe the walls wthin Nor seelinge anie more or other roomes then the gentlemens roomes Twoe pennie roomes and Stadge before remembred / nowe theiruppon the saide

Peeter Streete dothe cove̅n̅nte promise and graunte ffor himself his executo^{rs} and admīstrato^{rs} to and wth the saide Phillipp Henslowe and Edward Allen and either of them and thexecuto^{rs} and admīstrato^{rs} of them and either of them by theis pn̄tꝭ In manner & forme followeinge (that is to saie) That he the saide Peeter Streete his executo^{rs} or assignes shall & will att his or their owne

propper costꝭ & Chardges well woorkmanlike & substancyallie make erect, sett upp and fully finishe In and by all thinges accordinge to the true meaninge of theis pn̄tꝭ wth good stronge

and substancyall newe Tymber and other necessarie stuff All the saide fframe and other woorkꝭ whatsoever In and vppon the saide plott or ꝑcell of grounde (beinge not by anie aucthoretie

Restrayned, and haveinge ingres egres & regres to doe the same) before the ffyue & Twentith daie of Julie next Com̄einge after the date hereof And shall alsoe at his or theire

like costes and Chardges Provide and finde All manner of woorkemen Tymber Joystꝭ Rafters boordꝭ dores boltꝭ hinges brick Tyle lathe lyme haire sande nailes leede Iron Glasse

woorkmanshipp and other thinges whatsoever wch shalbe needefull Convenyent & necessarie for the saide fframe & woorkꝭ & eu^{r}ie ꝑte thereof And shall alsoe make all the saide

fframe in every poynte for Scantlingꝭ lardger and bigger in assize Then the Scantlinges of the Timber of the saide newe erected howse, Called the Globe

And alsoe that he the saide Peeter Streete shall furthwth aswell by himself As by suche other and soemanie woorkmen as shalbe Convenient & necessarie enter into and

vppon the saide buildinges and woorkes And shall in reasonable manner proceede therein wthoute anie wilfull detraccōn vntill the same shalbe fully effected and

finished / In consideracōn of all wch buildingꝭ and of all stuff & woorkemanshipp thereto belonginge The saide Phillipp Henslowe & Edwarde Allen and either of

them ffor themselues theire and either of theire executo^{rs} & admīstrato^{rs} doe Joynctlie & seu^{r}allie Coven̄nte & graunte to & wth the saide Peeter Streete his executo^{r}s & adm̄istrato^{r}s by

theis pn̄tꝭ That they the saide Phillipp Henslowe & Edward Allen or one of them Or the executo^{r}s adm̄istrato^{r}s or assignes of them or one of them Shall & will well & truelie paie or

Cawse to be paide vnto the saide Peeter Streete his executo^{rs} or assignes Att the place aforesaid appoynted for the erectinge of the saide fframe The full som̄e of ffower hundred & ffortie

Poundes of lawfull money of Englande in manner & forme followeinge (that is to saie) Att suche tyme And when as the Tymberwoork of the saide fframe shalbe rayzed & sett upp by the saide Peeter Streete his executo^rs or assignes, Or w^th^in Seaven daies then next followeinge Twoe hundred & Twentie poundes And att suche time and when as the saide fframe &

woorkẹ shalbe fullie effected & ffynished as is aforesaide Or w^th^in Seaven daies then next followeinge, thother Twoe hundred and Twentie poundes w^th^oute fraude or Coven

Prouided allwaies and it is agreed betwene the saide parties That whatsoever som̃e or som̃es of money the saide Phillipp Henslowe & Edward Allen or either of them

or thexecuto^rs or assignes of them or either of them shall lend or deliver vnto the saide Peter Streete his executo^rs or assignes or anie other by his appoyntem^te or consent ffor or

concerninge the saide Woorkẹ or anie ꝑte thereof or anie stuff thereto belonginge before the raizeinge & settinge upp of the saide fframe, shalbe reputed accepted taken & accoumpted in

ꝑte of the firste paym^te aforesaid of the saide some of ffower hundred & ffortie poundes And all suche som̃e & som̃es of money as they or anie of them shall as aforesaid lend or deliver betwene

the razeinge of the saide fframe & finishinge thereof and of all the rest of the saide woorkẹ Shalbe reputed accepted taken & accoumpted in ꝑte of the laste paym^te aforesaid of the same

som̃e of ffower hundred & ffortie poundes Anie thinge abouesaid to the contrary notw^th^standinge / In witnes whereof the ꝑties abouesaid to theis p̃nte Indetures Interchaun

geably haue sett theire handes and Seales / Yeoven the daie and yeare ffirste abouewritten

P S

Sealed and deliu^r^ed by the saide Peter Streete
in the p^r^esence of me william Harris Pub Scr
And me frauncis Smyth appr to the said Scr /

[*endorsed*:]
Peater Streat ffor The Building of the ffortune

The back also bears the following acquittances and accounts, written for the most part in Henslowe's hand. The lineation here is not that of the MS., in which the sums in the left-hand margin are written vertically up the page.

1599

Receaued att thensealeinge heereof. in ꝑte of payem^t^ towardẹ stuff. } x^li^

more in pte of payment aforesayd the 17 of Jeneway to wm shepde bricklayer at the a poyntment of petter strette . . . . } xxxx^s

P S

more in earneste of xx & ode lodes of tymber vnto Richard deller bargman at the a poyntment of petter strette the some of . . . 19 of Jenewary 1599 . . } x^li

P S

more in earneste of xxxx lode of tymbȝ pd vnto m^r winche of the scaldinge howsse & m^r Baylle kepe of the stare chambȝ dore the 21 of Janewary 1599 at the apoyntment of petter strete the some of . . . . . . } xx^li

P S Receaved the said some of xx^li /
p me Robertū Baylye. /

more in pte of payment the 24 of Janewary 1599 wch was dd vnto [his] m^r stret man John Benyon wch came frome hime owt of the contrye to paye his sayers the some of } iij^li

bye mee John Benion

more receued in parte of pamente the firste daye of ffebuaree for the vse of my m^r Peeter Streate x^li by mee John benion . . . . } x^li

more pd in pt of the 5 of febreary 1599 ⟨at⟩ the apoyntment of petter streate vnto Richard deller for tymbȝ as maye a pere by his h⟨an⟩d the some of } iij^li xiij^s

by me Richarde dellare

more in pte of payment the 6 of febrearye 1599 vnto goodman duff[t]e for ix lode of tymbȝ the some of fyve pownd I saye . . . . } v^li

P S

mor in pt of payment this 7 ffebr. 99 my self for mens wages . . . . } viij^li

more the same tyme in pte of paym^t. for wydow martyns tymber . . . . } x^li

P S

more in pt of payment the 13 of febreary 1599 for dubell tenes & syngell tenes . . . . xj^s viij^d

more in pt of payment by edward alleyn when he was in the contrey wth hime . . . . v^li more pd in pt of payment the 15 of febreary 1599 vnto his man John Benion vpon a note from his m^r^ wth his hand to yt some of . . . . vij^li^ x^s^

By me John Benion

more in parte of payment the 19 of february 1599 to hym self for a mast . . . . xxv^s^

more ye same daye to radolph bemond in earnest for tymber . v^li^

ye marke of |—⟨ beomond

more in parte of payment the 21 of february 1599 to goodman Jordain in earnest for 30 load of tymber . . . . . . v^li^

Thomas Jordan

more in pte of payment the 22 of febreary 1599 vnto goodman Beaman for the vsse of petter strette for to paye his worckmen wageꝭ the some of . . . . viij^li^

Raffe |—⟨ Beamans marke

pd more in pt of payment 24 of febreary 1599 for dubell tennes & singell tennes some . . . . xj^s^ 8^d^

pd more in pt of paymente the laste of febreary 1599 when we wente into the contrey to m^r^ strete hime sellfe the some of . . . . x^li^

pd more in pt for syngell tenes & dubell tennes . . . . . [x]xj^s^ 8^d^

more ye 2 of march 1599 to streetꝭ boy Robart whartoun to carye downe to his m^r^ . . . . xx^li^

wittnesses william brollear Nicolas Seatton

Receaved by vs John Winche and Robert Bayly according to a note from m^r^ Peter Street directed dated the ffyveth of Marche the some of . . . . x^li^ x^s^./

J W Robert Baylye

mor ye 8 of march to his boy robart whartoun as wages. . . 8^li^

ye boyes R mark

pd vnto Goodman smithe the 13 of march 1599 for iij lode of tymbȝ the some of. . . . . xxxxv^s^

pd vnto streetꝭ mann willyam blacbourn ye 17 of march 1599 to cary downe to his master. . . . . v^li^

pd vnto goodman Jordayn the 18 of marche 1599 for timbȝ the some of . . . . v^li^

pd to beomand ye 20 of march 1599 for ye first faer of tymber . . . . v^li

I do acknoledg the reseat of all thes somes of money aboue written in wittnes whear of I haue sett to my mark

the marke of P S peter strett 180^li–18^s

173–18

Receaved more in pte of payment my self the 20 of march 1599 . . . . xl^s

pd vnto m^r strette to paye his worckmen the 22 of march 1599 . . . . v^li

more ye 25 of march to m^r street for tymber to beckley . . . . .ij^li

more ye Last of march to his boy Ro whartoun . on his bill . . . . v^li

more to w^m tyller brickk macker at the apoynt ment of strete 4 ma^rch 1600 . . . . xxxx^s

more to peter strete the 12 of Ap^rell 1600 to fetche vp pylles . . . . x^li

li s
Some of this is – 63 – 16 w^t ye former & this – 244 – 14

more payd to hew hewsse the 17 of ap^rell for tymb3 x^li & for bringe downe of a fare iij^li I saye payd . . . xiiij^li

pd more to hew hewssen the 25 of ap^rell 1600 for bringe a fare . . . . v^li

pd more to petter strete boye 26 of ap^rell 1600 Robart wharton . . . . v^li

pd more to petter strete the 28 of ap^rell 1600 to paye wages . . . . ij^li

pd to petter strete the 31 of ap^rell 1600 to paye for brickes & sande . . . . xx^s

pd ye 2 of may to crose & thrale sawyers 56^s–& to georg Jacson j^li in all . . . . iij^li xvj^s

pd to goodman Jordain ye Last of Aprill by bill for timber . . . . xxx^s

pd yᵉ forth of May to willyam Jonsoun for petter strete some of . . . . v^{li}

pd yᵉ sand man for viij lode of sande . . . . x^{s}

pd to John warner sayer . xxxviij^{s} & to Robart lithinge sayer 6 of maye . . . . xxj^{s} . lix^{s}

pd for tymbȝ to m^{rs} martyne the 6 of maye 1600. . . v^{li}

pd to the carpenters wch came frome winser the 8 of maye 1600 . . . . iiij^{li} vij^{s}

pd to the labereres at the eand of the fowndations the 8 of maye 1600 . . . . iij^{li} viij^{s}

pd to petter strette the 8 of maye 1600 . . . . x^{s}

pd to goodman shepde the 10 of maye 1600 . . . . . xxxx^{s}

li s 47 – 4 dd to my sone when he Ride to winser 15 of maye 1600 ix^{li} xvj^{s}

pd vnto the bargman Robart caine for a fayer bringinge iiij^{li}

pd vnto m^{r} strete man the 19 of may to cary into the contrye . . . . xix^{s} vj^{d}

dd to goodman Beamand to carye into the contrey 19 of maye. xj^{li}

pd to the ⟨carters⟩ man the 19 of maye 1600 . . . . . vij^{s}

pd vnto the carpenters for ij lode & hallfe of tymbȝ 1600 . . . . xxxv^{s}

pd to the carmen for carenge of tymbȝ . . . . xxij^{s} vj^{d}

21 of may pd for a fayer 4^{li} yᵉ brewer 10^{s} sherwood 7^{s} street hymself 10^{s} . . . . v^{li}–vij^{s}

23 of maye pd vnto the Brewer of maydenhed hary smyth . . . . xxviij^{s}

pd ye 23 of may in yᵉ cuntrye to dyvers. . . . . . . v^{li}–xij^{s}–viij^{d}

pd yᵉ 24 of may being satterday for wagis to Ro. wharton . . . . vj^{li}–xiiij^{s}

pd yᵉ 24 of maye 1600 in earneste of xij lode of lathes . . . . v^{li}

pd m^r^ william for ix thowsand of brickes [24]
30 of maye . . . . iiij^li^ x^s^

pd the 27 of maye to petter stretę boye w^m^
wharton . . . . x^s^

pd the 30 of maye for ij lode & hallfe of tymbȝ
1600 . . . . xxx^s^ vj^d^

pd the 31 of may pd wages. sayers & carege &
strete . . . . viij^li^

Lent vnto m^r^ strete the 5 of June 1600 to fetche his hores frome m^r^ Ierlandes owt of pane . . . } iiij^li^

pd ye 6 of June to garrett for 30 bordę & 18 d
for carryag of them . . . . xxij^s^–vj^d^

pd ye 6 of June to Ro: wharton – xij^d^ to beomand
for carriag. . . . . xj^s^

to street to buy carte wheels ye 6 of June . . . . . . xv^s^

ye 7 being satterday for wagis & sawyers & cartes . . viij^li^

ye 10 to street to pasify hym. . . . . iiij^s^

ye 11 to goodman Laurenc . . . . v^li^

Manuscript not in the Dulwich collection. In his *Henslowe Papers* (1907), p. 127, Greg cited a note 'sold a few years ago as an Ireland forgery', but which he printed as genuine. This fragment is now MS. X.d.261 in the Folger Shakespeare Library. Dr J. G. McManaway kindly supplied us with photostats of the document, which measures 8 inches by a maximum of 4 inches, and is covered with scribble in Henslowe's hand, including his own name and the names and phrases 'John Whitte', 'Jhone Willsone sitizen & haberdaher [*sic*] of london', 'Alleyn', 'M^r^ dorington', 'Samell Rowley dew m̄ fortune Smy'. Its main interest is the undated note by Rowley printed below; Henslowe recorded payments for *Tom Strowd* in the *Diary* in 1601 (see above, pp. 170–82). Between the request and the signature is written in Henslowe's hand the sum '45–2–00'.

M^r^ hincheloe I praye ye delyver to John Daye thurtye shyllyngs
whych Is vpon the thurd parte of Tom Strowde
Samuell Rowlye

APPENDIX 2

PLAYHOUSE INVENTORIES NOW LOST

The following inventories of properties, costumes and play-books were first printed by Malone in his *The Plays and Poems of William Shakespeare* (1790), vol. I, part II, pp. 300–7. He wrote, p. 289, 'In a bundle of loose papers [i.e. at Dulwich College] has also been found an exact inventory of the Wardrobe, playbooks, properties, &c. belonging to the lord Admiral's servants'. These papers have since disappeared. There is no reason to doubt that the lists were genuine, and were probably, if the spelling is a guide, in Henslowe's hand. They were reprinted by Greg, *Henslowe Papers*, pp. 113–23. The first five lists are dated March 1598; Greg thought that they were drawn up 'at the time of the amalgamation of the Admiral's and Pembroke's men in the winter of 1597/8', but the companies joined in October 1597 (*Diary*, ff. 27v, 43v). However, a statement of debt was acknowledged by the sharers between 8 and 13 March 1598, and the lists would appropriately belong to this year. It is just possible that they were made in 1599, when there was no playing during most of March (f. 48v), but the evidence within the lists points to the earlier year, except for two items of doubtful interpretation (see l. 80 and notes). The last two lists can be dated by reference to the *Diary* as not earlier than August 1598, and probably not much later than this. In the list of play-books only one, *Vayvode*, seems out of place as added to the stock in January 1599, but it was in production in August 1598, and its appearance in the list is best explained as an accident; see l. 198 and n. Only a few of the last list of costumes can be certainly traced in the *Diary*, but more may be concealed in the loans to buy 'divers things' which often appear there. The notes to these lists are largely based upon the thorough work of Fleay in his

Chronicle History of the London Stage (1890), and Greg; conjectural identifications are marked with a query, and perhaps little reliance is to be placed upon the connecting of a property with a specific play. Difficult words are noted in the Index and Glossary at the end of this volume.

The booke of the Inventary of the goods of my Lord Admeralles men, *tacken the* 10 *of Marche in the yeare* 1598.

Gone and loste.

Item, j orenge taney satten dublet, layd thycke with gowld lace.

Item, j blew tafetie sewt.

Item, j payr of carnatyon satten Venesyons, layd with gold lace.

Item, j longe-shanckes[1] sewte.

Item, j Sponnes dublet pyncket.

Item, j Spanerd gyrcken.

Item, Harey the fyftes[2] dublet.

Item, Harey the fyftes[2] vellet gowne.

Item, j fryers gowne.

Item, j lyttell dublet for boye.

The Enventary of the Clownes Sewtes and Hermetes Sewtes, with dievers other sewtes, as followeth, 1598, *the* 10 *of March.*

Item, j senetores gowne, j hoode, and 5 senetores capes.

Item, j sewtte for Nepton;[3] Fierdrackes sewtes for Dobe.[4]

Item, iiij genesareyes gownes, and iiij torchberers sewtes.

Item, iij payer of red strasers, and iij fares gowne of buckrome.

Item, iiij Herwodes cottes, and iij sogers cottes, and j green gown for Maryan.[5]

Item, vj grene cottes for Roben Hoode,[5] and iiij knaves sewtes.

Item, ij payer of grene hosse, and Andersones[6] sewte. j whitt shepen clocke.

---

(1) *longe-shanckes*] *Longshanks*, played as 'ne' 29 August 1595 (*Diary*, f. 12v).

(2) *Harey the fyftes*] first played 28 November 1595 (*Diary*, f. 14).

(3) *Nepton*] Fleay and Greg suggest Neptune in *Selio and Olympo* (?=Heywood's *Golden Age*), but this is mere conjecture; see Chambers, *E.S.* III, 344.

(4) *Dobe*] unexplained; an actor 'Dab' figures in the plot of *The Battle of Alcazar*, which may belong to late 1597 (Chambers, *E.S.* II, 175 and n.); cf. l. 130 below, and pp. 329 ff.

(5) *Maryan...Roben Hoode*] the two parts of *Robin Hood* (*The Downfall* and *The Death of Robert Earl of Huntington*) were licensed for performance 28 March 1598 (*Diary*, f. 45).

(6) *Andersones*] ? an actor; as Greg notes, Sir Cuthbert Anderson is a character in Greene's *James IV*, but there is no evidence that this play belonged to the Admiral's Men.

Item, ij rosset cottes, and j black frese cotte, and iiij prestes cottes.

Item, ij whitt sheperdes cottes, and ij Danes sewtes, and j payer of Danes hosse.

Item, The Mores lymes, and Hercolles[1] lymes, and Will. Sommers[2] sewtte.

Item, ij Orlates[3] sewtes, hates and gorgetts, and vij anteckes cootes.

Item, Cathemer[4] sewte, j payer of cloth whitte stockens, iiij Turckes hedes.[5]

Item, iiij freyers gownes and iiij hoodes to them, and j fooles coate, cape, and babell, and branhowlttes[6] bodeys, and merlen[7] gowne and cape.

Item, ij black saye gownes, and ij cotton gownes, and j rede saye gowne.

Item, j mawe[8] gowne of calleco for the quene, j carnowll hatte.

Item, j red sewt of cloth for pyge,[9] layed with whitt lace.

Item, v payer of hosse for the clowne, and v gerkenes for them.

Item, iij payer of canvas hosse for asane,[10] ij payer of black strocers.

Item, j yelow leather dublett for a clowne, j Whittcomes[11] dublett poke.

Item, Eves bodeyes,[12] j pedante trusser, and iij donnes hattes.

Item, j payer of yelow cotton sleves, j gostes sewt, and j gostes bodeyes.

Item, xviij copes and hattes, Verones sonnes hosse.[13]

Item, iij trumpettes and a drum, and a trebel viall, a basse viall, a bandore, a sytteren, j anshente, j whitt hatte.

Item, j hatte for Robin Hoode,[14] j hobihorse.

Item, v shertes, and j serpelowes, iiij ferdingalles.

Item, vj head-tiers, j fane, iiij rebatos, ij gyrketruses.

Item, j longe sorde.

---

(1) *Hercolles*] *I Hercules* was played as 'ne' 7 May 1595, and *II Hercules* 23 May 1595 (*Diary*, ff. 11v, 12v).

(2) *Will. Sommers*] Henry VIII's fool; he cannot be linked with any known Admiral's play at this date.

(3) *Orlates*] unexplained.

(4) *Cathemer*] unexplained.

(5) *Turckes hedes*] possibly, as Greg suggests, for use in *The Battle of Alcazar*, the plot of which calls for dead men's heads as properties, and may belong to 1597 (see l. 17 and n.).

(6) *branhowlttes*] a woman's gown was bought for *Branholt*, 26 November 1597 (*Diary*, f. 43v).

(7) *merlen*] perhaps a character in *Uther Pendragon*, played as 'ne' on 29 April 1597 (*Diary*, f. 26v).

(8) *mawe*] unexplained; ? for *The Set at Mawe*, played as 'ne' 14 December 1594 (*Diary*, f. 10v).

(9) *pyge*] John Pig the boy actor, cf. ll. 102, 104, 105, 166 below, *Diary*, f. 37v, and p. 282 above.

(10) *asane*] unexplained.

(11) *Whittcomes*] ? an actor.

(12) *Eves bodeyes*] play not identified.

(13) *Verones sonnes hosse*] for a character in *An Humorous Day's Mirth*, which encourages the identification of Chapman's play with the *Comedy of Humours*, first played 11 May 1597 (*Diary*, f. 26v); cf. l. 119 and n.

(14) *Robin Hoode*] see l. 20 and n. above.

The Enventary of all the apparell for my Lord Admiralles men, *tacken the* 10 *of marche* 1598.—*Leaft above in the tier-house in the cheast.*

Item, My Lord Caffes[1] gercken, & his hoosse.
Item, j payer of hosse for the Dowlfen.[2]
Item, j murey lether gyrcken, & j white lether gercken.
Item, j black lether gearken, & Nabesathe[3] sewte.
Item, j payer of hosse, & a gercken for Valteger[4]
Item, ij leather anteckes cottes with basses, for Fayeton.[5]
Item, j payer of bodeyes for Alles Pearce.[6]

The Enventary tacken of all the properties for my Lord Admeralles men, *the* 10 *of Marche* 1598.

Item, j rocke, j cage,[7] j tombe, j Hell mought.
Item, j tome of Guido,[8] j tome of Dido,[9] j bedsteade.
Item, viij lances, j payer of stayers for Fayeton.[5]
Item, ij stepells, & j chyme of belles, & j beacon.
Item, j hecfor[10] for the playe of Faeton,[11] the limes dead.
Item, j globe, & j golden scepter; iij clobes.
Item, ij marchepanes, & the sittie of Rome.[12]
Item, j gowlden flece;[13] ij rackets; j baye tree.
Item, j wooden hatchett; j lether hatchete.
Item, j wooden canepie; owld Mahemetes head.[14]
Item, j lyone skin;[15] j beares skyne; & Faetones[16] lymes, & Faeton[11] charete; & Argosse heade.[17]
Item, Nepun[18] forcke & garland.

---

(1) *Lord Caffes*] perhaps Caiaphas (Malone's suggestion; Dekker was paid for a prologue and epilogue to *Pontius Pilate*, 12 January 1601/2; cf. *Diary*, f. 96).
(2) *Dowlfen*] ? Dauphin in *Henry V*; cf. l. 10 above (Fleay).
(3) *Nabesathe*] unexplained.
(4) *Valteger*] *Vortigern*, played as 'ne' 4 December 1596 (*Diary*, f. 25v).
(5) *Fayeton*] *Phaeton*, bought of Dekker on 15 January 1597/8 (*Diary*, f. 44).
(6) *Alles Pearce*] *Alice Pierce*, in production December 1597 (*Diary*, ff. 37v, 43v).
(7) *cage*] ? perhaps for *Tamburlaine*; see l. 71 and n.
(8) *Guido*] first played as 'ne' 19 March 1597 (*Diary*, f. 26).
(9) *Dido*] *Dido and Aeneas*, in production January 1597/8 (*Diary*, f. 44).
(10) *hecfor*] unexplained.
(11) *Faeton*] see l. 52 and n.
(12) *sittie of Rome*] required in *Dr Faustus* (Fleay).
(13) *gowlden flece*] ? for *Hercules*; cf. l. 25 and n. (Greg).
(14) *Mahemetes head*] ? for *Mahomet*, first listed 14 August 1594 (*Diary*, f. 9v).
(15) *lyone skin*] ? for *Hercules*; see l. 25.
(16) *Faetones*] see l. 52 and n.
(17) *Argosse head*] ? Argus's head for *Jupiter and Io* in *Five Plays in One*, played as 'ne' 7 April 1597 (*Diary*, f. 26); so Greg.
(18) *Nepun*] Neptune; see l. 17 and n.

Item, j crosers stafe; Kentes woden leage.[1]
Item, Ierosses head,[2] & raynbowe; j littell alter.
Item, viij viserdes; Tamberlyne[3] brydell; j wooden matook.
Item, Cupedes bowe,[4] & quiver; the clothe of the Sone & Mone.
Item, j bores heade[5] & Serberosse[6] iij heades.
Item, j Cadeseus;[7] ij mose banckes, & j snake.
Item, ij fanes of feathers; Belendon[8] stable; j tree of gowlden apelles;[9] Tantelouse tre; jx eyorn targates.
Item, j copper targate, & xvij foyles.
Item, iiij wooden targates; j greve armer.
Item, j syne for Mother Readcap;[10] j buckler.
Item, Mercures wings;[11] Tasso picter;[12] j helmet with a dragon; j shelde, with iij lyones;[13] j eleme bowle.
Item, j chayne[14] of dragons; j gylte speare.
Item, ij coffenes; j bulles head; and j vylter.[15]
Item, iij tymbrells, j dragon in fostes.[16]
Item, j lyone; ij lyon heades; j great horse[17] with his leages; j sack-bute.
Item, j whell and frame in the Sege of London.[18]
Item, j paire of rowghte gloves.
Item, j poopes miter.[19]
Item, iij Imperial crownes; j playne crowne.

---

(1) *Kent's woden leage*] perhaps for *The Wise Man of West Chester* (?=*John a Kent*) played as 'ne' 2 December 1594 (*Diary*, f. 10v).

(2) *Ierosses head*] ? Iris's head, perhaps for *I Hercules*, if this is Heywood's *Silver Age*; see l. 25 and n., and E. Schanzer, *Rev. English Studies*, n.s. XI (1960), 18–20.

(3) *Tamberlyne*] first listed 28 August 1594 (*Diary*, f. 10).

(4) *Cupedes bowe*] ? for *Dido and Aeneas*, see l. 57 (Fleay); or for *Five Plays in One*, see l. 67 and n. (Greg).

(5) *bores heade*] ? for *2 Hercules*, if this is Heywood's *Brazen Age*; see l. 70 and n.

(6) *Serberosse*] Cerberus; ? for *1 Hercules*; see l. 70 and n.

(7) *Cadeseus*] caduceus; ? for *1 Hercules*.

(8) *Belendon*] *Belin Dun*, played as 'ne' 8 June 1594 (*Diary*, f. 9).

(9) *tree of gowlden apelles*] for *1 Fortunatus*, first listed 3 February 1595/6 (*Diary*, f. 14v), if this may be traced in Dekker's *Old Fortunatus*.

(10) *Mother Readcap*] bought December 1597 (*Diary*, ff. 37v, 43v).

(11) *Mercures wings*] ? for *1 Hercules*; see l. 70 and n.

(12) *Tasso picter*] for *Tasso's Melancholy*, played as 'ne' 11 August 1594 (*Diary*, f. 9v). As Greg says, if Malone's conjecture that this is the picture paid for in July 1598 (*Diary*, f. 47v) be accepted, then these lists must be dated March 1599 (see headnote).

(13) *shelde...lyones*] ? for Richard I in *I Robin Hood* (cf. l. 20 and n.; so Greg); or for *The Funeral of Richard Cœur de Lion*, bought June 1598, though this would necessitate dating the lists from March 1599; see headnote.

(14) *chayne*] unexplained.

(15) *vylter*] ? philtre.

(16) *fostes*] *Dr Faustus* first listed 30 September 1594 (*Diary*, f. 10); cf. l. 62 and n.

(17) *horse*] ? the horse of the Greeks in *Troy*, played as 'ne' 22 June 1596 (*Diary*, f. 21v).

(18) *Sege of London*] first played 26 December 1594 (*Diary*, f. 11).

(19) *poopes miter*] ? for *Pope Joan*, played 1 March 1592 (*Diary*, f. 7).

Item, j gostes crown; j crown with a sone.[1]
Item, j frame for the heading in Black Jone.[2]
Item, j black dogge.
Item, j cauderm[3] for the Jewe.

The Enventorey of all the aparell of the Lord Admeralles men, *taken the* 13*th of Marche* 1598, *as followeth*:

Item, j payer of whitte saten Venesons cut with coper lace.
Item, j ash coller satten doublett, layed with gold lace.
Item, j peche coller satten doublett.
Item, j owld white satten dublette.
Item, j bleu tafitie sewtte.
Item, j Mores cotte.
Item, Pyges[4] damask gowne.
Item, j black satten cotte.
Item, j harcoller tafitie sewte of pygges.[4]
Item, j white tafitie sewte of pygges.[4]
Item, Vartemar[5] sewtte.
Item, j great pechcoller dublet, with sylver lace.
Item, j white satten dublet pynckte.
Item, j owld white satten dublet pynckte.
Item, j payer of satten Venesyan satten ymbradered.
Item, j payer of French hosse, cloth of gowld.
Item, j payer of cloth of gowld hosse with sylver paines.
Item, j payer of cloth of sylver hosse with satten and sylver panes.
Item, Tamberlynes[6] cotte with coper lace.
Item, j read clock with white coper lace.
Item, j read clocke, with read coper lace.
Item, j shorte clocke of taney satten with sleves.
Item, j shorte clocke of black satten with sleves.
Item, Labesyas clocke,[7] with gowld buttenes.
Item, j payer of read cloth hosse of Venesyans, with sylver lace of coper.
Item, Valteger[8] robe of rich tafitie.
Item, Junoes cotte.[9]

---

(1) *sone*] ? sun, for use in *Phaeton*; see l. 52 and n.
(2) *Black Jone*] see below, l. 185 and n.
(3) *cauderm*] the cauldron in *The Jew of Malta*, first listed 26 February 1592 (*Diary*, f. 7).
(4) *Pyges...pygges*] John Pig the actor, cf. l. 32 and n.
(5) *Vartemar*] ? *Valteger* or *Vortigern*; cf. l. 51 and n.
(6) *Tamberlynes*] cf. l. 71 and n.
(7) *Labesyas clocke*] for Labesha in *An Humorous Day's Mirth* (Fleay); see l. 38 and n.
(8) *Valteger*] see l. 51 and n.
(9) *Junoes cotte*] ? for *I Hercules*; see l. 70 and n.

Item, j hode for the wech.
Item, j read stamel clocke with whitte coper lace.
Item, j read stamel clocke with read coper lace.
Item, j cloth clocke of russete with coper lace, called Guydoes clocke.[1]
Item, j short clocke of black velvet, with sleves faced with shagg.
Item, j short clocke of black vellet, faced with white fore.
Item, j manes gown, faced with whitte fore.
Item, Dobes cotte[2] of cloth of sylver.
Item, j payer of pechecoler Venesyones uncut, with read coper lace.
Item, j read scarllet clocke with sylver buttones.
Item, j longe black velvet clock, layd with brod lace black.
Item, j black satten sewtte.
Item, j blacke velvet clocke, layd with twyst lace blacke.
Item, Perowes sewt,[3] which Wm Sley[4] were.
Item, j payer of pechcoler hosse with sylver corlled panes.
Item, j payer of black cloth of sylver hosse, drawne owt with tufed tafittie.
Item, Tamberlanes[5] breches of crymson vellvet.
Item, j payer of sylk howse with panes of sylver corlled lace.
Item, j Faeytone[6] sewte.
Item, Roben Hoodes[7] sewtte.
Item, j payer of cloth of gowld hose with gowld corlle panes.
Item, j payer of rowne hosse buffe with gowld lace.
Item, j payer of mows coller Venesyans with R.[8] brode gowld lace.
Item, j flame collerde dublet pynked.
Item, j blacke satten dublet, layd thyck wyth blacke and gowld lace.
Item, j carnacyon dubled cutt, layd with gowld lace.
Item, j white satten dublet, faced with read tafetie.
Item, j grene gyrcken with sylver lace.
Item, j black gyrcken with sylver lace.
Item, j read gyrcken with sylver lace.
Item, j read Spanes dublett styched.
Item, j peche coller satten casse.
Item, Tasoes robe.[9]
Item, j murey robe with sleves.

---

(1) *Guydoes clocke*] see l. 57 and n.

(2) *Dobes cotte*] see l. 17 and n.

(3) *Perowes sewt*] unexplained.

(4) *Wm Sley*] belonged to Strange's or Admiral's Men in 1590/92, when he appears in the plot of *2 Seven Deadly Sins*; later to Chamberlain's Men. Henslowe sold him a jewel October 1594 (*Diary*, f. 15). See Chambers, *E.S.* II, 340.

(5) *Tamberlanes*] see l. 71 and n.

(6) *Faeytone*] see l. 52 and n.

(7) *Roben Hoodes*] see l. 20 and n.

(8) *R.*] unexplained.

(9) *Tasoes robe*] see l. 80 and n.

Item, j blewe robe with sleves.
Item, j oren taney robe with sleves.
Item, j pech collerd hallf robe.
Item, j lane robe with spangells.
Item, j white & orenge taney skarf spangled.
Item, Dides robe.[1]
Item, iij payer of basses.
Item, j white tafitie sherte with gowld frenge.
Item, the fryers trusse in Roben Hoode.[2]
Item, j littell gacket for Pygge.[3]
Item, j womanes gown of cloth of gowld.
Item, j orenge taney vellet gowe with sylver lace, for women.
Item, j black velvet gowne ymbradered with gowld lace.
Item, j yelowe satten gowne ymbradered with sylk & gowld lace, for women.
Item, j greve armer.
Item, Harye the v.[4] velvet gowne.
Item, j payer of crymson satten Venysiones, layd with gowld lace.
Item, j blew tafitie sewte, layd with sylver lace.
Item, j Longeshankes[5] seute.
Item, j orange coller satten dublett, layd with gowld lace.
Item, Harye the v.[4] satten dublet, layd with gowld lace.
Item, j Spanes casse dublet of crymson pyncked.
Item, j Spanes gearcken layd with sylver lace.
Item, j wattshode tafitie dublet for a boye.
Item, ij payer of basses, j whitte, j blewe, of sasnett.
Item, j freyers gowne of graye.

A Note of all suche bookes as belong to the Stocke, and such as I have bought since the 3d of March 1598

Blacke Jonne[6]
Woman will have her will.[7]
The Umers.[8]
Welchmans price.[9]

---

(1) *Dides robe*] for *Dido and Aeneas*; see l. 57 and n.
(2) *Roben Hoode*] see l. 20 and n.
(3) *Pygge*] see l. 32 and n.
(4) *Harye the v.*] see l. 10 and n.
(5) *Longeshankes*] see l. 7 and n.
(6) *Blacke Jonne*] not otherwise known; see l. 91.
(7) *Woman will have her will*] paid for February–May 1598 (*Diary*, ff. 44v, 45v).
(8) *Umers*] *Comedy of Humours*; see l. 38 and n.
(9) *Welchmans price*] ? *The Welshman's Prize*; probably *The Famous Wars of Henry I*, paid for March 1598 (*Diary*, f. 45).

Hardicanewtes.[1]
King Arthur,[2] life and death.
Borbonne.[3]
1 p^{t} of Hercules.[4]
Sturgflaterey[5]
2 p^{te} of Hercoles.[6]
Brunhowlle.[7]
Pethagores.[8]
Cobler quen hive.[9]
Focasse.[10]
Frier Pendelton.[11]
Elexsander and Lodwicke.[12]
Alls Perce.[13]
Blacke Battman.[14]
Read Cappe.[15]
2 p. black Battman.[16]
Roben Hode, 1.[17]
2 p^{t} of Goodwine.[18]
Roben Hode, 2.[19]
Mad mans morris.[20]
Phayeton.[21]
Perce of Winchester.[22]
Treangell cockowlls.[23]
Vayvode.[24]
Goodwine.[25]

---

(1) *Hardicanewtes*] played October–November 1597 (*Diary*, f. 27v).

(2) *King Arthur*] paid for April–May 1598 (*Diary*, f. 45v).

(3) *Borbonne*] played November 1597 (*Diary*, f. 27v).

(4) *1 p^{t} of Hercules*] see l. 25 and n.; bought of Slater 16 May 1598 (*Diary*, f. 45v).

(5) *Sturgflaterey*] ? *Strange Flattery* (Chambers); ? *Stark Flattery* (Greg); not otherwise known.

(6) *2 p^{te} of Hercoles*] see l. 25 and n.; bought of Slater 16 May 1598 (*Diary*, f. 45v).

(7) *Brunhowlle*] *Branholt*; see l. 29 and n.

(8) *Pethagores*] *Pythagoras* played as 'ne' 16 January 1595/6 (*Diary*, f. 14); bought of Slater, 16 May 1598 (*Diary*, f. 45v).

(9) *Cobler quen hive*] ? *The Cobbler of Queenhithe*; *The Cobler* was paid for in October 1597 (*Diary*, ff. 37, 43v).

(10) *Focasse*] *Phocas*, played as 'ne' 19 May 1596; bought of Slater 16 May 1598 (*Diary*, ff. 15v, 45v).

(11) *Frier Pendelton*] *Friar Spendleton*, played as 'ne', 31 October 1597 (*Diary*, f. 27v).

(12) *Elexsander and Lodwicke*] first played 14 January 1597; bought of Slater 16 May 1598 (*Diary*, ff. 23, 45v).

(13) *Alls Perce*] *Alice Pierce*; see l. 53 and n.

(14) *Blacke Battman*] *1 Black Bateman*, paid for May–June 1598 (*Diary*, ff. 45v, 46).

(15) *Read Cappe*] *Mother Redcap*; see l. 79 and n.

(16) *2 p. black Battman*] paid for June–July 1598 (*Diary*, f. 47).

(17) *Roben Hode, 1*] see l. 20 and n.

(18) *2 p^{t} of Goodwine*] paid for June 1598 (*Diary*, f. 46).

(19) *Roben Hode, 2*] see l. 20 and n.

(20) *Mad mans morris*] paid for June–July 1598 (*Diary*, f. 47).

(21) *Phayeton*] see l. 52 and n.

(22) *Perce of Winchester*] paid for August 1598 (*Diary*, f. 49).

(23) *Treangell cockowlls*] *The Triplicity of Cuckolds*, bought March 1598 (*Diary*, f. 44v).

(24) *Vayvode*] in production August 1598 (*Diary*, f. 49v); but it was bought for the company from Alleyn 21 January 1598/9 (*Diary*, f. 53), and Greg supposes that Henslowe forgot that it did not belong to the stock in August or September when this list was made. No other plays bought after the end of August 1598 appear in the list.

(25) *Goodwine*] *Earl Goodwin and his Three Sons*, paid for March–April 1598 (*Diary*, ff. 45, 45v).

A Note of all suche goodes as I have bought for the Companey of my Lord Admirals men, *sence the* 3 *of Aprell*, 1598, *as followeth*:

	£	s.	d.
Bowght a damaske casock garded with velvett[1]	0	18	0
Bowght a payer of paned rownd hosse of cloth whiped with sylk, drawne out with tafitie, Bowght j payer of long black wollen stockens,	0	8	0
Bowght j black satten dublett. Bowght j payer of rownd howsse paned of vellevett.	4	15	0[2]
Bowght a robe for to goo invisibell Bowght a gown for Nembia[3]	3	10	0
Bowght a dublett[4] of whitt satten layd thicke with gowld lace, and a payer of rowne pandes hosse of cloth of sylver, the panes layd with gowld lace[4]	7	0	0
Bowght of my sonne v sewtes[5]	20	0	0
Bowght of my sonne iiij sewtes[5]	17	0	0

(1) *damaske...velvett*] Henslowe lent 20*s.* to buy one on 7 April 1598 (*Diary*, f. 45).

(2) Henslowe lent £4. 13*s.* 4*d.* to buy a suit of satin on 25 July 1598 (*Diary*, f. 48); Greg suggests that this may 'refer to the same transaction'.

(3) *Nembia*] unexplained.

(4) *dublett...lace*] Henslowe financed the purchase of such articles for £7 on 9 May 1598 (*Diary*, f. 45v).

(5) As Greg notes, these suits may be among the items listed in MS. I. 30.

APPENDIX 3

ACTORS' NAMES IN DRAMATIC PLOTS

Six dramatic 'plots', or outlines for the prompter's use, are extant, and a seventh, *I Tamar Cam*, now lost, was printed by Steevens in the Variorum edition of Shakespeare (1803), III, 414. There is reason for thinking that all were at one time in the possession of the Admiral's Men, and they may all have belonged once to the MSS. at Dulwich College. Only one is now there, oddly that of *2 Seven Deadly Sins* (MS. XIX), which names actors exclusively of Strange's Men. The remaining five are collected in the British Museum MS. Additional 10449. They were discussed by Greg in his *Henslowe Papers* (1907), pp. 127–54, where transcripts of the main plots were printed. Chambers commented on them at various places in his *Elizabethan Stage* (1923), vol. II, and references are given in headnotes to the plots in the following pages. They were all reprinted, with facsimiles, tables, and a full discussion of dating and other problems, in Greg's *Dramatic Documents* (2 vols. 1931). Two of the plots date from about 1590–2, a period when Strange's Men and the Admiral's Men were collaborating (see Chambers, *E.S.* II, 120–2, 138–9; Greg, *Dramatic Documents*, I, 16–23); the others date from 1597 to ?1602–3, and clearly were used by the Admiral's Men. Two of the plots, those of *2 Fortune's Tennis* and *Troilus and Cressida*, are severely mutilated.

The plots are considered here in their presumed chronological order, though this is still under debate. Except in the case of the first, *The Dead Man's Fortune*, which provides only four names of actors, these names are given in alphabetical order under three headings: Master Actors (i.e. those who are given the honorific 'Mr', indicating a sharer or senior member of a company), adult actors, and boy actors. The name recorded in the plot is given first (original punctuation and capitals are not kept), and then, where it differs, the name by which the actor is usually known. Conjectural identifications are prefixed by a question mark.

(1) *The Dead Man's Fortune*

The date and authorship of this play are not known. The plot contains the names of only a few actors. Both Chambers, *E.S.* II, 136, and Greg, *Dramatic Documents*, I, 16–19, assign it to *c.* 1590, a period when Strange's and the Admiral's Men were working in collaboration. Nothing further is known of Darlow, or 'b samme', who, Greg thinks, may be Sam Rowley. Robert Lee sold a play called *The Miller* to the Admiral's Men in 1598 (*Diary*, f. 44v).

Burbage (Richard Burbage).
Darlowe
Robert Lee
b samme (also listed as sam)

(2) *2 Seven Deadly Sins*

The plot probably relates to the play *Four Plays in One*, performed by Strange's Men on 6 March 1592 (*Diary*, f. 7). This appears to have been a revival of Richard Tarlton's play on *The Seven Deadly Sins*, written for the Queen's Men about 1585 (Chambers, *E.S.* III, 496–7). The actors named all seem to have belonged specifically to Strange's Men, and can nearly all be traced later at one time or another among the personnel of the Chamberlain's or King's Men. For this reason Greg thinks that it was acted 'about 1590 by Strange's Men alone at the Curtain' (*Dramatic Documents*, I, 19). Several of these actors also figure in the *Diary* or other Dulwich MSS.; among them are Richard Cowley, Thomas Pope, William Sly, and, later of Worcester's Men, Christopher Beeston, John Duke, William Kemp and Robert Pallant.

Master actors

Mr Brian (George Brian)
Mr Phillipps (Augustine Phillips)
Mr Pope (Thomas Pope)

Adult actors

Kitt (? Christopher Beeston)
R. Burbage (Richard Burbage)
Harry (? Henry Condell)
R. Cowley (Richard Cowley)
John Duke
Tho. Goodale
J. Holland (John Holland)
Ro. Pallant (Robert Pallant)
John Sincler
W. Sly (William Sly)
Vincent

(3) *Frederick and Basilea*

This play was performed as 'ne' by the Admiral's Men 3 June 1597 (*Diary*, f. 27). The evidence is fairly strong that the plot belongs to this time: Martin Slater, who is named among the actors in it, left the company in July 1597 (*Diary*, f. 27v); Richard Jones and Thomas Downton, who are not named, had been with Pembroke's Men (Chambers, *E.S.* II, 131–4), but returned to the Admiral's Men respectively in August and October 1597 (*Diary*, ff. 232v, 232). See also Chambers, *E.S.* II, 149–50; Greg, *Dramatic Documents*, I, 25.

Master actors

Mr Allen (Edward Alleyn)
Mr Dunstann (James Donstone or Tunstall)
Mr Juby (Edward Juby)
Mr Martyn (Martin Slater)
Mr Towne (Thomas Towne)

Adult actors

Richard Alleine (Richard Alleyn)
Black Dick
Ed. Dutton (Edward Dutton)
Tho: Hunt
Robt leadb; ledbeter (Robert Ledbetter)
Charles (Charles Massey)
Sam (Samuel Rowley)

Boy actors

Griffen
Dick; E. Dutton his boye (Dick Juby)
Pigg (John Pyk or Pig)
Will
T. Belt
Saunder (? Alexander Cooke)
Ro. Go (Robert Gough)
Ned
Nick (? Nicholas Tooley)
Will

(4) *Troilus and Cressida* (fragment)

This fragment of a plot probably belongs to about April 1599, when Dekker and Chettle were at work on a play of this title (*Diary*, f. 54v). Hunt does not have the addition of 'Mr' in the plot of *Frederick and Basilea* (1597), and Jones had left the company by February 1602 (*Diary*, f. 104), so that the plot must have been drawn up between these limits. See Chambers, *E.S.* II, 158–9; Greg, *Dramatic Documents*, I, 26.

Master actors

Mr Hunt (Thomas Hunt)
Mr Jones (Richard Jones)

Adult actors

Stephen (? Stephen Maget)

Boy actors

Mr Jones his boy (? James; cf. *Diary*, f. 13v)
Pigg (John Pyk or Pigg)

(5) *The Battle of Alcazar*

The date of this plot has been much debated. Chambers, *E.S.* II, 173–7, argued for a late date after Edward Alleyn's resumption of acting late in 1600 and the removal of the Admiral's Men to the Fortune Theatre. An upward limit is provided by the death of Richard Alleyn in November 1601 (Chambers, *E.S.* II, 299). The play does not appear in the lists made by Henslowe up to 5 November 1597 (*Diary*, ff. 27, 27v), and the plot cannot belong to a period earlier than August 1597 when Shaa joined the company (*Diary*, f. 232v), or, probably, than 8 December 1597, when Kendall was hired as an actor (see above, p. 268). Greg, however, makes a strong case for dating the plot in 1598 (*Dramatic Documents*, I, 38–40); his argument depends upon his claims that the honorific 'Mr' in the plots always indicates a sharer, and that Richard Alleyn and Thomas Hunt, who are given it in this plot, had ceased to be sharers by 10 July 1600, for their names are omitted from the list of this date in the *Diary*, f. 70. But there is no evidence that Edward Alleyn acted between his retirement late in 1597 (*Diary*, f. 43) and 1600, and the evidence outside the plots that Richard Alleyn and Thomas Hunt were sharers is not strong. Both dates raise difficulties, but on the whole we prefer the late date. The play is by George Peele, dates from about 1589, and was printed in 1594; this plot must relate to a revival, one which provoked Jonson's satire in his *Poetaster* (1601). It should be noted that Chambers came to accept Greg's date for this plot; see Greg, *Dramatic Documents*, I, 40–2.

Master actors

Mr Ed: Allen (Edward Alleyn)
Mr Rich: Allen (Richard Alleyn)
Mr Doughton (Thomas Downton)
Mr Hunt (Thomas Hunt)
Mr Jones (Richard Jones)
Mr Jubie (Edward Juby)
Mr Charles (Charles Massey)
Mr Sam (Samuel Rowley)
Mr Shaa (Robert Shaa)
Mr Towne (Thomas Towne)

Adult actors

W. Cartwright (William Cartwright)
Tho: Drom
Anthony Jeffes
H. Jeffes (Humphrey Jeffes)
W. Kendall (William Kendall)
Ro: or Robin Tailor (Robert Tailor)

Boy actors

Mr Allen's boy (? John Pyk or Pig)
Dab (? = Dobe of the Inventories, p. 317, l. 17)
Harry
Jeames (James)
Dick Jubie (Richard Juby)
Parsons (Thomas Parsons)
Georg Somersett
Mr Towne's boy

(6) *2 Fortune's Tennis* (fragment)

Dekker was paid for a book called *Fortune's Tennis* on 6 September 1600 (*Diary*, f. 70v). It could have been an old book, and Greg dates the plot 1597–8, partly because the cast-list, so far as the fragment shows it, is similar to that of *Frederick and Basilea*; partly because Charles Massey and Sam Rowley are named in it without the honorific 'Mr', and, as Greg thinks, are for this reason not likely to have been sharers at the time; see *Dramatic Documents*, I, 26, 30. However, the absence of 'Mr' from the one appearance in the fragment of Massey and Rowley may not be significant; see Introduction, pp. xxxviii ff., for further comments on their status. It is simpler to accept the probable date of this plot as between September 1602 and the time of Singer's retirement, early in 1603. Chambers thinks it may be Munday's *Set at Tennis* of December 1602 (*Diary*, f. 108v), but there is no evidence; see *E.S.* II, 177.

Master actors

Mr Singer (John Singer)

Adult actors

W. Cartwright (William Cartwright)
Ch⟨..⟩l⟨ (Charles Massey)
Pau⟨ (? Pauy or Paus; perhaps not a player's name)
Sam (Samuel Rowley)
R. Tailor (Robert Tailor)
Tho (? Hunt, Rowley, Parsons, Towne or Downton)

Boy actors

dic⟨ (? Richard Juby)
Ge⟨ ; somerton (? George Somerset)

(7) *1 Tamar Cam*

Henslowe lists as 'ne' Part II of this play on 28 April 1592, when it was played by Strange's Men (*Diary*, f. 7), and again, played by the Admiral's Men, on 11 June 1596 (f. 21 v); Part I is listed as 'ne' on 6 May 1596 (f. 15 v). Martin Slater left the company in July 1597 (*Diary*, f. 27 v), and his non-appearance among the actors named in the plot is evidence that this does not belong to the revival of 1596. The book of 'Tambercame' was sold to the company by Edward Alleyn on 2 October 1602 (*Diary*, f. 108), and the plot almost certainly relates to a revival after this date. If Singer retired from acting in 1603 (see Chambers, *E.S.* II, 177; he is last named in the *Diary*, f. 109, as receiving payment for his play 'Syngers vallentary' on 13 January 1603), the plot cannot have been made much later than the date of Alleyn's transfer of the book. See also Greg, *Dramatic Documents*, I, 27–8.

Master actors

Mr Allen (Edward Alleyn)
Mr Burne, Bourne, Boorne (William Birde)
Mr Denygten (Thomas Downton)
Mr Jubie (Edward Juby)
Mr Charles (Charles Massey)
Mr Sam (Samuel Rowley)
Mr Singer (John Singer)
Mr Towne (Thomas Towne)

Adult actors

W. Cartwright (William Cartwright)
A. Jeffs (Anthony Jeffes)
H. Jeffs (Humphrey Jeffes)
W. Parr (William Parr)

Boy actors

Mr Denygten's little boy
Jack Grigerie (Jack Gregory)
Jeames (James)
Jack Jones
Dick Jubie (Richard Juby)
Tho. Parsons (Thomas Parsons)
George (George Somerset)

Supernumeraries, who appear only in the procession at the end

Ned Browne (Edward Browne)
Old Browne
Gibbs
Gedion (Gideon)
Rester
Tho: Rowley

Boy actors

Little Will Barne
Gils his boy (Giles's boy)
Jeames (James)

INDEXES AND GLOSSARY

1. NOTE ON THE INDEXES AND GLOSSARY

In the Indexes and Glossary all the references are to page numbers. There are three sections. The first is an index of the titles of plays mentioned; the principal alternative spellings are cross-indexed, and odd forms of titles are printed in brackets after the main listing, where titles are given in the modernised form used by E. K. Chambers and others as a standard mode of reference. The figures within brackets indicate the number of times (more than once) that a title is mentioned on a page. The second section comprises a general index and a glossary of difficult terms. This lists persons, places, companies, theatres, and subjects relating to the theatrical material. Where it is appropriate, the standard modern form of a name is used for the main listing, and some prominent or strange forms are cross-indexed; for other names, the spelling of the manuscript is given. The glossary is not comprehensive, but aims at explaining, where possible, the most puzzling spellings and the rare or specialised words that appear in the manuscripts. A page reference is given for each item in the glossary; a plus-sign after the page number indicates that the spelling or word occurs several times. The third section is an index of the years cited in the *Diary* and supplementary material; with its help the events of any one year as recorded in entries scattered through the documents may be traced. Dates are sometimes entered in the documents according to the Old Style calendar, in which the year ended on 25 March; if it is clear that, for instance, an entry dated January 1593 belongs to 1594 in the New Style or present-day calendar, the years are listed as follows: 1593 (= 1594), and 1594 (as 1593). If there is any doubt at all, the year is simply listed as it appears in the document.

2. INDEX OF PLAYS

 22-2

3. GENERAL INDEX AND GLOSSARY

4. INDEX OF YEAR-DATES